The Lutheran Church Among Norwegian-Americans

Volume II, 1890-1959

The Lutheran Church Among Norwegian-Americans

A History of the Evangelical Lutheran Church

by
E. CLIFFORD NELSON

AUGSBURG PUBLISHING HOUSE
Minneapolis   Minnesota

THE LUTHERAN CHURCH AMONG NORWEGIAN-AMERICANS
A History of the Evangelical Lutheran Church
© 1960 Augsburg Publishing House

Library of Congress Catalog Card No. 60-6438

Manufactured in the United States of America

To Lois and Our Children

    Dagmar Elizabeth
    David Jensen
    Naomi Jeanette

Preface

That there can be no absolutely impartial presentation of history is generally admitted today. It is wishful thinking to imagine that one can get an objective view of "what actually happened" (Ranke). History, and not least church history, is accessible only as it is interpreted; it becomes a living thing only when the historian is himself deeply concerned as a person in that with which he deals. The historian's involvement, therefore, militates against an objective detachment. At the same time he must be aware of his own standpoint and make allowances for his possible prejudices, exercising a constant self-criticism in relation to them. This principle of controlled involvement has guided the writing of this and the previous volume.

In conjunction with this observation it should be said that two possible attitudes may develop in the heart and mind of the church historian. One may be an attitude of cold cynicism, resulting from a close scrutiny of much church activity done in the name of Christ but which sometimes hardly comports with the spirit of Christ. The other is a growing wonder at the mercy and patience which God exercises toward His people. The writer has tried to see a tiny segment of church history—the history of The Evangelical Lutheran Church—as an evidence of God's activity and as a vivid witness to His grace and patience. It cannot be gainsaid that the witness of the Spirit has often been corroded and frustrated by the perversities and parochialisms of God's people among the Norwegian-American Lutherans. The so-called "non-theological factors" in church history have too often been merely a polite way of disguising original sin. The writer, however, has taken heart in the knowledge that the Spirit's presence in the church is not proved by the absence of sin but in the willingness to confess sin. When The Evangelical Lutheran Church has exhibited this attitude, it has been blessed; and there are evidences of such blessing in the story. On the other hand, there have been some unpleasant, even ugly, episodes in the life of the church. The telling of them has given no pleasure—is it ever pleasant to confess sins and foibles? Some events, which one might prefer to omit and forget, have been included in order to present a balanced picture. The result has been that the history of the church is not a self-congratulatory narrative designed to please the faithful, but a serious attempt at honest historiography. It is hoped that the reader will remember that God often turns the strange and perverse ways of men to His praise.

In acknowledging the assistance of those who have aided the author the name of Dr. Eugene L. Fevold must be mentioned first. It is doubtful that the task of completing this history would have been accomplished without his collaboration. In the first place, he generously assumed an extra burden of teaching in order that the undersigned might devote the major portion of his time during the third quarter of the academic year 1958-1959 to additional research and reworking of the manuscript for both volumes. Moreover, he graciously wrote the section on home and foreign missions in Chapter IV, "The Expanding Church," of this second volume. In addition, he has read the entire manuscript and offered helpful criticisms which have prevented errors in fact and interpretation.

Besides those to whom appreciation was expressed in the Preface to Volume I grateful mention should be made of those who have read portions of the manuscript for Volume II: Dr. A. N. Rogness, president, the Reverend J. V. Halvorson and Dr. W. A. Quanbeck, professors, Luther Theological Seminary; Dr. F. A. Schiotz and Dr. Raymond M. Olson, president and stewardship director, respectively, of The Evangelical Lutheran Church; and Dr. Theodore Tappert, professor, Lutheran Theological Seminary, Philadelphia, Pennsylvania.

Of special value to the writer have been collections of private and institutional documents and letters. Thanks are due to Messrs. Ray and George Mohn, Northfield, Minnesota, for the use of the T. N. Mohn Correspondence; to Dr. Karen Larsen and Miss Ingeborg Larsen, Northfield, Minnesota, for permission to examine those items of the Laur. Larsen Papers in their possession; to Dr. C. M. Granskou, president of St. Olaf College, Northfield, Minnesota, for allowing access to the L. W. Boe Correspondence; to Dr. William Larsen, president of the United Evangelical Lutheran Church, Blair, Nebraska, for permission to see the letter files of N. C. Carlsen; to Dr. J. A. Aasgaard, president emeritus of The Evangelical Lutheran Church, for the use of the manuscript minutes and other documents relative to the 1917 merger; to Miss Margaret J. Hort, librarian, Krauth Memorial Library, Lutheran Theological Seminary, Philadelphia, for microfilm copies of the H. G. Stub-F. H. Knubel Correspondence; and to my father-in-law, Mr. J. K. Jensen, Janesville, Wisconsin, for his personal letter files and documents relative to Lutheran unity.

OCTOBER, 1959　　　　　　　　　　　　　　　　　　E. C. N.

Chronology

1890—June 13
    Organization of The United Norwegian Lutheran Church.
1891—
    Beginning of Augsburg Controversy.
1891—
    Concordia College (academy) begun.
1893—
    United Church's mission work in southern Madagascar begun.
1893—September
    United Church Seminary ("Sacharias School") begun.
1893—November
    "The Friends of Augsburg" organized.
1894—
    Pacific Lutheran University (academy) begun.
1896-1898—
    Litigation over Augsburg Seminary
1897—June
    Lutheran Free Church organized.
1897—September 15-22
    Lanesboro (Minnesota) Free Conference.
1900—December
    Lutheran Church of the Brethren organized, Milwaukee, Wisconsin.

1901—March 28-30
: Unity conference, St. Paul: Presidents and Theological Faculties of the Norwegian Synod and United Church.

1903—
: Waldorf College (academy) begun.

1905—
: New unity talks initiated by Hauge's Synod.

1906—March 30
: Theses on Absolution approved.

1906—October 16-19
: Theses on Lay Activity approved.

1908—April
: Theses on the Call and Conversion approved.

1908—November 10-13
: Joint Union Committee discussed Election.

1910—December 13-14
: Joint Meeting, United Church Seminary, St. Paul; withdrawal of Synod members.

1911—April 18
: Southern Wisconsin Pastoral Conference of United Church adopts resolutions favoring immediate union.

1911—November 21-24
: New Joint Union Committee, St. Paul.

1912—
: *The Lutheran Hymnary* published.

1912—
: Norwegian Synod authorized mission in China.

1912—February 22
: "The Madison Agreement" (*Opgjør*), Madison, Wisconsin.

1912—June 6-12
: United Church Convention adopted Union Report, Fargo, North Dakota.

1912—
: Hauge's Synod in Red Wing approved Union Report.

1913—Spring
: *Bønskrift* ("Petition") objects to merger; "Minority" in Synod appears.

1913—June
: Extraordinary convention of Norwegian Synod.

1914—Hauge's Synod postpones action on Articles of Union.

Chronology

1914—
: United Church approves Articles of Union.

1914—
: Synod votes approval over large "Minority"; "Peace Committee" appointed.

1915—April
: Joint Union Committee; Synod approves interpretation of *Opgjør*.

1915—June
: Joint Union Committee votes name of church, "The Norwegian Lutheran Church of America," and prepares constitution.

1916—
: "Austin Agreement."

1917—
: Formation of Lutheran United Mission (China).

1917—June 6-8
: Synodical meetings approved resolution of Joint Union Committee to accept Synod minority into new church.

1917—June 8
: Three synods ended separate existence.

1917—June 9
: Norwegian Lutheran Church of America organized.

1917-1925
: H. G. Stub's presidency.

1918—June 14
: Norwegian Synod of the American Evangelical Lutheran Church organized.

1918—
: National Lutheran Council organized.

1919—
: "The Chicago Theses" and "The Essentials of a Catholic Spirit" drafted by Stub and F. H. Knubel, respectively.

1920—
: The Lutheran Church of China begun.

1923—
: United Lutheran Theological Seminary in Madagascar founded.

1923—
: Lutheran World Convention begun in Eisenach, Germany.

1925—
: Norse-American Centennial.

1925-1954—
: J. A. Aasgaard's presidency.

1925—
    "The Minneapolis Theses" drafted.
1927—
    Control of Schreuder Mission in Zululand transferred to NLCA.
1929—
    Lutheran World Convention in Copenhagen.
1930—October 29-31
    American Lutheran Conference organized.
1935—
    Lutheran World Convention, Paris.
1943—
    Centennial of NLCA.
1943—
    Decision reached to begin mission work in South America.
1944—
    Full-time executive secretary of Charities authorized.
1944—
    Full-time director of Home Missions authorized.
1945—
    Full-time director of Evangelism authorized.
1946—June 13
    Change of name to The Evangelical Lutheran Church.
1947—
    First Assembly, Lutheran World Federation, Lund, Sweden.
1948—
    First Assembly, World Council of Churches, Amsterdam, Holland; ELC rejects membership.
1948—
    Norwegian Conference established.
1949—January
    Inter-Lutheran unity discussions begin.
1949—
    Withdrawal of American missions from Red China.
1949—
    ELC Japanese mission begun.
1949—
    ELC mission begun in Hong Kong.
1950—
    ELC mission begun in Formosa.

Chronology

1950—
    Independent Malagasy Lutheran Church established.

1950—
    ELC enters unity discussion with UELC and ALC.

1952—
    "The United Testimony" approved by ELC.

1954—
    F. A. Schiotz elected president of ELC.

1954—
    American Lutheran Conference dissolved.

1956—
    ELC approves union documents for TALC.

1956—
    ELC joins World Council of Churches.

1957—August
    Third Assembly, Lutheran World Federation, Minneapolis.

1958—
    Mission work begun in French Camerouns and Equatorial Africa.

1958—
    Brazil mission begun.

1958—
    The new Lutheran Service Book and Hymnal published.

Contents

CHAPTER   PAGE

Part I. *Formation of the United Church. The Augsburg Controversy (1890-1900)*

I. Planning the Union 3
II. Achieving the Union 23
III. The Augsburg Controversy 38

Part II. *The Churches Merge (1900-1917)*

IV. The Expanding Church 85
V. Forward to *Opgjør* 129
VI. The Union of 1917 183

Part III. *A Heritage Meets a New Era (1917-1959)*

VII. An Interpretation of the Heritage 229
VIII. The Church Discovers America 241
IX. The Church Discovers Other Churches 281

Appendix

A. 1890 Constitution and Bylaws 333
B. Danish-Norwegian Liturgies 342

xvii

C. Union Documents (1906-1912) 344
D. Constitution and Articles of Union With
   "An Interpretation" (1917) 359

Index 373

Illustrations

Insert between pages 28 and 29

Gjermund Hoyme, First President of the United Church
United Church Seminary, St. Paul, Minnesota
Concordia College, Moorhead, Minnesota
Pacific Lutheran College, Tacoma, Washington
Augustana College and Normal, Sioux Falls, South Dakota
Theological Faculties, ca. 1900
   United Church
   Hauge's Synod
   Norwegian Synod
Representative Rural Church of the ELC

Insert between pages 172 and 173

Union Committee, 1912
Union Committee, 1915
Church Presidents 1916-1917
   H. G. Stub, Norwegian Synod
   T. H. Dahl, United Church
   C. J. Eastvold, Hauge's Synod
Merger Convention, 1917

Other Leaders in the Merger
  J. N. Kildahl, United Church
  C. K. Preus, Norwegian Synod
  M. G. Hanson, Hauge's Synod
Presidents of the Church 1917-1960
  H. G. Stub, 1917-1925
  J. A. Aasgaard, 1925-1954
  F. A. Schiotz, 1954-1960
Presidents of the Seminary 1917-1960
  M. O. Bøckman, 1917-1930
  T. F. Gullixson, 1930-1954
  A. N. Rogness, 1954-
Mission Countries of the ELC
ELC Home Missions (1944-1957)

Insert between pages 268 and 269

  Augustana College, Sioux Falls, South Dakota
  Concordia College, Moorhead, Minnesota
  Luther College, Decorah, Iowa
  Pacific Lutheran College, Parkland, Washington
  St. Olaf College, Northfield, Minnesota
  Augustana Academy, Canton, South Dakota
  Waldorf College, Forest City, Iowa
  Institutions of Charity
  Mrs. T. H. Dahl, First President of the W.M.F.
  L. W. Boe, ELC Pioneer in Inter-Lutheran Cooperation
  Lutheran Churches in America

PART ONE

Formation of the United Church

❦

Augsburg Controversy
(1890-1900)

CHAPTER ONE

Planning the Union

The congregations established in America by Norwegian immigrants reflected the diverse religious tendencies of the homeland. Although there was but one church (the Church of Norway) in the old country, emphases deriving from the significant Haugean Revival (early 19th century) clashed with the traditional piety of the Established Church. Both viewpoints were perpetuated on the American frontier.

Low-church Haugean immigrants, led by an uneducated but earnest layman, Elling Eielsen, formed the Eielsen Synod in 1846 (changed in 1876 to Hauge's Norwegian Evangelical Lutheran Synod in America). Representatives of a more traditional Lutheranism formed in 1853 what came to be known as the Norwegian Synod. Led by university-trained clergymen from Norway, the conservative Norwegian Synod found itself affected by the point of view held by the German Missouri Synod. Close association with the latter in the area of ministerial education soon influenced the Norwegian Synod to the point that it began to look upon itself as the sole advocate of orthodoxy among Norwegian-Americans. However, by 1870 a clearly defined third tendency appeared. Individuals who found the ecclesiastical atmosphere to left and to right unacceptable sought to walk a middle way but concluded by forming two new church bodies, the Norwegian Augustana Synod and the Norwegian-Danish Conference.

Although some expressions of interest in church unity were made in the fifteen-year period after the Civil War, actual attempts to reduce the multiplicity of church groups originated in 1880. Before fruits of the interest in union were to be realized, however, the church suffered further fragmentation when the Norwegian Synod was split over the Election Controversy of the eighties. The seceders, the so-called Anti-Missourians, immediately assumed leadership in the union movement which brought the Augustanans and the Conference with the Anti-Missourians into the United Norwegian Lutheran Church in America (1890).

The steps leading to the formation of the United Norwegian Lutheran Church included a series of "free conferences," in which the participating individuals were without official standing, and after 1883 "joint conferences," in which the members were chosen by the several bodies. Results of these meetings convinced the church leaders in the Conference, the Norwegian Augustana Synod, the Anti-Missourian Brotherhood, and to a lesser degree in Hauge's Synod that the time was ripe for definite consideration of organic union. To that end each group named representatives to a joint committee on union.

Discussion of Merger Plans

The Eau Claire Meeting, 1888

Pastor P. A. Rasmussen, as chairman of the Anti-Missourian committee, called the joint committee on union to meet at Eau Claire, Wisconsin, August 15 to 23, 1888. This and the later meeting at Scandinavia, Wisconsin, were to be two of the most significant union meetings of the eighties.

Upon arrival of the committee members it was discovered that there was full representation from all except Hauge's

Synod, which sent only Professor Bergsland and Pastor Eisteinsen.[1] G. Hoyme was chosen chairman. The other officers were P. A. Rasmussen, vice-president; J. N. Kildahl, secretary; and A. Wright, assistant secretary. Thereupon, three sub-committees were elected: (1) the committee on constitution (Dahl, Ellestad, Rasmussen, Hatlestad, Eisteinsen, and Klove), (2) the committee on doctrinal settlement (Lysnes, Schmidt, Bergsland, Olsen, Swenson and Kirkeli), and (3) the committee on articles of union (Sverdrup, Wright, Eisteinsen, Kildahl, Hoyme, Aaslaksen, and Venem).

The joint committee accomplished a monumental task in preparing a complete plan for the consummation of the proposed merger, and since its labors proved to be determinative for the future of the church, we must examine in some detail the proceedings of the meeting.[2]

The doctrinal settlement was to cause the most discussion. The above-named sub-committee on doctrine prepared a report of nine points. When the joint committee failed to approve it, a new committee, consisting of four theological professors (Lysnes, Sverdrup, Schmidt, and Bergsland) was elected. This group brought in a report which all approved.[3]

The first paragraph of the doctrinal settlement *(Opgjør)* was significant for the reason that it announced the basis on which union between these synods would occur:

(1) .. we regard our harmonious subscription to the Holy Scriptures, the confessions of the Norwegian Lutheran Church, and the catechism now in use in our synods and congregations as a completely sufficient

---

[1]This was unmistakable evidence of the lack of a genuine interest in Hauge's Synod for the proposed union. For the membership of the joint committee on union see Vol. I, ch. XIV, pp. 334-335.

[2]The report of the joint committee was printed and widely circulated through the synodical organs previous to the joint meeting at Scandinavia, Wisconsin, November, 1888. The complete report appeared as a supplement to *Lutheraneren*, XXII (October 6, 1888). See editorial comments, p. 319. It is conveniently printed also in J. A. Bergh, "Historisk Inledning," in N. C. Brun (ed.) *Fra Ungdoms Aar* (Minneapolis: Augsburg Publishing House, 1915), pp. 20-26. Cf. "Kirkelige Efterretninger," *Lutherske Vidnesbyrd*, VII (1888), 572-574; "Kirke- og Missions-efterretninger," *Budbæreren*, XX (1888), 575; "Kirkelige Efterretninger," *Lutheraneren*, XXII (1888), 280. For the Norwegian Synod's sharp criticism of the report see "Fælleskomiteens Indstilling til Fællesmødet," *Evangelisk Luthersk Kirketidende*, XV (1888), 637-643.

[3]Bergh, "Historisk Inledning" in Brun (ed.), *op. cit.*, p. 19.

basis for church union, since there is evidence of no official act on the part of any of the synods in denial of the Scripture and the confessions.[4]

It will be noted that this paragraph revealed the hand of Sverdrup who had fought against the dogmatism of Missouri. This union was not to be based on Missourian theses, but upon Scripture, the Augsburg Confession, Luther's Small Catechism and Pontoppidan's *Explanation* of the catechism.

The second paragraph proclaimed that the old doctrinal differences had been settled to the extent that they did not now prevent church union. It was intimated that complete agreement did not exist but that the unsolved problems did not justify continued division.

Paragraph three admitted that the ecclesiastical strife of the past was unseemly and deplorable. In many instances "carnal indiscretion and party spirit" had contributed unnecessarily to the controversies and schisms.

The fourth paragraph was the longest in that it set forth the five previously disputed doctrines on which they were now united. They were: the atonement and justification, the gospel, absolution, the observance of Sunday, and election. This last paragraph may appear to be a contradiction of paragraph one. However, an explanation was made that the inclusion of this in the report was merely a statement of what was commonly believed by the four synods and not a set of theses to be accepted by the forthcoming joint meeting of the synods.[5] With this in mind the following items were included:

Concerning Atonement and Justification

Pastor J. N. Kildahl's statement of these doctrines at the Willmar meeting the previous year and approved by it were now accepted by the joint committee.[6] Of significance was the inclusion of sentences rejecting the designation of the world's

---

[4]*Ibid.*, p. 20. Tr. in E. L. Fevold, "The History of Norwegian-American Lutheranism, 1870-1890" (Unpublished Ph.D. dissertation, University of Chicago, 1951), p. 426.
[5]Bergh, "Historisk Inledning" in Brun (ed.), *op. cit.*, p. 20. Paragraph nine declares that paragraph four is merely an "account" ("en redegjørelse").
[6]See Vol. I, ch. XIV, p. 329.

redemption as the justification of the world. "Justification" should be used only of God's judicial act when the individual sinner comes to faith.

Concerning the Gospel

Two items were held forth as expressions of the existing unity on this doctrine: (1) the content of the gospel is not dependent upon man's relation to it, and (2) no person is saved without conversion and faith.

Concerning Absolution

The free conference at Gol and the Norwegian-Danish Conference in 1886 had adopted a doctrinal statement on this subject which was now accepted by the joint committee.[7] A supplemental explanation requested by a few was included because it drew a clear distinction between the subjective and objective aspects of absolution: it is always an *offer* of forgiveness and only an *impartation* of forgiveness when believed. Furthermore, the different liturgical practices in administering absolution ought not be considered divisive.

Concerning the Observance of Sunday

Luther's explanation of the third commandment in the catechism was considered an adequate statement of this matter.

Concerning Election

Pontoppidan's answer to Question 548 in his *Sandhed til Gudfrygtighed* was accepted as a satisfactory statement of this admittedly difficult theological question. In the same breath, it was said "our union is not to be a hindrance to continued work for agreement and union of all Norwegian Lutherans in America."[8]

---

[7] See Vol. I, ch. XIV, pp. 326-327.
[8] The obvious conclusion to draw is that this statement looked toward the Norwegian Synod whose leaders considered "Question 548" an inadequate statement of the doctrine of election.

It will be noted from the articles included in paragraph four that the committee's doctrinal conclusions were based largely upon the statement drawn up and accepted by the free conferences and joint meetings of the eighties.

The fifth paragraph, dealing with lay activity, was later to be subjected to criticism by Hauge's Synod. Consequently it is herewith reproduced:

> Concerning the activity which is generally known among us under the term *Christian lay activity,* we declare that we are convinced that it has been of great blessing in our church and for our people, and we believe that it ought to be most warmly recommended and promoted among us. We do not regard this activity in its proper manifestation to be any infringement upon the pastoral office and, therefore, do not regard it to be in any conflict with Article XIV of the Augsburg Confession. Where such activity is exercised in ordered congregations, it ought, in so far as possible, to be coordinated with the rest of the congregation's spiritual program *(opbyggelsesarbeide).*[9]

The sixth paragraph of the doctrinal settlement made cooperation in practical matters a primary goal without setting aside the importance of preserving the revealed truth. The next paragraph spoke of the need of "regenerated Christians"[10] in the pastoral and teaching offices. The eighth paragraph requested the exercise of Christian brotherliness toward each other through the official organs and in general church contacts lest the union work be stymied. The last paragraph said that the forthcoming joint meeting would take official action only on paragraphs one, five, six, seven and eight.[11]

The second major accomplishment of the Eau Claire meeting was the preparation of a proposed constitution for the new church. Bergh indicated that Sverdrup, more than any other individual, was responsible for the constitution and plan of union.[12] The knotty problem of how the union could be con-

---

[9]Translation in Fevold, *op. cit.,* p. 428.
[10]Although one is aware of the concern expressed in this paragraph, the careful reader will note that anxiety over the presence of vital spirituality in the leaders of the church involved the framers of this paragraph in a bit of redundancy. One is tempted to ask the question (re "regenerated Christians"), "Is there any other kind?"
[11]Bergh, "Historisk Inledning" in Brun (ed.), *op. cit.,* p. 22.
[12]J. A. Bergh, *Den norsk lutherske Kirkes Historie i Amerika* (Minneapolis: Augsburg Publishing House, 1914), p. 365.

summated without any one of the synod's harboring the feeling that it had been absorbed by another synod was solved by Sverdrup. He suggested that the correct procedure would be for all contracting synods to change their present constitutions into the constitution of the proposed new church. The synodically-unorganized Anti-Missourians would simply adopt the proposed constitution, and then all would easily flow into one body.[13]

The constitution agreed upon at Eau Claire stipulated that the name of the new organization should be "The Norwegian Lutheran Free church in America."[14] Once again the hand of Sverdrup was evident, but already a rift was beginning to appear. A motion to reconsider the name was defeated. As was to become clear later, the Old School of the Conference was opposed to incorporating the New School concept of a "free church" into the name of the new body.[15] Furthermore, the editor of the Norwegian Synod periodical, watching the formation of this new church from a distance, ridiculed the proposed name and with ill-concealed sarcasm said, "Free church! Does that imply the existence of a state church in America? Surely no church body in America exists other than as a free church."[16]

Other provisions of the constitution stipulated that the new synod should be composed of congregations (not pastors), that there should be annual conventions of the synod, that the synod be divided into districts (not *administrative* districts as was the case with the Norwegian Synod), and that representation at the annual synod should be one lay delegate from each congregation and the pastor. Seminary professors were also to be given the right to vote.[17] Officers of the church were

[13]*Ibid.*, p. 377.
[14]Several other names were considered: "The United Norwegian Lutheran Church in America" (the proposal of the subcommittee on constitution), "The Fellowship (*Samfundet*) for the Norwegian Lutheran Church in America," "The Norwegian Lutheran Augustana Synod," and "The Norwegian Lutheran Augsburg Synod." Bergh, "Historisk Inledning" in Brun (ed.), *op. cit.*, p. 19.
[15]*Ibid.*, p. 29. N. C. Brun, a militant Old School man, was instrumental in getting the proposed name altered to "The United Norwegian Lutheran Church in America" at the joint meeting in Scandinavia, Wisconsin, October, 1888.
[16]"Fælleskomiteens Indstilling til Fællesmødet," *E. L. K.*, XV (1888), 659.
[17]This provision was not consistent with the fact that the synod was to be composed only of congregations.

to be president, vice-president, secretary, treasurer, and parish visitors. No provision was made for a synodical church council to deal with church business between the annual synods, as was the case in the Norwegian Synod.

Thus it can be seen that the proposed constitution provided a congregational-synodical form of church government which revealed a fear of centralized control. When the Norwegian Synod's official organ commented that this constitution was virtually the same as the Synod's constitution, it neglected to recognize that among the Norwegian-American Lutheran groups the Synod, as witnessed by its powerful church council, was more inclined towards centralization of authority.[18]

The third major accomplishment of the joint committee at Eau Claire was the working out of the proposed articles of union. These included the conditions to be fulfilled and the practical procedure to facilitate the consummation of the union. One of the first stipulations was that Augsburg Seminary in Minneapolis be the divinity school of the new church. Theological professors were to be paid from the interest of a fund of which the Augustanans were to contribute $15,000; Hauge's Synod, $20,000; the Conference, $50,000, and the Anti-Missourians a sum large enough to provide income for two professors. The faculty was to be composed as follows: two professors from the Anti-Missourians, two from the Conference, one from the Norwegian Augustana Synod, and one from Hauge's Synod.

Incorporation of the church body was to take place as soon as possible and to it each of the contracting parties was to transfer ownership of all school property debt-free. Preparatory departments of Augsburg and Red Wing Seminaries, the academy at Canton, South Dakota, and the school at Beloit, Iowa, were to be maintained for at least one year.[19] Church

---
[18] "Fælleskomiteens Indstilling . . ." *E. L. K.*, XV (1888), 660.
[19] The statement regarding "the school at Beloit" is a mistake. The educational institution of the Norwegian Augustana Synod was moved from Marshall, Wis., to Beloit, Iowa, in 1881. It consisted of an academy, a college course, and a theological course. In 1884 the academy and college departments were moved to Canton, S. Dak., the seminary remaining in Beloit until it was merged with Augsburg Seminary in 1890. In other words, there was no school at Beloit to continue "for at least one year" after 1890. Interview

periodicals and publishing concerns were to be merged. All debts must be liquidated before the union, and the freedom of the local congregation was not to be jeopardized by the new organization.[20]

The following schedule for the accomplishment of the merger was set up: the committee's report would be sent to a joint meeting of lay and clerical delegates from the four synods. The resolutions adopted there would then be sent to the annual conventions of each body in 1889. If approved by the conventions, the proposed constitution and the articles of union would be sent to the congregations for approval. They in turn were to act before the synodical conventions of 1890. In 1890 all the synodical meetings would be held simultaneously in the same city at which time the proposed constitution would be a pending motion for a change of constitution. This would apply to all except the Anti-Missourians for whom the proposed constitution would be a pending motion for constitution. Thus each would adopt identical constitutions and would flow into one church body. With these details thoroughly thought through and the report apparently unanimously approved,[21] the next step was the assembling of the delegates for the joint meeting.

The Joint Meeting at Scandinavia, Wisconsin, 1888

Perhaps the largest representative gathering of Norwegian-American Lutherans up to this time was the assembly at Scandinavia, Wisconsin, November 15-21, 1888.[22] Virtually all of

---

with the Rev. Olaf Lysnes, son of Prof. David Lysnes of Augustana Seminary (4-13-59). Cf. Norlie, *History of the Norwegian People in America* (Minneapolis: Augsburg Publishing House, 1925), p. 281.

[20]Because some of the articles of union were to be the subject of bitter conflict in what was to be known as "The Augsburg Controversy," they are reproduced in translation and may be found in the Appendix.

[21]Emanating from Hauge's Synod was an indication that this group was increasingly hesitant about union. Professor Bergsland wrote that through an error the official report of the joint committee failed to include his opposition to paragraph two of the doctrinal settlement which declared that all old doctrinal disagreements no longer existed. H. H. Bergsland, "En Oplysning," *Budbæreren*, XX (1888), 655.

[22]Bergh, *Den n. luth. Kirkes Hist. i Am.*, p. 378. Cf. Bergh, "Historisk Inledning" in Brun (ed.), *op. cit.*, p. 28.

the previous conferences among the Norwegian-American Lutheran groups had been for the purpose of arriving at doctrinal unity through discussion. The Scandinavia meeting, however, was for the sole purpose of considering the report of the joint committee on union and other related matters. According to the announcement of the meeting, each congregation of the four church groups, as well as independent Lutheran congregations, had the right to send a voting delegate. Other voting members should be the pastors, theological professors, and members of the joint committee.[23]

On the whole, the meeting at Scandinavia was characterized by a spirit of good-will and harmony. The differences of opinion which appeared were centered mainly on Part One (the doctrinal settlement) of the report,[24] and the chief objections were raised by members of Hauge's Synod. The final suggestion of this part of the report had been that paragraphs one, five, six, seven and eight be adopted. This was done with the exception of paragraph six (dealing with cooperation in practical matters) which was removed as unnecessary.[25] The discussion on paragraph one, which set forth the doctrinal basis of the union, revealed that several members of Hauge's Synod were opposed to it.[26] Likewise, when the conference came to vote on paragraph five (dealing with lay activity) and paragraph six (asking for the exercise of mutual brotherliness), Hauge's Synod men either abstained from voting or voted against the proposals.[27] Later several Haugeans requested that paragraphs two, three, and four of the doctrinal settlement be reviewed since they would be unprepared to discuss the articles of union until that had been done. The request was granted.[28] Thereupon ten members of Hauge's Synod presented three

---
[23]"Fællesmødet i Foreningssagen," *Lutheraneren*, XXII (1888), 352.
[24]*Supra*, pp. 5-8.
[25]"Om Fællesmødet i Scandinavia," *E. L. K.*, XV (1888), 768-773, 784 f.
[26]*Fællesmødet i Scandinavia, Wisconsin. Fra 15de til 21de November 1888* (Wittenberg, Wisconsin: Waisenhusets Bogtrykkeri, n. d.), p. 5. The footnote indicates that Pastors O. Hanson, M. G. Hanson, Utheim, Oppegaard and Sandven did not vote for paragraph one.
[27]*Ibid.*, p. 8. The official Hauge's Synod organ protested the way in which approval of paragraph five had been "forced through." "Fra Fællesmødet," *Budbæreren*, XX (1888), 750.
[28]"Om Fællesmødet i Scandinavia," *E. L. K.*, XV (1888), 785 f.

proposals: (1) they wanted the word "easily" removed from the following explanation concerning justification and the atonement (para. 4a): "We will not accede in introducing or sanctioning the new usage of language in consequence of which the redemption of the world is presented as a general justification of the world, whereby justification by faith is *easily* [italics not in original] overshadowed." It was their conviction that such an overshadowing of justification would *necessarily* follow. (2) They requested the omission of the explanatory remarks in paragraph 4c, which stressed the subjective and objective aspects of absolution. (3) They requested the inclusion *in the constitution* of a paragraph approving and encouraging lay activity as practiced by "the friends of Hauge" in Norway. Five of the ten Haugeans felt this should be a part of the unalterable section of the constitution.[29] These proposals were referred to the joint committee which granted the first two requests but denied the third. The assembly adopted the recommendation of the committee.[30] With this disposed of, the conference proceeded to adopt an important motion introduced by Professor Oftedal, approving the doctrinal statements prepared by the joint committee as now amended. The motion also stated that the old doctrinal conflicts should now be considered settled and buried, and that the committee be commended for its work.[31] President G. Hoyme expressed the wish that these conflicts might be buried twenty fathoms in the earth from which they ought not rise again like ghosts to frighten the common people.[32]

The proposed constitution was accepted with a few significant alterations. In the first place, the name recommended by the joint committee was rejected. As mentioned above, the proposed name, "The Norwegian Lutheran Free Church in America," was undoubtedly the handiwork of Professor Sverdrup. At Scandinavia Professor Schmidt (Anti-Missourian) and

---
[29]*Ibid.*, pp. 786 f.
[30]*Ibid.*, pp. 800 f.
[31]*Ibid.*, pp. 801 f.
[32]Th. N. Mohn, "Fællesmødet i Scandinavia, Wisconsin," *Lutherske Vidnesbyrd*, VII (1888), 762.

Pastor N. C. Brun (Conference—Old School) worked against the adoption of this name. Although the reports indicate that the opposition centered ostensibly in the presumptuous all-inclusiveness of such a name, the real reason was no doubt the dislike of these latter men for Sverdrup's concept of a "free-church." The majority approved the change of name to "The United Norwegian Lutheran Church in America."[33] Defeated on the matter of name, the New School men (Sverdrup and Oftedal) proposed that the constitution be altered to permit one *or two* lay delegates from each congregation. This was an expression of their concern for a people's church and free congregations. It was assumed that more lay representation would prevent synodical domination of the congregation. This motion was carried.[34]

In order to mollify the unhappy Haugeans and to give a more positive recognition to lay activity, Pastor M. O. Bøckman proposed that there be introduced into the statement of the church's objectives the assurance that it "promotes Christian lay activity." The amended constitution received the approval of the assembly.[35]

With the doctrinal section and the proposed constitution agreed upon, the conference turned to the articles of union. These too were accepted with only minor alterations and little opposition. The major disagreement was over the establishment of a professors' fund. Again it was the delegates of Hauge's Synod who voiced their disapproval, voting against the recommendation which included an allocation of $20,000 to be provided by Hauge's Synod. They warned that there was no possibility of union if this were made one of the conditions. However, the original recommendation stood and was adopted.[36] With the addition of a new paragraph stipulating that previously independent congregations now entering the union

---

[33] *E. L. K.*, XV (1888), 787. The editor points out that the name adopted was quite as faulty as the one rejected, as far as being a description of the new church.
[34] *Ibid.*, pp. 788 f.
[35] *Ibid.*, pp. 802, 803.
[36] *Ibid.*, p. 805.

should contribute to the professors' fund according to ability, the remainder of the report was adopted.[37] Thereupon, Pastor J. Olsen of the Conference moved that a committee of sixteen —four men from each group—be selected to present the cause of union at the 1889 meetings of the conferring groups.[38]

Before the conference was concluded a remarkable event occurred, namely, the celebration of Holy Communion. It was remarkable because never before among Norwegian-American Lutherans had there been a service of Holy Communion in which there was intersynodical participation as far as pastors were concerned. The service was conducted by two pastors, one from the Conference and the other from the Augustana Synod. Bergh, who records the event, declares that it was in this hour, not in 1890, that the United Norwegian Lutheran Church was formed.[39]

Unquestionably the Scandinavia meeting had accomplished much for the cause of union. In reality, its achievements were a testimony to the thorough preparation by the Eau Claire committee and to the value of the numerous conferences of the eighties which revealed the existence of an essential unity and fostered understanding and toleration of opposing views. Naturally the lay delegates who attended these meetings were much impressed and upon returning to their local parishes became ardent advocates of union. The only exception to this was within Hauge's Synod where a feeling of dissatisfaction was mounting.[40]

One evidence of the spirit engendered by the Scandinavia meeting and now prevalent within the Conference, the Augustana Synod and the Anti-Missourian Brotherhood was a poem written by Pastor L. M. Biørn of the Anti-Missourians. Expressing the profound piety of this immigrant folk, so many of whom had been seafaring people, the poem reveals the

[37] *Ibid.*, p. 806.
[38] *Loc. cit.* A proposal that this committee visit the annual convention of the Norwegian Synod was laid on the table.
[39] Bergh, *Den n. luth. Kirkes Hist. i Am.*, p. 379.
[40] Bergh, "Historisk Inledning," in Brun (ed.), *op. cit.*, p. 32.

nautical thought patterns which colored even the ecclesiastical hopes of these Norwegian-Americans at the dawn of the final decade of the 19th century:

Man Has Yearned

Man has yearned for brotherhood
Endless days in every clime.
Night ensued where long he stood
Gazing from the shores of time.
Hark, glad voices echo song!
Heart be still, in faith be strong!
Lift your beacon, Norsemen, rise!
Yonder the ship approaches the shore;
Banner and flag triumphantly soar.

Envy had to move aside;
Homeless was the wanton pride.
Wheresoe'er they took their plight,
Doors were closed, though late at night.
Friend with friend united stand;
Brother clasps a brother's hand.
Strong and mighty was the Lord.
Humbly adore Him; praise Him and sing!
Hide thee, O hide thee under His wing![41]

Synodical Reaction to Scandinavia

As already intimated the only serious opposition to the union movement was that which appeared in Hauge's Synod. The other groups were expected to give enthusiastic approval to the recommendations of the Scandinavia meeting.

Hauge's Synod, 1889.—In its early years, Hauge's Synod had indicated an interest in the cause of church union. But with the passing of time, circumstances led the synod to entertain certain misgivings about mergers with other Lutherans. The important conference held at Chicago in 1885 had witnessed the presence of representatives of Hauge's

---

[41]Bjørn, "Fra Scandinavia," *Lutherske Vidnesbyrd,* VII (1888), 781. Translation by Oscar R. Overby, 1951.

Synod, but none appeared at successive meetings at Gol (1886) and Willmar (1887). In 1885 the annual convention of Hauge's Synod had refused to name a committee to meet with committees of other synods in planning another joint meeting. Indications of this trend within Hauge's Synod were already apparent at the Chicago (1885) meeting. The reason given for the failure to continue in the union movement was the feeling that internal dissension within the Conference and the Norwegian Synod militated against real union.[42] The participation of the Haugeans in the meetings of 1888 was only over the protest of several members at its annual convention of that year.[43] Moreover, when the joint committee assembled at Eau Claire, only two out of seven members of the Hauge's committee were on hand, whereas there was full attendance on the part of the others.[44]

When the important Scandinavia meeting convened, it was evident that the same spirit persisted within the Hauge's delegation. Nevertheless, this synod was quite well represented, indicating that the congregations had responded to the plea of the official organ of the synod to send delegates. However, the editor was not convinced that sufficient unity of faith and practice (especially the latter) existed to warrant a merger.[45] It will be recalled that, when the Haugean delegates appeared at Scandinavia, they objected to certain sections of the union report. Thereupon, major concessions were made to appease them.[46] But despite this gesture of appeasement, Hauge's Synod leaders and pastor remained cool towards the proposed merger.

The real storm within Hauge's Synod broke out in the months just preceding its 1889 convention. The few who argued for the union were inundated by a flood of articles which insisted that union was premature. It was rumored that "the friends

---
[42]"Kirkekrønike," *E. L. K.*, XII (1885), 488.
[43]See Vol. I, ch. XIV, p. 334.
[44]*Supra*, pp. 4-5.
[45]"'Til Hauges Synodes Menigheder, Prester og Professorer!" *Budbæreren*, XX (1888), 699 f.
[46]*Supra*, pp. 13-14.

of union" would secede from the synod, but one of the leading advocates of the merger, Pastor J. Eisteinsen, assured his readers that this was not the case.[47] The secular paper, *Skandinaven*, as well as the Haugean *Budbæreren*, carried a number of articles which revealed the reasons for the Haugean opposition to the union. In the first place, absence of real unity of spirit precluded union.[48] The major objection raised by the Haugeans was the absence of "living" Christianity in the ranks of the other church bodies.[49] Pastor J. N. Kildahl, who appreciated the evangelistic emphasis of Hauge's Synod and who had the confidence of the Haugeans, sought to convince them of the genuineness of the piety in the other synods and to persuade them to participate in the 1890 union.[50] Typical of many Haugean objections was that concerning lay activity. Would the new church give proper emphasis to it?[51] Nothing must be permitted which would cause it to be minimized.[52] P. A. Rasmussen endeavored to assure these questioners that the Anti-Missourians were favorably disposed towards lay activity.[53] Always a matter of great concern to Haugeans was the question of liturgy and clerical vestments, toward which they exhibited a profound distaste. Would the merger force upon them the liturgy of the Church of Norway and the use of cassock, stole, and *prestekrave* (fluted collar) by the pastors?[54] Furthermore, there was altogether too much emphasis on money in this plan of union (Hauge's Synod was allocated $20,000 towards the establishment of an adequate professors' fund).[55] Moreover, there was serious question in the minds of some whether Augsburg Seminary (the proposed divinity school for the new church) would be in a better situation to

---

[47] I. Eisteinsen, "Ikke Splittelse men Forening," *Budbæreren*, XXI (1889), 215-218.
[48] J. S., "Nogle Spørgsmaal til Hauges Synode i Anledning Foreningssagen?" *Skandinaven*, December 26, 1888, p. 2; A Haugean, "Et Par Bemærkninger om Foreningssagen," *Skandinaven*, May 1, 1889, p. 2.
[49] O. O. Bergh, "Foreningssagen," *Budbæreren*, XXI (1889), 133 ff.
[50] J. N. Kildahl, "Til Brødre og Søstre i Hauges Synode," *Skandinaven*, January 31, 1889, p. 7.
[51] Th. Hansen, "Foreningssagen," *Budbæreren*, XXI (1889), 181 ff.
[52] A. Haavik, "Lægmandsvirksomheden," *Budbæreren*, XXI (1889), 214.
[53] P. A. Rasmussen, "Til lidt bedre Forstaaelse," *Skandinaven*, March 13, 1889, p. 7.
[54] O. O. Bergh, *op. cit.*, p. 134.
[55] "Er Foreningssagen et specielt Pengespørgsmaal?" *Skandinaven*, March 27, 1889, p. 2.

train "living witnesses for the Lord's church" than the Hauge's seminary at Red Wing.[56]

In the midst of all this discussion an old and familiar voice, that of August Weenaas, was heard again. Now living in Norway, this former president of Augsburg Seminary and Red Wing Seminary, sent a letter to the editor of *Budbæreren* indicating that he had been eagerly watching the union movement in America and was sorry to see the attitude of his friends in Hauge's Synod. He wanted to speak a "good word" for the cause of union and to give a reminder that union would demand self-denial and self-sacrifice, not least within Hauge's Synod.[57]

Despite this "plain talk" by Weenaas, the rank and file of Hauge's Synod showed little inclination to enter a union with the other churches. Even before the annual convention in 1889, it was a foregone conclusion that Hauge's Synod would officially withdraw from the merger movement. The convention was held at Trinity Church, Chicago, June 12-22, 1889. President Østen Hanson reported that, as a result of the many expressions of opinion against union, it was his conviction that Hauge's Synod was not yet prepared to enter the forthcoming united church.[58] Nevertheless, a considerable amount of time was devoted to a discussion of the decisions reached the previous autumn, and the committee selected at Scandinavia was given an entire afternoon session to present the cause of union. Despite the presence and appeal of such highly-respected leaders as Rasmussen and Kildahl of the Anti-Missourians and Hoyme of the Conference, no step was taken to approve the union proposals. Finally, a motion was adopted stating that it was advisable to lay the matter aside until it had been given further thought and consideration.[59] In this way, Hauge's Synod effectively removed itself from the union

---
[56]A. H. Raae, "Foreningssagen," *Budbæreren*, XXI (1889), 124.
[57]"Til 'Budbærerens' Redaktion!" *Budbæreren*, XXI (1889), 198-201.
[58]"Referat af Hauges norsk evangelisk lutherske Synodes 44de Aarsmøde . . . 1889," *Budbæreren*, XXI (1889), 407-408.
[59]*Ibid.*, pp. 435-436. Only three pastors and two laymen requested that their negative votes be recorded in the minutes. *Ibid.*, p. 437.

movement until 1905, when it took the initiative in the new union movement which culminated in the 1917 merger.

Anti-Missourian Brotherhood 1889.—It was a keen disappointment that Hauge's Synod withdrew from the proposed merger, but fortunately this action did not dampen the enthusiasm of the other groups. The Anti-Missourians held their convention May 30-June 5, 1889, at Hanley Falls, Minnesota, and adopted the merger plans with only a few changes. The subject of Christian lay activity was raised, because, as one pastor put it, many charged the Anti-Missourians with teaching that lay activity ought to be confined to the conducting of family devotions.[60] Professor Schmidt prepared the following resolution, later adopted, in order to clarify the Anti-Missourian position on Christian lay activity:

> By Christian laymen's activity we understand:
> (1) Not only the conducting of family devotions, the Christian instruction of children, Christian conversations and reproofs between individual persons, but that with the individual congregations there be conducted meetings for edification *(opbyggelsesmöder)*, and gathering for joint prayer, mutual reproof, instruction, exhortation and the promotion of the fear of God.
> (2) That one make use of such gifts of grace which the Lord of the Church may have bestowed upon Christian laymen, in order to produce, through the proclamation of the Word, awakenings and warnings in wider circles also.[61]

Turning from the topic of lay activity, the Anti-Missourians approved the proposed constitution and adopted an explanatory resolution which showed the characteristic concern of the Norwegians to preserve the autonomy of the local congregation: "We approve this constitution with the understanding that the synod *[samfundet]* in relation to the individual congregation is advisory, not legislative."[62]

Realizing that the articles of union allocated a sum of $50,000 to be raised for the professors' fund by the Anti-Missourians, a spirited and optimistic discussion was held on this

---

[60]*Beretning om det andet aarlige Møde af det Anti-missouriske Broderskab . . . 1889* (Northfield, Minnesota: Northfield Publishing Company, 1889), p. 14.
[61]*Ibid.*, p. 14, 57.
[62]*Ibid.*, p. 23.

matter. It was agreed by all that "where there is a will, there is a way," and that with proper preaching of the Word, emphasizing the place of money in the Kingdom, the funds would be forthcoming.[63] A committee, with Pastor P. A. Rasmussen as chairman, was chosen to direct the ingathering of funds among the congregations in order to comply with the articles of union.[64] It was patent that the Anti-Missourians were approaching 1890 hopefully and with determination.

The Norwegian Augustana Synod, 1889.—As was to be expected, no opposition to the proposed union was raised at the annual meeting of the Norwegian Augustana Synod held at Highland Prairie, Minnesota, May 22-30, 1889. A minor discussion occurred relative to the possibility of Missourian remnants in the doctrinal position of the Anti-Missourians. This was a mere ripple, however, and on the motion of Pastor O. A. Solem, the synod passed the following resolution: "Resolved, that we adopt the proposed constitution, articles of union, and doctrinal settlement of the Scandinavia meeting according to the joint meeting's resolution, paragraph 18 and 19."[65] Thus the Augustanans cast their lot with the hoped-for united church, awaiting only the favorable decisions of the individual congregations, who, according to the above-mentioned paragraph nineteen, were now to consider the proposal.

The Conference for the Norwegian-Danish Evangelical Lutheran Church, 1889.—The 1889 meeting of the Conference was held in Grundy, Illinois, June 19-26. In his report to the church, President Hoyme called attention to the favorable action of the Anti-Missourians and the Augustanans on the merger proposal. He mentioned that, although Hauge's Synod was not yet ready, perhaps within a year's time, this church

[63]*Ibid.*, pp. 23-25. It is interesting to note the difference between the attitudes of the Anti-Missourians and Hauge's Synod on this matter. Professor Schmidt insisted that money played an important part in God's kingdom. The Haugeans gave the impression that there was a taint of unspirituality about the emphasis on money in the union movement. *Supra*, p. 18.
[64]"Fond," *Lutherske Vidnesbyrd*, VIII (1889), 392. Instead of $50,000 the Anti-Missourians raised almost $90,000 in this campaign. "Det Anti-missouriske Broderskabs Aarsmøde," D. C. Jordahl and G. T. Lee, *Fællesmødet for "Den forenede Kirke"* . . . *1890* (Minneapolis: Fædrelandet og Emigranten Publishing Company, 1890), p. XI.
[65]"Kirkelige Efterretninger," *E. L. K.*, XVI (1889), 382. The motion was passed without a negative ballot. Three or four abstained from voting.

would also become a part of the new organization. It was his hope that the Conference would now give its endorsement to the merger.[66]

When the union report was presented, the doctrinal statement was examined point by point and unanimously adopted. The same procedure was followed in the consideration of the constitution. This, too, was unanimously approved.[67] When the convention came to the articles of union, the question was raised whether the Conference could actually fulfill the condition of providing a fund of $50,000. The president of the board of trustees, Sven Oftedal, had reported that the professors' fund in the Conference was considerably short of the required sum. Despite the fact that the report showed over $55,000, worthless notes, current indebtedness, and other circumstances reduced the sum by approximately $22,000.[68] It was consequently decided that a campaign be begun immediately to raise the required sum and that the participation of the Conference in the 1890 merger be made contingent upon the successful completion of this financial drive.[69] President Hoyme was elected director of the campaign.[70] An ardent advocate of union, Hoyme was calculated to press this venture to a successful conclusion. This is precisely what happened. Under his direction, the goal was over-subscribed and the way made clear for the union.[71]

Thus the respective annual synodical meetings of the year 1889, with the exception of Hauge's Synod, gave enthusiastic approval to the union proposals. During the subsequent year the entire matter was considered on the parish level, and each congregation was to report its decision to the synodical president prior to the next annual meeting. The stage was now set for the dramatic and eagerly anticipated events of 1890.

---
[66] *Beretning . . . Konferentsen . . . 1889*, p. 16.
[67] *Ibid.*, p. 65.
[68] *Ibid.*, pp. 26-29.
[69] *Ibid.*, p. 82.
[70] *Ibid.*, p. 56.
[71] "Beretning . . . Konferentsen . . . 1890," in *Beretning om Det 1ste Aarsmøde for Den forenede norsk-luth. Kirke i Amerika . . . 1890* (Minneapolis: Trykt i den forenede norsk-luth. Kirkes Trykkeri, 1890), pp. 54-56. United Church reports will henceforth be abbreviated to *Beretning . . . Den f. Kirke . . . (year)*.

CHAPTER TWO

Achieving the Union

By previous arrangement all three church bodies held the annual conventions of 1890 in the city of Minneapolis. Each convened separately on June 11, and concluded its existence as an independent body. A committee of two from each church body assured itself that the conditions of union had been fulfilled by all participants. Its affirmative report was adopted by each convention.[1] The congregations of the three churches had given their unreserved approval to the union. Of the 788 congregations which belonged to the conferring synods not one was reported as voting against the union.[2] Each group now proceeded to adopt the constitution of The United Norwegian Lutheran Church in America.[3] The Anti-Missourians did so after expressing the opinion that the new church body ought to be advisory rather than legislative in relation to the individual congregations.[4] As previously mentioned, for the Norwegian Augustanans and the Conference this step of adopting the United Church constitution meant a change of their old constitutions; but for the Anti-Missourians it meant the adoption of a constitution for the first time. This was in harmony with

---
[1]*Beretning* . . . *Den f. Kirke* . . . *1890*, p. 124. Brief minutes of each of the three conventions which preceded the merger convention are included.
[2]Bergh, *Den n. luth. Kirkes Hist. i Am.*, p. 383.
[3]*Beretning* . . . *Den f. Kirke* . . . *1890*, pp. 4, 6, 8.
[4]*Ibid.*, p. 6.

the articles of union.[5] Thus, by adopting a common constitution the three groups became one. Before the dissolution of the then existing bodies, each convention selected professors for the joint seminary. The choices were as follows: For the Conference, Georg Sverdrup and Sven Oftedal; for the Anti-Missourians, F. A. Schmidt and M. O. Bøckman; and for the Norwegian Augustanans, D. Lysnes.[6] In addition, the Conference took two significant actions. In the first place, it elected Professor Sven Oftedal and Oley Nelson to three-year terms on the board of trustees for the Augsburg Seminary.[7] In the second place, it passed the following resolution:

    1. The board of trustees of the seminary is authorized to amend its articles of incorporation so that the board instead of being elected at and by the annual meeting of the Conference, shall be elected at and by the annual meeting of the United Norwegian Lutheran Church.
    2. The name shall be abbreviated from the Norwegian-Danish Evangelical Augsburg Seminary to simply Augsburg Seminary.[8]

The first of these matters was to play a significant role in the tragedy that followed the formation of the United Church.

Following the dissolution of each body, the merger plan called for a joint meeting of the three delegations in Trinity Church. On the morning of June 13, the Anti-Missourians, having assembled again at St. Paul's Church, and the Norwegian Augustanans, having gathered at Augsburg Seminary, formed a procession and marched to Trinity Church where the Conference delegation awaited them. The editor of *Vort Blad* described the event as follows:

    At ten o'clock, Friday forenoon, preparations were made at the Conference church for the coming of the other groups. The members of

---

[5]Paragraph eighteen: ". . . In case the annual conventions in 1889 approve these proposals, the proposed constitution shall be a pending motion for change of constitution in the formerly organized bodies, and can consequently be adopted by them at their annual conventions in 1890. As far as the Anti-Missourians are concerned, it will be a pending motion for constitution, which can be adopted at their annual meeting in 1890." Bergh, "Historisk Inledning," in Brun (ed.), *op. cit.*, p. 25.
[6]*Beretning . . . Den f. Kirke . . . 1890*, pp. 4, 5, 7.
[7]"Konferentsens Aarsmøde, 1890," in *Fællesmødet for "Den forenede Kirke,"* . . . *1890*, p. XIX. The Conference had never been incorporated; only the Seminary had legal status.
[8]"*Beretning . . . Konferentsen . . .*" in *Beretning . . . Den f. Kirke . . . 1890*, p. 4.

the Conference were asked to take their places as near the main door as their large number permitted. By sitting closely together in and between the pews in the commodious church, about half of the forward part of the church remained empty. And soon the Anti-Missourians began to arrive. When they entered the church, they were greeted by the standing assembly with the hymn . . .: "God's Word Is Our Great Heritage."
. . . After a short moment of waiting members of the Augustana Synod began to enter, and they were greeted with the first stanza of "Praise to Thee and Adoration."

More than 2000 people, the great majority of whom were men, now filled the church from altar to door, and this assembly sang . . . "Thee God We Praise." Many of us undoubtedly thought of the many other solemn occasions in the past when *Te Deum* had resounded in the Church; but probably seldom had it been sung with greater power than when these 2000 male voices sang it out of hearts filled with profound feeling. . . . And who at that moment could help but see, not only ourselves and our children, who down through the ages and generations should walk united upon their way to church, but also that greater gathering when the hosts of the Lord's Church would meet from east and from west, from north and from south, around the throne of His glory. And I suppose we should not be ashamed to have shed the tears of repentance and humility, joy and gratitude at that moment. It would have been good for you too, dear reader, to have sung and wept with us.

Thereupon we confessed our faith and prayed the Lord's Prayer audibly together, and no "eloquent" prayer of praise whatever could have taken the place of the simple words which mother and father and the Church of the Lord had taught each one of us in the Catchism.[9]

It was immediately apparent that 2000 people standing in that crowded church could not conduct the official business of organizing a new synod. Therefore, the convention withdrew from Trinity and marched two by two to Augustana Church, 11th Avenue South and 7th Street, the mother-church of the Swedish Augustana Synod in Minneapolis. As organist Dahle played improvisations on "A Mighty Fortress Is Our God," "Praise to the Lord, the Almighty" and other Lutheran chorales the long procession found its way into the church. After the singing of the Battle Hymn of the Reformation, Pastor P. A.

---
[9]Bergh, *Den n. luth. Kirkes Hist. i Am.*, pp. 383-385. (Translation by J. R. Lavik).

Rasmussen, the "father" of the union movement, led the assembly in prayer.[10]

Professor Oftedal, upon motion by Pastor Biørn, was elected temporary chairman, and Pastor Kildahl, upon motion by Professor Sverdrup, was elected temporary secretary.[11] A brief discussion then occurred concerning the necessity of adopting the constitution since each group had already done so. Pastor Hoyme, with customary clarity of expression, said that it was not necessary in and by itself to do so, since the constitution was already adopted. But the present assembly should vote on the constitution, not as if they were adopting a new instrument, but as a ratification of the previous actions. With this explanation, the assembly unanimously approved the constitution.[12] The election of officers for the new church body resulted in the following: Pastor G. Hoyme of the Conference, president; Pastor L. M. Biørn of the Anti-Missourians, vice-president; Pastor J. N. Kildahl also of the Anti-Missourians, secretary; and Mr. Lars Swenson of the Conference, treasurer.[13]

According to the constitution the new synod was divided into non-administrative districts. Nineteen such geographic areas were formed and in each one a pastor was designated as "visitator."[14] As an indication that the United Church was determined to press the matter of Lutheran union among Norwegian-Americans, two union committees were elected, one to nego-

[10] *Fællesmødet for "Den forenede Kirke"* . . . 1890, pp. 3-5.
[11] *Ibid.*, p. 5. In light of what was to transpire in a very short time, it is significant to observe the relation between the "New School" Conference men (Sverdrup and Oftedal) and the Anti-Missourians (Biørn and Kildahl).
[12] *Ibid.*, p. 6.
[13] *Ibid.*, pp. 8, 11, 12. Hoyme was not immediately prepared to accept the office. The constitution did not stipulate whether the presidency should be a full-time position. The presidents of the three previous synods had served congregations. Hoyme, who was pastor of the large Eau Claire (Wisconsin) congregation and last president of the Conference, felt that his experiences qualified him to point out the inadvisability of the president of the new body serving a congregation. *Ibid.*, p. 9. At Sverdrup's suggestion a committee was appointed to study the matter and report. *Ibid.*, p. 13. The committee, consisting of Pastors C. O. Braaten, T. H. Dahl and O. A. T. Solem, prepared a resolution, which was adopted, indicating that the presidency was full-time and that the annual salary was to be $1,500 plus traveling expenses. *Beretning . . . Den f. Kirke . . . 1890*, pp. 113, 120-121. As was anticipated, Hoyme accepted the position. *Fællesmødet . . . 1890*, pp. 15, 52.
[14] *Beretning . . . Den f. Kirke . . . 1890*, p. 111. A "visitator" was an active pastor whose duty it was to visit each parish triennially ("if possible") to determine "the state of the church" and to assist in settling parish problems. This office proved to be, on the whole, rather ineffective.

tiate with the Norwegian Synod, the other, with Hauge's Synod.[15] President Hoyme, always ready to speak for a united Lutheran church, had given expression to his high hopes for speedy union with both Hauge's Synod and the Norwegian Synod in his last presidential address to the Conference.[16] Clearly he did not contemplate twenty-seven additional years of deliberations with these two synods. As it was Hoyme, Biørn and Hatlestad, all prominent in the union movement, were not to live to see the next great step in the merging of the church.

The three official organs were merged and a new weekly, *Luthersk Kirkeblad,* edited by the theological faculty, was to take the place of the former papers.[17]

That the new church was prepared to promote an intensive home mission program to gather in the Norwegian diaspora all the way from the Mississippi Valley to the Pacific Northwest and thus to meet the challenge provided by the successive waves of Norwegian immigration was clearly indicated by the lengthy discussion and manifest interest in the allocation of mission funds to the various areas. Ten thousand dollars was to be provided for the coming year's program and the Home Mission Committee was to call a superintendent to organize and oversee the work.[18]

Two resolutions which indicated to some extent the influence of the American environment upon these Norwegian-American churchmen concerned the liquor traffic and the mission work of other Protestant bodies among the Norwegian immigrants. Despite their European background the Norwegians gave evidence of vigorous advocacy of the prohibition movement,

---

[15]*Ibid.,* p. 112. The former: Pastor T. H. Dahl, Professor M. O. Bøckman, Professor D. Lysnes, Pastor N. Iversen, and Pastor G. Rasmussen. The latter: Pastor P. A. Rasmussen, Dr. F. A. Schmidt, Pastor G. Hoyme, Pastor J. C. Jensen, Pastor J. A. Bergh.

[16]*Ibid.,* p. 29. "That day is not far off," he said.

[17]*Ibid.,* pp. 112, 119. The merging papers were *Luthersk Vidnesbyrd* of the Anti-Missourians, *Lutheraneren* of the Conference, and *Luthersk Kirketidende* of the Augustana Synod. The first issue of *Luthersk Kirkeblad* continued the numbering of *Lutheraneren,* and was dated August 16, 1890. In January, 1891, it began independent numbering designating the first issue as No. 1, Vol. I. The report of the publications committee expressed the hope that the new organ would be comparable to Dr. W. A. Passavant's paper, *The Workman. Ibid.,* p. 88.

[18]*Ibid.,* pp. 118-119. Cf. *Fællesmødet* . . . *1890,* pp. 29-39.

urging pastors and people to oppose "the ungodly and ruinous traffic."[19] The second resolution was a strenuous objection to the practice of some of the larger American Protestant denominations, particularly the Congregationalists, in proselyting the Scandinavians.[20]

Perhaps the most portentous of all the decisions of the convention was the adoption of a resolution which made St. Olaf College, Northfield, Minnesota, "the college of the United Church." St. Olaf's School had been founded in 1874 by Pastor B. J. Muus and had been without synodical affiliation, although it had been offered to the Norwegian Synod.[21] When the Election Controversy split the Synod, the Anti-Missourians rallied to the support of St. Olaf and generally considered it their college, despite the fact it was an independent institution. With the formation of the United Church, the hope grew among the supporters of the college that the new church body would accept St. Olaf as one of its educational institutions. The board of trustees of the school offered to transfer it to the United Church and accordingly, when the committee on educational institutions made its report to the convention, it included resolutions pertaining to St. Olaf College.[22]

Those portions of the committee report which bear upon the proposed transaction are as follows:

(2) It is incumbent upon the Board of Directors [of Augsburg Seminary] in conjunction with the theological faculty to prepare the necessary regulations with reference to the division of labor among the theological professors at the school.

(6) The committee proposes that the school directors maintain the academy at Canton, South Dakota and the college department of Augsburg Seminary for the coming year in the same manner as heretofore.

(8) (a) St. Olaf's College at Northfield, Minnesota, shall be the college of the United Norwegian Lutheran Church.

---

[19]*Beretning* . . . *Den f. Kirke* . . . 1890, p. 122.

[20]*Ibid.*, pp. 122-123. The resolution: " . . . we . . . do hereby most earnestly protest against the proselytism among our people as unjust, unchristian, pernicious in its effect upon the church of God and an insult to our church and our nationality, and do most earnestly request the denominations concerned to desist therefrom."

[21]W. C. Benson, *High on Manitou. A History of St. Olaf College, 1874-1949* (Northfield, Minnesota: St. Olaf College Press, 1949), p. 38.

[22]*Fællesmødet* . . . 1890, pp. 52 ff.

Gjermund Hoyme
First President of the United Church

United Church Seminary, St. Paul, Minn.

Concordia College, Moorhead, Minnesota

Pacific Lutheran College, Tacoma, Washington

Augustana College and Normal, Sioux Falls, South Dakota

THEOLOGICAL FACULTIES ABOUT 1900

United Church

M. O. Bøckman    E. G. Lund    E. Kr. Johnsen    F. A. Schmidt

Hauge's Synod

H. H. Bergsland    M. G. Hanson

Norwegian Synod

H. G. Stub    Joh. Ylvisaker    J. B. Frich    W. M. H. Peterson

A Typical ELC Rural Church

(b) The United Norwegian Lutheran Church at the present meeting shall nominate twenty-five candidates of the former Anti-Missourians, twenty-five of the former Norwegian-Danish Conference, and ten of the former Augustana Synod, and the board of trustees of St. Olaf College shall elect of the Anti-Missourian candidates fifteen, of those of the Conference fifteen, and of those of the Augustana Synod five, as members of a new board of trustees of St. Olaf College.

(c) Seven members of the board of trustees shall retire each year, and a new election shall take place. The United Church shall nominate each year fourteen candidates, and the board of trustees shall supplement itself by electing new members from these candidates.

(d) The United Norwegian Lutheran Church pledges itself to support St. Olaf College in such a manner that it may continue to be a college which will meet the requirements that the times demand of an institution of this kind.

Hardly had the report been presented when Professor Sverdrup arose to speak against the adoption of Paragraph Two which stipulated that the directors as well as the faculty should determine what and where the professors should teach. Sverdrup maintained that the directors would be unqualified to make such decisions. Furthermore, he insisted that this resolution limited the theological professors to teaching in the seminary but not in the preparatory or college department of the school. This, he said, would strike at the very heart of Augsburg's educational program and would mean the ruination of the school.[23] For, according to Sverdrup's "program" which had been carried out at Augsburg for fifteen years, there was to be an integrated educational plan with the preparatory, college, and seminary departments cut of the same cloth. As a matter of fact, theological professors were to teach in the preparatory department as well as in the seminary, thus giving the whole program the orientation which Sverdrup conceived was proper in a Christian educational institution.[24] As if he were thinking, "There is more in this than meets the eye," Sverdrup bluntly asked, "As a theological professor and one who has the welfare of the school at heart, I wish to know

[23] *Ibid.*, p. 54.
[24] A. Helland, *Georg Sverdrup, The Man and His Message 1848-1907* (Minneapolis: The Messenger Press, 1947), p. 52.

precisely what the committee's meaning is in this matter?"[25] Sensing that this was perhaps a well-timed blow at his pet theory of education and an attempt to remove the college department at Augsburg in order to make room for St. Olaf College, he insisted that a board of directors would be quite incompetent to deal with the problems arising in the new faculty composed of professors representing differing traditions.

At this point Pastor P. G. Østby, an Old School opponent of Sverdrup from the days of the sharpest cleavages in the Conference, together with President Mohn of St. Olaf College, argued that it would be ridiculous for a church convention to establish a schedule for a theological school. The proper agency for this was the board of directors and the faculty.[26] Sverdrup seemed to have little support in the assembly, for one after another spoke in behalf of the committee's proposal. Finally Professor Schmidt suggested, as a sort of compromise, that the committee's recommendation be adopted with the understanding that the faculty be given free hands to determine the teaching schedule. This was adopted.[27]

In the afternoon of the same day, Tuesday, June 17, the convention reached the highly-charged Paragraph Eight which, if adopted, would commit the United Church to support St. Olaf College. As an indication of the temper of the meeting, a motion to consider this paragraph point by point was defeated.[28] Realizing the way the wind was blowing, Sverdrup's intimate friend and colleague, Professor Oftedal, rose and declaimed that, "as it is important to have a good seminary, it is likewise important to have a good college." In such a significant matter as this, he would like to have the paragraph considered point by point, but since there would hardly be time for that, it was

---
[25]*Fællesmødet* . . . *1890*, p. 54.
[26]When one reads the stenographic report of this exchange, one is quick to sense a subtle shift in argument. Østby and Mohn impute to Sverdrup the suggestion that the synod convention determine school details. Anybody could see that this would be a cumbersome way to handle the matter. Sverdrup, however, had said nothing about the synod; he was arguing for a narrowing of responsibility to the faculty alone, where, as president, he hoped to preserve intact his *menighedsmæssig presteuddannelse*, built upon the presupposition that Augsburg was an indissoluble whole: preparatory, college and seminary as one.
[27]*Fællesmødet* . . . *1890*, p. 56.
[28]*Ibid.*, p. 64.

his considered judgment that the paragraph be voted on as a whole. Pastor B. Tollefsen, a New School Conference man, then moved that the whole paragraph be turned over to the Board of Directors of Augsburg for consideration until the next annual synodical meeting. Thereupon, a stream of speakers, pastors, professors and laymen, spoke in favor of Paragraph Eight. One of the delegates stressed the fact that St. Olaf College was a "great gift" which the United Church could not afford to refuse, especially in view of Augsburg Seminary's report to the synod of overcrowded conditions.[29] Professor Schmidt, emphasizing that he carried no special brief for St. Olaf College and that he had been originally opposed to this arrangement, now felt that the only thing to do was to adopt this proposal. If the new church valued the fact that the former Conference had contributed a divinity school, it should set equal store by the present opportunity to obtain control of a college. He continued with the following significant declaration:

> Furthermore, I believe that Augsburg Seminary will be too small to be both a seminary and a college. It would be, therefore, more to the point if the preparatory division could be separated from Augsburg and be an independent school. Thus the seminary could be by itself, and the preparatory school likewise, wherever it may be located. Men have always come back to the conclusion that it is best not to have the two institutions [college and seminary] together.[30]

The observation of most significance in connection with Schmidt's idea is that what he expressed openly was precisely what Sverdrup feared was the motive for making St. Olaf the college of the United Church. The articles of union had specified that Augsburg should be the seminary of the United Church, that the preparatory department of Augsburg (including the college) should be maintained, as is, for at least one year. In other words, there was no guarantee that Augsburg's college department should continue in perpetuity. But Sverdrup said no more. Manifestly the convention wanted St.

---
[29] *Ibid.*, p. 66.
[30] *Ibid.*, pp. 67-68. It is interesting to note that Professor Schmidt gave expression to an educational policy practiced today in the major Protestant bodies.

Olaf College, and when Pastor J. A. Bergh proposed that even as the resolutions with reference to Augsburg Seminary and the election of its professors had been unanimously adopted, so also this matter regarding St. Olaf ought to have the unanimous approval of the assembly. Without permitting him to finish his speech, voices were raised calling for the question. Therewith, Tollefson's motion that Paragraph Eight be turned over to the Augsburg Board of Directors was defeated, and the original proposal in its entirety was adopted, thus making St. Olaf College an institution of the United Church.[31]

The next morning, Wednesday, June 18, President Hoyme called for the report of the committee on elections. Among other offices to be filled was the presidency of Augsburg Seminary, and nominated for this position was Professor Georg Sverdrup. Before bringing the matter to a vote, the president read a letter from Sverdrup (who had absented himself) in which the latter expressed himself as being unprepared to assume the office and therefore must decline the nomination. Immediately Pastors Rasmussen, Roalkvam, and Ellestad presented a resolution expressing appreciation of Sverdrup's leadership, and that it would be a loss to the United Church not to have him as president. Similar expressions of opinion were heard from all quarters and when the vote was taken Sverdrup was unanimously elected.[32] As directors for Augsburg Seminary the following were elected: Professor Sverdrup, chairman, Professor Bøckman, Pastors J. N. Kildahl, H. Roalkvam, T. H. Dahl, H. M. Sætterlie, J. C. Jensen, O. J. Hatlestad, and Mr. A. A. Klove.[33]

Paragraph Seven of the articles of union stated that the new church body was to be incorporated as soon as possible. This

---
[31]*Ibid.*, p. 70.
[32]*Ibid.*, pp. 75-78. M. O. Bøckman of the Anti-Missourians was elected vice-president. It is interesting to note that Sverdrup's name does not appear in the proceedings as a speaker after the rough handling he had received on the matter of the relationship between the Board of Directors and the faculty. Whether he left the assembly and did not return, is not clear from the minutes. (The late Professor George Ellingson, St. Olaf College, was present at the 1890 convention and has told the writer that Sverdrup left the church in anger.) His voluble friend, Oftedal, was much in evidence and had something to say on almost every subsequent question.
[33]*Ibid.*, p. 112.

simple statement of what appeared to be an ordinary and to-be-assumed requirement was in reality a keen desire based upon the confused experiences of the former Conference which had never been incorporated, a fact which was to involve the United Church in years of bitterness in the matter of obtaining legal control of Augsburg Seminary and the "professors' fund" of the Conference. The Conference property was legally under the board of trustees of Augsburg Seminary which had incorporated itself under the laws of Minnesota in 1872, with amendments in 1877.[34] The articles of union obligated each synod to raise a specified sum, such funds to be pooled in the new church to endow the chairs of theology at Augsburg Seminary.

When the legal committee was ready to report, its spokesman, Professor Oftedal,[35] proposed to the convention that, because of the shortness of time and the difficulties involved in incorporating the new church, a committee on incorporation be elected by the assembly to arrange the necessary legal requirements and then present the matter at the next synodical meeting.[36] Several objections to this procedure were raised, chief among them being the belief that the requirements implicit in the articles of union bound the church to incorporate itself at this meeting. The chief argument for this was that the synodical funds were to be turned over to "the incorporated church."[37] A lay delegate, Mr. Iver Larsen, made a substitute motion that a committee on incorporation be elected and that it go to work immediately so that incorporation could take place at this meeting.[38] Against this, Professor Oftedal urged the assembly to make haste slowly. However, the convention was not to be deterred and Larsen's motion was adopted. The

---

[34]*In the District Court of the State of Minnesota in and for the Fourth Judicial District and County of Hennepin . . . Application of Nils C. Brun et al. against Sven Oftedal et al.* (Minneapolis: North Star Printing Company, 1897), pp. 7-8, 22-25. Cf. *Beretning . . . Konferentsen . . . 1877*, pp. 45, 46, 79.
[35]Besides Oftedal, the committee consisted of Consul Halle Stensland and Pastor A. Wright.
[36]*Fællesmødet . . . 1890*, p. 80.
[37]Article eight of the articles of union. Bergh, "Historisk Inledning," in Brun (ed.), *op. cit.*, p. 25.
[38]*Fællesmødet . . . 1890*, p. 83.

committee on incorporation began its work immediately and on Wednesday afternoon reported that it was not feasible to incorporate at this meeting and that the original proposal to have articles of incorporation prepared for the next annual convention be carried out. In light of this Larsen's motion was rescinded and the committee's suggestion approved.

A third item in the committee's report, however, met with even more discussion and caused no little confusion. The committee on incorporation proposed that the vexing problem of what to do about the funds subscribed for the professors' endowment be solved by requesting that these monies be turned over to the incorporated board of trustees of Augsburg Seminary to be held in trust until the convention of 1891. Again indicative of the temper of the meeting, a substitute motion that the three individual funds be held by the original parties until the following year was adopted by a large majority.[39] This was confusion worse confounded, for the original synods no longer existed. Once more a motion to reconsider was approved and the committee's original solution of the problem was adopted by the assembly.[40] Thus it came about that the unincorporated United Church authorized the turning over of its special funds to the board of trustees of the incorporated Augsburg Seminary.

With the business of organizing a new church completed, the concluding session of the convention was moved from the Swedish Augustana Church to the Colosseum of the University of Minnesota where over five thousand people gathered for a festival service of thanksgiving on Wednesday evening, June 18. Several speeches were made in which expression was given to the joy in the hearts of thousands over the consummation of the union efforts. President Gjermund Hoyme climaxed the occasion with the dramatic words:

Return to your homes, pastors and lay delegates, and let the church bells ring from every tower—let them ring so their sound will echo among Norway's mountains and will declare to the mother church that

[39] Ibid., pp. 104, 106. The vote was 234 to 145.
[40] Ibid., p. 108.

her emigrated and separated sons and daughters have found one another.[41]

Despite the disparaging comments of the editor of *Evangelisk Luthersk Kirketidende* (Norwegian Synod organ), the events of the year 1890 made this one of the two most significant dates in the history of Norwegian-American Lutheranism.[42] With this merger, the number of Norwegian Lutheran synods was once more reduced to four. The new synod became the largest of the four church bodies, and as years went on, its influence was to be commensurate with its numerical strength. A total of 688 congregations had accepted the constitution and articles of union by the time of the meeting of 1890. Of these 379 were of the former Conference, 268 of the Anti-Missourians, and 41 of the Norwegian Augustana Synod. Furthermore, thirty-one independent congregations were received into the United Church at the 1890 convention, making a total of 719 congregations. The clergy roll included 260 names.[43] The total membership was inexact because the 1890 report did not include these statistics. Furthermore, the status of the congregations of the former Conference and Norwegian Augustana Synod which had not reported their actions on the matter of union was somewhat uncertain.[44] The secretary's report for 1891 revealed the difficulty in ascertaining the exact membership of the synod because many congregations, not formally members, regarded themselves to be such and sent in parochial reports. On the other hand, as was usually the case, some parishes failed to report their statistics. On the basis of the secretary's report, an estimate has been made that in 1890, the United Church numbered approximately 830 congregations, with 83,500 confirmed members and 152,200 baptized mem-

[41]Brun (ed.), *op. cit.*, p. 44.
[42]"Kirkelige Efterretninger," *E. L. K.*, XVII (1890), 458-459. The other date is 1917 when the Norwegian Lutheran Church of America was formed.
[43]*Beretning . . . Den f. Kirke . . . 1890*, pp. 114, 151-170.
[44]Bergh says that these congregations became members of the United Church if they had not taken specific action against the merger, since the synodical constitutions were only revised. "Historisk Inledning," in Brun (ed.), *op. cit.*, p. 40. President O. J. Hatlestad's 1890 report to the Norwegian Augustana Synod confirms Bergh by the statement that silence was regarded as consent. *Beretning . . . Den f. Kirke . . . 1890*, pp. 39 f. The articles of union do not clarify this matter.

bers.[45] The other two major synods among the Norwegian Lutherans, Hauge's and the Synod, were considerably smaller. In 1890, the former numbered 65 pastors, 185 congregations, 12,741 confirmed members, and 22,279 baptized members.[46] The Norwegian Synod, through its district reports, showed a clergy roll of 187 names. Congregations numbered 516 with 51,534 confirmed members and 94,166 baptized members.[47] For the first time since its organization, the Norwegian Synod now found itself greatly outnumbered, being approximately two-thirds the size of the new church body. In fact, the United Church in 1890 was larger than the Synod and Hauge's Synod combined.

The formation of the United Church marked the end of one epoch and the beginning of a new as far as Norwegian-American Lutheranism was concerned. The old era of divisions, jealousies and doctrinal strife was all but over. To be sure, another twenty years was to elapse before there was doctrinal agreement among all Norwegian-American Lutherans, but nevertheless, the age of major schisms on questions of doctrine was ended. Two problems which the United Church had settled to its own satisfaction remained to agitate Hauge's Synod on the one hand and the Norwegian Synod on the other. These were the questions of lay activity and divine election respectively. Until a satisfactory understanding could be reached on these matters the Norwegians would remain in three separate major ecclesiastical households. The union of these churches was not to come till 1917, but it was apparent now that "*Søndringens tid ær forbi*" ("the day of fragmentation is past").[48] The struggles of the previous years had developed a religious awareness among the people, had produced some able theologians among an immigrant folk, and had led the warring factions

---
[45]Brun (ed.), *op. cit.*, pp. 45 f.
[46]*Beretning . . . Hauges Synode . . . 1891*, pp. 8 f. Only 53 pastors sent in parochial reports. Eielsen's contempt for "protokol" was hard to shake in Hauge's Synod.
[47]The 1890 statistics are to be found in the district reports for 1891. *Beretning . . . Østlige Distrikt . . . 1891*, pp. 74-77; *Iowa Distrikt . . . 1891*, pp. 118-121; *Minnesota Distrikt . . . 1891*, pp. 98-101.
[48]Quoted in K. Gjerset, "Historical Review of the United Norwegian Lutheran Church in America" in O. N. Nelson (ed.), *History of the Scandinavians and Successful Scandinavians in the United States* (Minneapolis: O. N. Nelson, 1893), I, 242.

to a better and deeper understanding of each other. Not least important was the slowly-learned lesson of patience and tolerance, showing forbearance in minor points and charity in consideration of opposing views. In this respect, the United Church had, on the whole, made a happy solution of the major issues, and had combined in its new organization a concern for churchliness and order together with the zeal and devotion characteristic of the Haugean spirit. In this way, the United Norwegian Lutheran Church in America represented a center in church life and thought around which, it was hoped, all parties could eventually unite. But before we can continue the study of the union movement among the Norwegian-American Lutherans, we must pause to examine one of the bitterest and most unpleasant episodes in the life of the church, the controversy over the transfer of Augsburg Seminary to the United Church and the subsequent formation of the Lutheran Free Church.

CHAPTER THREE

The Augsburg Controversy

The efforts of the Norwegian-Americans to find each other religiously were often interrupted by conflict. At times it seemed that the union movement was but a succession of spurts between periods of strife. Hardly had an attempt at good will taken on momentum when it became bogged down in disputes and disagreements. One clear example was the circumstance associated with the merger of 1890. The hope had been expressed by at least one of the synodical presidents that the union of 1890 would serve to hasten the eventual amalgamation of all Norwegian-American Lutherans. Thus 1890 was not to be considered in any way terminal but rather an inducement to immediate and continuing efforts in the cause of church union.[1] This hope was also implicit in the dramatic words spoken at the festival service which marked the consummation of the union.[2]

Hardly had the echoes of President Hoyme's earnest oratory died away when rumblings of dissent were heard. By 1891 these had broken out into the open, and in the succeeding seven years the church was rent by one of the most bitter conflicts in its history, the controversy concerning the control of Augsburg Seminary. For the first time in Norwegian-Amer-

[1] See G. Hoyme's presidential report, *Beretning . . . Den f. Kirke . . .* 1890, p. 29.
[2] *Supra*, pp. 34-35.

38

ican Lutheran history, the church was exercised over a question of major importance which was non-doctrinal in nature.[3] Absolution, "justification of the world," and election were all but forgotten in the battle that raged around Augsburg Seminary in Minneapolis. It is to the tracing of this conflict that we now turn our attention.

1890-1891: The First Year of the United Church

It should be pointed out that the 1890 merger brought together elements in Norwegian-American Lutheranism which, though obviously not irreconcilable, nevertheless were in some respects historically antagonistic. In the enthusiasm surrounding the merger the differences were submerged and attempts were made to forget the mutual grievances of the past. However, there were inflammable materials in the 1890 merger. The Conference men, especially the New School, harbored a dislike for Missourian dogmatism which they suspected was present even among the so-called Anti-Missourians.[4] Furthermore, the Conference was allied with the Augustanans who had vivid recollections of 1870 when, as they felt, Weenaas and Clausen had ridden roughshod over them.[5] It was clear, therefore, that the dying embers of old fires could be fanned into flames. All that the situation required was an "incident." This incident was provided in the decision of the first assembly of the United Church in 1890 to make St. Olaf College of Northfield, Minnesota, an institution of the United Church.[6]

Before 1890 St. Olaf College had been a school without definite ecclesiastical moorings. In its earlier days it had sought unsuccessfully the support and favor of the Norwegian Synod.[7] The Synod felt that it had its hands full in maintaining Luther

---
[3]The previous disagreements on such matters as lay activity had not generated the heat which this one did.
[4]Schmidt and Muus were "Missourian" Anti-Missourians, except for their view of election. Both of these men, prior to the Election Controversy, were vigorous advocates of Norwegian Synod "orthodoxy" in the earlier disputations with such Conference men as Weenaas, Sverdrup, and Oftedal.
[5]Augustanan Pastor Wright insisted his negative vote on some of the articles of union be recorded. Bergh, "Historisk Inledning," in Brun (ed.), *op. cit.*, p. 24.
[6]*Supra*, p. 32.
[7]Benson, *op. cit.*, pp. 37-38, 48-49.

College, Decorah, Iowa, and a seminary at Madison, Wisconsin. With the rise of the Election Controversy in the Norwegian Synod, the Anti-Missourians began to speak of St. Olaf as "our college." When the schism occurred in 1887, the Anti-Missourians established a seminary on the St. Olaf campus, the decision having been reached in 1886 that "St. Olaf's School" should become a "college."[8]

Since the Anti-Missourian Brotherhood was not officially organized and had no legal status as a church body, and since St. Olaf College was controlled by a private corporation, the institution did not enter into the preliminary negotiations regarding the union of the churches in 1890. No provision could be made in the articles of union regarding St. Olaf College because it was only indirectly connected with one of the contracting parties. However, it was public knowledge that the Anti-Missourians considered St. Olaf as "our college."[9] Therefore, it was not strange that the Anti-Missourians, once the union was an accomplished fact, urged upon the new church body the acceptance of the offer of the St. Olaf College corporation to transfer ownership of the school to the United Church. As we have seen, this was discussed at length and approved by a large majority in the United Church.[10]

However, a minority in the United Church led by the former New School Conference men, Sverdrup and Oftedal, interpreted this action on the part of the church as a clever maneuver by the former Anti-Missourians in conjunction with the generally anti-Augsburg Old School men[11] and the Nor-

---

[8]*Ibid.*, p. 53. The official change of name did not occur until June 20, 1889. *Ibid.*, p. 58.
[9]See the published minutes of the Anti-Missourians, *Beretning . . . af det Anti-missouriske Broderskab . . . 1889*, pp. 46-47. One of the subjects discussed at this meeting was "Hvad skal vi gjøre med vort College?" ("What shall we do with our college?")
[10]*Supra*, pp. 28-32.
[11]There is no evidence of collusion between the Anti-Missourians and the Old School men as intimated in L. Lillehei (ed.), *Augsburg Seminary and the Lutheran Free Church* (Minneapolis: n. n., 1928), p. 99. Mohn's letters before 1890 reveal no communication with such Old School men as N. C. Brun, J. A. Bergh, and N. E. Boe. The only Conference men with whom he corresponded on this issue were New School men Sverdrup and Oftedal, and Pastor Hoyme. "Mohn Manuscript Letters," IV (January 4, 1890-July 24, 1891). Hoyme was a loyal Augsburg man, although he vigorously opposed Sverdrup and Oftedal in their refusal to transfer Augsburg to the United Church. He felt that St. Olaf should not replace Augsburg's collegiate department. Hoyme expressed this view to Dr. C. A. Mellby, professor emeritus at St. Olaf. Hoyme's son-in-law, Dr. J. A. Aasgaard, second president of The Evangelical Lutheran Church, confirmed this view to the writer.

wegian Augustanans to destroy or at least to impair Augsburg Seminary, which embodied Sverdrup's pet theory of ministerial education.[12] The historian of the New School, Andreas Helland, maintains that the decision to accept St. Olaf College came as a complete surprise to the New School men who, if they had suspected in 1888 that St. Olaf would be involved in the union, would not have participated in it. He further states, without documentation, that, upon inquiry by the New School men at the drafting of the articles of union, assurances were given that St. Olaf College was not a factor to be considered in the union, and therefore not to be included in the articles of union.[13]

It is true that the articles of union quite explicitly stated that Augsburg Seminary was to be the divinity school *(presteskole)* of the new church body.[14] There was no argument on this matter and the merging churches accepted this as a foregone conclusion. However, with the action which made St. Olaf a college of the United Church, there arose a difference of opinion. The argument simmered down to this: what is a divinity school? Is a divinity school a specialized three-year course in the study of theology, or is it a nine-year course embracing, besides theological studies, a preparatory and college training in which the spirit of the theological department is the guiding principle for the whole? The friends of St. Olaf were prepared to assume the former, or the traditional position, that a divinity school is a *theological* seminary. The friends of Augsburg, however, were committed to the latter view, for it was this that Sverdrup had fought to establish at Augsburg Seminary, an integrated educational program for the training of ministers for a free Lutheran Church in America.

The articles of union also included references to the preparatory departments of Augsburg Seminary and the academy of the Augustanans at Canton, South Dakota. Article Ten stated that these departments should be maintained, as they had been

---

[12] *Supra*, pp. 29-31.
[13] A. Helland, *Augsburg Seminar gjennem femti aar* (Minneapolis: Folkebladet Trykkeri, 1920), pp. 222-223. Cf. G. T. Lee and D. C. Jordahl, *Forhandlingerne ved Den forenede Kirkes tredie Aarsmøde . . . 1892* (Chicago: "Amerika"s Forlag, 1892), pp. 122-123.
[14] Bergh, "Historisk Inledning," in Brun (ed.), *op. cit.,* p. 24.

in the past, for at least one year after the merger.[15] Apparently Sverdrup and his Augsburg friends had accepted this article without question, for as we have shown, Sverdrup was one of the leading spirits in drafting the plan of union.[16] Now, however, the friends of Augsburg Seminary saw in the adoption of St. Olaf a threat to the preparatory and college department at Augsburg. St. Olaf, they reasoned, was to become *the* college of the church, replacing the pre-seminary department at Augsburg, leaving only a theological school. This was to do violence to the whole Sverdrup program of education, making of Augsburg but a burlesque of a ministerial training institution, a head without a body.

At the center of the argument, therefore, were two divergent views on the purposes of church-supported educational institutions. On the one side was Sverdrup's conception that church schools were primarily intended for the education of ministers, and, therefore, the whole course of study must have a special stamp. This was *menighedsmæssig presteuddannelse*. This view tended to exclude any other type of education from the purview of the church. The church should not take any major responsibility for educating men in other professions or for providing a Christian emphasis in general culture.

The other view was embodied at St. Olaf College where Muus and the other founders of the school had sought to establish an educational institution unlike any then existing among Norwegian-Americans. Other schools were chiefly interested in preparing men for theological study or for teaching in the congregational or parochial schools.[17] But at St. Olaf the curriculum was to be more inclusive. Without precluding preparation for the ministry or teaching, this school was to provide a general Christian education, stressing the meaning of Amer-

---
[15] *Ibid.*, p. 25.
[16] *Supra*, p. 8.
[17] *Luther College Through Sixty Years 1861-1921* (Minneapolis: Augsburg Publishing House, 1922), pp. 27, 45-46. Cf. K. Larsen, *Laur. Larsen* (Northfield, Minn.: Norwegian-American Historical Association, 1936), pp. 137, 140-141. This is illustrated by the Luther College graduation certificate which contained the words: "Dismissed to the theological seminary." Gerald Thorson, "The Novels of Peer Strømme," *Norwegian-American Studies and Records*, XVIII, 144.

ican citizenship and the importance of taking one's place as a Lutheran Christian in the social and economic community. Muus, and especially Mohn, the first president, realized that the future depended not only on pastors but also on well-trained and consecrated laymen and lay-*women*. Here was an institution, therefore, which was also "radical" in departing from the prevailing patterns by advocating coeducation.[18]

It was this concept of education which Sverdrup quickly stigmatized as "humanist" and "secular."[19] Pastors prepared for the seminary at St. Olaf would, because of their training in Latin and Greek authors, pagan philosophy and morals, suffer a handicap in the Christian ministry. Humanistic training, as above described, would tend to undermine the religious life of youth from Christian homes.[20] Furthermore, the position maintained by the Rev. Th. N. Mohn, the outspoken president of St. Olaf College, that the college with its broad and liberal curriculum should be independent of the theological seminary was looked upon by Sverdrup as being not only truncated but dangerous.[21] Rather, said Sverdrup, the training of pastors must be in conformity with the nature, origin, and goal of the "free congregation." From the "free congregations" young men would come to Augsburg. Here they would be trained to go back to the congregations as servants of God. Sverdrup's chief

---

[18]Benson, *op. cit.*, pp. 23-24, 44-45, 76, 92.

[19]Georg Sverdrup, *Samlede Skrifter* (Minneapolis: Frikirkens Boghandels Forlag, 1910), III, 214-225. Under the general title, "Humanismen og Presteuddannelsen" (Humanism and Ministerial Education"), Sverdrup discussed "Humanisternes Ufred" ("The Dissension of [caused by] the Humanists"), "Humanismens Princip" ("The Principle of Humanism"), "Den humanistiske Forkvakling af Sjælelivet" ("The Humanist's Impairment of Spiritual Life"), and "Humanismens Ufolkelighed" ("Humanism's Lack of Feeling for the People"). It was this emphasis on "humanism" which made St. Olaf, "a common secular college" unfitted to prepare Christian pastors. *Ibid.*, pp. 217-218 and Lillehei (ed.), *op. cit.*, p. 138.

[20]Some of the Anti-Missourian pastors were concerned that there might be some truth to the charges that St. Olaf was undermining the Christianity of its students. To one pastor who inquired about this, President Mohn wrote a lengthy letter in which he gave him "the facts" regarding the religious and moral character and influence of each of the faculty members. "Mohn Manuscript Letters," IV (January 4, 1890-July 24, 1891), 381, to Pastor H. Roalkvam, December 24, 1890.

[21]C. A. Mellby, *St. Olaf College, Through Fifty Years, 1874-1924* (Northfield, Minnesota: n. n., 1925), pp. 28-29. Cf. Benson, *op. cit.*, p. 92. Surely Sverdrup's charge of "humanism" (Sverdrup's definition: ". . . the presupposition and point of departure of humanism is this that men are good by nature . . ." *Samlede Skrifter*, III, 218) at St. Olaf was so ridiculous that one wonders how such a brilliant and scholarly man, as he unquestionably was, could make such a statement.

purpose was to conduct the school in such a way that it did not lead out of the congregation, but ever deeper into it.[22]

It was to be Sverdrup's conclusion in 1891 and the years that followed that he and his colleague Oftedal, together with "the friends of Augsburg" must fight the transfer of Augsburg Seminary to the control of the United Church, under which, they feared, the institution would lose its distinctive character.[23]

The school year 1890-1891 began optimistically at both St. Olaf and Augsburg.[24] However, suddenly and without warning an event occurred which, because of its explosive character, changed the whole situation. The popular Norwegian language newspaper, *Skandinaven,* published two letters written by an Augsburg student to a "Mr. A. Erikson."[25] The letters, sharp criticisms of the preparatory and college department at Augsburg, were interpreted by the friends of Augsburg as an overt attempt to undermine Augsburg in favor of St. Olaf. They felt that their suspicions were confirmed when it was revealed that the letters had been sent to a relative of the student ("Mr. A. Erikson") who was Dr. A. E. Egge, a professor at St. Olaf College. It was Professor Egge who had made the letters public through the columns of *Skandinaven.*[26] References to the incident were made in Professor Sverdrup's report to the United Church convention in 1891,[27] but names were not mentioned until the report of 1892, and then it was revealed that the student, Thorstein Egge, had apologized and was no longer a student at Augsburg.[28] Professor Egge's actions were discussed

[22]Sverdrup, "Menighedsmæssig Presteuddannelse," *Samlede Skrifter,* III, 234.
[23]Lillehei (ed.), *op. cit.,* p. 138.
[24]Benson, *op. cit.,* p. 75; Helland, *Augsburg Seminar,* pp. 242-243.
[25]"Til Overveielse," *Skandinaven,* January 7, 1891, p. 2. The two letters were dated December 10 and 12. The first was a general criticism of Augsburg as an educational institution. The second letter was a severe castigation of Augsburg's unabashed contempt for *Kundskaben* (knowledge) in general culture and subjects other than those which centered in God's Word.
[26]Professor Sverdrup's agitation over the appearance of these criticisms is witnessed by the fact that he called into his office those students whom he suspected, because of their previous synodical affiliation, of having knowledge of the letters. Professor emeritus C. A. Mellby at St. Olaf told the writer that Sverdrup had quizzed him.
[27]*Beretning* . . . *Den f. Kirke* . . . *1891,* p. 94.
[28]*Beretning* . . . *Den f. Kirke* . . . *1892,* p. 87. Egge, a sickly individual, transferred to the seminary of the Norwegian Synod and was later ordained. He died young. Cf. Helland, *Augsburg Seminar gjennem femti aar,* pp. 244-245, and Norlie (ed.), *Who's Who,* p. 124. C. A. Mellby, a classmate at Augsburg described Egge as a neurotic introvert.

at the convention in 1892 but no disciplinary action was taken.[29] The same summer, however, he was relieved of his teaching duties at St. Olaf College.[30]

Even before the personages of the "Egge affair" came to light, another incident added coals to the fire. Professor F. A. Schmidt, a veteran of many doctrinal battles, now entered the ecclesiastical lists by writing, as a member of the Augsburg theological faculty, a series of articles in which he expressed the opinion that the United Church was not bound to maintain Augsburg's preparatory department longer than one year. Furthermore, what value was there in so doing? Granted there were two sides to the question of ministerial education, it would appear that to avoid undesirable uniformity and one-sidedness in pastors, to say nothing of a marked party-spirit, the church would be best served by separating its colleges from its theological seminaries.[31]

As was to be expected, the New School Augsburg men immediately began to write articles attacking Schmidt, to which Schmidt in turn found it necessary to reply.[32] The sharp exchange came to a climax when Schmidt charged Sverdrup and Oftedal with dominating the Augsburg faculty and causing a spirit of disunity to prevail among the students as well as the

---

[29]*Beretning . . . Den f. Kirke . . . 1892*, pp. 168-169.

[30]For biographical data see O. M. Norlie (ed.), *School Calendar 1824-1924* (Minneapolis: Augsburg Publishing House, 1924), p. 152, and John A. Hofstead, *American Educators of Norwegian Origin* (Minneapolis: Augsburg Publishing House, 1931), p. 49. Egge was of the conviction that the educational policy at Augsburg was provincial and not calculated to meet the demands which American society would make upon future pastors, teachers, and other leaders trained in small church colleges. The method of pseudonymity which he employed to promote his views would, however, hardly win support even in circles sympathetic to his attitude. The reaction among Augsburg sympathizers was naturally one of righteous indignation. C. K. Birkeland, *Brydninger i Den Forenede Kirke* (Minneapolis: C. Rasmussen's Bogtrykkeri, 1892), pp. 8 f. President Mohn of St. Olaf at first took a detached view of the fracas, saying that Dr. Egge was old enough to answer for himself. "Mohn Manuscript Letters," V (July 25, 1891-July 3, 1893), 23, to Pastor P. A. Rasmussen, August 10, 1891. However, a year later Mohn found it necessary to let Egge go, recommending a long rest to overcome the nervousness which rendered him unable "to communicate his knowledge to others, . . . to interest his students and keep good discipline in the class." *Ibid.*, 308, to Dr. Andrew Fossum, July 15, 1892.

[31]F. A. Schmidt, "Er de forberedende Afdelinger ved Augsburg Seminar en Bestandel af den forenede Kirkes Presteskole?" *Folkebladet*, February 18, 1891, p. 1. *Folkebladet* (the privately-owned mouthpiece of the New School in the former Conference) carried a number of articles in which favorable reference was made to St. Olaf College. *Folkebladet*, January 14, 1892, p. 2; January 28, 1891; February 11, 1891, p. 4; November 19, 1890, p. 6.

[32]"Prof. Schmidts Angreb paa Augsburg Seminarium," *Folkebladet*, February 25, 1891, p. 5. F. A. Schmidt, "Svar paa Tiltale," *Folkebladet*, March 4, 1891, p. 4.

teachers.[33] Later on Schmidt apologized for the unrestrained manner in which he had expressed himself, but retracted none of his views regarding the discontinuance of the Augsburg preparatory department.[34]

By this time the whole church was aware that the "school question" was fraught with explosive elements which threatened the continued well-being of the newly-formed United Church. The editor of *Luthersk Kirkeblad*, the new organ of the United Church, commented that since opinions were divided so sharply it appeared that discussion would necessarily continue until the matter was settled by the forthcoming annual meeting.[35]

In the earlier stages of the debate, President Mohn's letters show that he deplored the resurgence of strife in the church but expressed his conviction that the storm would quickly pass. At all events, he would not involve himself in the fight but would leave it to the decision of the church in convention.[36] In other letters he declared his dislike of the methods employed, perhaps referring to the pseudonymous ways of Professor Egge. He was outspoken in his disapproval of Schmidt's manner of attack, but implied that Schmidt would be out of character employing any other device ("each man to his own method").[37] As far as disposition of the "school question" was concerned, he naturally was sympathetic to the argument which favored St. Olaf and felt it necessary to prepare for the inevitable showdown at the church convention of 1891.[38]

It can be easily understood that the supporters of Augsburg Seminary interpreted the published criticism of their educational institution as emanating from the leadership of the old

---

[33]F. A. Schmidt, "Om Stillingen paa Augsburg," *Folkebladet*, April 15, 1891, p. 4 (reprinted from *Skandinaven*).
[34]F. A. Schmidt, "Erklæring," *Folkebladet*, May 27, 1891, p. 4. Schmidt blamed his choleric outburst on the fact that at the time of writing he was sick with "la grippe"!
[35]"Kirkelige Efterretninger," *Kirkeblad*, I (1891), 170.
[36]"Mohn Manuscript Letters," IV, 434 (n. d., but perhaps February, 1891), to Pastor O. J. Hatlestad.
[37]*Ibid.*, p. 437, March, 1891, to Pastor E. J. Homme.
[38]*Ibid.*, p. 430, February 27, 1891, to Pastor Oftedal; p. 431, February 28, 1891, to Pastor Quam; p. 441, (n. d.), to Pastor Thorkveen.

Anti-Missourian Brotherhood in general and the friends of St. Olaf College in particular. Here was a concerted effort by the latter, so they believed, to disparage Augsburg in the eyes of the church. It was not strange, therefore, that Augsburg's leaders began to look with questioning eyes at the United Church and with animosity towards its rival institution in Northfield, Minnesota. This was the situation which had developed during the autumn and winter of 1890-1891.

One more matter which requires consideration before attempting to trace the course of the controversy is the fact that the old Conference had never been incorporated.[39] In order to hold and receive property the board of trustees of Augsburg Seminary, elected by the third annual convention of the Conference, incorporated itself on July 23, 1872, as "The Norwegian-Danish Evangelical Lutheran Augsburg Seminary."[40] The Conference, however, was not persuaded of its legal status and in 1875 directed the board of trustees to investigate and report whether the church body itself could be incorporated.[41] The following year the board reported as follows:

> That the church body cannot be incorporated directly; that [it] can be incorporated only through a corporation of the same nature as the present Augsburg Seminary . . . and that the Conference ought to retain the present Augsburg Seminary corporation; that the present corporation is lawful and efficient except in one particular, namely, as to the election of the board of trustees.[42]

In view of this, it was recommended that the Conference annually elect the Augsburg board of trustees, consisting of five members. Furthermore, it was recommended that application

---
[39]There was no law in the state of Minnesota providing for the incorporation of church bodies before 1885. Cf. *State of Minnesota ex. rel. Nils C. Brun and Others v. Sven Oftedal and Others*, Minnesota Reports, LXXII (St. Paul, Minnesota: Frank P. Dufresne, 1899), 508.
[40]*Beretning . . . Konferentsen . . . 1872*, p. 33. The elected members of the board of trustees were Pastors O. Paulson (chairman), Amon Johnson, T. H. Dahl, and laymen A. Tharaldsen and K. Olsen. The articles of incorporation, signed by the above named trustees, are to be found in *Beretning . . . Konferentsen . . . 1877*, pp. 45-47.
[41]*Beretning . . . Konferentsen . . . 1875*, p. 69. The articles of 1872 were defective in that they failed to make provisions for the admission of new members to the corporation. Furthermore, although they provided for trustees, they did not expressly state by whom they were to be elected.
[42]*Beretning . . . Konferentsen . . . 1876*, p. 34.

be made to the state legislature to amend the articles in accordance with the foregoing resolution.[43] In 1877 the Minnesota legislature passed a special act ratifying the elections of the trustees and confirming their previous acts. The articles of incorporation were also amended so that the Conference henceforth could elect the trustees of the corporation.[44]

Despite the curative act of 1877, doubt was still entertained by various members of the church whether the Conference, through the Augsburg Corporation, was secure in the possession and ownership of the seminary property. The matter was discussed at the annual conventions of 1879 and 1880.[45] However, the board of trustees assured the convention of the impossibility of more direct control but that its property was quite secure under the existing arrangement.[46]

For seventeen years after 1873, the Conference elected trustees for Augsburg Seminary, thus assuming a prerogative which legally belonged to the corporation of Augsburg Seminary. Despite the legislation of 1877 which was calculated to remedy the defects of the original act of incorporation and to give the Conference more direct control over its seminary by the election of trustees, the seminary strictly speaking remained in the hands of the original five incorporators, who, significantly, were the trustees of Augsburg Seminary elected by the Conference in 1872.[47] Nevertheless, the annually elected trustees were given the exclusive management and control of the property and temporal affairs of the seminary and each year made reports to the Conference under whose direction they did their work. Meanwhile, the original incorporators held no meeting, neither exercising nor asserting their authority over the seminary. Furthermore, although two or more of the in-

---
[43]*Ibid.*, p. 35.
[44]*Beretning . . . Konferentsen . . . 1877*, p. 43.
[45]*Beretning . . . Konferentsen . . . 1879*, p. 66, and *Beretning . . . Konferentsen . . . 1880*, pp. 29, 68.
[46]*Ibid.*, p. 43. In 1883 the Conference passed a resolution directing the board of trustees to have the articles of incorporation of the seminary changed so that thereafter the elections of trustees should be staggered. The object of this amendment was that the terms of office of only a part of the whole board should expire in any one year. *Beretning . . . Konferentsen . . . 1883*, p. 79; *Beretning . . . 1886*, pp. 18, 20.
[47]*. . . Nils C. Brun . . . v. Sven Oftedal . . .*, Minnesota Reports, LXXII, 498-500.

corporators were present at every meeting of the Conference from 1873 to 1890 and although in subsequent years some of them were elected trustees, none of them interposed any objection to the right of the church body to elect trustees and to manage the affairs of the seminary.[48] This was a confused state of affairs, the details and the significance of which were quite unknown to most if not all the leaders and members of the Conference in 1890.

When the Conference entered upon negotiations with the other churches to form the United Church, it agreed with the others to turn over its property to the new church as soon as the latter was incorporated.[49] Presumably to facilitate the transfer the Conference at its 1890 meeting authorized the board of trustees of the seminary to amend its articles of incorporation so that the board, instead of being elected by the annual meeting of the Conference, could be elected by the United Church.[50] This was one of the final acts of the Conference.

When the United Church convened in its first assembly, it learned that it was unable to incorporate itself immediately as it had been hoped. Consequently, the matter of incorporation was turned over to a committee whose report would be a major item of business in 1891. In the meantime, the funds of the former Anti-Missourians and the Augustanans were turned over to the board of trustees of the incorporated Augsburg Seminary to be held in trust until the United Church should adopt articles of incorporation.[51] This was the situation when the United Church concluded its first annual meeting.

As we have seen, the autumn and winter months of 1890-1891 witnessed events which threatened a rift in the newly united church. Nevertheless, the work of the church went on

[48]*Ibid.*, p. 505.
[49]Articles of union, No. 8 and 22, *supra*, pp. 10 f. Cf. Bergh, "Historisk Inledning," in Brun (ed.), *op. cit.*, pp. 24-25. According to Article 22 the respective boards of trustees were to function until the new corporation was formed and then immediately transfer the properties. This article became known as "Article 23" when the articles of union were increased in 1889. *Beretning . . . Konferentsen . . . 1889*, p. 65. Hereinafter it will therefore be referred to as "Article 23."
[50]*Supra*, p. 24.
[51]*Supra*, p. 34.

and the committee on incorporation engaged a lawyer to draft articles of incorporation.[52] The committee met at Augsburg Seminary, March 3, 1891, and, after minor changes, adopted the articles prepared by its counsel, A. Ueland.[53] In commenting on this, President Hoyme, who reported the meeting, said hopefully, "Soon the property which belongs to the United Church can be turned over to the church."[54] That the wish was the father of the thought, is, in the light of what was happening, a warranted conclusion, but little did he know or suspect that seven years of strife would come and go before the Augsburg question would be settled.

1891: The Emerging Controversy

The first week in April the official organ of the United Church carried the announcement that the second annual convention of the church would be held at Kenyon, Minnesota, June 17-25. Among other significant items, it said, the incorporation of the church would be given special attention.[55] Chief among the "other significant items" was the disposition of the school question.

When the convention delegates assembled, there was an air of tense anticipation as President Hoyme began his annual report.[56] After a review of the state of the church, he proceeded to a consideration of those matters which threatened to make the United Church "the disunited church."[57] Expressing his

---

[52]Legal counsel for the United Church was Andreas Ueland, son of the famous Haugean peasant, Ole Gabriel Ueland, who represented the *bønder* in the Norwegian parliament. See C. G. O. Hansen, *My Minneapolis* (Minneapolis: privately published, 1956), p. 31; Andreas Ueland, *Recollections of an Immigrant* (New York: Minton, Balch & Co., 1929).

[53]G. Hoyme, "Samfundets Inkorporation," *Luthersk Kirkeblad*, I (1891), 186-187. The articles were printed (in English) that people of the church might acquaint themselves with them before the annual meeting in June.

[54]*Loc. cit.*

[55]*Luthersk Kirkeblad*, I (1891), 224.

[56]Birkeland, *op. cit.*, p. 9.

[57]In some circles it was being said that *Den forenede Kirke* (the United Church) had become *Den uforenede Kirke* (The Disunited Church). T. H. Dahl, *Fred og Strid eller Lidt Foreningshistorie* (Stoughton, Wisconsin: Trykt i "Normannen"s Trykkeri, 1894), p. 29.

The Augsburg Controversy 51

concern over the harm done in the church because of the newspaper war regarding Augsburg Seminary, he nevertheless was able to rejoice that there now seemed to be peace in the theological faculty.[58] If changes in educational policy and institutions were desirable and necessary, he said, the church was in duty bound to make them. Perhaps open discussion would reveal that it was for the benefit of the church, even this year, to discontinue the preparatory department at Augsburg and turn over the training of pre-seminarians to the college which the church already possessed. Be that as it may, the proper forum for this discussion was the church convention, not the newspapers!

With this said, the president called the attention of the convention to other school matters and then turned to the problem of incorporating the church body. In compliance with the order of the church, the committee on incorporation was now prepared to present articles of incorporation. If the incorporation were carried through according to the prepared articles, then the property which rightfully belonged to the church would be immediately turned over to the board of trustees elected by this convention.[59]

On Friday, June 19, the report of the committee on incorporation was heard.[60] President Hoyme distributed to the members of the convention copies of his comments made in the columns of *Luthersk Kirkeblad* which had reported the meeting of the committee of incorporation with Attorney Ueland.[61] In these comments Hoyme had expressed his opinion that the

---

[58]*Beretning om Det andet Aarsmøde for Den forenede norsk-lutherske Kirke i Amerika . . . fra 17de til 25de Juni, 1891,* p. 19. In addition to these published minutes of the meeting, a helpful summary of the proceedings may be found in "Kirkelige Efterretninger," *Luthersk Kirkeblad,* I (1891), 408-409 and 424-427.

[59]*Beretning . . . Den f. Kirke . . . 1891,* p. 22. The last convention of the Conference in June 1890 had elected Professor Oftedal and Mr. Oley Nelson of Slater, Iowa, to three-year terms on the board of trustees. *Beretning . . . Den f. Kirke . . . 1890,* p. 4. The other members were Ole Aanstad, Theodore Helgeson (terms expired 1891) and Halvor Engemoen (term expired 1892). Two of these trustees, Nelson and Aanstad, later opposed Oftedal and his cohorts in their refusal to turn over the Augsburg property to the United Church.

[60]*Luthersk Kirkeblad,* I (1891), 424.

[61]*Supra,* p. 50.

incorporation of the church would clear the way for the transfer of the properties which were now held by the boards of trustees of St. Olaf and Augsburg. The question was raised whether the convention might hear Ueland's "opinion" on the transfer of the school properties to the new corporation. To this President Hoyme answered that, since the document was lengthy and its reading would consume the convention's precious time, and since the articles themselves were the work of Ueland, it would hardly be necessary to read the document to which he (Hoyme) had made reference in his annual report.[62] Furthermore, since the "opinion" dealt with the question of transfer of property and not with the articles of incorporation consideration of it at this time would be out of order.[63] The discussion was thus confined to the articles of incorporation. After a few alterations were made, the convention adopted the report and proceeded to incorporate itself according to Minnesota law.[64] Trustees elected

[62] *Beretning . . . Den f. Kirke . . . 1891*, pp. 22-23.
[63] Birkeland, *op. cit.*, p. 21. A number of questions have been raised regarding Hoyme's action at this juncture. At the March meeting of the committee on incorporation, Ueland was asked for a written "opinion" as to the feasibility of having the property of the colleges, controlled by the church, transferred to that body after the proposed incorporation should be effected. *Beretning . . . Den f. Kirke . . . 1892*, pp. 198-205. Meanwhile, Hoyme reported the committee meeting through the columns of the church paper and expressed his opinion that the way would be now clear for the transfer of the properties which rightfully belonged to the United Church. *Supra*, p. 50. On June 4, 1891, Ueland sent his "opinion" to President Hoyme (who made passing reference to it in his annual report) and in it expressed his view that "the proposed transfers would be beyond their (the Augsburg and St. Olaf corporations) corporate power to make, and that the transfers could be hindered or set aside at the instance of a donor of the property or of the state if an attempt was made to do this." However, continued the "opinion," although the transfers would be voidable, they would not be void. "Until attacked and set aside by the court they would be operative and vest title in the new corporation." Hoyme's reason for not making this "opinion" public at the convention in 1891 was no doubt his belief that the Augsburg trustees would turn over this property without question once the incorporation was effected. Assured by Ueland that this would be a valid and binding transfer unless "attacked and set aside by the court," this would provide a solution of a troublesome question which might be stirred up anew with the publication of Ueland's opinion. The weakness of Hoyme's reasoning lay in this that he did not realize the deep-seated fears of the Augsburg group and their genuine dislike of St. Olaf College. When Oftedal and his friends later learned of the "opinion," they immediately accused Hoyme of bad faith and then began to hold forth the law as making it impossible to transfer the Augsburg property, thus concealing their real motives (for not transferring) behind a legal convenience. Whether the controversy would have been settled more quickly had Hoyme read the "opinion" in 1891 is consequently a highly moot question. From the vantage point of the present it would seem that his actions showed an absence of his customary foresight and understanding and can be attributed only to his sincere but ill-executed concern for the peace of the United Church.
[64] *Beretning . . . Den f. Kirke . . . 1891*, pp. 154-157.

by the convention were: A. A. Klove, Halle Steensland, and Professor Oftedal (three-year terms); O. Aanstad, L. K. Aaker, and Iver Larsen (two-year terms); and Oley Nelson, O. Hoff, and N. Jacobsen (one-year terms).[65]

Those who were present at the convention considered the debate on the school question the matter of greatest moment.[66] Essentially the topic of the debate was: What shall be done with the preparatory department at Augsburg Seminary? Shall it be continued in conjunction with the theological department or not? In reality there were three proposals before the convention. One came directly from the board of trustees of the Augsburg Seminary and the other two were majority and minority reports from Committee No. 1 which had been charged with preparing resolutions on the basis of the main convention reports.[67]

The first of these proposals had been prepared by Professor Sven Oftedal and was presented to an *ad hoc* meeting of the Augsburg board held in connection with the convention at Kenyon.[68] Oftedal's resolution laid out a new set of conditions for the transfer of Augsburg and stipulated that they should not be acted upon until the 1892 convention. Moreover, they were not to be altered or reconsidered except by a two-thirds

---

[65]*Ibid.*, pp. 148-149. It will be noticed that three members of this board were already members of the Augsburg board: Oftedal, Aanstad (Onstad) and Nelson. The latter two were unsympathetic to Oftedal's plans to retain Augsburg in the control of its trustees. Cf. Oley Nelson and Ole O. Onstad, *The Controversy As to the Responsibility of the Augsburg Board of Trustees to the United Norwegian Lutheran Church of America from 1890 to 1893* (N. p.: n. n., n. d.), pp. 1-9. Furthermore, it should be pointed out that two of St. Olaf's most ardent supporters, Steensland and Larsen, were elected members of the United Church board of trustees. Larsen had served as treasurer of the Anti-Missourian Brotherhood and a trustee of St. Olaf College. In reporting this 1891 election, the Norwegian Synod's official organ made special note of the fact that of the 526 votes cast the highest number was received by Larsen (504), and the lowest by Oftedal (414). *E. L. K.*, XVII (1891), 454.

[66]*Ibid.*, p. 469 and *Luthersk Kirkeblad*, I (1891), 426. The editor of *E. L. K.* called it *"det mest brændende Spørgsmaal"* ("the question which generated most heat") and the reporters for the *Luth. Kirkeblad* described Wednesday, June 24, as the convention's "most critical day."

[67]*Loc. cit.*

[68]"At the meeting in Kenyon in 1891 there were present from this Board, Oftedal, Helgeson, Engemoen and Nelson. No formal notice was given by the President [Oftedal] that a Board meeting should be held at Kenyon, and for that reason Ole Onstad, a member of the board, was not present. Nevertheless, the President called the four members present together for a Board meeting and presented the . . . resolution." Nelson and Onstad, *op. cit.*, p. 1.

vote of the assembly.[69] The impossible and preposterous nature of the resolution was clear to the convention which quickly and emphatically voted it down.[70]

As noted above, Committee No. 1 presented majority and minority reports on the touchy school question. The latter represented the feelings of the most outspoken supporters of St. Olaf College and proposed that the Augsburg preparatory departments be united with St. Olaf at Northfield. This resolution, too, was defeated.[71]

The majority report, a compromise proposal, said: "Because of the circumstances the preparatory departments of Augsburg Seminary shall continue to function for the time being in conjunction with the divinity school of the church body." This proposal was almost unanimously adopted.[72] The wording of this resolution clearly indicated that the church body as a whole did not consider Augsburg an indissoluble unit. The continuation of the school as heretofore was based not on convictions regarding educational policy but on the existing untoward "circumstances." Furthermore, it intimated that this was a temporary expedient *("indtil videre")*. Finally, the resolution revealed that the church recognized only the theological department of Augsburg as its "divinity school." There was an obvious differentiation between the "preparatory departments" and the divinity school. In other words, the resolution did not define the undivided Augsburg Seminary as "the divinity school of the church body."

Another item of importance in this connection was the decision of the church to postpone action on the proposed new

---

[69]The resolution may be found in Dahl, *op. cit.*, pp. 44-45. A rough translation will be found in Nelson and Onstad, *op. cit.*, pp. 1-2. Nelson tells that he refused to sign the resolution and intended to wire Onstad to come immediately to Kenyon. Oftedal, however, talked him out of this and agreed that, if the proposal caused controversy in the church, it would be reconsidered at the next meeting of the board. Thus assured, Nelson signed the resolution which Oftedal presented to the United Church.
[70]*Luthersk Kirkeblad*, I (1891), 426. It has been pointed out that the adoption of this resolution would have meant the virtual annulment of the articles of union in that now, a whole year after the union had been consummated, entirely new conditions for carrying out the union were being foisted upon the church. Dahl, *op. cit.*, pp. 45-51.
[71]*Luthersk Kirkeblad*, I (1891), 426.
[72]*Loc. cit.*

constitution of Augsburg Seminary until 1892.[73] The significance of this act becomes clear when it is known that article one of the constitution perpetuated the Augsburg concept of ministerial education.[74]

Before adjournment, the church ordered the board of trustees of Augsburg Seminary to transfer to the trustees of the United Church the fund of the Anti-Missourians which had been held in trust by the former since the previous year.[75] Furthermore, the debt on St. Olaf College must be liquidated by the members of the former Anti-Missourian Brotherhood and the property of the school turned over to the church debt-free as soon as possible.[76] The resolution which was to have most immediate bearing on the school question was that which authorized the appointment of a nine-man committee to study the problem of educational institutions in the church and make a report at the next annual convention.[77] This came to be known as "the college committee."

When the Kenyon convention of the United Church adjourned, the chief problems for which solution had been sought at this meeting still remained to vex the church. The feeling between Augsburg and St. Olaf mounted in intensity. The rift between the factions in the church widened.[78] Moreover, the United Church, though incorporated, still did not have legal possession of the property and funds which were to have been transferred to it according to the articles of union.

1892-1893: From Strife to Schism

The next two years witnessed no improvement in the situation. In the months immediately after the Kenyon meeting

[73]*Ibid.*, p. 427. Cf. *Beretning . . . Den f. Kirke . . . 1891*, p. 141.
[74]*Ibid.*, p. 95.
[75]*Beretning . . . Den f. Kirke . . . 1892*, p. 147.
[76]*Ibid.*, p. 142.
[77]*Loc. cit.* The committee was to be appointed at the 1891 meeting by President Hoyme. However, there is no indication in the minutes that he did so. This confirms the statement by Birkeland, *op. cit.*, p. 39, that he forgot to do so, and the committee was not appointed till in the following winter. This committee met in March of 1892. "Kirkelige Efterretninger," *Luthersk Kirkeblad*, II (1892), 218. Cf. *Beretning . . . Den f. Kirke . . . 1892*, pp. 23ff.
[78]"Er det en Krigserklæring?" *E. L. K.*, XVII (1891), 503 f.

there was a sharp exchange between the boards of trustees representing the church and Augsburg Seminary. A meeting of "the college committee" in the spring of 1892 prepared fuel for the fire at the next annual convention. This in turn was followed by an amendment of Augsburg's original articles of incorporation to permit a membership increase in the corporation. With this accomplished the Augsburg faction made renewed demands on the United Church, which acknowledged the impasse and established a new seminary in 1893. Therewith a loosely knit group known as "The Friends of Augsburg" under the leadership of Professors Sverdrup and Oftedal was formed and the schism was an accomplished fact.

The details of the events leading up to the convention of 1892 are not readily accessible. However, it appears that the two above-mentioned boards met separately in July, 1891, at Minneapolis.[79] Three of the newly elected members of the board of trustees for the United Church were also members of the Augsburg board. They were Oftedal, Nelson and Onstad (Aanstad).[80] Oftedal was chairman of the latter and Iver Larsen of the former.[81] Nelson reports that the Augsburg board was very reluctant to transfer the Anti-Missourian and Augustana funds held in trust since 1890. However, when Onstad and Nelson threatened to engage an attorney, Oftedal yielded and agreed to write out a transfer receipt which included a provision that the United Church trustees give a guarantee to protect the interests of Augsburg. This condition was not accepted by the church trustees until it had been greatly modified by Oftedal.[82] However, nothing was done at the Augsburg meeting regarding the transfer of the seminary property and funds. In fact, no further action was taken until after the beginning of the new year. Nelson and Onstad, fearing that Oftedal would not call a meeting to transfer the property, sent out a circular letter to the board members urging a meeting before the end of January, 1892. This plea was heeded and the board met at

---

[79]Nelson and Onstad, *op. cit.*, p. 2.
[80]*Supra*, p. 53.
[81]*Beretning . . . Den f. Kirke . . . 1892*, pp. 73, 82.
[82]Nelson and Onstad, *op. cit.*, pp. 3-4.

Augsburg Seminary, January 5, 1892.[83] At this meeting, it was again evident that no transfer would be made.[84] Oftedal had obtained a copy of Ueland's "Opinion" two weeks earlier and said that, on the basis of it, it appeared questionable whether the transfer could be made. Therefore, he would not transfer the holdings until the board had received a legal opinion.[85] A motion was made and carried that Oftedal prepare a Norwegian translation of Ueland's "Opinion" and seek to have it printed in several newspapers in the event President Hoyme refused to make the document public.[86] With this, the board adjourned to reassemble at the call of the chairman.

The committee to study the school question, appointed by President Hoyme, consisted of the following men: Professors Sverdrup, Mohn and Tuve, Pastors T. H. Dahl, J. N. Kildahl, O. J. Hatlestad, and laymen O. Onstad, A. A. Klove, and Iver Larsen. Of these Professor Sverdrup declined to serve.[87]

The committee met March 22-25 in Minneapolis,[88] and organized itself by electing Pastors Dahl and Kildahl chairman and secretary, respectively. Without further ado the committee agreed to seek an opinion from Dean W. S. Pattee of the Law School of the University of Minnesota regarding a method whereby Augsburg and St. Olaf could be legally transferred to the United Church.[89] Pattee, together with Attorney Selden Bacon, prepared a statement which suggested that the Augsburg and St. Olaf corporations should amend their articles of incorporation to permit the delegates attending the convention of the United Church to be the corporations of both col-

---
[83]The minutes of this meeting were published. "Referat fra Møde i Board of Trustees for Augsburg Seminarium," *Luth. Kirkeblad*, II (1892), 74-75. They confirm, in general, the Nelson and Onstad account.
[84]The board of five members voted consistently as follows: Oftedal, Engemoen, and Helgeson against the transfer; Nelson and Onstad for the transfer. This three to two vote effectively stymied all action toward cooperation with the United Church.
[85]Nelson and Onstad, *op. cit.*, pp. 6-8.
[86]*Luth. Kirkeblad*, II (1892), 75.
[87]*Ibid.*, p. 218. This committee was made up of persons who might be expected to be unsympathetic to the Augsburg board of trustees, excepting of course Professor Sverdrup who did not serve. President Hoyme sought to get replacements for Sverdrup from the Augsburg faculty but all declined. *Beretning . . . Den f. Kirke . . . 1892*, p. 24.
[88]The committee report will be found in *ibid.*, pp. 181 ff.
[89]This action indicates that Judge Ueland's "Opinion," though not yet published, was known by the church leaders, who consequently entertained serious questions about the possibility of legal transfer.

leges. This meant that the United Church delegates sitting at different times would be successively the Augsburg Corporation and the St. Olaf Corporation. Each corporation would have legal right to elect trustees. This arrangement, said Pattee and Bacon, would give the United Church full control and ownership of both schools.[90]

The school problem dominated the church convention at Dawson, Minnesota, June 15-23, 1892.[91] It was apparent immediately that the Augsburg faction was in no mood to accept the Pattee-Bacon solution of the transfer problem.[92] After a lengthy discussion, Professor Bøckman finally introduced a resolution in five parts which crystallized the sentiment of the convention and sought to bring the debate to an end.[93] Item one proposed that the convention accept Point One[94] of the college committee's report as it pertained to Augsburg Seminary. Item two required that the board of trustees of Augsburg Seminary in agreement with this point and the state law settle its relations to the United Church with respect to Augsburg Seminary. Item three required that the board give its reply at the present meeting. In case an official answer could not be given at this meeting, item four provided that an unofficial answer would satisfy the church, if it was understood that the reply would be legalized and sent to the chairman of the board of trustees of the church by September 1, 1892. Item five softened the whole demand by stating that if neither official nor unofficial replies were forthcoming at this meeting, the Augsburg board must send an answer to the chairman of the trustees of the church by September 1, 1892. The assembly

---

[90]The general plan, dated March 24, 1892, and later details, dated May 24, 1892, are to be found in *ibid.*, pp. 182-184, 185-188.
[91]In addition to the official minutes of the meeting, the writer has used a stenographic report of the entire proceedings: G. T. Lee and D. C. Jordahl (eds.), *Forhandlingerne ved Den forenede Kirkes tredie Aarsmøde i Dawson, Minnesota, fra 15de til 23de Juni 1892*. The latter is to be found in the archives of the Norwegian-American Historical Association, Northfield, Minnesota.
[92]*Beretning . . . Den f. Kirke . . . 1892*, p. 24. Lee and Jordahl (eds), *Forhandlingerne . . . Dawson . . . 1892*, pp. 4-35, 40.
[93]*Ibid.*, pp. 111 ff. Cf. *Beretning . . . Den f. Kirke . . . 1892*, pp. 156 ff.
[94]"The committee recommends that Augsburg Seminary and St. Olaf College transfer their property to the United Church according to the plan presented by L. S. Pattee and Selden Bacon." *Ibid.*, p. 184.

approved each of the items, amending the first so that it applied exclusively to Augsburg Seminary.[95]

At this point in the convention, Wednesday afternoon, June 22, Professor Sverdrup asked for the floor and spoke for two and a half hours.[96] Beginning with references to the fact that Oftedal and he had been accused of filibustering *(Udhalerpolitik)* at this convention, he wanted to point out that the "politics" which had really caused strife and pain to the church was the action of those who supported St. Olaf College. In the light of this and the financial burden which St. Olaf had thrust upon the church, it was his conviction that the whole matter be referred to the congregations for ultimate decision.[97]

The next day Pastor J. N. Kildahl, long a supporter of St. Olaf and one of the moving spirits in the union movement,[98] picked up Sverdrup's suggestion of the day before and called for a referendum of the whole school matter to the congregations.

Kildahl explained that he, as a member of "the college committee," had hoped that its report would bring peace to the

---

[95]*Ibid.*, p. 158. When the convention considered the school report as it pertained to St. Olaf, a similar action was taken. The Augsburg board had, in 1891, refused to turn over the property because, as they said, it was contrary to law. When this was acknowledged by the United Church at its 1892 convention and a legal method was devised to facilitate the transfer, it was to be expected that if the question of illegality had been the real hindrance as far as the Augsburg board was concerned, the property would have been transferred immediately. The continuing refusal of the board to comply made it necessary for its leaders to justify their actions by criticizing the Pattee-Bacon plan. Two charges were consequently levelled against it: (1) it was ponderous and impracticable; (2) it did not bestow ownership upon the congregations. Helland, *Augsburg Seminar*, p. 226. Coincidentally this identical plan was already being successfully employed in the Norwegian Synod which exercised its ownership and control over Luther College by this method. Lee and Jordahl (eds.), *Forhandlingerne . . . Dawson . . . 1892*, p. 75. It is interesting to note that The Evangelical Lutheran Church continues to use this same plan in its control of Luther and St. Olaf. Cf. *Annual Report . . . The Evangelical Lutheran Church, 1950* (Minneapolis: Augsburg Publishing House, 1950), pp. 526-528. As to Helland's second charge, the incorporation of Augsburg Seminary also failed to place ownership directly in the hands of the congregations. The figment of congregational control was the leading principle involved in Sverdrup's "free church" ideas, which even he found difficult of realization.

[96]Lee and Jordahl (eds.), *Forhandlingerne . . . 1892*, pp. 122, 132. One of the delegates interposed the remark, before Sverdrup began speaking, that debate was limited to five minutes. Sverdrup answered sharply that no limitations had been applied to the present session and he would talk as long as he pleased.

[97]*Ibid.*, p. 130.

[98]Kildahl was to succeed Mohn as president of St. Olaf and continue his concern for the union movement by working unceasingly for better relations among the Norwegian Lutheran church bodies, a labor which bore fruit in the merger of 1917.

church. He was convinced now that it would not. It was his opinion that it was not right and proper to refer the matter to the congregations, since the representatives of the congregations two years before had voted unanimously to adopt St. Olaf as the college of the church. But the current convention made it obvious that nothing could be accomplished in solving this troublesome problem under the prevailing circumstances. For that reason alone he was proposing a resolution for referendum.[99] Although St. Olaf was dear to him, should the congregations vote against it, he would abide by their decision. He hoped that the opposing side would demonstrate the same willingness should the vote go against Augsburg.[100]

The Augsburg faction spoke heatedly against the above resolution and proposed a substitute which made only St. Olaf the subject of referral to the congregations. This was voted down and the Kildahl resolution was adopted.[101]

The delegates to the 1892 convention of "the disunited church" had barely returned to their homes when a new development in the controversy gave indication that the recently adopted resolutions at Dawson carried little promise of bringing about the hoped-for settlement. The new turn of events centered around a rapid and cleverly executed move by Professor Oftedal, the Augsburg trustees, and the original incorporators of the institution. This was the amending of the articles of incorporation increasing the membership of the corporation in order to assure the friends of Augsburg that their interests would be protected. When the general church public learned what had happened, the question was asked, "What will this lead to?"[102]

The Pattee-Bacon plan adopted by the convention in June had stipulated that the delegates to the United Church become

---

[99]*Beretning . . . Den f. Kirke . . . 1892*, p. 159. Cf. Lee and Jordahl (eds.), *Forhandlingerne . . . 1892*, pp. 130-131.
[100]*Ibid.*, pp. 131-132.
[101]*Ibid.*, p. 141.
[102]"Om Augsburg Seminar," *E. L. K.*, XX (1892), 631-633. The editor of the Norwegian Synod publication reports this most recent action by the Augsburg group and then comments: "What this will lead to is not pleasant to contemplate. Oftedal has maneuvered the situation so that the church body either yields to him or—it will burst asunder." These words proved prophetic.

the corporation of Augsburg Seminary. In order to accomplish this, it would be necessary for the old Augsburg Corporation to amend its articles of incorporation. Suggested amendments had been prepared by the legal counsel and were presented to the church in convention.[103] Furthermore, Pattee and Bacon expressed their opinion that the power of amendment resided in the original five incorporators of Augsburg Seminary. Lest there be any question of the legality of this procedure it was further suggested that the present Augsburg board of trustees also adopt the amendments. The opinion concluded: "By the adoption of the method suggested, the Seminary can readily, easily and inexpensively put itself under the control, and become representative of the United Church, with perfect lawfulness."[104]

President Mohn of St. Olaf had learned the details of the Pattee-Bacon plan before the Dawson convention and wrote to a member of the United Church board of trustees as follows:

> The Conference has never been incorporated, but Augsburg Seminary has. Five men incorporated Augsburg, and the lawyers are of the opinion that the five incorporators are the corporation. It is therefore of the greatest consequence to get the original five to pass the amendments.[105]

Whether this letter prompted the succeeding events or not is uncertain. Nevertheless, it is known that President Hoyme and Pastor T. H. Dahl, one of the original Augsburg incorporators and a member of the Board of Directors for the educational institutions of the United Church, wrote a letter to Pastor Ole Paulson, the chairman of the Augsburg Corporation of 1872,[106] asking him to call a meeting of these five men for the purpose of amending the articles to permit the transfer according to the Pattee-Bacon plan.[107] Paulson complied with

---
[103]*Beretning . . . Den f. Kirke . . . 1892*, pp. 188-190.
[104]*Ibid.*, pp. 186-187.
[105]"Mohn Manuscript Letters," V (July 25, 1891-July 3, 1893), 287, to Mr. Iver Larsen, Decorah, Iowa, June 2, 1892.
[106]*Beretning . . . Konferentsen . . . 1877*, pp. 45-47.
[107]Lee and Jordahl (eds.), *op. cit.*, p. 70.

the request, but only two of the incorporators responded by meeting at the designated time and place.[108]

The 1892 convention came and went with a worsening of the whole situation. It was then that Oftedal and his friends conceived the idea of amending the original articles of incorporation while the incorporators were still living, so that the corporation "might acquire the right of perpetual succession."[109] To this end attorneys were retained and on the basis of their counsel a meeting was called for August 3, 1892, to be held at the seminary in Minneapolis.[110] Present at the meeting were the members of the board of trustees for Augsburg Seminary and four of the original incorporators.[111] Except for the abortive attempt of President Hoyme and Pastor Dahl, this was the first legal meeting of the Augsburg Corporation since its inception in 1872. During the intervening twenty years, the church body (the Conference), rather than the corporation, had presumed to elect trustees for the institution. Therefore, to obviate any legal uncertainty, counsel had been given now that both the original incorporators and the present board adopt the proposed amendments of the incorporating articles.[112]

The chief feature of the amendments was a provision to increase the corporation from five to at least thirty members,

---

[108]These men were Paulson and a Mr. K. Olsen. When Paulson related this incident at the church convention in 1892, he caused laughter by saying that Hoyme and Dahl had informed him that they thought that Olsen was dead. He wrote to him nevertheless and the only man who appeared at the meeting besides himself was the "dead" man. *Loc. cit.*

[109]Lillehei (ed.), *op. cit.*, p. 107.

[110]The legal firm of Jackson and Atwater of Minneapolis prepared an opinion, dated July 27, 1892, which confirmed the opinions of Ueland, Pattee and Bacon regarding the illegality of transfer, recommended a plan for perpetuating the present interests of Augsburg Seminary, and criticized the Pattee-Bacon plan as "unwieldy." *In the District Court of the State of Minnesota in and for the Fourth Judicial District and County of Hennepin . . . March 1-17, 1897 . . . Affidavits of Sven Oftedal, et al.* (Minneapolis: North Star Printing Company, 1897), pp. 117-119.

[111]T. H. Dahl was not present. The minutes of this meeting have not been accessible to the writer. However, the document by Nelson and Onstad, *op. cit.*, is readily available, and though written prejudicially by minority members of the Augsburg board, gives an adequate account of what transpired. A report of the meeting with the new articles and by-laws will be found in "Referat af Mødet til amendere Augsburg Seminariums Inkorporationsartikler," *Luth. Kirkeblad*, II (1892), 713-716.

[112]*District Court . . . Minnesota . . . March 1-17, 1897. Sven Oftedal, et al.*, p. 118. To give the action the appearance of ecclesiastical endorsement, appeal was made to the last official act of the old Conference which authorized the board of trustees to amend the Augsburg articles of incorporation.

said members to be drawn from the United Church. Membership in the corporation was by a majority vote for the first thirty. Beyond that number a two-thirds vote was required. Expulsion "for good and sufficient reasons" was also by two-thirds vote.[113] Oftedal introduced the amendments with the statement that their adoption would facilitate the transfer of the Augsburg property to the United Church.[114] That this was not quite the case was apparent in the course of the meeting when it was declared that the increase in the membership of the corporation was rather to secure the control of Augsburg by its friends.[115] Oftedal produced a list of men who could be "trusted" and these were forthwith elected to membership in the corporation. By this time both Johnson and Onstad had left the meeting, and Nelson alone registered his negative vote. The election completed, Nelson submitted his resignation from the office of trustee to which he had been elected earlier and left the meeting.[116]

This action by the Augsburg Corporation lent an air of futility to the communication from the chairman of the United Church board of trustees to the Augsburg board calling attention to the resolution of the church which requested that Augsburg Seminary be transferred according to the Pattee-Bacon plan by September 1, 1892. It was now September 26, and no answer had been made. Therefore, chairman Iver Lar-

[113] A copy of the amendments will be found in *District Court . . . Minnesota . . . January 29, 1897, Affidavits of Nils C. Brun, et al.*, pp. 123-126.
[114] Nelson and Onstad, *op. cit.*, pp. 9-10.
[115] One of the original incorporators, Pastor Amund Johnson, was disillusioned by the tactics of Oftedal and his friends and joined Nelson and Onstad in opposing their moves. Said Johnson: "If I understand Oftedal correctly in explaining the new 'Articles of Incorporation,' it would be easier to transfer the Augsburg property over to the United Norwegian Lutheran Church. . . . But I see that I was mistaken in that idea." When Nelson proposed that the thirty members of the corporation be apportioned according to the former church affiliations—fifteen to the old Conference, ten to the Anti-Missourians, and five to the Augustanans—he was answered as follows by Pastor Paulson: "Mr. Nelson, if I have understood you correctly, you have stood for the transfer of Augsburg into the hands of its enemies, but Mr. Nelson, we will not have now three against two, but will have twenty-nine against one [Onstad was not re-elected as a trustee at this meeting], and will build a wall around Augsburg so high that no Anti-Missourian can fly over it; so thick that no Augustanan can break through, and so deep that no 'gammelretning' [Old School] can dig under it; a wall that is permanent for Augsburg Seminary." *Ibid.*, p. 14.
[116] The trustees elected were the same as elected by the Conference in 1890, with the exception of Onstad. They were: Nelson, Helgeson, Engemoen, Oftedal, and Paulson, the latter replacing Onstad. *District Court . . . Minnesota . . . January 29, 1897*, p. 59.

sen requested that this be done "as soon as possible."[117] To this Oftedal answered as follows:

> ... I am personally of the opinion that the said resolution was annulled by a later resolution of the United Church (Minutes 1892, p. 159) by which the question concerning transfer was referred to a new vote of the congregations and a subsequent decision by the Annual Meeting of the United Church in accordance therewith. ... As a step toward an early adjustment of the present difficulties the Articles of Incorporation of Augsburg Seminary have been amended *in a manner which will materially simplify the question as to giving the United Church—as an unincorporated church society (in its non-corporate capacity) control of Augsburg Seminary in a legal and mutually satisfactory manner.*[118] [Italics supplied.]

It will be noted that Oftedal misrepresented the purpose of the referendum voted at the Dawson meeting. The referendum was not to decide whether Augsburg Seminary was to be transferred or not. The church had already decided that matter affirmatively. Rather the referendum was to feel the pulse of the congregations regarding the support of the two rival institutions and to that end the resolution asked, "Shall the United Church maintain and carry on both St. Olaf College and the college department at Augsburg Seminary?"[119] In the second place, Oftedal presented the amending of the articles of incorporation of Augsburg in such a light as to make it appear that the action was taken to hasten and facilitate the transfer. The available sources hardly substantiate such an interpretation.

The attitude of St. Olaf's leaders at this time is well expressed in a letter which President Mohn wrote to Consul Halle Steensland in the autumn of 1892. Discussing the question, "Shall St. Olaf be given up?" Mohn wrote as follows:

> My position in this question can be briefly stated thus: We, Anti-Missourians ought to yield wherever we can do so with a good conscience. That the Church must have a *college* from which to draw the material for its clergy is my firm conviction, and I cannot give that up

---
[117]*Beretning . . . Den f. Kirke . . . 1893*, p. 103.
[118]*Ibid.*, p. 104.
[119]*Beretning . . . Den f. Kirke . . . 1892*, p. 159.

without violating my conscience, but the *place* [italics supplied] of the college is not at all a matter of conscience, hence the Anti-Missourians ought not to cling stubbornly to St. Olaf when it comes to the question of place, and should the Church whose property St. Olaf now is, conclude to give it up the friends of the college ought to take the decision with good grace and not consider ourselves insulted or slighted by the Church. We brought the college to the Church because we thought the Church would be benefited by it; if the Church can do better without St. Olaf, very well, then St. Olaf better withdraw, but the fight for the college will go on just the same. . . .[120]

Shortly after the first of the year, it appeared that Mohn's premonition about St. Olaf was to be realized. Returns on the congregational referendum were pouring into the office of President Hoyme. Although there was considerable confusion as to the precise meaning of the referendum and therefore in the manner of voting, it was clear that a majority of the congregations desired only one educational institution. The majority favored Augsburg on the condition that complete control be obtained by the United Church.[121]

The fourth annual assembly of the United Church was held in the Swedish Tabernacle, one of the larger church buildings in Minneapolis, June 7 to 15.[122] The delegates who listened to President Hoyme's annual message must have noted a mood of sadness and weariness as he commented about the contentious spirit which was plaguing the church. He maintained that the strife had set the church back many years in its development and its essential work was suffering.[123] Turning to a consideration of the specific ills of the church, he mentioned first of all the action of the Augsburg Corporation in amending its articles. Of this he said that as long as Augsburg was con-

[120]"Mohn Manuscript Letters," V (July 25, 1891-July 3, 1893), 398, to Halle Steensland, Madison, Wisconsin, November 18, 1892.
[121]"Menighedernes Stemmegivning i Collegesagen," *Luth. Kirkeblad*, III (1893), 170. It is doubtful that the congregations were voting for the educational principles represented by the two schools. Rather the very practical matter of financing two institutions was a major consideration, as witnessed by the number of articles appearing in *Luth. Kirkeblad* during the latter part of 1892 and the months before June, 1893, which dealt with financial shortages in the United Church. St. Olaf was costing the United Church more than any one other single institution. *Luth. Kirkeblad*, II (1892), pp. 635-636, and *ibid.*, III (1893), *passim*. The final report on the referendum is to be found in *Beretning . . . Den f. Kirke . . . 1893*, p. 190.
[122]"Vort Aarsmøde, 7de til 15de Juni," *Luth. Kirkeblad*, III (1893), 425-429.
[123]*Beretning . . . Den f. Kirke . . . 1893*, p. 16.

trolled by a self-perpetuating board, independent of and not accountable to the church, its leadership was placing itself beyond those influences which the constitution demanded. In fact, those principles to which Augsburg had been historically committed, namely the rights and the freedom of the congregations, were now being violated by this very group which stood wilfully beyond the reach of the congregations of the United Church.[124]

In light of this situation and the results of the school referendum, he recommended that the church dissolve its relationship with St. Olaf College. He hoped that, in view of the difficulties which were besetting the church, the St. Olaf board of trustees would look upon this action with understanding and charity. This done, it became the duty of the church once more to demand complete control of Augsburg Seminary and to assert that its promise to operate the school was conditioned on the realization of this provision. To implement this Hoyme proposed that the church require such transfer by June 30, 1893, and the adoption of the necessary amendments to the articles of incorporation, "*in extenso,* in words and phrases."[125]

These were militant words and a weary church, eager to lift itself above the clutch of conflict and contentious circumstance, was quick to respond to its president's proposals. The decision to rescind the 1890 action regarding St. Olaf was carried through without serious division of opinion. Thereupon, the delegates turned their attention to explicitly worded resolutions regarding Augsburg Seminary. Beginning with the promise that the United Church would not support any school which it did not own and control,[126] the delegates adopted a resolution which demanded transfer of Augsburg Seminary before the closing of the convention or, at the latest, by July 15, 1893, together with the adoption by the Augsburg Corporation of the proposed amendments to its articles of incorporation.[127] Should the Augsburg corporation and its trustees comply, the

[124] *Ibid.,* pp. 20-21.
[125] *Ibid.,* pp. 22-23.
[126] *Ibid.,* p. 194.
[127] *Ibid.,* pp. 194, 195-202.

United Church promised (1) not to mortgage the school property for the debts of the church, (2) to maintain the preparatory department in conjunction with the theological department as heretofore, but reserving the right, through the Augsburg Seminary Corporation, to make such improvements as deemed necessary, and (3) to limit use of the endowment fund to the payment of salaries to the theological professors. Furthermore, the church extended itself by making provision for amendments and concessions should the Augsburg board desire to negotiate, but having first indicated its willingness to transfer before the deadline. The plan of transfer, however, must not be essentially altered.[128]

Finally, the church, faced with the seriousness of its position and desirous of making provision for the future, resolved that, in case the said requirements were not met by the Augsburg Corporation, the board of trustees of the United Church together with the Board of Directors should arrange to remove the United Church divinity school from the Augsburg premises and establish a seminary in temporary quarters until the next annual meeting.[129]

The foregoing actions were completed on Wednesday afternoon, June 14.[130] Just before the session concluded, Professors Oftedal and Sverdrup submitted their resignations as theological professors "in the service of the United Church." Oftedal gave as the reason for his resignation that

... the unjust treatment of which I have been the object from the side of the majority since the union was consummated, and especially at the last three annual conventions, has convinced me that I do not in the United Church enjoy the confidence which is necessary for a fruitful and blessed cooperation in a teaching position in theology.[131]

Sverdrup's resignation read as follows:

Since the annual convention of the United Church has with an overwhelming majority voted down every motion tending to an amicable

[128]*Ibid.*, p. 202.
[129]*Ibid.*, p. 203.
[130]*Ibid.*, p. 202.
[131]*Ibid.*, p. 185.

settlement concerning Augsburg Seminary, and as this irreconcilable attitude according to my conviction points back to a deep-seated disagreement with the principles for the training of pastors and for church work that is represented by Augsburg Seminary, I am forced to resign as theological professor in the service of the United Norwegian Lutheran Church in America from December 31st of this year.[132]

The next morning both resignations were accepted by the church.[133]

In light of what was to happen on Wednesday evening, it should be noted that the resignations were carefully worded and explicitly referred to service in the United Church. There was no resignation from the faculty of Augsburg Seminary.

On the evening of the very day during which the resolutions regarding Augsburg were adopted by the United Church and the professors' resignations were presented, over two hundred lay and clerical delegates held a meeting in the chapel of Augsburg Seminary.[134] Most of these "friends of Augsburg" were former members of the Conference (New School). Those present pledged themselves to support the seminary and urged Oftedal and Sverdrup to continue as professors at Augsburg. This was the first public evidence that the minority within the United Church looked upon itself as a distinct, and if need be, autonomous group.[135]

During the summer of 1893 two events widened the breach between the church and "the friends of Augsburg." In the first place, two days after the assembly had adjourned, Professor Oftedal and Mr. H. Engemoen took possession of the property of Augsburg Publishing House by force. This action resulted in litigation which continued until June 4, 1894, at which time the court judged that the property did not belong

---
[132]*Ibid.*, pp. 185-186.
[133]*Ibid.*, p. 188.
[134]Though no minutes were published, a record of the proceedings may be found in *Referat fra Mødet af Augsburgs Venner . . . fra 21de til 23de November 1893* (Minneapolis: "Folkebladet"s Trykkeri, 1894), p. 17. Cf. Lillehei (ed.), *op. cit.*, p. 110.
[135]It was this group which became known officially as "The Friends of Augsburg," holding annual meetings from November, 1893-June, 1897. At the latter meeting action was taken transforming "The Friends" into the Lutheran Free Church. C. J. Carlsen, *The Years of Our Church* (Minneapolis: The Lutheran Free Church Publishing Company, 1942), p. 32.

to the Augsburg board of trustees, but rather to the United Church.[136]

The second event, distinctly colored by the difficulties over the publishing house, was the exchange of notes between the United Church and the Augsburg board regarding the transfer of the seminary. The notes were little more than a dreary reiteration of the opposing points of view, concluding with the Augsburg board's statement that "before God, it must have quite essential changes in the entire plan of transfer . . . ."[137]

The situation was obviously deadlocked and both parties were intransigent. Therefore, the trustees and the Board of Directors of the United Church took action to remove its school from the Augsburg premises and appointed a sub-committee to arrange the necessary details.[138] The following resolutions were the most significant:

> 1. In connection with the theological department there shall, if possible, be established a preparatory department.[139]
> 2. The name of the ecclesiastical school of the United Church shall be: The United Church Seminary.[140]

A letter embodying these decisions was sent to all the faculty members at Augsburg Seminary. In addition, the letter said that whereas Professors Sverdrup and Oftedal had resigned as of December 31, 1893, and as it would injure the school "to begin the school year with five theological professors and continue with but three in the middle of the school year," the two named professors would be excused from any instruction during the present year, and Professors Bøckman, Schmidt and Lund in conjunction with the newly-called professors for the preparatory departments would arrange the course of in-

---

[136]*Beretning . . . Den f. Kirke . . . 1894*, pp. 104-105.
[137]*Beretning . . . Den f. Kirke . . . 1894*, pp. 105-111.
[138]*Ibid.*, pp. 23-24, 111-112. Cf. the original resolution of the church, *Beretning . . . Den f. Kirke . . . 1893*, pp. 202-203.
[139]The Augsburg principle of education was to be followed *in toto*. Cf. M. J. Stolee, "Det teologiske seminarium," in Brun (ed.), *op. cit.*, p. 135. Called to teach in the preparatory departments were O. A. Strafs, M. Steensland, P. J. Eikeland, and C. A. Mellby. *Beretning . . . Den f. Kirke . . . 1894*, p. 24.
[140]Colloquially it was known as the "Sacharias School," because the owner of the building which housed the school was Sakarias Anderson, a Swedish contractor. The location was 26th and Franklin Avenue, Minneapolis, Minnesota. C. G. O. Hansen, *My Minneapolis* (Minneapolis: privately published, 1956), p. 96.

struction. This school arrangement was to be "temporary," that is, until the church's rights with regard to the Augsburg Seminary property could be finally determined.

The reaction to this by the Augsburg group was immediate and blunt. Professor Sverdrup charged that the United Church was not moving *its school* to another location; it was establishing *a completely new school*. This act, therefore, was unhesitatingly described as a transgression of the articles of union which had obligated the United Church to support Augsburg Seminary.[141] Under the circumstances, action such as embodied in the resolution of Trinity Church near the Augsburg campus was to be expected. Accusing the United Church of breaking the covenant of union, the congregation declared itself morally obligated to support Augsburg rather than "the new divinity school."[142] A dozen congregations passed similar resolutions and the nucleus of a schismatic group was formed.[143] Representatives of these congregations assembled as "The Friends of Augsburg" in Minneapolis, November 21-23, 1893, and heard speeches by both Oftedal and Sverdrup reviewing the difficulties in the United Church over Augsburg Seminary and pointing up the impossibility of their amicable and satisfactory solution.[144]

Sverdrup concluded his address by saying that the union movement had regressed to the days before 1890. Whereas disunity now prevailed, "The Friends of Augsburg" must continue the work of the church. Separation from the United Church had cut them off from financial help in the matter of an educational and missionary program; therefore they would soon have to assume the duty of meeting the requirements for carrying on the necessary functions of a church body.[145]

---

[141]G. Sverdrup, "Om Foreningssagen," *Samlede Skrifter*, IV, 159-160. Cf. *Referat fra Mødet af Augsburgs Venner, 1893*, pp. 62-64; Helland, *Augsburg Seminar*, p. 229.

[142]*Beretning . . . Den f. Kirke . . . 1894*, p. 26. Sverdrup and Oftedal were members of this congregation, Oftedal having served as its pastor at one time.

[143]Helland, *Georg Sverdrup*, p. 150. Helland says the United Church caused its own schism by dismissing the congregations which did not abide by the constitution of the United Church. Cf. President Hoyme's proposals and the church's action regarding the schismatic congregations, *Beretning . . . Den f. Kirke . . . 1894*, pp. 27, 197.

[144]*Referat fra Mødet af Augsburgs Venner, 1893*, pp. 14-40, 50-64.

[145]*Ibid.*, p. 63. Sverdrup here had reference to action taken by the United Church in 1893, which limited expenditure of home mission funds to those missionaries who would

Before the meeting adjourned, resolutions were adopted which sought to reopen the way to a transfer of the Augsburg property to the United Church. To this end it was resolved that the offending paragraph twenty-three of the articles of union be amended so as to permit transfer by a ninety-nine year lease and that, on this basis, negotiations be resumed with the United Church.[146] But no transfer was to be made until the United Church accepted the guarantees demanded by "The Friends of Augsburg." Included in these "securing guarantees" were the provisions that Sverdrup and Oftedal were to be theological professors of the United Church, and should they die or resign within five years, their replacements should be approved by the Augsburg board of trustees. Moreover, the endowment funds which were set apart for Augsburg Seminary should be placed in the hands of the Augsburg Corporation which should continue as in the past and which should execute a ninety-nine year lease in accordance with the foregoing resolutions.[147] To carry out the negotiations a committee of union was appointed to present this matter to the 1894 convention of the United Church.[148]

This action in 1893 brought to a conclusion another phase of the conflict. Up to 1893, there had been no schismatic moves. Now, however, the two opposing parties were clearly visible to all concerned and the positions of each had been definitely stated. Thus 1893 marked a major turning point in the controversy.

1894-1898: The Church in Court

Court action in the dispute had already begun in connection with Augsburg Publishing House which Oftedal and Engemoen had forcibly occupied two days after the conclusion of the

---

be faithful to the church body. *Beretning . . . Den f. Kirke . . . 1893.* p. 216. The next year the United Church passed a resolution limiting ordination only to seminary graduates who declared themselves willing to subscribe unreservedly to the constitution and the work of the church body. *Beretning . . . Den f. Kirke . . . 1894,* p. 196. "The Friends of Augsburg" were accordingly permanently organized at this meeting in 1893. *Referat . . . Augsburgs Venner, 1893,* p. 85.
[146]*Ibid.,* p. 72.
[147]*Ibid.,* pp. 87-88.
[148]*Ibid.,* p. 87.

1893 convention.[149] This matter was shortly turned over to a court of law for adjudication. The judge issued an order that the official organ of the United Church, *Luthersk Kirkeblad*, must refrain from printing partisan articles favoring either side until judgment had been rendered. Meanwhile, the privately-owned *Folkebladet* carried the Augsburg cause to the people. The officials of the United Church, frustrated by this circumstance, began publishing on August 31, 1893, a paper known as *Samfundet*.[150] The editor of the new paper engaged in a hot exchange with the editor of *Folkebladet*, finally charging him with dishonesty. The libel suit which followed ended when a fine of one dollar was placed on *Samfundet*.[151]

In the meantime, Professor Oftedal had thought better of the whole Augsburg Publishing House matter and, under date of September 18, 1893, proposed to the United Church that the Augsburg board would be willing to settle out of court.[152] This was rejected and the case was continued in court. Final judgment was made on June 5, 1894, in favor of the United Church.[153]

The next two years saw only a worsening of the situation. The 1894 convention of the United Church saw no evidences of rapprochement.[154] "The Friends of Augsburg" initiated fund-

[149]*Supra*, p. 68. The records give the following account of the appropriation: "During the noon hour of June 17, while Mr. Swenson was at the post-office and the clerks were eating lunch, the foreman of the composing room opened the office safe to obtain a manuscript. Just as he opened it, Oftedal and Engemoen entered, took possession of the safe, changed the combination with the help of an expert and re-locked it. Thereupon, the personnel of the publishing house was evicted, the building locked, and a watch placed over it. When Mr. Swenson returned at 3:00 P.M. he was told that he was no longer treasurer of Augsburg Seminary and that his office was now held by Mr. Engemoen." *Beretning . . . Den f. Kirke . . . 1894*, p. 98.

[150]Brun (ed.), *op. cit.*, p. 49. A complete file of this periodical is to be found in the archives of the Norwegian-American Historical Association, Northfield, Minnesota. The paper continued publication until August, 1895. At that time it was joined with *Luth. Kirkeblad* and appeared henceforth as *Lutheraneren*, the name of the official organ of the former Norwegian-Danish Conference. *Ibid.*, p. 63.

[151]The historian of Augsburg Seminary, A. Helland, speaks of this judgment (without mentioning the amount of the fine) as a vindication of Editor Birkeland. Cf. his *Augsburg Seminar*, p. 235. As a matter of fact the opposite appears to have been true. Birkeland had previously served a congregation in Badger, Iowa, which had dismissed him because of dishonesty. The congregational minutes which recorded the affair and upon which *Samfundet* based its charge were not admitted to court. In light of this, the judge stipulated the fine of one dollar. "Saka," *Samfundet*, April 24, 1895, p. 6.

[152]*Beretning .. . Den f. Kirke . . . 1894*, pp. 100-101. The letter fairly drips with piety and Bible passages, a rather different approach than that made on June 17th.

[153]*Ibid.*, pp. 104-105.

[154]See *Beretning . . . Den f. Kirke . . . 1894*, passim.

raising to guarantee the present and future operation of the seminary,[155] indicating by this action that the point of no return had been reached.

Meanwhile, one of the most highly respected Norwegian missionaries in India, L. O. Skrefsrud, was conducting a speaking tour in America. Dismayed by the scandal of church controversy, he sought valiantly to bring the two contending parties together. However, his plan of peace was misinterpreted by both sides and ultimately rejected.[156]

Two events at the 1895 convention of the United Church served to widen the already impassable gulf. One was the refusal of the convention to seat Professors Sverdrup and Oftedal as delegates from Trinity congregation in Minneapolis. The second was the expulsion of twelve congregations which supported the Augsburg board of trustees.[157] Oftedal described this as "unchristian and unrighteous," and then proceeded to lead the board in amending the articles of incorporation to dissociate the seminary from the United Church.[158]

This step led a group of individuals in the United Church to seek legal opinion "concerning the right of the United Church to control Augsburg Seminary." The opinion maintained that the United Church, as the successor to the Conference, had the right to control the seminary. It had elected no trustees because it expected the former trustees to turn over the property. Since attempts at peaceful transfer had failed, the opinion continued, the United Church at its next convention should elect trustees for Augsburg. Should they be denied the right to manage the property by the acting trustees, they should take appropriate legal steps to compel transfer.[159]

In June, 1896, this privately sponsored "opinion" was re-

---

[155]*Beretning* . . . *af Augsburgs Venner* . . . *fra 9de til 12te Oktober 1894*, pp. 52-53, 58-59, 76-77.

[156]*Beretning* . . . *Den f. Kirke* . . . *1895*, pp. 179-182.

[157]A thirteenth congregation withdrew. *Ibid.*, pp. 180-181, 191.

[158]*Beretning* . . . *Augsburgs Venner* . . . *1895*, p. 31. See also *District Court* . . . *Minnesota* . . . *January 29, 1897*, pp. 72, 143-144.

[159]*Opinion of Andreas Ueland and Emanuel Cohen Concerning the Right of the United Church to Control Augsburg Seminary*, April 2, 1896 (Minneapolis: n. n., 1896), pp. 1-21. This document is to be found in the library of Luther Theological Seminary, St. Paul, Minnesota. A Norwegian translation will be found in *Lutheraneren*, II (May 21, 1896), 327, 330-332.

ported to the United Church and its recommendations were formally approved.[160] On July 1 the newly elected trustees formally demanded transfer of the Augsburg property.[161] "The Friends of Augsburg" in convention instructed the Augsburg trustees to use all lawful means to keep the school from falling into the hands of its enemies.[162] This, of course, propelled the matter into the civil courts.

The trustees of the United Church sought unsuccessfully to use the name of the state against the acting trustees of Augsburg, Sven Oftedal *et al.*[163] The attorney general denied the application for the following significant reasons: The election of the trustees for Augsburg Seminary up to 1890 by the Conference was a misconception of the legal character of the Augsburg corporation. The Augsburg corporation was an independent entity apart from the Conference. The curative act of 1877, whereby the Conference (or, after 1890, the United Church) was to be permitted to elect trustees for the seminary, was a manifest violation of the constitution. "As a Corporation . . . the Seminary stands upon its own feet and contains within itself the requisite legal machinery for effectuating the purposes of its being. In short, the United Church has no voice whatever in the election of trustees."[164] Nothing daunted, the United Church trustees instructed their attorneys to carry the case to the District Court. In mid-October, Judge R. D. Russell of the District Court in Hennepin County (Minneapolis) handed down a decision in favor of the United Church.[165]

In his "Memorandum" Judge Russell pointed out that the question underlying this whole case was the identity of the members of Augsburg Seminary from 1870 to 1892, at which

---
[160]*Beretning . . . Den f. Kirke . . . 1896*, pp. 21-22, 185. Trustees elected were: O. Onstad and Lars Swenson, who had served on the Augsburg board before the schism; N. C. Brun, an Old School Conference pastor; L. F. Clausen, son of the first president of the Conference, C. L. Clausen; and O. A. Veblen, brother of the famous economist Thorstein Veblen. *Ibid.*, pp. 165-166.
[161]*District Court . . . Minnesota . . . January 29, 1897*, pp. 76-77.
[162]*Beretning . . . Augsburgs Venner . . . 1896*, p. 49.
[163]*Beretning . . . Den f. Kirke . . . 1897*, pp. 215-216.
[164]*District Court . . . Minnesota . . . January 29, 1897*, pp. 145-151.
[165]"Dommen i Augsburgsagen," *Lutheraneren*, III (1897), 706-707, 722-723, and 725. Cf. *Beretning . . . Den f. Kirke . . . 1898*, p. 230.

latter date the original incorporators asserted a right as sole members to amend the articles, elect other members, and through them the trustees. It was Judge Russell's decision that the seminary was not created by the incorporators but by the Conference. And since the Conference had merged with the United Church, the latter assumed the privileges of the former. For this reason judgment was ordered in favor of the trustees elected by the United Church for Augsburg Seminary.

It was precisely at the point where Judge Russell had placed his finger that the argument centered. But it was apparent that his interpretation of the law was faulty and would soon be challenged.[166] While steps were being taken to protect the endowment fund, which was a part of the Augsburg property to be transferred, the old Augsburg trustees appealed the case to the Supreme Court.[167]

On June 9, 1898, the Supreme Court reversed the decision of the lower court.[168] The Supreme Court maintained that Augsburg Seminary, founded in 1869, had no legal existence until it was incorporated in 1872 by the five men who were named as the first board of trustees. The articles of incorporation were defective in that they failed to provide for admission of new members to the corporation. The so-called curative act of the Minnesota legislature of 1877, which ratified election of trustees for the seminary by the Conference, was unconstitutional.[169] Therefore, according to Minnesota law, the five original incorporators of 1872 were the corporation of Augsburg Seminary. These alone had the legal right to amend the articles of incorporation. Thus the Augsburg corporation existed as a legal entity wholly distinct from the church body, which could exercise no control over it and had no power to elect trustees or in any way to supervise its acts. Although the

---
[166]The Augsburg leaders were already indicating their intentions of appealing the case to the Supreme Court of Minnesota. *Lutheraneren*, III (1897), 784.
[167]*Beretning . . . Den f. Kirke . . . 1898*, p. 230. Cf. *Beretning om Frikirkens 2det Aarsmøde . . . 1898*, p. 17.
[168]*Nils C. Brun and Others v. Sven Oftedal and Others*, Minnesota Reports, LXXII (1898), 498-516. The main decision was written by Justice Wm. Mitchell. A concurring opinion was by Justice Thomas Canty.
[169]*Ibid.*, pp. 499-500.

original corporation did not function as such for twenty years, it nevertheless retained the right to exclusive control; it had not lost its franchise or property. Therefore, in 1892, when the United Church asked the Augsburg trustees to amend the articles of incorporation so as to provide for the election of trustees by the United Church,[170] they were answered by a meeting of the original incorporators, who amended the articles and increased the membership by adding "friends of Augsburg" to the corporation. The claim of the United Church that the original incorporators had acquiesced in the control of Augsburg by the Conference in no way altered the legal status of the Augsburg corporation. Said Judge Mitchell:

> The right to be a corporation is a franchise. This franchise resides in the corporation itself. It is a privilege not existing at common law, but only given by the express authority of the state. Unlike a conventional contract between natural persons, the state is party to it, and when the legislature has prescribed the nature and extent of the franchise, and how it shall be exercised, the courts will never permit it to be enlarged or changed by a usage or custom in violation of the statute.[171]

Judge Canty concurred, but developed his opinion a bit further:

> This corporation was so irregularly organized, and has been so irregularly conducted, that it seems . . . there is no way to appoint de jure officers for it. . . . We have, then, an irregular anomalous corporation, whose past acts were at one time legalized, but the terms of its officers and members expired, and there is no legal way to appoint new officers or members. The relators [the United Church trustees for Augsburg] are therefore not legal officers of the corporation.[172]

Despite Canty's questioning of the present legal status of the Augsburg corporation, it was at least clear that the United Church trustees for Augsburg could not qualify under the law as officers of the Augsburg corporation.[173]

The sole question in the case was a legal one. On this both

---

[170]*Supra*, pp. 60-61.
[171]*Ibid.*, p. 514.
[172]*Ibid.*, p. 516.
[173]Seventeen years later, in 1915, the following statement was made: "It is consequently an open question to this day whether there is any owner of Augsburg Seminary according to Minnesota law." Brun (ed.), *op. cit.*, p. 118.

The Augsburg Controversy 77

Supreme Court justices were in agreement. They had been called upon to decide whether the trustees for Augsburg elected by the United Church had legal title to the offices. It was patent that they could not hold such title and therefore the decision of the lower court must be reversed.

On the other hand, the court noted, it had not been called upon to judge the "ethical character" of the case or of the parties involved. If it were the intention of the United Church to establish its moral rights, to prove that it, as the successor of the Conference, enjoyed the same rights to Augsburg as did the latter body, then this case was being tried in the wrong court. It was indicated that the whole matter could have been more justly disposed of in a court of equity.[174]

Both church bodies, the United Church and the Lutheran Free Church (organized in 1897 by "The Friends of Augsburg"), were in convention when the decision was made known.[175] The news was received with sober rejoicing by the latter.[176] The former, though unhappy over the reversal, was not dismayed. In fact, the assembly seemed to take heart from the judge's opinion that a court of equity was the proper forum for this case. Consequently a resolution was passed and a committee named to carry on the work of seeking justice.[177]

While the committee was making plans to place the Augsburg case before a court of equity, mutual weariness over the processes of law led to the feeling that the other side might desire to "settle."[178] With this in mind, Mr. L. F. Clausen, secretary of the committee for the United Church, wrote a letter to Professor Oftedal suggesting the possibility of a satisfactory settlement out of court.[179] Oftedal had already left on a vaca-

---

[174]"But, if it [the United Church] has any such right of which it has been deprived, a court of equity is equal to every emergency, and its machinery and process are sufficiently flexible to meet it." *Nils Brun and Others v. Sven Oftedal and Others*, Minnesota Reports, LXXII (1898), 511.
[175]The United Church met June 8-16 in St. Paul; the Free Church June 8-12 in Minneapolis.
[176]*Beretning . . . Frikirkens 2det Aarsmøde . . . 1898*, p. 55.
[177]*Beretning . . . Den f. Kirke . . . 1898*, pp. 230-232. The Committee: N. C. Brun, L. F. Clausen, and O. A. Veblen.
[178]Brun (ed), *op. cit.*, p. 118. *Beretning . . . Frikirkens 3die Aarsmøde . . . 1899*, pp. 27-28.
[179]*Beretning . . . Den f. Kirke . . . 1899*, p. 254.

tion trip to Europe, but the letter was opened by other members of the board, who agreed to meet with the United Church committee to discuss settlement.[180]

At a meeting held in Minneapolis on July 20 and 21, 1898, the committee of the United Church and Mr. O. Hoff and Professor A. M. Hove representing Augsburg Seminary adopted a memorandum of settlement.[181] The settlement had the following main provisions: (1) The Augsburg Seminary corporation was to transfer to the United Church all its right, title and interest in and to all of the fund known as the Endowment or Professor Fund. This amounted to forty-eight thousand, six hundred and eleven dollars and fifty-nine cents. (2) Augsburg was to transfer to the United Church that portion of the library which had belonged to the former Augustana Synod and the books acquired prior to January, 1876 (i.e., during the presidency of August Weenaas). (3) On the other hand, the United Church was to surrender all its claims to the property (except that above enumerated) in possession of the Seminary corporation. This meant that the Augsburg campus and buildings, valued at approximately the same figure as the property transferred to the United Church, should remain in the hands of the Seminary corporation. (4) Finally, it was agreed that both parties henceforth were to claim that this was an "equitable, complete and final settlement between the parties."

Thus, after almost a decade of bitter ecclesiastical strife and acrimonious exchange between prominent personalities in the church, the deplorable "Augsburg Controversy" had become history. Among the results of the conflicts several are to be noted. As was to be expected the general benevolence and missionary program of the church suffered. Although the foreign mission program expanded during these years, its growth was less than it might have been had the conflict not occurred. As it was, foreign mission interest and benevolent im-

---

[180]Apparently Oftedal anticipated such a move for he left instructions with the vice-chairman of the board, Mr. Olaf Hoff, to communicate with him by private "telegraph code." In this way, he said, it would be possible to confer inexpensively regarding the conditions of settlement. Helland, *Augsburg Seminar*, p. 238.

[181]The memorandum is to be found in the official minutes (1899) of both the United Church (pp. 254-263) and the Free Church (pp. 30-33).

pulses were stunted by the consuming passions of contention.[182]

A second result was the further fragmentation of the church. The merger of 1890 had been hailed as a significant move towards the union of the separated sons and daughters of the Church of Norway in America. And so it was. But now the seeds of disunity which were present in the 1890 merger had germinated and fructified into schism. "The Friends of Augsburg" met originally as a separate group in 1893. The following year, 1894, was Augsburg's twenty-fifth anniversary. Sverdrup used the occasion to fan the fires of loyalty by directing "The Friends" to champion the ideals upon which Augsburg was built.[183] Against the background of the strife with the United Church, which was charged with lordly and dictatorial tactics,[184] it was not surprising that there developed a persecution complex among the minority, which, in turn, engendered an uncompromising spirit of allegiance to Augsburg. This reached its climax in the year 1896, when at the annual convention of "The Friends of Augsburg" a committee was selected to draft a set of principles and rules for carrying on church work.[185] The report of this committee was entitled "Rules for a Lutheran Free Church," and bore the unmistakable stamp of Sverdrup and his friend Oftedal.[186] The report was adopted and by this action "The Friends of Augsburg" became the Lutheran Free Church.[187]

The Lutheran Free Church has no other constitution than the document which came to be known as "Guiding Principles and Rules of the Lutheran Free Church." There are twelve "principles" and fifteen "rules" for church work. Chief among the former is the emphasis on the local congregation as "the right form of the kingdom of God on earth."[188] The congregation governs its own affairs under the authority of the Word

---

[182]J. Tharaldsen, "Historisk Oversigt," *Beretning . . . Den f. Kirke . . . 1901*, p. LXIV.
[183]Sverdrup, "Augsburgs Principer," *Samlede Skrifter*, III, 15-23.
[184]Helland, *Georg Sverdrup*, p. 148.
[185]*Beretning . . . Augsburgs Venner . . . 1896*, p. 47.
[186]*Beretning . . . Frikirken . . . 1897*, pp. 47-50.
[187]*Ibid.*, pp. 59-60. Cf. Carlsen, *The Years of Our Church*, p. 32.
[188]Professor Sverdrup prepared a commentary on the principles entitled "Om Den lutherske Frikirkes 'ledende Principer,'" *Samlede Skrifter*, III, 265-293.

of God and the Spirit, and acknowledges no other ecclesiastical authority or government as a higher tribunal. The church body is a free association or conference of free congregations for the purpose of mutual help in carrying out such work as is beyond the ability of the individual congregation. But such a conference of free congregations cannot, in a Lutheran free church, impose on the individual congregation any duty or obligation. It can only present motions and requests to congregations and individuals.[189]

The "rules" provide a very simple organization for the Lutheran Free Church. An annual conference of the congregations determines what activities will be recommended to the congregations. The only officers are a president, vice-president, and secretary, However, each annual meeting elects a highly important "Committee on Organization," an "Ordinator," a superintendent of Home Missions, and the Board of School Directors for Augsburg Seminary. The various branches of church work are not carried on by the church body as such but by boards, members of which are nominated by the annual conference.[190]

The Lutheran Free Church does not have legal corporate existence, but receives gifts and legacies through its Board of Organization which is incorporated.[191] Through its other boards this small church conducts an extensive program of home and foreign missions, secondary and higher Christian education, charities and publications.[192]

---

[189] It has been pointed out that the years produced a definite alteration in Sverdrup's ideas of the relationship between free congregations and the church body. In the early eighties Sverdrup could speak in favor of the authority of a church body. In fact, as late as 1890, when the United Church adopted its constitution and a group of Anti-Missourians wished to restrict the United Church to advisory rather than legislative functions, Sverdrup spoke against such a narrowing of church power. He wanted to know nothing of "Copperheads" who exalted congregational independence. However, the experiences of the nineties caused Sverdrup to change his views and by 1897, he had said farewell forever to the synodical principle. J. O. Evjen, "Georg Sverdrup," *Real-Encyclopädie für protestantische Theologie und Kirche*, XXIV, 553. Cf. Sverdrup, *Samlede Skrifter*, II, 141-142.

[190] Nominees are made for the following: Lutheran Board of Missions, Board of Home Missions, Augsburg Seminary Corporation, and Board of Trustees of Augsburg Seminary.

[191] Carlsen, *op. cit.*, p. 109. The other boards are likewise incorporated, varying in size from fifteen to one hundred members who are chosen from nominees made by the annual conference of the Lutheran Free Church. *Ibid.*, p. 110.

[192] Carlsen, *op. cit.*, pp. 114-200. The center of activity is Augsburg College and Seminary. 1959 enrollment: approximately 1000 (includes 28 seminarians).

The third major result of the controversy was to be seen in the unification and solidifying of the United Church. The potential differences represented in the divergent traditions which merged in the United Church were seen to disappear as all made common cause against the Augsburg faction. When the rumblings of ecclesiastical warfare died away in 1898, the United Church found itself ready to turn its attention again to St. Olaf College which it had abandoned in 1893 in the interests of peace. The college had lived a hand-to-mouth existence in the intervening years, but in 1899 the United Church voted once more to adopt the institution as its college and promised unequivocally to support it.[193] Equipped with a seminary[194] and a college and supported by a unified and loyal constituency, the United Church was prepared to take a leading part in the resumption of the union movement during the first years of the new century. Strangely enough, the years of conflict over Augsburg Seminary did not serve to quash union interest among the leaders of the United Church. Almost every annual meeting heard reports from the committee on relations with other bodies. Moreover, several union conferences were held during the last decade of the 19th century. At these meetings the United Church was the moving spirit. With the Augsburg matter settled, the church could once again give undivided attention to the union movement. This it did, and the cause moved steadily forward to its consummation in 1917.

[193]*Beretning . . . Den f. Kirke . . . 1899*, pp. 308, 310-312. For an account of St. Olaf between 1893 and 1899, see Benson, *op. cit.*, pp. 79-95.

[194]The temporary quarters on Franklin Avenue in Minneapolis gave way to a new building in St. Anthony Park, St. Paul, in 1900. This is the present site of Luther Theological Seminary of The Evangelical Lutheran Church.

PART TWO

The
Churches
Merge
(1900-1917)

CHAPTER FOUR

The Expanding Church

During the last three decades of the nineteenth century the churches had made beginnings in education, inner, home, and foreign missions.[1] As the new century dawned, therefore, the churches were faced with the tasks which grew out of the organizations already established and the programs which clearly had to be initiated, if the church was to continue its mission in the New World.

It was undeniable that the bitter theological and ecclesiastical controversies of the late nineteenth century had stunted the evangelistic and benevolent work of the churches. But as the wounds of warfare healed, churchmen, lay and clerical, turned as if in an act of penance to what surely must be their proper occupation, Christian works, common worship, and the quest for unity. This chapter will be devoted to the first two of these items. The union movement will be dealt with later.

The Great Plains to the Coast

There was a marked ebb and flow to the tide of Norwegian immigration, for its strength and extent were closely related to economic conditions prevailing in both Norway and the United

---
[1] See Chapter XIII of Volume I.

States. The great migration of the decade of the 1880s extended into the early nineties and then, largely as a result of the economic depression following the Panic of 1893, it declined until the turn of the century. The early years of the twentieth century saw the tide flowing strongly again, continuing until the outbreak of World War I.[2] The destination of most of these "newcomers" was the Midwest, as had been the case previously. However, it was difficult to obtain land in the older settlements of northern Illinois, southern Wisconsin, northern Iowa, and southern Minnesota. Consequently, for them the frontier with its promise of unclaimed land was progressively farther west and north—in northern Minnesota, the Dakotas, Montana, Canada, and the Pacific Northwest. These regions comprised the area of greatest home mission challenge and activity in the period 1890 to 1917.

After 1890 home missions continued to receive top priority in the synods.[3] At its convention that year the Norwegian Synod adopted the following resolution: "The Synod acknowledges that the home mission is the mission lying nearest at hand and ought to be vigorously supported."[4] This sentiment was expressed frequently by leaders of the Synod, and its activities were carried on in accord with it. The same conviction guided the leadership of both the United Church and Hauge's Synod. For example, President M. G. Hanson of Hauge's Synod reported in 1900: "As a synod this mission [home missions] obviously must hold first place with us. . . ."[5]

Established congregations frequently felt the "pull" of the northwestwardly moving frontier, some of them experiencing distressing losses of membership. In 1900 Secretary Løhre of Hauge's Synod reported that membership statistics revealed significant gains for his synod on the frontier, but it was actually losing ground in the old centers of strength.[6] A decade

---
[2] C. Qualey, *Norwegian Settlement in the United States* (Northfield, Minn.: Norw.-Am. Hist. Assn., 1938), pp. 5-7.
[3] J. C. K. Preus (ed.), *Widening the Frontier* (Minneapolis: Augsburg Publishing House, 1929), pp. 11-15.
[4] *Beretning . . . Synoden . . . 1890*, p. 64.
[5] *Beretning . . . Hauges Synode . . . 1900*, p. 10.
[6] *Ibid.*, pp. 35-36.

later President Stub of the Norwegian Synod described the same problem facing older congregations of his synod in Illinois, Wisconsin, Iowa, and, to a lesser extent, Minnesota, from which "year after year caravans have gone to North and South Dakota, Montana, the West Coast, and Canada."[7] This meant that home mission work could not be neglected in the older areas of settlement. Furthermore, there were several "islands" of Norwegian settlement east of the Mississippi River which constituted a mission challenge because of the sizable number of immigrants attracted to them. This was the case in northern Wisconsin and Michigan, especially the Upper Peninsula, and in such metropolitan areas as New York City and Chicago. Thus, it is not surprising that it was the Eastern District of the Norwegian Synod that gave significant attention to the home mission program of that organization. In 1895 it budgeted $5000 for that purpose.[8]

Norwegian Synod work on the eastern seaboard began in 1860, and the following thirty years witnessed the establishment of a small number of congregations in New York, New Jersey, Maryland, and the New England states. Responding to the growing number of immigrants who settled in metropolitan New York and vicinity, the Norwegian Synod and the United Church established about fifteen congregations in that area and in neighboring New Jersey in the late nineteenth and early twentieth centuries.[9] Hauge's Synod attempted only limited mission work east of Chicago.

In Chicago all three synods engaged in concentrated home mission activity. From 1890 to 1917 approximately twenty-five or thirty Norwegian Lutheran congregations were established in Cook County. Hauge's Synod was an active participant, beginning seven congregations in addition to the two already located in Chicago.[10]

In the period under discussion the area of the most concen-

[7] *Beretning . . . Synoden . . . 1911*, p. 35.
[8] H. Halvorsen (ed.), *Festskrift . . .*, p. 297.
[9] O. M. Norlie (ed.), *Norsk Lutherske Menigheter i Amerika, 1843-1916* (Minneapolis: Augsburg Publishing House, 1918), I, 851-860.
[10] *Ibid.*, I, 51-63.

trated home mission endeavor was the portion of the Upper Midwest which included northwestern Minnesota, the Dakotas, northeastern Montana, and the prairie provinces of Canada. Settlement of the fertile Red River Valley had begun about 1870, but over a period of many years Norwegian immigrants continued to come in large numbers, thickly populating much of the region, until northwestern Minnesota and eastern North Dakota became one of the areas of the heaviest concentration of Norwegian Lutherans in the entire nation. The line of the frontier steadily moved westward across the Dakotas in the last two decades of the nineteenth century and into the early years of the twentieth century. Norwegian settlements and congregations were spread across the entire northern third of the state of North Dakota in an unbroken chain, following the route of the Great Northern Railroad, and spilling over into northeastern Montana. The western counties of both North and South Dakota, never heavily populated, were settled by Norwegians after the turn of the century. The western Dakotas, particularly south and west of the Missouri River, known as the Missouri Slope District of Hauge's Synod, was described as late as 1917 as "almost entirely a mission field."[11]

The tremendous growth in the number of congregations in these frontier areas was reflected in organizational changes in the synods. In the Norwegian Synod, for example, the Minnesota District had extended to the Pacific Coast. In 1893 the Pacific District was organized, and in 1908 the Northwestern District, composed of North Dakota, Montana, Manitoba, Saskatchewan, and Alberta was created. Consequently, the drastically reduced Minnesota District was now confined to the state of the same name. Nevertheless, in 1916 President Bjørgo was able to report that although the Minnesota District had become the smallest of the Synod's districts in geographical size it was the largest in membership.[12] Similar reorganizations of districts were necessitated in the United Church and Hauge's Synod.

[11]*Beretning* . . . *Hauges Synode* . . . 1917, p. 31.
[12]*Beretning* . . . *Minnesota distrikt, Synoden* . . . 1916, p. 157.

Shortly after 1900 the state of Montana was regarded as a particularly promising mission field. President P. A. Hendrickson of the Northwestern District of the Synod in 1911 overoptimistically expressed the opinion that Montana would eventually become as Scandinavian as North Dakota.[13] In 1917 the superintendent of home missions for the United Church, in like manner, went on record to the effect that the great home mission field of the future would be Montana.[14] In 1890 there were only three Norwegian Lutheran pastors and four congregations in the entire state. By 1920 the number had increased to thirty-five pastors and one hundred fifty congregations, the greatest growth having occurred after 1910.[15] The congregations were chiefly concentrated in northeastern Montana, to which Norwegian immigrants were flocking early in the 1900s, and then extended westward across the northern part of the state to the Rocky Mountains, thus continuing the pattern of settlement characteristic of North Dakota.

In the rugged, sparsely-settled Rockies, Norwegian Lutheran work was confined to a few clusters of congregations in western Montana, northern Idaho, and eastern Washington. It was nearly non-existent in Wyoming (one congregation), Utah (one congregation and one preaching place), and Nevada (two preaching places), but in Colorado several Synod and United Church congregations and preaching places were established in the early 1900s in addition to the Synod congregation in Denver which dated from 1881.[16]

While interest in the West Coast as a place of settlement for Norwegians began in the 1870s, "not until the 1890s did the Pacific region present anything like a challenge to the Middle West as a place of settlement and then only on a limited scale."[17] The stepped-up influx of settlers into Washington and

[13]*Beretning . . . Nordvestlige distrikt, Synoden . . . 1911*, p. 121.
[14]*Beretning . . . Den forenede Kirke . . . 1917*, p. 419.
[15]O. M. Grimsby, "The Contribution of the Scandinavian and Germanic People to the Development of Montana," (Unpublished Master's thesis, U. of Montana, 1926), p. 122.
[16]Norlie (ed.), *Norsk . . . Menigheter . . .*, 1843-1916, II, 320-325, 328-332, 376, 379, 382-383.
[17]K. O. Bjork, *West of the Great Divide* (Northfield, Minn.: Norw.-Am. Hist. Assn., 1958), p. 9.

Oregon after 1890 resulted in expansion and intensification of efforts by the Synod and the United Church. The Puget Sound area saw the greatest concentration of Norwegians, and it was there that Norwegian Lutheran church work was most intensive. By 1891 the United Church had five pastors serving in Washington and the Synod had six.[18] When the Pacific District of the Synod was created (1893), it included fifteen pastors, eight of whom were in Washington, two in Oregon, and five in California.[19] The Synod's Pacific District required financial subsidies from other districts over a period of many years, remaining primarily a home mission district with a small membership.[20] Early high expectations for home mission progress in the Pacific Northwest did not fully materialize but it continued to be a home mission field of primary importance. In 1910 N. J. Ellestad, the veteran promoter of home missions in the United Church, was appointed assistant superintendent for home missions on the West Coast, a position he held for a couple of years.[21] Hauge's Synod was relatively inactive in the Far West. As late as 1916 its president reported that there were only four parishes in the five states of Montana, Idaho, Washington, Oregon, and California.[22]

The settlements and congregations in Oregon, considerably fewer in number than in Washington, were located primarily in the northwestern part of the state.[23] California had a sizable number of Norwegian settlers, but in this period home mission work did not flourish. Several congregations were organized by the United Church and the Norwegian Synod, and also a few by Hauge's Synod, but many of the congregations and preaching places were soon discontinued.[24]

Canada was the goal of numerous Norwegian settlers in the two decades prior to World War I. The great majority came

---
[18]*Ibid.*, pp. 516-518.
[19]H. Halvorsen (ed.), *Festskrift* . . . , p. 102.
[20]J. Halvorson, "Den norske Synode," in Norlie (ed.), *Norsk . . . Menigheder* . . . , 1843-1916, II, 700-701.
[21]Olaf Guldseth, "Indremissionen" in Brun (ed.) *Fra Ungdoms Aar*, p. 208.
[22]*Beretning . . . Hauges Synode . . . 1916*, p. 52.
[23]Norlie (ed.), *Norsk . . . Menigheter 1843-1916*, II, 252-263.
[24]*Ibid.*, I, 1046-1059.

from the United States to "take up land" in the prairie provinces of Manitoba, Saskatchewan, and Alberta, Saskatchewan becoming the most Norwegian of the provinces. At an earlier date the Norwegian Synod had carried on home mission work in the eastern provinces of Quebec and Ontario, the origins going back to 1862 and 1876 respectively, and the United Church had attempted some work in the same localities in the later 1890s, but these efforts were not permanent, having been given up prior to the year 1900. Six Synod congregations organized in Manitoba in 1876 were taken over by the Icelandic Synod in 1885.[25]

Of the three synods uniting in 1917 "the United Norwegian Lutheran Church did by far the most" in establishing congregations in Canada.[26] The United Church began work in Vancouver and New Westminster, British Columbia, in 1890-1891. In 1899 it organized a congregation in the Wetaskiwin district of Alberta, in 1903 began its work in Saskatchewan, and in the following years saw its home mission work in the prairie provinces blossom. H. C. Holm, home mission superintendent of the United Church from 1901 to 1906, was an enthusiastic promoter of work in the Canadian field. It was under the leadership of Bersvend Anderson that the first congregation of Hauge's Synod was begun at Bardo, Alberta, in 1895. The beginnings of Norwegian Synod activity in central and western Canada date from 1903 when a congregation was established near Northgate in Saskatchewan.[27]

Between 1890 and 1916 approximately four hundred thirty Norwegian Lutheran congregations of all synods, including the Lutheran Free Church, were organized in Canada, plus about one hundred twenty preaching places. At the time of the union about three hundred forty congregations and preaching places were still maintained in the four western provinces, and in that year the Norwegian Lutheran Church in Canada had forty-

---
[25]Harold O. P. Engen, "A History of the Evangelical Lutheran Church of Canada" (Unpublished Bachelor's thesis, Luther Theological Seminary, Saskatoon, Canada, 1955), pp. 4-9. (Mimeographed.)
[26]*Ibid.*, p. 5.
[27]*Ibid.*, pp. 10-12, 20, 66, 75.

nine pastors, thirty-seven of them coming from the United Church, six from the Norwegian Synod, five from Hauge's Synod, and one from the Lutheran Free Church.[28]

Statistics compiled by O. M. Norlie reveal that 2,629 Norwegian Lutheran congregations and preaching places had been started in the United States and Canada prior to 1890. By 1916 this total had increased to 6,764.[29] However fifty per cent of the latter were soon dissolved or merged with other congregations.[30] Despite the zeal and earnestness with which the Norwegian synods confronted the home mission challenge they could not keep up with the pace set by immigration. It is estimated that by 1914 about twenty-five percent of the immigrants and their immediate descendants held membership in the Lutheran synods, the membership total being somewhat over five hundred thousand while the Norwegian population of the nation, including Norwegian-born and those of Norwegian ancestry, was estimated at about two million.[31] Speaking to the convention of the United Church in 1917 President T. H. Dahl sought to emphasize the magnitude of the home mission task by pointing out that over one million Norwegian-Americans had no church affiliation.[32]

The organizational setup developed by the Norwegian Synod for the supervision of home missions differed from that utilized by the United Church and Hauge's Synod. Each district maintained its own home mission treasury, and each district president, in addition to his other duties, was a home mission superintendent and was paid from home mission funds. Under this system there was no synodical home mission committee or superintendent. However, it worked effectively, and during this period the Synod excelled in home mission work. After having experienced heavy losses of membership as a result of the Election Controversy and having restored a unity of spirit,

---
[28]*Ibid.*, pp. 86-87.
[29]Norlie (ed.), *Norsk . . . Menigheter . . . 1843-1916*, II, 678, 1125.
[30]*Ibid.*, II, 492-677; Norlie, *History of the Norwegian People in America*, p. 360.
[31]Norlie (ed.), *Norsk lutherske prester i Amerika, 1843-1915*, pp. 46, 49, 52.
[32]*Beretning . . . Den f. Kirke . . . 1917*, p. 298.

it was natural that the Synod would exert strenuous efforts to replace its losses.

When the United Church was organized in 1890 a synodical mission committee was created. By decision of the convention of 1891 the office of home mission superintendent was established, and able leadership was provided by the men who occupied the position in subsequent years: N. J. Ellestad, 1892-1900 (except for some brief intervals); H. C. Holm, 1900-1906; Oluf Glasoe, 1907-1914; and G. A. Larsen, 1914-1917. Another important synodical official was the home mission secretary. From 1904 responsibilities for missions were divided between two committees, one for home and the other for foreign missions. M. Sæterlie served as secretary for both committees and as editor of the synodical mission periodical. In 1910 Olaf Guldseth was chosen home mission secretary, which office he held until the merger in 1917, while Sæterlie continued as foreign mission secretary.[33]

In its supervision of home mission work the practice of Hauge's Synod was similar to that of the United Church. In 1894 the synodical mission committee was relieved of its responsibilities for foreign missions as a result of the organization of the China Mission Committee, making it possible to devote all its efforts to the cause of home missions. Hauge's Synod was divided into several districts, eventually eleven of them, but, as with the United Church, the direction of home mission work remained in the hands of the synodical committee. In 1900 the election of a home mission superintendent was authorized.[34] However, the Haugeans experienced difficulty in getting men to accept and retain the position. Of the various superintendents selected only A. O. Oppegaard served over a period of several years.[35]

In order to increase interest and to encourage financial support of home missions the synods encouraged the work of

[33]For a helpful survey of the home mission program of the United Church see Olaf Guldseth, "Indremissionen" in Brun (ed.), *Fra Ungdomsaar*, pp. 199-219.
[34]*Beretning . . . Hauges Synode . . . 1900*, p. 79.
[35]Norlie (ed.), *Norsk lutherske prester i Amerika, 1843-1915*, p. 169.

women's societies, the holding of annual mission festivals in each congregation or parish, the setting apart of the offering on special occasions, special mission services at synodical and district meetings, and the use of synodical periodicals for publicizing home mission news.[36] District superintendents, mission superintendents and secretaries had a special responsibility for stimulating interest and providing leadership, but especially in the earlier years a large number of pastors were engaged in home mission activities in their communities. Furthermore, frequently pastors of established congregations, professors, and students did home mission work on a short-term basis, particularly during the summer months.

To provide new congregations with financial assistance for the construction of church buildings each synod set up a church extension fund. The Synod set the example in 1892, followed by the United Church in 1897 and Hauge's Synod in 1910. In none of the synods did this fund engender an enthusiastic response. However, at the time of the merger President Stub reported that over a period of twenty-five years two hundred forty-six congregations had been assisted with the building of churches and that the Synod's church extension fund had grown to $115,000.[37] The same year the United Church reported about $40,000 in its fund, and in 1916 Hauge's Synod reported an amount slightly in excess of $8,000.[38]

A significant number of special home mission activities was carried on by the synods, this being particularly true of the Norwegian Synod and the United Church, whose greater resources made it possible for them to assume broader responsibilities than Hauge's Synod. A number of mission enterprises carried on by the Norwegian Synod and regarded at the time as foreign missions would today be included under the category of home, or American, missions. These special missions were established to minister to Alaskan Eskimos and Nor-

[36]*Beretning* . . . *Synoden* . . . *1890*, pp. 64-65; *Beretning* . . . *Østlige distrikt Synoden* . . . *1891*, p. 52.
[37]*Beretning* . . . *Synoden* . . . *1917*, p. 135.
[38]*Beretning* . . . *Den f. Kirke* . . . *1917*, p. 342; *Beretning* . . . *Hauges Synode* . . . *1916*, p. 182. A report concerning the status of the extension fund of Hauge's Synod was inadvertently omitted from the 1917 report.

wegians, Norwegian Mormons in Utah, American Indians, and American Negroes.[39]

The Alaska mission was begun in 1894 when Pastor T. L. Brevig was commissioned by the Norwegian Synod to serve as missionary at Teller, Alaska, where he was to serve as a schoolteacher for the United States government. Brevig devoted many years to this difficult field, serving there from 1894 to 1917, with the exception of several rather lengthy absences.[40] Authorized in 1890, a mission in Salt Lake City was begun in 1892, and a small congregation was organized in that year. The purpose of the mission was to reclaim Norwegians who had been won over to Mormonism.[41] This Mormon mission attracted considerable support, but the work was difficult and the fruits meager. In due time this "foreign" mission was taken over by the Home Mission Committee of the Iowa District. However, the Utah mission was discontinued in 1912 after twenty years of earnest but frustrating work.[42] The Synod undertook no work of its own among the Negro population, but contributions from individuals and congregations were frequently sent to the Synodical Conference for its Negro mission. Mention has been made previously of the origin in 1884 of the Synod's mission to the American Indians in the vicinity of Wittenberg, Wisconsin.[43] For some years this was regarded as the chief "foreign" mission of the Synod. Special emphasis was placed on educational work for the Indian children, and the Synod was fortunate to have dedicated leadership for this work over a long period of time from layman Axel Jacobson.

The seamen's and immigrants' missions of the Norwegian Synod in New York City were begun in the 1870s through the leadership of Pastor Ole Juul. At the time of the 1917 merger

[39]For an example of the practice of counting these activities as foreign missions see H. G. Stub's presidential report, *Beretning . . . Synoden . . . 1911*, p. 45.
[40]For an account of Brevig's work based on his own records see J. Walter Johnshoy, *Apaurak in Alaska* (Philadelphia: Dorrance & Co., 1944). A review of the beginnings of the mission may be found in the pamphlet, *En kort historisk oversigt over synodens Alaskamission og dens nuværende kaar og krav* (N. p., Committee for the Alaska Mission, Synod, 1905).
[41]A. G. H. Overn, "Utahmissionen," in Halvorsen (ed.), *Festskrift* . . . .
[42]Norlie, (ed.), *Norsk lutherske Menigheter i Amerika, 1843-1916*, II, 379.
[43]Vol. I, p. 285.

seamen's missions were maintained in New York, Boston, San Francisco, and Galveston.[44] In each of these localities a seamen's pastor sought to be of assistance to Norwegian sailors, visiting them in ships, hospitals, and boarding homes; distributing Christian literature; conducting services; and maintaining a reading room.[45] The mission assisted thousands of immigrants with counsel, encouragement, spiritual help, and in some cases, lodging. The United Church did not officially undertake work among seamen, but it did establish an immigrant mission in New York City in 1906. The position of pastor for immigrants, however, was combined with the pastorate of one of the United Church congregations.[46] World War I practically put an end to immigration for a few years and greatly reduced the need for the immigrant missions.

In 1901 the United Church manifested its concern for a spiritually neglected element of the population by calling Pastor C. M. Larson to work among the deaf, dumb, blind, and other handicapped persons in the state institutions at Faribault, Minnesota. Larson served in this capacity until 1912 when he was succeeded by B. J. Rothnem. In Sioux Falls, South Dakota, Pastor H. O. Bjorlie ministered to the deaf and dumb in addition to his parish duties. Especially through the interest and activity of Pastor N. Lunde the United Church was alerted to another field of service which was badly neglected, work among prisoners.[47]

Although the Norwegian immigration was overwhelmingly rural, it was increasingly obvious that the American city was also a challenging home mission field. A significant element of the later immigration settled in the larger cities, especially Brooklyn, Chicago, and the Twin Cities. Moreover, many second and third generation Norwegians were leaving the countryside for the urban centers. After the turn of the century reports and addresses of synodical leaders frequently

---
[44]*Beretning* . . . *Synoden* . . . *1917*, pp. 138, 154.
[45]*Ibid.*, p. 120.
[46]Guldseth, "Indremissionen," in Brun (ed.), *Fra Ungdomsaar*, p. 217; *Beretning* . . . *Den f. Kirke* . . . *1917*, pp. 401-402.
[47]Guldseth, "Indremissionen," in Brun (ed.), *Fra Ungdomsaar*, pp. 216-217.

underscored the importance of city mission work. The following excerpt from the 1917 report of Home Mission Superintendent Larsen of the United Church is quite typical:

There is one area of home mission work concerning which I want to make you particularly conscious at this time, and that is the city mission. . . . That the United Church has undertaken an extensive home mission work is evident from the results, but this work has concentrated primarily on the rural areas or smaller cities. Naturally something has been done in the larger cities, but it has not been, and still is not, adequate for the need. I believe, therefore, that in the future the church should devote more of its attention to this phase of missions and lay more emphasis upon it than earlier. . . . Thousands of our people live in the larger cities. They are not so scattered but what they can be found. In Chicago alone it is estimated that there are between seventy and one hundred thousand of them, and even in Minneapolis there are fifty thousand. And the situation is not better in other large cities. Moreover, let us not forget that they not only are outside the church, which is bad enough, but also no small part of them have so fallen into sin and vice that they must be reckoned as belonging to 'the slums.' Surely it is worthwhile to give special attention to this type of mission! These poor people are also our brothers.[48]

The awakened feeling of responsibility for their countrymen in the cities prompted the Norwegian Synod and the United Church, and to a lesser degree Hauge's Synod, not only to establish an increasing number of city congregations, but also to support city missions and missionaries, who assumed responsibility for chaplaincy, institutional, and relief work, somewhat in the spirit of the European concept of the inner mission. Pastor Ellestad, formerly home mission superintendent for the United Church, was appointed city missionary for Chicago in 1907. His responsibility was to assist home mission congregations in Chicago and to carry out visitations in the hospitals and elsewhere.[49] The earliest city mission of the Norwegian Synod was also in Chicago, originating in 1905, and thus antedating the United Church's work by two years.[50] In 1907 the United Church took over the independently-operated Bethesda Mission in Brooklyn and conducted it as a slum, or rescue,

---
[48]*Beretning* . . . *Den f. Kirke* . . . *1917*, pp. 419-420.
[49]Guldseth, "Indremissionen," in Brun (ed.), *Fra Ungdomsaar*, p. 214.
[50]*Beretning* . . . *Synoden* . . . *1917*, p. 213.

mission. When in 1913 the position of city missionary was also created, the United Church was able to carry out a rather effective social service program. The scope of its efforts is revealed in the report of the Bethesda and city missions of Brooklyn presented to the United Church in 1917 by J. C. Herre and C. O. Pedersen. The report covers such activities as youth work, the rescue mission, maintenance of a day nursery, a summer camp for children, maintenance of an industrial mission, the distribution of clothing and food to the needy, evangelistic work, assistance in finding employment, and the operation of a book store.[51] In 1917 the United Church had city and/or hospital missionaries in Brooklyn, Chicago, Minneapolis, and St. Paul.[52] By that time the Synod was supporting missionaries in the same cities and, in addition, in San Francisco and Seattle.[53] A paragraph from the report of Pastor Otto Juul covering about an eight-month period when he was serving as Minneapolis city missionary in 1916-1917 is typical:

> Up to the first of May I had visited the hospitals 101 times and had shared the Word of God with about 800 patients; in addition I had made eighty house calls in carrying out my duties. I have been present in children's court once or twice a week, have been at the rescue home thirty-four times, and have frequently visited the jails and various charitable and disciplinary institutions in and around the Twin Cities, and have been of some assistance in procuring work for several people.[54]

Evangelism is closely identified with home missions. Hauge's Synod, the most pietistic of the three synods under discussion, actively promoted evangelistic work within its districts. Both laymen and pastors were used as evangelists. The general tendency in the Haugean group was increasingly in the direction of regulated lay preaching, with the districts at their annual meetings selecting lay preachers for a stipulated period of service.[55] The annual reports of the synodical pres-

---
[51]*Beretning . . . Den f. Kirke . . . 1917*, pp. 400-401, 412-416.
[52]*Ibid.*, pp. 400-403.
[53]*Beretning . . . Synoden . . . 1917*, p. 138.
[54]*Ibid.*, p. 215.
[55]For a critique of this tendency to supplant the free lay activity of an earlier time see

ident, in which he reviewed the work of the synod, district by district, characteristically reveal a primary concern for prayer meetings, special evangelistic services, and spiritual revival.[56] Many apparently believed that it was unnecessary to appoint synodical evangelists, but in 1916 one was selected. When he did not accept the call, the secretary reported: "And so this year also we as a synod are without a regular evangelist."[57]

The United Church likewise approved of orderly evangelistic activity as a means of spiritual revival and of nurturing Christian life in its congregations. In 1909 the synodical home mission committee was entrusted with the responsibility for calling evangelists. They were to be paid from synodical home mission funds. Congregations desiring the services of an evangelist were to make the necessary arrangements with the home mission committee.[58] Several men served as synodical evangelists for short periods of time, and there seemed to be considerable enthusiasm for their work.[59] However, the home mission committee did not always encourage this work; consequently it did not keep the position of synodical evangelist filled at all times, to the obvious disappointment of Secretary Guldseth.[60] The Norwegian Synod believed that the parish pastor is the only evangelist required and thus made no provision for any type of synodically-promoted evangelism, either by pastors or laymen.[61]

One of the most irritating problems confronting the Norwegian Lutheran synods during these years was that relating to the use of the English language. This was especially acute in the cities, where non-Lutheran churches often had an easy time in winning adherents from the younger generation of Nor-

---
[ature] G. M. Bruce, "Hauges synode," in Norlie (ed.), *Norsk . . . Menigheter . . . 1843-1916*, II, 683-685.
[56]See, e.g., J. J. Ekse's report in *Beretning . . . Hauges Synode . . . 1916*, pp. 41-62.
[57]*Beretning . . . Hauges Synode . . . 1917*, pp. 28-30.
[58]Jens C. Roseland, *Samfunds-Haandbog* (Minneapolis: Augsburg Publishing House, 1913), pp. 86-87.
[59]Guldseth, "Indremissionen," in Brun (ed.), *Fra Ungdomsaar*, p. 218.
[60]*Beretning . . . Den f. Kirke . . . 1917*, p. 404.
[61]J. Halvorson, "Den norske synode," in Norlie (ed.), *Norsk . . . Menigheter . . . 1843-1916*, II, 692.

wegians who preferred English. The problem, of course, was most pressing in the areas of earliest settlement.

The situation at about the turn of the century may be illustrated by reference to Hauge's Synod. In 1901 during one entire day of the annual meeting sessions were conducted in the English language. Several papers dealing with the language question were read, discussed, and printed as part of the annual report. Pastor K. O. Eittreim of Creston, Illinois, read a paper, entitled "Demand for English Work in Our Synod."[62] In answer to the question, "Is there such a demand in our Synod?", he referred to the situation in his two congregations. In one Sunday school the demand for English was constantly increasing, that for Norwegian was steadily decreasing; in the other English was used exclusively except in the adult Bible class. In one of his confirmation classes eleven of the pupils used English and ten used Norwegian; in the other twenty used English and only two used Norwegian. In the young people's Luther League only English was used. The hostess for Ladies' Aid meetings would frequently request that he conduct devotions in English. He reported that English was requested for two-thirds of the weddings for which he officiated, and for funerals it was almost invariably requested for all or a part of the service. He conducted Sunday evening services in English. Then he went on to say:

> But the demand is not equally great in all parts of our Synod. . . . This demand for English work, reminds me of a ship coming in from the sea. The demand happens to come from the east, and we, who are farthest east, see most of it. We are beginning to see the hull over the horizon, while you who are farther west, except in the larger cities and in school centers perhaps, see only the tops of the masts. But whether we see it or not, the ship is coming! It is a mighty ship, and is laden with the choicest blessings to our Synod, if we are prepared to receive them![63]

In the portion of his paper dealing with the question "How shall we meet this demand?", Pastor Eittreim put his finger

---
[62]*Beretning* . . . *Hauges Synode* . . . *1901*, pp. 149-152.
[63]*Ibid.*, p. 150.

on a couple of pressing needs. Pastors must be trained in both English and Norwegian, for "in our present stage of transition we must do efficient work in both languages, according to the need." Furthermore, since so many children were receiving religious instruction in English, provision would have to be made for more Sunday morning services in English: ". . . if we have trained and confirmed them in the English language, we do them a great injustice when we compel [sic] them to henceforth take the means of grace either in a strange tongue or at the evening service."[64]

Obviously Pastor Eittreim was serving a parish more advanced in its Americanization than most Norwegian Lutheran parishes at that time, or he would not have been assigned such a topic, but the problem of transition to English would soon become crucial nearly everywhere and unfortunately there was no way in which it could be solved easily. Inevitably there would be a whole generation deeply involved in a difficult period when the two languages would have to be used simultaneously. Frequently there was a lack of foresight in tenacious adherence to the old and, of course, it was possible to go to the other extreme and effect precipitous change without regard for the older generation. However, the persistent danger was that of alienating the younger generation from the Lutheran Church through tardiness in transition.[65]

From about 1900 various devices were used by all three synods to promote English work. Special committees, boards, and organizations were created. The English Conference of the United Church is an example. It was composed of those pastors and laymen of the United Church who wished "to foster the English work in our Church as the requirements of our people may demand."[66] The synods took the necessary steps to provide English books, tracts, catechisms, hymnbooks, and periodicals, sometimes individually and at other times

---
[64] *Ibid.*, p. 151.
[65] For a discussion by pastors of the synod at the next annual meeting see *Beretning . . . Hauges Synode . . . 1902*, pp. 146-147.
[66] J. Roseland, *Samfunds-Haandbog* (1913), pp. 98-99.

cooperatively. Each synod began an English periodical: the Synod, *Lutheran Herald* (1905); United Church, *The United Lutheran* (1907); and Hauge's Synod, *The Lutheran Intelligencer* (1910). All three cooperated in the preparation of an English hymnal, *The Lutheran Hymnary* (1912).

The whole problem of language transition raised a question as to the extent of the home mission responsibilities of the Norwegian Lutheran synods. In 1914 Mission Superintendent Oluf Glasoe expressed it in the following words:

Up to this point our home mission activity has been confined to work among "our countrymen," who have generally settled in larger settlements in city or country and thus were sufficiently numerous in each such locality that they could undertake religious work for themselves and order it in accordance with their particular needs as to language and creed. In contrast, a generation of those of Norwegian background is now growing up whose "language of the heart" is English, and very often they do not understand Norwegian at all—at any rate, not to the degree that they receive any benefit from a Norwegian sermon. Moreover, there naturally enough are more and more "mixed marriages" in which one partner is not of Scandinavian background and usually not of our faith. If we are not to lose the Lutheran partner in such a marriage, we must seek to win the other for the Lutheran faith. There are already a large number involved in this situation.

These circumstances make it indispensable for us to use English as well as Norwegian, and it will naturally follow that *we also, in accord with the Lord's commission will bring the Gospel to all without regard to their parentage.*

Consequently, our home mission activity in the future must be somewhat different from what it has been when we, like Peter, come to see that our task is more extensive than we had previously thought. It will also be more difficult, since the field will be primarily the cities, specifically the large cities, where we shall deal with many people of other religious faiths and convictions, if they have any at all.

Is it not, therefore, absolutely necessary that not only Norwegian Lutherans but *all Lutherans should cooperate in vigorous activity in order not only to preserve our Lutheran heritage for our own but also to enable others to participate in the truth unto salvation as we have it in our Lutheran Church?*[67]

The transition to the use of English seems to have pro-

---

[67]Oluf Glasoe, *Omsorg for sine egne* (Minneapolis: Augsburg Publishing House, 1919), pp. 581-582.

ceeded at approximately the same rate in all three synods. On the eve of the 1917 merger about one in every four or five services was conducted in English. However, for confirmation instruction and Sunday school teaching English was used about fifty per cent of the time, with the scale still slightly tipped to the Norwegian side, while perhaps two-thirds of the youth organizations no longer used Norwegian. In general, the use of English was farthest advanced in the cities and the areas of earliest settlement.[68] In his report to the United Church Secretary Roseland called attention to "the amazing rapidity with which work in the English language has accelerated in recent years." Having quoted figures revealing the extent of transition to English, he observed that this was the case "despite the persistence with which our clergy have championed the use of the Norwegian language in religious work." An enthusiastic advocate of the use of English, he felt that any hindrances placed in the way of a natural language transition would have fateful consequences for the church's future in this country.[69] The general situation, however, is revealed in a resolution passed by the United Church at the same convention which received Roseland's report. It took note of the evidence showing a decided trend to the use of English but urged congregations and pastors "to hold fast to the Norwegian language where it will not hinder the growth and progress of the kingdom of God."[70]

Asia and Africa

By 1890 a high degree of interest in foreign missions had been awakened within the constituency of the Norwegian-American churches. As noted earlier, a number of factors contributed to the growth of this interest: intersynodical mission meetings, visits of Norwegian missionaries, the special interest of P. A. Rasmussen and other pastors, and the pub-

[68]*Beretning . . . Hauges Synode . . . 1917*, p. 29; *Beretning . . . Synoden . . . 1916*, pp. 314, 317, 321, 324, 326; *Beretning . . . Den f. Kirke . . . 1917*, pp. 324-326.
[69]*Beretning . . . Den f. Kirke . . . 1917*, pp. 325-326.
[70]*Ibid.*, pp. 437, 455.

licity given to foreign mission work in religious periodicals.[71] It was quite natural that the activities of two mission societies based in Norway would be of particular concern to the mission-minded: The Norwegian Mission Society (NMS), with fields in South Africa and Madagascar, and the Schreuder Mission in South Africa. By 1890 two Norwegian-American Lutherans had gone overseas as missionaries, namely, J. P. Hogstad and E. H. Tou of the Conference, who went to Madagascar in the service of the NMS. Furthermore, by that date two independent (*i.e.*, not synodically-sponsored) mission societies had been formed, The Zion Society for Israel (1878) and The Norwegian Evangelical Lutheran China Mission Society (1890).

In the period 1890-1917, characterized by widespread mission enthusiasm, each of the three synods which merged in 1917 embarked on a foreign mission program of its own. By 1917 flourishing missions had been established in China and Madagascar, and close ties had been knit with the NMS field in Natal (Zululand), South Africa.

China[72]

As recounted earlier, a growing concern for bringing the gospel to the Chinese, stimulated by the visits of Norwegian missionaries, crystallized in the formation of the China Mission Society in 1890.[73] Initially all officers and members of the board were from Hauge's Synod, but membership was not restricted by synodical lines. By 1892 the United Church was represented on the board and in a few years dominated it. The Reverend H. N. Ronning and his sister Thea were called to be the Society's missionaries to China where they began

---
[71] Vol. I, pp. 282-289.
[72] For a convenient historical summary see Rolf A. Syrdal, "The History of the United Mission," in *White Unto Harvest* (Minneapolis: Augsburg Publishing House, 1934), pp. 5-42.
[73] Vol. I, p. 289. A group of pastors and laymen attending the annual meeting of Hauge's Synod brought the society into being. They desired to follow the organizational pattern of the Norwegian Mission Society and to secure intersynodical support for their undertaking. Rolf A. Syrdal, "American Lutheran Mission Work in China" (Unpublished Ph.D. Dissertation, Drew University, 1942), pp. 17-21.

work in 1891. However, Daniel Nelson was the first Norwegian-American Lutheran to go to China as a missionary, for he arrived in China a year earlier than the Ronnings, even though he did not have the official support of the Society or any other organization.

At its annual convention in 1891 Hauge's Synod decided to begin a mission in China and requested the China Mission Society to dissolve. It became apparent that many preferred the independent society to a synodical organization, but a period of three-cornered negotiations involving the Society, Hauge's Synod, and the United Church brought no agreement. Finally, in 1894 Hauge's Synod severed connections with the Society, and the missionaries, who up to that time had a double or ambiguous allegiance, declared which mission they would serve. The break with the China Mission Society did not seem to handicap the Hauge's Synod mission, and its band of missionaries, some of whom were initially with the Society, promoted an aggressive and effective mission program, sustained by staunch support. The China Mission Society turned more and more to the United Church for support and in 1903 was taken over by that church. It was the China Mission Society that laid the foundations for the China mission of the United Church.[74]

The formal transfer of the China Mission Society (1903-1904) gave a powerful impetus to missions in the United Church. Up to 1904 both home and foreign missions had been supervised by one board; now there were to be two. Pastor M. Sæterlie was designated as joint missions secretary and was to devote himself exclusively to that task. After 1910, when a further division of responsibilities was made, he was secretary only for foreign missions.[75]

In 1899 the Norwegian Synod decided to begin mission work in Japan and in 1900 sent J. R. Birkelund as a medical missionary. However, the Synod's first effort at oriental mis-

---
[74]*Ibid.*, pp. 23-26. It should be made clear that, during the decade 1894-1903, the United Church gave no official support to the China Mission Society.
[75]M. Sæterlie, *The Foreign Missions of the United Church, 1890-1915* (Minneapolis: Augsburg Publishing House, 1917), pp. 32-33.

sions proved abortive as Birkelund had to return home in 1902 because of the illness of his wife, and no one replaced him.[76]

Not until 1912 did the Norwegian Synod decide to begin a mission in China. Significant mission interest had developed among the students of Luther Seminary and in 1911 H. G. Stub, president of the Synod, made an earnest plea on behalf of missions, which eventuated in the decision of 1912. Pastor George Lillegaard was the Synod's first missionary, leaving for China that same autumn. J. R. Birkelund was appointed synodical mission secretary. The Synod mission had a brief history as the merger occurred a short time after its establishment.

In August, 1917, the three missions in China conducted by Hauge's Synod, the United Church, and the Norwegian Synod merged to form the Lutheran United Mission. The three mission fields were in the north central section of China in the provinces of Honan and Hupeh and included about seven million inhabitants.[77] The missionaries of the three synods knew one another rather well as they had engaged in a number of cooperative activities. By 1917 the pioneering period of the China mission was over, and a substantial program of education, evangelism, and medical missions had been established.

Madagascar and South Africa[78]

The mission committee designated by the United Church at its first annual meeting sought to clarify its relationship to the Norwegian Mission Society under whose auspices Hogstad and Tou, formerly of the Conference, were serving as missionaries in Madagascar. The committee explored the possibility of obtaining a separate field for the United Church in the southern part of that country. Pastors P. A. Rasmussen and Lars Lund attended the 1892 meeting of the NMS, at

---
[76]H. Halvorsen (ed.), *Festskrift* . . . , pp. 340-342.
[77]M. Sæterlie, "China," in Geo. Drach (ed.), *Our Church Abroad* (Minneapolis: Augsburg Publishing House, 1926), p. 141.
[78]See A. Burgess, *Zanahary in South Madagascar* (Minneapolis: Augsburg Publishing House, 1932) and A. Burgess, *Unkulunkulu in Zululand* (Minneapolis: Augsburg Publishing House, 1934).

which time it offered to turn over to the United Church a field in southern Madagascar. This offer was gratefully accepted by the United Church at its 1893 convention.[79] The unfortunate controversy which resulted in the withdrawal of the Lutheran Free Church from the United Church produced difficulties on the mission field. Hogstad and Tou aligned themselves with the Free Church, and the western portion of the field in southern Madagascar was turned over to that body. Hogstad, however, later returned to the United Church. The first years of mission activity were made particularly difficult by the unrest accompanying the French conquest of Madagascar, 1895-96, with the resultant encouragement of Roman Catholicism, and by the prevalence of illness among the missionaries. As noted earlier, the United Church reorganized its mission setup in 1904 after it took over the China Mission Society. This inaugurated an era of expansion and intensification of foreign mission effort which greatly benefited both the Madagascar and China fields. Indicative of the United Church's desire to insure mission leadership was the appointment in 1911 of Madagascar missionary M. J. Stolee to a seminary professorship in missions and practical theology.

Before they emigrated many Norwegians had been stirred to a lively interest in the NMS mission to the Zulus in Natal, which was begun by H. P. S. Schrueder in 1843. Friction between Schreuder and the society caused him to sever connections with the NMS in 1873, and thereafter he was supported by the Committee for the Mission of Schreuder. The Norwegian Synod became interested in the Schreuder Mission, especially after Pastors Nils and Hans Astrup went to Zululand in the early 1880s to carry on Schreuder's work.[80] President Laur. Larsen of Luther College, whose wife was a sister of the Astrup brothers, did much to stimulate interest in the Schreuder Mission. In the 1890s two of his daughters went to the Zulu field as teachers. Ties with the Schreuder Mission were

---
[79] Sæterlie, *The Foreign Missions of the United Church, 1890-1915*, pp. 7-10.
[80] Vol. I, p. 285.

further established when in 1890 three sons of missionaries came to Luther College as students, two of whom, Johannes Astrup and Heinrich Otte, returned to Zululand as missionary pastors.[81] Although the Norwegian Synod provided workers and financial support for the Schreuder Mission, it remained under the supervision of the Norwegian Committee until 1927 when the Norwegian Lutheran Church of America assumed full responsibility for the Zulu field.

In 1917 the official foreign mission effort of the newly-formed church body included the merged work of the three synods in China and the field of the United Church in Madagascar. The total missionary forces, including wives, numbered one hundred twenty-eight, ninety-four in China and thirty-four in Madagascar.[82] Furthermore, it assumed responsibility for continued support of the Schreuder Mission in South Africa. The work being conducted among American Indian and Alaskan Eskimos was also regarded as foreign mission activity.[83]

"The Gospel of the 'Inasmuch' "

The term "Inner Mission" entered the Protestant ecclesiastical vocabulary in Germany where Johann Heinrich Wichern (1808-1881) aroused Christians to their responsibility towards homeless children and the aged, the sick and the destitute. He defined it as "the collective and not isolated labor of love which springs from faith in Christ, and which seeks to bring about the internal and external renewal of the masses within Christendom who have fallen under the dominion of those evils which result directly or indirectly from sin. . . ."[84] The extension of this interest to American Lutheranism is closely associated with the name of William Alfred Passavant, whose labors among the underprivileged led him to promote the

---
[81] A. Burgess, "Burning Zeal," in J. C. K. Preus (ed.), *Norsemen Found a Church*, pp. 347-349.
[82] *Ibid.*, p. 360.
[83] *Beretning . . . Den Norsk Lutherske Kirke i Amerika . . . 1917*, p. 559.
[84] Quoted in G. M. Bruce, *Ten Studies on the Lutheran Church* (Minneapolis: Augsburg Publishing House, 1932), p. 83.

building of hospitals, orphanages, and other institutions of mercy. With the help of Theodore Fliedner he introduced the female diaconate to American Protestantism.[85]

Among Norwegian-Americans in the late nineteenth century the Reverend E. J. Homme was the most successful advocate of the eleemosynary enterprise.[86] His initiative and intensity of purpose directly or indirectly served to awaken the churches to the necessity of organized charities. However, the first years saw only small progress. By 1890 three children's homes had been founded, the Homme Home (1882), Wittenberg, Wisconsin; the Martin Luther Home (1889), Madison— later, Stoughton—Wisconsin; and the Beloit Children's Home (1890), Beloit, Iowa.[87] Two deaconess homes and hospitals, one in Brooklyn (1883), the other in Minneapolis (1889) were under way. This was the extent of organized charity.

During the next period of years, 1890-1917, numerous institutions of mercy were established by church bodies or private associations made up of Norwegian Lutheran pastors and lay folk. The outreach of this work is evident from lists and statistics compiled by O. M. Norlie.[88] In the period before the union of 1917 the following church-related institutions, supported either by the churches or independent groups within the churches, were begun:

Children's Homes

Martha-Maria, Poulsbo, Washington, estab. 1891 (Luth. Free)

Lake Park, Lake Park, Minnesota, estab. 1895 (United Church)

---
[85]G. H. Gerberding, *Life and Letters of W. A. Passavant, D.D.* (Greenville, Pa.: The Young Lutheran Co., 1906), *passim.*
[86]See Volume I, Chapter XIII. Cf. Beulah Folkedahl, *A Dream Come True, The Homme Homes at Wittenberg* (Wittenberg, Wisconsin: Nels and Ruth Englund Paulsen, 1956). *passim.*
[87]Homme also cared for a few old people as early as 1882. Therefore, this date is considered the beginning of this phase of Christian charity among the Norwegian-Americans. Folkedahl, *op. cit.*, p. 155.
[88]See *History of the Norwegian People in America*, pp. 426-433.

Bethesda, Beresford, South Dakota, estab. 1896 (Hauge's Synod)
Wild Rice, Twin Valley, Minnesota, estab. 1898 (Norw. Synod)
Norwegian Lutheran, Edison Park, Illinois, estab. 1898 (Independent)
Parkland, Everett, Washington, estab. 1900 (Norw. Synod)
Bethesda, Willmar, Minnesota, estab. 1905 (Luth. Free)
Children's, Brooklyn, New York, estab. 1915 (Independent)

Homes for the Aged

Norwood Park, Chicago, Illinois, estab. 1896 (Independent)
Bethesda, Willmar, Minnesota, estab. 1898 (Lutheran Free)
Skaalen, Stoughton, Wisconsin, estab. 1900 (Norw. Synod)
Norw. Christian, Brooklyn, New York, estab. 1902 (Independent)
Josephine, Stanwood, Washington, estab. 1908 (Norw. Synod)
Ebenezer, Poulsbo, Washington, estab. 1908 (Luth. Free)
Bethesda, Beresford, South Dakota, estab. 1910 (Hauge's Synod)
Sarepta, Sauk Center, Minnesota, estab. 1910 (Luth. Brethren)
Bethesda, Chicago, Illinois, estab. 1910 (Independent)
Northwood, Northwood, North Dakota, estab. 1910 (Independent)
Lyngblomsten, St. Paul, Minnesota, estab. 1912 (Independent)
Aase Haugen, Haugenville, Iowa (later to Decorah), estab. 1914 (United Church)
Glenwood, Glenwood, Minnesota, estab. 1914 (Norw. Synod)
Ebenezer, Minneapolis, Minnesota, estab. 1916 (Independent)

Hospitals[89]

Lutheran, Sioux Falls, South Dakota, estab. 1894 (Norw. Synod)
Lutheran Deaconess, Chicago, Illinois, estab. 1896 (United Church)
Norwegian-American, Chicago, Illinois, estab. 1896 (Independent)
St. Olaf, Austin, Minnesota, estab. 1896 (Independent*)
Bethesda, Crookston, Minnesota, estab. 1898 (Independent*)
Deaconess, Grand Forks, North Dakota, estab. 1899 (Independent)
Lutheran, LaCrosse, Wisconsin, estab. 1899 (Norw. Synod)
St. Paul, St. Paul, Minnesota, estab. 1901 (Norw. Synod)
Ebenezer, Madison, Minnesota, estab. 1902 (Independent*)
Deaconess, Northwood, North Dakota, estab. 1902 (Independent*)
St. Luke's, Fergus Falls, Minnesota, estab. 1903 (Independent*)
Deaconess, Grafton, North Dakota, estab. 1904 (Independent*)
Luther, Eau Claire, Wisconsin, estab. 1907 (Independent*)
St. Luke's, Fargo, North Dakota, estab. 1908 (Independent*)
Good Samaritan, Rugby, North Dakota, estab. 1910 (Independent)
Wittenberg, Williston, North Dakota, estab. 1911 (Independent)
Central Iowa, Story City, Iowa, estab. 1914 (Independent)
Dawson Surgical, Dawson, Minnesota, estab. 1915 (Independent)
Luther, Watertown, South Dakota, estab. 1915 (Independent)

---

[89] The independent hospitals marked with an asterisk received their chief support from congregations and individuals of the United Church.

Fairview, Minneapolis, Minnesota, estab. 1916 (Independent)

Moe, Sioux Falls, South Dakota, estab. 1917 (Independent)

Miscellaneous

Several miscellaneous inner mission institutions, like the above-listed "independent" hospitals, carried on their work by means of voluntary gifts from church people. Chief among them were the Luther Home (hospice), Minneapolis, Minnesota (1904); the Seamen's Mission, Seattle, Washington (1907); the Siloah Scandinavian Mission, Seattle, Washington (1907); and the Seamen's Mission, Galveston, Texas (1910).

Before concluding this section it should be noted that the inner mission program had grown out of and was nurtured by pietism. Furthermore, it bore the characteristically pietistic hallmark of "mission," that is, the institutions and programs were evangelistically and individualistically orientated. Charities were a means to an end, a good and Christian end, the "saving of souls." Despite this motivation there was among the Norwegian-American Lutherans no real appreciation of the Lutheran social ethic. The "social gospel" from which they turned in understandable abhorrence was not yet seen as one of the ways by which the church was being awakened to Christian *social* action. This was to come, but two world wars would lie between. Meanwhile, Christian welfare was directed solely to rescuing individuals, the lost, the homeless, the straying—the least of Christ's brethren. "The Gospel of the 'Inasmuch'" grew hands and feet.

"How They Love Education!"

One of the few English-speaking Lutherans "from the East" who understood the Norwegians was Dr. G. H. Gerberding, who taught theology at Chicago Lutheran Seminary and Northwestern Lutheran Seminary (Minneapolis) during the first quarter of the twentieth century (1894-1927). In his autobiography, Gerberding spoke glowingly of the Norwegians whom he met on the Great Plains:

And how they love education. How they will plan and how ready they are to sacrifice and to suffer that their children may have an education. I actually saw large families living in sod shacks on the open prairie sending a boy or a girl to Concordia College [Moorhead, Minnesota]. Am sorry to say that I have not seen anything like this among the Germans.[90]

Although Gerberding's comparison might not have been fair to the Germans, he was not exaggerating the educational interest of the Norwegians. By 1900 they had established institutions on at least three educational levels: secondary, collegiate, and professional. On the secondary level, parochial schools and academies were being organized in various areas. On the collegiate level there were no less than five institutions: Luther College, Decorah, Iowa; Augsburg Seminary (with a college department), Minneapolis, Minnesota; St. Olaf College, Northfield, Minnesota; Augustana College, Canton, South Dakota; and Red Wing Seminary (with a junior college department), Red Wing, Minnesota. On the professional level there were normal schools and theological seminaries. Normal schools at Sioux Falls, South Dakota, Wittenberg, Wisconsin, and Madison, Minnesota, prepared teachers for public as well as church schools. The theological seminaries in 1900 numbered four: Luther Seminary, St. Paul, Minnesota (The Norwegian Synod), Augsburg Seminary (The Free Church) and the United Church Seminary (United Norwegian Lutheran Church), Minneapolis, Minnesota, and Red Wing Seminary (Hauge's Synod), Red Wing, Minnesota.[91]

The expansion of the educational program of the churches during the next two decades was to occur on the secondary and collegiate levels.

On the secondary level the most prominent feature of the

---

[90] G. H. Gerberding, *Reminiscent Reflections of a Youthful Octogenarian* (Minneapolis: Augsburg Publishing House, 1928), p. 150.
[91] For a summary to 1914 see M. K. Bleken, "De Norsk-Amerikanske Skoler," in J. B. Wist (ed.), *Norsk-Amerikanernes Festskrift 1914* (Decorah, Iowa: The Symra Co., 1914), pp. 245-265.

era was what has been called "the academy movement." Numerous private church high schools were organized, usually by groups of congregations, in the states of the upper Mississippi valley. Great initial interest led many to assume this kind of education would be a permanent characteristic of the Norwegian Lutherans in America.[92] However, from the very beginning there was resistance from those who advocated support of "genuine public education among the Scandinavian people."[93] In the end this view was to prevail, partly for its own merits, partly for financial reasons and changes in educational philosophy. Meanwhile, however, almost forty academies, twenty-five of which were founded after 1890, were experiencing varying degrees of prosperity.[94]

Among the more flourishing schools, some of which had been founded before 1890, were the following (listed with total enrollment during the life of each academy): Augsburg (Lutheran Free Church), with an accumulated total of 2,247 students; St. Olaf (United Church), 6,592 students; St. Ansgar (United Church), 2,868; Red Wing (Hauge's Synod), 5,025; Willmar (Norwegian Synod), 7,110; Augustana (United Church), 5,943; Concordia (United Church), 9,890; Park Region (Norwegian Synod), 7,983; Jewell (Hauge's Synod), 4,236; Lutheran Ladies Seminary (Norwegian Synod), 4,129; Pacific Lutheran (Norwegian Synod), 4,950; Pleasant View (United Church), 4,250; Gale (Norwegian Synod), 2,920; Waldorf (United Church), 6,272; Spokane (United Church), 2,679; Oak Grove Ladies Seminary (Free Church), 3,595; and Camrose (United Church), 2,716.[95] Among the normal schools the most prominent were the Lutheran Normal School (Norwe-

---

[92]For a survey of the academy movement see B. H. Narveson, "The Norwegian Lutheran Academies," *Norwegian-American Studies and Records*, XIV, 184-226. Although we have spoken of the "normal schools" as professional schools, it should be pointed out that they were actually academies with teacher training courses.

[93]*Ibid.*, pp. 192-193.

[94]For a list of the academies see *ibid.*, pp. 217-221.

[95]*Loc. cit.* It should be pointed out that the synodical designation is accurate only in a general way. With the exception of the academy or preparatory departments of the synodically-operated schools (Luther, Augsburg, St. Olaf, Red Wing, and Augustana), most of the academies were controlled by independent boards or corporations or by congregations within a specific church body.

gian Synod), Sioux Falls, South Dakota, and the Lutheran Normal School (United Church), Madison, Minnesota. The former had been the normal department at Luther College for twenty years (1865-1885). Discontinued in 1886 it was reestablished at Sioux Falls in 1889. Following the union of 1917, this school was merged (1918) with Augustana College of Canton under the name Augustana College and Normal.[96]

The United Church, at its first convention in 1890, authorized the establishing of the normal school which opened its doors in 1892 at Madison, Minnesota.[97] Before it became one of the casualties of the depression years, the Madison Normal had enrolled about 2,500 students, ninety per cent of whom served the church as teachers in congregational schools of religion. In 1926 the normal department was discontinued. The school operated as an academy until 1932.[98]

Actually two philosophies of education faced each other in the years the academies and normal schools were being built. Those who supported the movement were convinced that the best way to preserve the faith of the fathers was to provide schools where both secular and religious subjects would be taught, the idea being that the secular learning would be carried on in a religious atmosphere. To this end the teachers would be Lutherans who were motivated by personal consecration to the cause.[99]

The group which opposed this type of education included two quite different segments. One was anticlerical, approaching the problem in a liberal and democratic spirit. It saw public education as a positive good and urged the immigrants,

---

[96] Norlie, *History of the Norwegian People*, p. 278. Cf. S. A. Jordahl, *Memorial History Lutheran Normal School . . . 1889-1918* (n. p.: n. n., n. d.), *passim*. It should be mentioned that local interests at Canton resented the transfer of Augustana College to Sioux Falls. The result was the operation of Canton Lutheran Normal School, 1920-1926. The school at Sioux Falls dropped its normal department in 1926 and henceforth was known simply as Augustana College.

[97] H. O. Hendrickson (ed.), *In Retrospect, A History of the Lutheran Normal School, Madison, Minnesota, 1892-1932* (Lake Mills, Iowa: Graphic Publishing Company, Inc., 1958), pp. 2-4.

[98] *Ibid.*, pp. vi, 22, 103-105, 107-111. In 1943 it was decided to establish a home for the aged on the site of the LNS. This institution, known today as the Madison Lutheran Home, was begun in 1944 and is owned by The Evangelical Lutheran Church. *Ibid.*, p. 16.

[99] This point of view is the thesis of an apology for the academies written by O. M. Norlie, *The Academy for Princes* (Minneapolis: Augsburg Publishing House, 1917), *passim*.

as enlightened Americans, to make common cause lest they be overrun by the spirit of the Norwegian Synod.[100] The other segment was made up of churchmen chiefly associated with the New School of the Norwegian-Danish Conference. Sverdrup, for example, insisted that the congregation was responsible only for religious instruction. The public school was responsible for general education. If the state undertook religious instruction, the result would be a dead and empty church. If the church undertook general education, the result would be priestly rule.[101]

Among the church people, therefore, the two attitudes toward the church schools could be summarized as follows: (1) one group sought to "save" the children for the Lutheran faith by an educational system built upon the principles of segregation and indoctrination; (2) the other group, no less interested in saving their children, looked upon indoctrination as the responsibility of the home and the church, but each youth must live out the principles of Christianity in the crucible of the public school.

Despite the fact that academies evoked no little opposition in some quarters of the church, the cause was generally popular at the turn of the century. One of the reasons for this was that the villages and small cities of the Upper Midwest possessed poorly-equipped and inadequately-staffed high schools. Moreover, many communities had no high schools at all; the district grade school was the sole representative of public education. In this situation, the privately-owned and church-related boarding school filled a distinct educational need.

The parents who sent their sons and daughters to the academies and normal schools were assured of a wholesome religious environment and a solid academic curriculum. The

---
[100]Blegen, op. cit., II, 257.
[101]Sverdrup, "Commonskolen," Samlede Skrifter, I, 358-384. Sverdrup discusses "the Common [Public] School and Christianity," "Luther and the Folk School," and "The American Folk School." Actually, however, Sverdrup was not consistent. Although he was friend of the public school, his own theory of ministerial education led him to include an academy or high school department at Augsburg Seminary.

catalog of the Glenwood Academy, for example, stipulated that the students must attend daily chapel services and divine worship on Sunday. Students were strictly forbidden to use tobacco, to attend theaters and dances, or to visit saloons, pool halls, and bowling alleys.[102]

The curriculum of most of the schools exhibited a variety of courses: college preparatory, commercial, normal, and parochial normal offerings. One of the better academies (Albert Lea) provided curricular fare that would warm the heart of many an educator today. The language courses, in addition to English, included German, Latin, Greek, and Norwegian. In mathematics the offerings were arithmetic, algebra, and geometry. Religion, ethics, history, geography, civil government, botany, physiology, zoology, "natural phelosophy" [sic], commercial subjects, music, penmanship, and physical culture completed the curriculum.

Extracurricular activities were not neglected. "Lyceum courses," lectures, literary and debating societies, school publications, and athletics all competed for the students' somewhat limited leisure.[103]

During a period of a dozen years, before and after 1900, the academies were quite enthusiastically supported. Enrollments increased year by year until a peak was reached in 1907.[104] But from that time to the Great Depression the academies experienced losses. The struggle for existence became increasingly severe until ultimately all but a handful were forced to close their doors.[105]

The reasons for the demise of the academies are to be sought in a complex of circumstances: the problems of the second generation immigrant, the question of financial and student

---

[102]Glenwood (Minnesota) Academy, *Twelfth Annual Catalog* (1905); cited in Narveson, *op. cit.*, pp. 207-208.

[103]A typical day's schedule:

6:30 Rising bell	10:00 Recitations	6:00 Supper
7:00 Breakfast	12:00 Dinner	7:00 Devotions
8:00 Recitations	1:30 Recitations	7:30 Study
9:30 Devotions	4:00 Recreation	10:00 Lights out

Ibid., p. 214.
[104]Norlie, *History of the Norwegian People*, p. 374.
[105]Narveson, *op. cit.*, p. 215.

support, the real or imagined conflict in educational philosophies. In fact, some of the causes for the decline were interlocked with others and simply cannot be examined in isolation. For example, there was the problem of Americanization. There was little that the second generation prized more highly than being identified with America. To many the high school was a symbol of America, whereas the academy was a reminder of the Old World which their parents had left—for good! In the early years, especially, all instruction in the academies had been carried on in the Norwegian language with a twofold purpose, to preserve the faith of the fathers (which, they suspected, underwent erosion in being translated into English) and to conserve something of the heritage from the motherland. The early years of the twentieth century saw a gradual shift to the use of English, but the change was not sufficient to provide compelling reasons for supporting the academies. To the children of the immigrants the academies still represented an alien culture. The public high school, however, was American, and with this they wanted to be associated.

It was not strange, therefore, that the church-related boarding schools began to note a decline in attendance before 1910. The lowered enrollment meant lowered income, lowered income meant lowered ability to compete with the tax-supported high schools. The latter ordinarily provided better equipment and higher salary schedules for teachers; moreover, they soon established the reputation of being "progressive," whereas the academies, clinging to the traditional disciplines, were regarded as "old-fashioned."

Strenuous efforts were made by church leaders and members to halt the disintegration of the academy program, but to no avail.[106] After 1915 hardly a year went by without the discontinuance of at least one institution. At the close of the period under survey almost one-half of the academies had been closed.[107]

[106]For a typical plea see Norlie, *History of the Norwegian People in America*, p. 378.
[107]*Beretning . . . Den Norsk Lutherske Kirke . . . 1918*, pp. 99-100.

In other words, despite the fact that twenty-three academies were operating in 1917-1918, the death-knell had been sounded, and it was only left for the Great Depression to administer the *coup de grace*. In 1937 but three schools remained: Augustana Academy, Canton, South Dakota (associated with the Norwegian Lutheran Church of America); Oak Grove Ladies Seminary, Fargo, North Dakota (Lutheran Free Church); and Outlook College (academy department), Saskatchewan, Canada (Norwegian Lutheran Church of America).[108]

The academy movement had seen its day, but during its years of popularity it had borne some notable fruits. Norlie has pointed out, as a sort of *apologia pro vita academiarum*, that these schools reached more young people than any other church schools of the time. Moreover, the academies and normal schools were a part of the preparatory training for theological study of nearly all Norwegian-American pastors during the seventy-five-year period, 1850-1925.[109]

Deplore, as many did, the passing of the academies, it should be noted that religious direction, given to the lives of many young people, did not disappear with the closing of these schools. What was once credited in good measure to the influence of academies and normal schools continued in a new milieu characterized especially by the church-sponsored summer camps for youth and the extensive program of the Luther League climaxed by the religious and emotional appeal of the giant youth conventions.

On the collegiate level the educational program of the churches saw less vigorous growth. The five colleges (Luther, Augsburg, Augustana, St. Olaf, and Red Wing) remained the sole representatives of higher education (with the exception of the theological schools) throughout the period, 1900-1917. However, the roots of at least three additional institutions, which were to achieve collegiate status later, were in

---
[108]Narveson, *op. cit.*, p. 215, n. 46. Cf. "Christian Education Through Twenty Years," *Annual Report, Norwegian Lutheran Church of America* . . . *1938*, pp. 77-80.
[109]Norlie, *op. cit.*, p. 378.

this period: Concordia College, Moorhead, Minnesota; Pacific Lutheran College, Parkland, Washington; Waldorf (Junior) College, Forest City, Iowa.[110]

Concordia College was begun as an academy in 1891 by an incorporated association of congregations affiliated chiefly with the United Church. Having acquired the former Bishop Whipple School (Episcopal) property in Moorhead, the school grew rapidly and by 1913 added a four-year college department offering the degree of Bachelor of Arts. The first collegiate class was graduated in 1917.[111] The same year Park Region Luther College, Fergus Falls, Minnesota, was merged with Concordia. Park Region was owned by the Norwegian Synod, which in 1917 merged with the United Church and Hauge's Synod.

On the West Coast another Lutheran college was being born. Shortly after the Civil War Norwegian immigrants had begun to settle in the San Francisco area and the Pacific Northwest. The Norwegian Synod initiated home mission work on the Coast in the seventies, and this action drew the attention of the church leaders to the need of schools. In 1890 the Synod adopted a resolution encouraging the erection of a Lutheran high school in the West and authorized Pastor Bjug Harstad, president of the Minnesota District, to undertake a western trip to explore the possibilities of implementing the resolution.[112]

The same year (1890) members of Synod congregations in the area organized the Pacific Lutheran University Association,

---

[110]Other junior colleges were also founded but were later discontinued or merged with other institutions. Among the latter were Park Region Luther College, Fergus Falls, Minnesota, merged with Concordia (1917); Spokane College, Spokane, Washington, merged with Pacific Lutheran (1929); Clifton College, Clifton, Texas, merged with Texas Lutheran College, Seguin, Texas, (1954).

[111]Dr. J. A. Aasgaard, president emeritus of The Evangelical Lutheran Church, became president of Concordia in 1911. It was under his administration that Concordia achieved status as a college. Rasmus Bogstad, *The Early History of Concordia College* (Moorhead, Minnesota [?]: n. n., 1942 [?], pp. 3-35, 208. Cf. *Concordia College Catalog 1931* (Moorhead, Minn.: n. n., 1931), pp. 12-13. Dr. Aasgaard became president of The Evangelical Lutheran Church in 1925. He was succeeded at Concordia by Dr. J. N. Brown; his successor was Dr. J. L. Knutson (1951-).

[112]W. C. Schnackenberg, "The Development of Norwegian Lutheran Schools in the Pacific Northwest from 1890 to 1920," (Unpublished Ph.D. dissertation, State College of Washington, 1950), pp. 20-23.

and four years later established Pacific Lutheran University at Parkland, Washington. The school retained this pretentious name until 1899 when it received accreditation as Pacific Lutheran Academy.[113]

The school lived a hand-to-mouth existence for a number of years. One of the chief reasons for this was the disunity among the Norwegian Lutherans and the resultant inability to concentrate on supporting one institution. Two of the other segments of Norwegian-American Lutheranism deemed it necessary to establish schools in the West; in fact, one group (the United Church) organized two: Columbia College, Everett, Washington, begun in 1909, and Spokane College, begun in 1907.[114] Meanwhile the Lutheran Free Church, after an abortive educational venture at Poulsbo, Washington, opened Bethania High School in Everett in 1904.[115] In other words, four schools sought the loyalties of churches which were hardly strong enough to support one!

After the union of 1917 Pacific Lutheran Academy was merged (1918) with Columbia College. The following year, however, Columbia closed its doors only to reopen in 1920 as Pacific Lutheran College in Parkland. The next year the curricular offerings were enlarged to qualify the institution as a junior college.[116]

Back in the Midwest, congregations of the United Church in northern Iowa established yet another school, Waldorf College at Forest City, Iowa. Begun as an academy in 1903 under the energetic leadership of the Reverend C. S. Salveson, the school added a junior college department in 1920 which has been continued to the present.[117]

---

[113]*Ibid.*, p. 151. Actually the "university" had never been more than a secondary school. In 1959 the college decided to readopt its original name, Pacific Lutheran University.

[114]*Ibid.*, pp. 223, 246.

[115]*Ibid.*, pp. 205-218. The school was discontinued in 1917.

[116]For an account of the involved details of the post-1917 years see *ibid.*, pp. 270-296. Spokane was merged with Pacific Lutheran College in 1929. Between 1931 and 1939 the institution became a "college of education"; in 1941, a liberal arts college.

[117]In 1936 the high school was discontinued. In 1945 the last two years of high school were added. From 1945 to 1955 Waldorf operated as a four-year junior college offering grades eleven through fourteen. In 1955 grades eleven and twelve were discontinud. Waldorf is today a two-year junior college. *Centennial Sketches* (Forest City, Iowa: The Forest City Centennial, Inc., 1955), p. 29. One of the significant facts about Waldorf

The Common Worship

Among Norwegian-American Lutherans there were three attitudes towards traditional liturgical practices. One, associated with the Norwegian Synod, looked upon the liturgy of the Church of Norway as the proper model for the ordering of public worship. The liturgy was something to be used and loved as a part of the rich devotional heritage of the Lutheran church. Furthermore, that which had been enjoined by royal decree upon the churches of Denmark and Norway was not to be lightly esteemed nor quickly altered on the American scene. The liturgy was an accepted part of the life of the church.

The polar opposite of this attitude was the view of the low-church segments as represented especially in the Eielsen Synod, Hauge's Synod, and the Lutheran Free Church. To these and other groups the liturgy and the whole idea of an ordered devotional life was repugnant. They reasoned that the liturgy was not only formal but a formalism, and thus liturgy was a hindrance to the free movement of the Holy Spirit. This could only be inimical to the life of the church. Services, therefore, should be simple, free of "order," and open to spontaneity.

Between these attitudes was a third, associated in a general way with the United Church. Actually, the majority of its congregations adhered to the traditional liturgy but found room for a certain amount of freedom. There was no strict insistence on the necessity of the liturgy and its accoutrements; nevertheless, it was considered good to worship in the manner prescribed by the *Ritual* of the Church of Norway. Generally speaking, therefore, the United Church and the Norwegian Synod represented a similar liturgical attitude, with the exception that the United Church did not look askance at prayer

---

College is that several of its presidents have become leaders in The Evangelical Lutheran Church educational circles. Dr. L. W. Boe (president, 1904-1915), became president of St. Olaf College. Dr. Martin Hegland (1915-1919), became chairman of the department of religion at St. Olaf College. President C. B. Helgen (1920-1929), later also joined the St. Olaf faculty. Dr. C. M. Granskou (1929-1932), later became president of Augustana College (1932) in Sioux Falls and in 1943 president of St. Olaf. Mr. J. L. Rendahl (1932-1943) became director of public relations at Concordia College. Acting president A. L. Halvorson (1950-1951) became professor of homiletics at Luther Theological Seminary, St. Paul. Dr. Sidney A. Rand (1951-1955) became executive director of the Department of Christian Education.

meetings and evangelistic services. In actuality, therefore, the public worship of the Norwegian-Americans took two forms: the liturgy of the Church of Norway and the informal service of Haugeans.

Norway's church shared the liturgy of the Church of Denmark. In fact, it was officially known as "The Church Ritual of Denmark and Norway." It was this order of service, modified through the years, which was generally used in American congregations.

With the introduction of the Reformation, the church in the Danish-Norwegian kingdom received an evangelical mass based on both of Luther's main liturgical works, *Formula Missae* and the *Deutsche Messe*. This was known as "The Ordinance" of 1542, a full and rich liturgical expression.[118]

Major revision towards simplification occurred in 1685 and was known as *Ritualet*. During the period of Pietism and Rationalism *Ritualet* of 1685 underwent rather severe changes. Pietism, fearing the dead hand of formalism, removed the formal prayers and limited the ceremonial parts. Rationalism, for different reasons, preferred a short service. By 1802 the service had suffered the following: the *Kyrie* was omitted; the Creed and *Gloria* were used alternately on every other Sunday and soon dropped completely; only the Epistle was read (in the interest of brevity the Gospel was read from the pulpit before the sermon); stanzas were omitted from hymns; the sermon, rationalistically oriented, was made more prominent. E. K. Johnsen comments, ". . . this was the Order of Service and its character at the time of the first Norwegian emigration to America and even down to 1887. . . . Its parts were: Opening Prayer, Hymn, Collect, Epistle, Hymn, Sermon, General Prayer, Blessing, Hymn, Collect, Hymn, Closing Prayer."[119]

---

[118] E. K. Johnsen, "The Liturgy of the Norwegian Lutheran Church," *Memoirs of the Lutheran Liturgical Association*, ed. by Luther D. Reed (Pittsburgh: The Association, 1906), VII, 37. Cf. E. Belfour, "The History of the Liturgy in the Lutheran Church in Denmark," *ibid.*, II, 57-73. See Appendix B for liturgical survey.

[119] *Op. cit.*, pp. 40-41. It was this eroded *Ritualet* to which J. W. C. Dietrichson pledged his congregation at Koshkonong, Wisconsin, in 1844. For a commentary on this "high church" liturgy see J. M. Rohne, *Norwegian American Lutheranism up to 1872* (New York: Macmillan, 1926), pp. 85-87.

By 1887 the Church of Norway had moved to a more conservative and traditional position in both theology and liturgy.[120] The new liturgy, based largely on the liturgy of the Bavarian Church, was produced by Pastors W. K. Hesselberg and Gustav Jensen, and promulgated by royal decree, January 8, 1887.[121] It was this service, rather than the 1802 denuded version of the 1685 *Ritual,* which came to be used in the Norwegian Synod and the United Church in the twentieth century. By 1902 an English translation was made by the United Church and later incorporated in *The Lutheran Hymnary* and the *Altar Book of the Norwegian Evangelical Lutheran Church.*[122]

The liturgy, known as *høimesse* (high mass), was led by the minister vested in a black robe which hung straight from the shoulders to within a few inches of the floor. Draped about the neck and hanging down the full length of the vestment was a stiffly-padded, satin-covered black stole, symbolizing the ministerial office. At the back of the neck the stole was raised to support a white fluted collar, three inches wide and an inch thick. On the occasion of the high festivals the pastor might wear a white surplice over his robe.

Participating in the liturgy was a lay assistant, a *klokker* (precentor), who read the opening and closing prayers from the chancel (standing outside the communion rail) and led the congregational responses and hymns. Regrettably, all too often the latter became cacophonous or soporific solos.

The minister entered the chancel from the sacristy, and at the close of the prelude knelt at the north (in an oriented church) side of the altar. While he knelt the *klokker* faced the congregation and read the Opening Prayer. The service then proceeded as follows:

---

[120] The spirit of conservative Lutheranism had grown from the forties. By 1887 when the more traditionally Lutheran liturgy was accepted, the theological currents had already begun to shift somewhat toward the late 19th century liberalism of German theology.

[121] *Salmonsens . . . Konversationsleksikon,* ed. Chr. Blangstrup (Copenhagen: Brøderene Salmonsen, 1898), VIII, 865. The new altar book was decreed by King Oscar, February 14, 1889. Cf. *Alterbog for den norske Kirke* (Kristiania: F. Beyer's Forlag, 1889), pp. 3-4. Cf. Johnsen, *op. cit.,* pp. 42-43.

[122] "The Short Form" was still used. Therefore, it was included in the Altar Book.

Hymn
Confession of Sin[123]
The Kyrie
The Gloria[124]
The Salutation (intoned)
The Collect (intoned)
The Epistle (congregation standing)
Hymn (in place of the customary Gradual)
The Gospel (congregation standing)
The Creed
Hymn
The Sermon (preceded by a pulpit prayer and closed by *Gloria Patri*)
The General Prayer (read in the pulpit, concluding with Lord's Prayer and Apostolic Benediction)
Hymn (here baptism and catechization of children might follow)
The Preface (intoned)
The Sanctus
The Exhortation
The Lord's Prayer (intoned)
The Words of Institution (intoned)
The Distribution
Hymn
Collect of Thanksgiving (intoned)
Salutation (intoned)
Benediction (intoned)
Hymn
Closing Prayer and Lord's Prayer (read by *klokker* while minister knelt)

Although the liturgy assumed the celebration of the Lord's Supper at each *høimesse,* the sacrament was usually administered at stated times during the year. When the Holy Communion was not celebrated, the hymn after the sermon was followed by the Collect for the Word, the Benediction, Hymn, and Closing Prayer.

The central part of the service was the sermon. The pastor was expected to preach on the text appointed for the day. The text, or pericope, as it was known, was one of three epistles

---

[123] The Absolution or Declaration of Grace was not used in Norway, but was added to the English translation in America. It was evidently taken from the Common Service of 1888.
[124] This included only the first line of the *Gloria in Excelsis.* The minister intoned: "Glory to God in the highest." The congregation sang: "And on earth peace good will toward men."

or three gospel selections. Originally the Church of Norway, like other Lutheran churches in Europe, used only the ancient, or primary, series of texts commonly known in the Church of Rome and the Church of England. However, the liturgical renewal in 1887 produced two additional series, essentially like those in the Church of Sweden. The new series was edited by Professors Gisle Johnson, A. Bang, and Pastor Sven Brun.[125]

If a person worshipped in a congregation of the Norwegian Synod after 1900, he could expect to be led in this order of service. This was generally true in the United Church as well. Some congregations of both church bodies continued to use the altered version of the 1685 *Ritual*, the so-called "Shorter Form," abbreviated during the eras of Pietism and Rationalism.[126] However, the pastors wore the traditional vestments, chanted certain portions of the service, and used the precentor as an assistant.

The second liturgical attitude among the Norwegians in America is perhaps best presented by summarizing the principles which guided the worship of Hauge's Synod. The liturgical orientation of this group and others like it grew out of a concern for religious life characterized by emphasis on personal Christianity, a regenerate church membership, evangelistic sermons, prayer meetings, and "lay activity," notably the right of laymen to preach. It was especially prayer and the preaching of repentance, conversion, and holiness that loomed large in the Haugean cultus.

G. M. Bruce has pointed out that Hauge's Synod with its strong lay emphasis eschewed the liturgy of the Church of Norway retaining only the formulas for the administration of the Lord's Supper and baptism.[127] Since the services of worship

---

[125] Johnsen, *op. cit.*, p. 42.
[126] "The Shorter Form" (*Den kortere Form*) is found in the English Altar Book (1902, 1915, 1934 editions) as well as in *Salmebog for Lutherske Kristne i Amerika* (Landstad's Salmebog) (Minneapolis: Den Forenede Kirkes Forlag, 1898), pp. 569-574. Whether one used the full service or "The Shorter Form," it was still known as *høimesse* (high mass).
[127] G. M. Bruce, "Hauge's synode," in Norlie (ed.), *Norsk Lutherske Menigheter i Amerika 1843-1916*, II, 687. This section on Haugean practices is largely a summary of what Professor Bruce calls *Kirkeskikke* (church customs), pp. 687–688. Cf. *Kirkeritual for Hauges Synodes Menigheder* (n. p.; m. n., 1905?) and *Udkast til Ritual-Forandring*, ed. G. M. Bruce *et al.* (Dell Rapids, S. Dak.: n. n., 1909). Both of the above pamphlets are in the Library, Luther Theological Seminary, St. Paul, Minnesota.

were patterned after the Haugean evangelistic or *opbyggelses-møter* (edifying meetings), it was to be expected that no fixed form would prevail. Fragments of the Church of Norway *Ritual* —in some instances altered, in others unchanged—might appear in the various congregations. A few ceremonies were retained, others were rejected, all without concern for liturgical uniformity or implied consequences. In none of the congregations did the divine service receive cultic structure.

If one attended a Haugean service in the late nineteenth or early twentieth century, he would note the traditional Norwegian Lutheran chancel arrangement: a free-standing altar at the center, the pulpit at one side and the baptismal font at the other. The pastor would appear from the sacristy without clerical garb, and lead the service of worship. The congregation would perhaps sing hymns from the familiar Landstad's *Salmebog*.[128] However, almost immediately the visitor would note disregard for the usual rubrics of the *Ritual*. After the opening hymn for example, the pastor might call on a layman to offer a free prayer. During the next hymn, the minister moved to the altar. If he oriented toward the altar, it would only be *before* turning to the congregation to read the collect for the day. Neither this nor any other part of the service would be chanted, nor would the sacrificial portions of the service be read facing the altar. The pastor might recite the Salutation, "The Lord be with you," but the congregation would not respond with the traditional, "And with thy spirit." During the reading of the lections the congregation might or might not rise. In at least one large congregation, says Bruce, the congregation remained seated for the Epistle and rose for the Gospel. The question whether communicants should stand or sit during the confessional address at the Lord's Supper or whether sponsors should stand or sit during baptism exercised some congregations, but no uniform practice was deemed desirable.

One of the more theologically significant problems was the

---

[128]Hauge's Synod (generally) and the United Church (wholly) used the significant hymnal of M. B. Landstad, published in Norway in 1869. The Norwegian Synod published its own hymnal in 1874. See P. M. Glasoe, "The Landstad-Lindeman Hymnbook," *The Lutheran Church*, I (October, 1938), 5 ff.

question of the relationship between absolution and Holy Communion. The "Old Constitution" (Eielsen) solved the problem by rejecting the customary Norwegian practice, the pronouncing of individual absolution with the laying-on of hands during the confessional service. Since Scripture said nothing of this in connection with the institution of the sacrament, and since Paul admonished each to examine himself, Haugeans generally maintained that the pastor should rather give a heart-searching exhortation and then conclude with the declaration that, according to God's Word, all repentant and believing sinners receive the forgiveness of sins in the name of the Father, and of the Son, and of the Holy Ghost.

Absolution by its very nature, said the Haugeans, was a private and not a public ceremony, and therefore, in its public and unconditional form, must be separated from the Lord's Supper. The danger of public absolution, even though a conditional form were used, was that unrepentant sinners would receive a false comfort and thus be unworthy communicants.

It is unmistakable that the overriding concern of the Haugean wing of Norwegian-American Lutheranism was the personal confrontation of men with the demands and promises of God's Word. Anything which seemed to obstruct the free course of this Word must be decried. One of the chief deterrents to spiritual life was formalism, and, according to Haugean reckoning, in the *Ritual* formalism was a self-evident and ultimate fact. Therefore, it must be cast out.

The variety of liturgical emphases and practices was one of the obstacles to the union of Norwegian-American Lutheranism. To ease the way for Hauge's Synod, the Articles of Union in 1917 made allowances for this variety, the Norwegian Synod and the United Church accepted a Haugean "Interpretation" of the articles on rites and ceremonies, and the joint seminary after the union provided special lectures on Haugean liturgical practices and usages. Eventually, however, very few congregations retained the practices of Hauge's Synod.[129]

[129] G. M. Bruce (ed.), *The Union Documents of the Evangelical Lutheran Church*, pp. 58-59, 68-69, and 69, n. 2.

CHAPTER FIVE

Forward to *Opgjør*

The years 1900-1912 are, in one respect, the most important in the history of the union movement among Norwegian-American Lutherans. During these years divisive practical and doctrinal problems which had plagued the church for decades were settled amicably. The question of lay activity was solved to the satisfaction of the majority in Hauge's Synod, and the doctrine of election was articulated to the satisfaction of the majority in the Norwegian Synod. Opposite tendencies which had existed in the church since pioneer days lost some of their sharpness and men of differing viewpoints began to draw closer together. For these reasons the first twelve years of the twentieth century were of great moment in Norwegian-American Lutheran history.

1890-1905: Union Interest Despite Church Conflict

The two major church bodies which did not enter the union of 1890, the Norwegian Synod and Hauge's Synod, kept the door partially open to further negotiations. In fact, in the year that the merger was consummated both of these churches gave expression to continuing interest in the task of gathering the

Norse peoples of America into one church.[1] The Norwegian Synod, however, approached the matter with traditional caution. In his annual message, President H. A. Preus went so far as to say that the departure of the Anti-Missourians from the Synod in 1887, and the non-participation of the latter in the 1890 merger was a blessing. His sentiments were expressed as follows:

> A purge *(en renselse)* has taken place within the body, and much that was incongruous has been sifted out. We have become fewer, but numbers are not the decisive factor. We stand united in the true faith, and faith is the victory that overcometh the world.[2]

Pastor U. V. Koren, one of the foremost leaders of the Synod, was no less forthright in the statement of his satisfaction over the turn of events which had left the Norwegian Synod outside the new United Church. In an address before the assembly, Koren judged the current union movement as an indication of doctrinal indifferentism and unionism. To be sure, he said, there had been no frontal attack on the Word of God, but the introduction of modifying elements tended to make truth relative and thus to undermine zeal for purity in doctrine. The insistence of pietism that "life" and not "doctrine" is the chief matter was once again apparent in the contemporary church. People could now conclude that it did not matter much what one *believed* just so one *lived* decently. Parodying Luther's well-known hymn based on the Apostles' Creed, he said,

> "Wir glauben all' an einem Gott,
> Christ, Jude, Türk und Hottentot."

The faith was being reduced to the least common denominator, and people were being offered works and rewards. "When we

---

[1] *Beretning . . . Synoden . . . 1890,* p. 73; *Beretning . . . Hauges Synode . . . 1890,* p. 54.

[2] *Beretning . . Synoden 1890,* p. 11. This instance of equating "the true faith" and "faith" was indicative of a tendency in "orthodoxy" which lay at the root of some of the trouble between the Synod and other church bodies. A weakness of the "orthodoxists" was their rationalistic approach to exegesis which was determined by their dogmatics. The New Testament seldom uses the word *pistis* (faith) in the sense of a *fides quae creditur* (a faith that is to be believed). The word is used religiously, not dogmatically as though it referred to a compendium of doctrine. Only a dogmatic exegesis of I John 5:4 (Preus' text) would equate "faith" and "the true faith" seen as a doctrinal system.

do *our* part, God will also do his" was an appealing but poisonous teaching. This, said Koren, was what happened when church unions were not built upon unity in the faith. Then they became products of church politics, indicating into whose hands power had come.[3]

Although Preus and Koren had sounded a dissonant note as far as the Synod's participation in the union movement was concerned, it was at this very meeting that clear and unmistakable statements were drafted showing a concern for the cause of union. The 1889 convention of the Minnesota District of the Norwegian Synod had memorialized the Synod to continue, as far as possible, negotiations with other Norwegian Lutheran groups looking to eventual merger. This significant document, discussed and acted upon at the 1890 convention, reiterated the Synod's concern for "the truth," and the necessity for "union on the basis of truth." The memorial noted that there were disruptive forces at work (the Anti-Missourians and those who now supported them, the Conference and the Augustanans), but the Synod should consider investing its union committee with authority to participate in joint meetings.[4] The convention proceeded to adopt a resolution which embodied the union hopes of the memorial.[5]

Thus it can be seen that there were signs which pointed toward the ultimate inclusion of most Norwegian Lutherans in a united church in America. Although this was not to come for another twenty-seven years, it is significant to note that once the concept of *one* church had gripped people's minds there were continual manifestations of earnest interest in and work for this goal. This was not confined to officially elected and authorized committees. Sometimes interested individuals came together on their own initiative to discuss the problem of union. An interesting record of the latter is to be found in the correspondence of President Th. N. Mohn of St. Olaf College.

[3]*Ibid.*, pp. 34-36.
[4]"Indstilling fra Komitteen angaaende Frikonferenser," *ibid.*, pp. 72-74.
[5]*Ibid.*, p. 74. A committee had been elected in 1887, consisting of Professors Frich and Larsen, and Pastors H. A. Preus, U. V. Koren, Harstad, and J. A. Thorsen. Two more names were added at the 1890 meeting: Professors Stub and Ylvisaker.

His letters reveal that in December, 1890, he was instrumental in promoting a private colloquy *(Samtale)* on the topic: "What Hinders Church Union Among Us?" Professors from the Norwegian Synod seminary, Augsburg Seminary, and St. Olaf College were present at the meeting held December 29-31, 1890, in Minneapolis. The discussion, according to Mohn, revolved around two doctrinal matters, absolution and synergism. Although there was some lack of unanimity in the presentation of the various points of view there was, nevertheless, a common agreement that all must consider one another as Lutherans.[6]

One of the fruits of the resolution on union adopted by the Norwegian Synod in 1890 was the initiation of union negotiations with the United Church. The latter body had elected a committee to discuss possible union with the Norwegian Synod.[7] The two committees met at Madison, Wisconsin, April 7-8, 1891.[8] It was decided at this meeting that each church body elect thirty representatives to confer on the problem of union. Hauge's Synod was also to be invited, but the meeting would be held if only two of the three parties responded. The suggested topic for discussion was "What Are the Requisites of Church Union?" This was to be approached with special reference to Paragraph One of the Scandinavia Agreement (1888). The second part of the discussion would be devoted to absolution or conversion.

The proposed meeting was held in Willmar, Minnesota, January 6-12, 1892, without representation from Hauge's Synod.[9]

---

[6]"Mohn Manuscript Letters," IV (January 4, 1890-July 24, 1891), 355, December 1, 1890, to Professor Georg Sverdrup; *ibid.*, p. 366, December 13, 1890, to Professor Sven Oftedal; *ibid.*, p. 376, December 22, 1890, to Professor J. B. Frich; *ibid.*, p. 377, December 22, 1890, to Professor H. G. Stub; *ibid.*, p. 392, January 2, 1891, to Pastor L. M. Bjørn; *ibid.*, p. 402, January 9, 1891, to Pastor B. J. Muus. Significantly President Mohn invited both Sverdrup and Oftedal to the colloquy, but both of them, consistent with their expressed preference for "cooperation" rather than "doctrinal discussion," declined the invitation.

[7]*Beretning . . . Den f. Kirke . . . 1890*, p. 112. The members of the committee were T. H. Dahl, M. O. Bøckman, D. Lysnes, N. Iversen, G. Rasmussen.

[8]"Møde i Madison, Wisconsin, den 7de og 8de April 1891," *Luthersk Kirkeblad*, I (May, 1891), 298. Dr. Schmidt and Pastor A. Wright, not originally members of the U. C. committee, substituted for Professor Bøckman (ill) and Professor Lysnes (deceased).

[9]Proceedings of the meeting were published. See *Referat af Forhandlingerne i Delegatmødet mellem Komiteer valgte af Synoden for den norske evang.-lutherske Kirke i Amerika og den forenede norske lutherske Kirke i Amerika, afholdt i Willmar, Minn., fra Onsdag den 6te Januar til Tirsdag den 12te Januar 1892* (Decorah, Iowa: Lutheran Publishing House, 1892), 123 pp.

Although no great strides toward the union of the Norwegian Synod and the United Church were taken, the meeting was nevertheless significant in that it revealed different points of view on ecclesiastical and doctrinal matters which had not been thoroughly discussed at previous intersynodical conferences. The first pertained to the question of prayer fellowship, and the second involved the inspiration of the Scriptures.

The Norwegian Synod, like the Missouri Synod, held to the position that participation in common prayer was to be denied unless there was complete doctrinal agreement. A Synod delegate, T. A. Torgerson, contended therefore that the sessions must not begin with prayer. The United Church representatives reluctantly allowed this, recognizing that the meeting would founder unless they made this concession.[10] The way was now cleared for a discussion of the main subject, namely the requirements for church union with special reference to Paragraph One of the Scandinavia Agreement.[11]

It was not long before the representatives of the Synod suggested an alteration in the wording of the paragraph defining the authority and verbal inspiration of the Scriptures.[12] Professor Bøckman, speaking for the United Church, replied that it was not pertinent to the discussion. He said they could not discuss all those questions on which other Lutherans were disunited. Like Stub, he held to *sola Scriptura*, but to make verbal inspiration, rather than Paragraph One, the basis for discussion was not proper.[13]

A lengthy and lively debate developed, revealing that the Synod persisted in its demand for exact definitions and that

---

[10]*Ibid.*, pp. 8, 9, 19, 44. The traditional position of the Synod was succinctly expressed by H. A. Preus. *Ibid.*, pp. 111-112.

[11]*Supra*, pp. 5-6. The paragraph reads: "We regard our harmonious subscription to the Holy Scriptures, the confessions of the Norwegian Lutheran Church, and the catechism now in use in our synods and congregations as a completely sufficient basis for church union, since there is evidence of no official act on the part of any of the synods in denial of the Scriptures and the confessions." Bergh, "Historisk Inledning," in Brun (ed.), *op. cit.*, p. 20.

[12]Stub and Preus charged Paragraph One with being an inadequate basis for church union. It was intimated that large portions of the Lutheran Church were in error in their views on the inspiration of Scripture and that the present statement was so worded that it could conceal almost any concept of inspiration. Therefore, the Synod would require a clear definition of the verbal inspiration of the Scriptures. *Referat . . . Willmar, 1892*, p. 4.

[13]*Ibid.*, pp. 4-5.

the United Church maintained the adequacy of the paragraph under discussion. The Synod men charged that there were Norwegian Lutheran pastors in America who had forsaken the "old Lutheran doctrine of inspiration" and were questioning the divine character of the Bible.[14] For this reason, inspiration was "the burning question of the day."[15] The response of the United Church men was that they were in essential agreement with the Synod on this question, but they did not want to make the doctrine of inspiration a condition of union. This was but to inject a new topic for controversy.[16]

President Hoyme of the United Church was the most articulate of the United Church representatives and crossed swords with the keenest of the Synod dialecticians, U. V. Koren. Hoyme said that he had come to Willmar with the desire to take at least one step towards uniting the Synod and the United Church. He was disappointed that the very man to whom everyone was looking for leadership in the union movement (Stub) had now raised an obstacle to union.[17] The authority of the Scriptures was unquestioned in the United Church. Its constitution and the constitutions of all the congregations committed the church to the divine character of the Bible. But now "something more is to be required, now the question of inspiration is also to be mixed in. . . ." Hoyme continued:

> Why, gentlemen, it seems as if you are trying to pick a quarrel with us. Are there not enough controversial questions already? Are the congregations to be burdened with more? Are we perhaps to sharpen our swords for the purpose of making new wounds?[18]

Hoyme reiterated his belief that the United Church stood foursquare on the authority of the Bible, but was reluctant to define the mode of inspiration. He said that it could not be denied that there were various views of this matter in the church of

---
[14]*Ibid.*, p. 12.
[15]*Ibid.*, p. 13.
[16]*Ibid.*, pp. 7, 14, 18, 28.
[17]Hoyme's speech covers over three pages of the printed proceedings of the meeting. *Ibid.*, pp. 27-30.
[18]*Ibid.*, p. 28.

the fatherland as well as in America. In fact, there was a real possibility that perfect agreement on inspiration did not even exist within the Norwegian Synod! Finally, Hoyme remarked that the famous Norwegian theologian, Professor Gisle Johnson, highly regarded by Synod men and United Church men alike, had recently said that the Lutheran church does not have any theory of inspiration. "Would one for this reason make a heretic of this venerable old man? May he bear his grey hairs with honor."[19]

Hoyme's speech apparently made a profound impression on the assembly, for despite Koren's attempt at rebuttal, the Synod delegation, in caucus, voted to withdraw its support from Stub's proposal to make of inspiration a new condition of union.[20] Therewith the conference elected a committee to prepare a statement to which all could give assent.[21] The committee presented the following:

> In regard to church union between the Synod and the United Church we consider the unanimous acceptance of the canonical books of the Holy Scriptures as God's revealed, infallible Word on the part of both church bodies as a fully sufficient basis for church union.
> *Note.* Our position in relation to Holy Scripture is given expression in Pontoppidan's answers to Questions 12, 15, and 18 in *Sandhed til Gudfrygtighed.*[22]

Once again a vigorous and prolonged debate developed,[23] but eventually the proposal was unanimously adopted as the expression of the conference.[24]

The Willmar colloquy drew to a conclusion with a discussion of the place of the Book of Concord among the confessional statements of the Norwegian Lutherans in America. Koren and Stub of the Synod expressed the view that subscription to the entire Book of Concord should be required of all

---
[19]*Ibid.,* p. 29.
[20]*Ibid.,* p. 32.
[21]The committee members: Hoyme, Stub, Bøckman, and Ylvisaker. *Ibid.,* p. 40.
[22]*Ibid.,* p. 49.
[23]*Ibid.,* pp. 49-83.
[24]*Ibid.,* p. 83. It is significant that Pastor Koren voted for the statement "with reservations." A copy of his opinion was incorporated in the minutes and was signed also by Pastors H. A. Preus, J. A. Thorsen, O. Juul, and Mr. Paul Vigenstad.

Lutherans. The United Church delegation, led by Professor Bøckman, opposed this on the ground that such action would be "sinful and thoughtless." For a congregation to claim as its confession a book containing several documents with which it had no familiarity would be immoral.[25]

On the whole, the Willmar meeting did little to bring the conferring parties any closer together.[26] On the other hand, neither did it cause any further separation. What it did do was to reveal that the two groups, which had taken opposite positions previously on other questions, now took differing views of prayer fellowship, inspiration, and the place of the Book of Concord.[27] Generally speaking, the Synod took a conservative and cautious view while the United Church took a more elastic view. Justification for our rather close scrutiny of this conference lies in the fact that the problems raised at that time continue to the present as some of the major issues in various segments of American Lutheranism.

Recognizing that the time for union had not come, the Willmar delegates made no provision for similar meetings in the future. The breach between the Norwegian Missourians and the Anti-Missourians was still too recent. The wounds of that conflict were still open. Furthermore, the United Church was engaged in an intramural battle which caused many to take a dim view of any new attempts at union.[28] Consequently, several years were to elapse before the calling of another free conference.

In the late summer of 1897, Pastor B. J. Muus took the

[25]*Ibid.*, pp. 104-105. The Book of Concord is a collection of six distinctly Lutheran confessions in addition to the ecumenical creeds. Of these, only two were generally known to the people, Luther's Small Catechism and the Augsburg Confession.

[26]When the colloquy ended, Hoyme said goodbye to Koren and offered him his hand. According to Hoyme's son-in-law, J. A. Aasgaard, Koren refused it.

[27]In fairness to both parties it should be said that on all three issues there was essential agreement. On prayer fellowship it was the feeling of all, even most of the Synod, that it was not right to deny corporate prayer. Regarding inspiration, both sides were agreed that the Bible is the Word of God, differing on the question whether the theory of inspiration should be made a condition for church union. Finally, both groups looked upon the Book of Concord as a correct exposition of Lutheran belief, but there was disagreement as to whether largely unknown documents, such as the Apology of the Augsburg Confession, the Smalcald Articles, and the Formula of Concord, ought to be foisted upon the churches as required Lutheran confessions.

[28]The Augsburg Controversy was moving toward its climax.

initiative in stirring up interest in a resumption of the union movement.[29] Obtaining the signatures of sixty-nine pastors of the three synods (Hauge's, United, and the Synod), Muus issued an invitation to a free conference to be held at Lanesboro, Minnesota, September 15-22, 1897.[30]

The subject for discussion, the doctrine of conversion, quickly led the disputants back to the Election Controversy of the eighties in which the question was asked, What, if any, is man's part in conversion? How to ascribe salvation solely to God (the Missourian emphasis) and not to detract from man as a responsible personality (the anti-Missourian emphasis) was the nub of the problem. At Lanesboro the Norwegian Missourians were led by Professor A. Mikkelsen, the anti-Missourians by Pastor B. J. Muus, and the Haugeans (who took the anti-Missourian position) by Pastor O. C. Meland.[31]

In the final analysis, said Muus, the argument distilled into an attempt to harmonize two things: (1) that it is God alone who works conversion, and (2) that conversion in a certain sense depends upon man himself. It is God who provides our salvation, but that salvation is contingent upon man's repentance.[32] To this Professor Mikkelson answered that he found too much emphasis on man and not enough on God. He said: "I also believe the ungodly must be converted; but I do not believe that he can do it himself."[33] To this Muus replied that he did not question that conversion was an act of God from first to last, but he insisted that man "in one way or another" must

---

[29]Muus was not affiliated with any synod at the time. Although he had taken an active part in the Anti-Missourian cause, he had not left the Norwegian Synod with his friends in 1887. Finally in 1896, he was virtually requested to leave the Synod, but the break did not come officially until 1898. *Beretning . . . Synoden . . . 1896*, pp. 116-118. Cf. *Beretning . . . Minnesota Distrikt . . . 1897*, pp. 29, 85. *Beretning . . . Minnesota Distrikt . . . 1898*, pp. 130-141.

[30]"Frikonferents," *Lutheraneren*, III (August, 1897), 514, 520. An interesting comment on the proposed conference is to be found in a clipping from *Amerika* incorporated in Ole Nilsen, "Scrap Book," (Unpublished collection of newspaper articles in the archives of the Norwegian-American Historical Association, Northfield, Minnesota), pp. 304-305. See also "Frikonferencen i Lanesboro," *E. L. K.*, XXIV (September, 1897), 572-573. A full report of the Lanesboro meeting was published. See J. A. Bergh, *Stenographisk Referat af Forhandlingerne ved Frikonferensen i Lanesboro, Fillmore County, Minn. 15de-22de September 1897*. (Orfordville, Rock County, Wisconsin, 1897).

[31]*Ibid.*, pp. 9, 13, 16, 20-37.
[32]*Ibid.*, p. 26.
[33]*Ibid.*, p. 27.

decide the matter. It is patent from the words of Scripture that it is man who must repent.[34] Pastor O. C. Meland maintained that man was given powers and capacities by the Holy Spirit so that he was not converted against his will. Man *permitted* God to work conversion in him. Repentance, contrition, and conversion constituted a change *within man,* who was not a stick or a stone but a being with a will.[35] From the moment God's call went out to a man and until the moment of regeneration came to him who accepted God's call, there was a consistent development in man under the creative activity of God's grace.[36]

Thus the discussion shuttled back and forth for a whole week. Neither side was in a mood to admit that the other side possessed insights into truth. In fact, the opposing sides stood out even more sharply than before. The significance of the meeting lay in this that substantially the same positions were to be maintained uncompromisingly for the next thirteen years. Although the stalemate was not to be recognized until 1910, it had already been reached in 1897.

For that reason the resolution of the Lanesboro meeting to continue the discussion at a subsequent free conference was largely an empty gesture.[37] This was borne out by the poor response to the invitation to the free conference at Austin, Minnesota, January 18-25, 1899.[38]

---

[34] *Ibid.,* p. 29.
[35] A major controversy had been going on at this time within Hauge's Synod between Meland and Professor H. Bergsland of Red Wing Seminary. Meland charged Bergsland with false teaching on the doctrines of the call, conversion, sanctification, and the church. Bergsland was accused of Pelagian leanings in granting spiritual powers to the natural man. O. C. Meland, *Redegjørelse for mine Anker mod Prof. H. Bergsland* (Red Wing, Minnesota: n. n., 1894), pp. 3, 11-24. Cf. E. K. Johnsen, *En Kort Udredning af de Læresporgsmaal som nu er oppe i Hauges Synode* (Chicago: Anderson Printing Company, 1895), 16 pp. For a time the controversy was heated and it appeared that Hauge's Synod would be split. Finally, in 1896, the synod declared that it found no heresy in Bergsland's teachings and the matter subsided. "Ved Aarsmødet," *Budbæreren,* XXVIII (June, 1896), 408. "Aarsmødet," *ibid.,* XXIX (June, 1897), 392, 397, 418-419.
[36] Bergh, *Referat . . . Lanesboro . . . 1897,* pp. 120-122.
[37] A committee of five, including Muus, Stub, and Meland, was charged with arrangements. *Ibid.,* p. 123.
[38] United Church representatives, twenty-one; Hauge's Synod, two; Norwegian Synod, one. The sole representative of the Synod was Pastor Rasmus Malmin. This is noteworthy because he was to become one of the most active participants in the union negotiations which led to the settlement of 1912. For a register of the names of men at Austin see G. O. Skaret and J. A. Bergh (eds.), *Referat af Forhandlingerne ved Frikonferentsen i*

The discussion at Austin centered around a set of theses on conversion prepared by Dr. F. A. Schmidt.[39] As was to be expected, the debate led nowhere and the conference ended without having contributed either negatively or affirmatively to the union movement. Its sole significance lay in that it sounded the death-knell of the large free conferences.[40]

One more meeting in the interest of union ought to be mentioned. In 1900 the Norwegian Synod determined to show that it had not given up the hope of reaching an understanding with other Norwegian Lutherans in America. Consequently the Synod adopted resolutions deploring the existing ecclesiastical divisions and inviting the presidents and the theological faculties of the United Church and Hauge's Synod to a colloquy on doctrine.[41]

Only the United Church accepted the invitation. Gathering at the Synod seminary in St. Paul, Minnesota, just before Easter, March 28-30, 1901, the synod presidents and professors gave evidence of reaching a common view of the assurance of salvation based upon the theses presented by President Hoyme. Thereupon resolutions were adopted to continue the discussions the next year. Previous to the next meeting, however, Professor F. A. Schmidt had published a partial account of the proceedings. As this was contrary to the wishes of the colloquy and since Schmidt described Hoyme's theses as a "compromise to bridge the chasm between truth and error,"[42] the Synod passed a resolution in 1902, requesting the United Church to replace Schmidt with another man who was less likely to be "a hindrance" to the cause of union. This the United Church

---

Austin, Minn., 18de-25de Januar 1899 (Decorah, Iowa: "Decorah Posten," 1899), pp. 3, 4, 22.
[39]Ibid., pp. 4-13.
[40]What was called a "Discussion Meeting" was held at Thor, Iowa, in 1900. Local in nature, it nevertheless brought together representatives of the Synod and the United Church. The debate on election revealed the traditional differences between the two sides. See Referat for Diskussionsmødet i Ullenvangs Menighed, Thor, Iowa. Den 16de og 17de Januar 1900 (Chicago: Trykt hos Anderson Co-operative Printing Company, 1900). pp. 3 et passim.
[41]Synodalberetning, 1900, Anden Del, pp. 68-69.
[42]U. V. Koren, "Hvorfor er der ingen kirkelig Enighed mellem norske Lutheranere i Amerika?" Samlede Skrifter, ed. Paul Koren (Decorah, Iowa: Lutheran Publishing House Bogtrykkeri, 1911-1912), III, 486.

refused to do; consequently no further discussions were held.[43]

Meanwhile, the United Church suffered its second schism.[44] In 1900 a group of congregations and pastors under the leadership of Pastor K. O. Lundeberg organized the Church of the Lutheran Brethren.[45] Despite the controversies between the churches, the 1890s had witnessed a religious "revival" among Norwegian Lutheran congregations in America. Called "the awakening of the nineties,"[46] it was not confined to any particular synod. Remarkably free of excesses and emotionalism, it was considered a veritable divine visitation. Nevertheless, sectarian influences began to exert themselves in a demand for "pure congregations."

It was in this context that the Church of the Brethren was born. Pastor Lundeberg, a former Anti-Missourian and now a member of the United Church, had visited Norway where he came in contact with a "free church" group of Donatist leanings.[47] Returning to America gripped with the thought of "pure congregations," Lundeberg began to practice his new beliefs by exercising strict discipline in his parish at Kenyon, Minnesota.[48] He felt that no Lutheran church group was sufficiently apostolic in the practice of church discipline and therefore

---

[43]H. Halvorson (ed.), *Festskrift* . . . *1853-1903*, pp. 286-287. Cf. *Beretning* . . . *Den f. Kirke* . . . *1901*, pp. 141, 206; *Beretning* . . . *Synoden* . . . *1902*, p. 57; *Beretning* . . . *Den f. Kirke* . . . *1902*, p. 261. The minutes refer to two pamphlets which appeared as a result of the colloquy of 1901 and the alleged incorrigibility of Dr. F. A. Schmidt. *Kirke-raadet for Synoden, Træk af Prof. Dr. F. A. Schmidts Færd* (Hamline [St. Paul], Minn.: 1903), pp. 3-38. The United Church elected a committee to draft an answer to this attack on Schmidt. *Beretning* . . . *Den f. Kirke* . . . *1903*, pp. 167, 193. This appeared in the form of a pamphlet: J. N. Kildahl, M. O. Bøckman, and N. J. Ellestad, *Kirkeraadet har talt ilde* (Minneapolis: Augsburg Publishing House, 1904). The authors took pains to answer each charge of the Synod and concluded by accusing the Synod of the defamation of Schmidt and urging it to confess its "great sin." *Ibid.*, p. 54.

[44]The first had been the withdrawal of "The Friends of Augsburg" (1893) who formed the Lutheran Free Church in 1897.

[45]*Religious Bodies: 1926* (Washington: United States Government Printing Office, 1929), II, 830-834. O. M. Norlie, *History of the Norwegian People in America* (Minneapolis: Augsburg Publishing House, 1925), pp. 362-364. Biographical data on Lundeberg will be found in Norlie, *et al* (eds.) *Norsk Lutherske prester i Amerika 1843-1913*, p. 248. See also the 50th anniversary publication: *The Church of the Lutheran Brethren in America . . . 1900-1950* (Fergus Falls, Minn.: Board of Publications, Church of the Lutheran Brethren, 1950).

[46]Helland, *Georg Sverdrup*, pp. 172-173.

[47]Bergh, *Den n. luth. Kirkes Hist. i Am.*, pp. 396-397.

[48]The direction of Lundeberg's church practice is indicated in an exchange of articles between him and Pastor B. J. Muus in the official organ of the United Church. See "En liden Bemerkning," *Lutheraneren*, III (1897), 514; B. J. Muus, "Spørgsmaal til Pastor Lundeberg," *ibid.*, p. 562; K. O. Lundeberg, "Svar til Pastor Muus," *ibid.*, pp. 658-659.

concluded he must establish a new one. Together with a recruit from the Lutheran Free Church, Pastor E. M. Broen, Lundeberg issued a call for a conference to be held at Milwaukee, Wisconsin. It was here that the Church of the Lutheran Brethren of America was organized in December, 1900.[49] By 1914, the church numbered eleven pastors, two professors, and three missionaries in China. It maintained a Bible School at Wahpeton, North Dakota.[50] In 1911, Pastor Lundeberg had acknowledged his error and rejoined the United Church,[51] but his former colleague, Pastor Broen, continued the work. In 1959, the church body had a baptized membership of 4,300.[52]

The schism of 1900 had no noticeable effect on the union movement. Our parenthetical consideration of this new religious development among Norwegian-American Lutherans is made merely to account chronologically for the formation of the Church of the Lutheran Brethren.

The first years of the twentieth century were not very auspicious for the cause of union. The negotiations between the Synod and the United Church were without fruit, and the future began to appear hopeless.

The United Church, committed to the task of furthering the cause of bringing all Norwegian Lutherans under one ecclesiastical roof, had seemingly exhausted every possibility of rapprochement. The man who had led the church since its inception in 1890, President Hoyme, and who was the moving spirit in every union effort, became ill in 1901.[53] Unable to be present at the annual convention of the United Church, he sent a greeting which urged the church to remember the cause of union.

---

[49] *Religious Bodies: 1926*, II, 833.

[50] Bergh, *Den n. luth. Kirkes Hist. i Am.*, p. 297. The school has been moved to Fergus Falls, Minn.

[51] Lundeberg gave as his reason for this action, in 1911, the fact that he had come to the conclusion that it was contrary to God's Word and the Augsburg Confession for "true Christians" to separate themselves from "worldly" congregations. He joined the United Church because (1) he had previously belonged to this church body, and (2) it was the only church truly interested in the union of all believers. K. O. Lundeberg, *Svar paa Spørgsmaal om Hvorfor jeg forlot Brodersamfundet og gik ind i Den forenede Kirke* (Minneapolis: Forfatterens forlag, 112 Seymour Avenue, S. E., n. d.).

[52] "Statistics on World Lutheranism," News Bureau, National Lutheran Council, New York, N. Y., May, 1959.

[53] Brun (ed.), *op. cit.*, pp. 349-350.

"Never be weary of praying and hoping that God will lead our beloved but separated church people into united and powerful cooperation on the basis of truth."[54]

Encouraged by this greeting, the church called an unofficial "free conference" in 1903.[55] Both the Norwegian Synod and Hauge's Synod declined the invitation to participate.[56] Therefore, there was a tone of hopelessness in the resolution adopted by the United Church in 1905, when it instructed the president of the church and the seminary faculty to do "what they could" to promote church union.[57]

The union interest had apparently reached its lowest point in 1904-1905. Then, without any previous indication, events took a new turn. At the very meeting which adopted the above doleful resolution a telegram was received from Hauge's Synod, convening simultaneously at Red Wing, Minnesota, announcing that it had elected a committee to consider union "with other Norwegian Lutheran synods" and urged the United Church to do the same.[58] It was this action of Hauge's Synod which initiated a new phase in the union movement.

1905-1911: From Agreement to Deadlock

The withdrawal of Hauge's Synod from the union activity of 1888-1889[59] had the result of removing this church body from active participation in the efforts toward union in the intervening years. At the same meeting in which it voted not to enter the proposed United Church, it had elected a committee to study the Scandinavia report and make necessary revisions which would permit Hauge's Synod to enter the merger at a later time.[60] This committee published its report in the official organ of the synod during the autumn of the same year to ac-

---

[54]*Beretning* . . . *Den f. Kirke* . . . *1902*, pp. 44-45.
[55]*Beretning* . . . *Den f. Kirke* . . . *1903*, p. 177.
[56]*Beretning* . . . *Den f. Kirke* . . . *1904*, pp. 44-45.
[57]*Beretning* . . . *Den f. Kirke* . . . *1905*, pp. 254-255.
[58]*Ibid.*, p. 277.
[59]*Supra*, pp. 17-19.
[60]"Referat af Hauges norsk evangelisk lutherske Synods 44de Aarsmøde . . . 1889," *Budbæreren*, XXI (1889), 437. The committee: Pastors A. O. Utheim, O. Hanson, A. O. Oppegaard, H. N. Rønning; Professor H. H. Bergsland; laymen I. Øien, H. M. Sande, E. O. Sigmundstad, O. E. Boyum, I. Duea.

quaint the congregations with what had been done.[61] The major revision, as was to be expected, occurred in the paragraph dealing with lay activity. Having felt that this feature of Hauge's Synod had not been adequately guaranteed by those contracting to form the United Church, the committee now took pains to define very carefully what it meant by "Christian lay activity."

During the nineties Hauge's Synod did not find it "practicable" to pursue the cause of union.[62] Moreover, by the end of the decade certain internal dissensions led the annual convention to postpone union negotiations indefinitely.

The situation within Hauge's Synod remained relatively unchanged for the next seven years. Then, at the annual meeting of 1905, a committee was elected to draft resolutions with respect to church union.[64] These resolutions, altered somewhat by the convention, called for the election of a union committee of five members to meet with similar committees from such other Norwegian Lutheran bodies as would be willing to negotiate.[65] Telegrams were immediately dispatched to the United Church assembled at Austin, Minnesota, and the Norwegian Synod meeting in Minneapolis, requesting that each appoint union committees. In both instances the church bodies complied.[66] In addition to these two churches, Hauge's Synod in-

---

[61] "Indstilling fra Hauges Synodes Timandskomite," *Budbæreren*, XXI (1889), 645-653.

[62] "Behandling af Timandskomiteens Instilling i Foreningssagen," *Beretning . . . Hauges Synode . . . 1890*, pp. 31-54. *Beretning . . . Hauges Synode . . . 1891*, pp. 36-37; *Beretning . . . Hauges Synode . . . 1892*, p. 34. *Beretning . . . Hauges Synode . . . 1893*, p. 44.

[63] *Ibid.*, p. 46. What the internal problems were is not clear from the official minutes. Vague references in the president's report to disturbances within many of the congregations, between pastors and people, and between professors at the seminary indicate the pervasive character of the difficulty. *Ibid.*, pp. 5-6. It has been suggested that the dissensions were largely repercussions of the controversy within the Red Wing Seminary faculty. G. M. Bruce, "A Brief History of Union Negotiations" in *The Union Documents of the Evangelical Lutheran Church*, p. 5. Cf. *Supra*, p. 138.

[64] *Beretning . . . Hauges Synode . . . 1905*, p. 135. The committee: Pastors G. O. Paulsrud, T. J. Oppedahl, and Professor M. G. Hanson.

[65] The members elected to the Union Committee: President C. J. Eastvold, Professor M. G. Hanson, Pastors K. C. Holter, A. O. Utheim and J. N. Sandven. *Ibid.*, p. 145. The requirements for union which had been prescribed by previous conferences, viz. Scandinavia (1888), were abandoned in favor of complete doctrinal agreement.

[66] *Beretning . . . Den f. Kirke . . . 1906*, pp. 235, 267; *Beretning . . . Synoden . . . 1905*, pp. 67-68. United Church committee: President T. H. Dahl and Professors M. O. Bøckman, F. A. Schmidt, E. K. Johnsen, C. M. Weswig and J. N. Kildahl. Norwegian Synod committee: President H. G. Stub, Professors O. E. Brandt, A. Mikkelson, and Pastors H. Halvorson and O. P. Vangsness.

vited the other Norwegian Lutheran synods in America to participate in the union movement. These groups were the Church of the Brethren, the Eielsen Synod, and the Free Church. Of these only the latter responded. The Free Church replied that it did not consider itself a synod, but would elect a committee to confer with Hauge's Synod about "cooperation."[67]

The union committees representing the United Church, the Norwegian Synod, and Hauge's Synod held three meetings during 1906. The first two were held in Minneapolis, January 17 and March 27-31. Both were conducted in a spirit of friendliness and genuine good will. Significantly the Norwegian Synod posed no objections to prayer-fellowship with the other committees. The joint meetings were opened and closed with common prayer.[68]

The major achievement of these first meetings was agreement on the doctrine of absolution. Five theses covering the various aspects of the controversy, which had been carried on among the synods since 1861, were unanimously adopted by the joint meeting. The report, signed by Eastvold (Hauge's), Johnsen (United), and Brandt (Synod), bore the date March 30, 1906, and was presented to each of the annual meetings of that year.[69] The first thesis defined absolution as "God's own absolving act through the ministry of the Word." The second and third theses explained that this absolution was a *declaration of grace* to the sinner, and that this grace, "offered, declared and bestowed by God in absolution" was appropriated by the sinner through faith. The seat of trouble in the days of the old absolution controversy had been the Norwegian Synod's definition of absolution as "a powerful impartation" of forgiveness. This had seemed to minimize man's subjective response to God's objective act. The above theses remedied this weak-

---
[67]*Beretning . . . Hauges Synode . . . 1906*, p. 12. The conference between the Free Church and Hauge's committees resulted in a series of recommendations with respect to cooperative work in several areas of Christian service, e.g., evangelistic meetings, deaconess work, foreign missions, etc. *Ibid.*, pp. 151-152.
[68]*Beretning . . . Den f. Kirke . . . 1906*, p. 49.
[69]A copy of the report will be found in *Beretning . . . Hauges Synode . . . 1906*, pp. 150-151. An English translation will be found in *The Union Documents of the Evangelical Lutheran Church*, p. 28.

ness, and thesis four assured the conferring parties that "absolution itself is always a real and valid absolution of God." The last thesis stressed it as a duty of the minister "to give conscientious attention to the profession in word and deed on the part of the confessors, lest the holy be given to the dogs and the pearls be cast before swine (Matt. 7:6)."[70]

The third meeting of the year, October 16-19, was also held in Minneapolis. This resulted in agreement on the troublesome problem of lay activity in the church. The document covering this subject was called "Lay Ministries in the Church." It was signed by the same representatives of the respective union committees.[71] Like the previous document, this one consisted of a set of theses, eight in number, together with supporting Scripture passages and citations from the Lutheran confessions. Thesis one asserted that God had given the church (this included the individual congregation) not only the means of grace, but also "the power of the keys, the office of the ministry and the gifts of grace." It was under the last phrase that lay activity was subsumed. The conclusion of the thesis was that the "congregation and the individual Christian in it" possessed all the gifts God had given the church (1 Cor. 3:21-23). The second thesis acknowledged the divine institution of the office of the ministry, which the congregation committed to those qualified for it (Eph. 4:11 and Titus 1:5). The third thesis confined the functions of the office of the ministry (except in emergency) to those properly called (Rom. 10:15, Heb. 5:4, Aug. Conf. Art. XIV). The next thesis addressed itself to the ecclesiastical-sociological principle of the Reformation, the priesthood of believers. It asserted that the office of the ministry and the priesthood of believers were not mutually exclusive. It was the right and duty of each Christian to be a priest

---

[70]It is significant that these propositions were virtually identical to those adopted by the Synod in 1874. *Beretning . . . Synoden . . . 1874*, pp. 18-61. These theses, previously prepared by Schmidt (then a member of the Synod), were unobjected to by Schmidt. Stub points out that the 1906 meeting is largely the answering of Schmidt's arguments against his own theses which he had forgotten were his. Stub, "Hvad staar iveien for de kirkelige enighedsarbeide blandt os?" *E. L. K.*, XXXVIII (1911), 254-255.

[71]*Beretning .. . Den f. Kirke . . . 1907*, pp. 62-64. English translation in *The Union Documents . . . E. L. C.*, pp. 28-30.

"in his own station" (Luther's concept of vocation) and to use his God-given opportunities and gifts for the edification of individuals or "assemblies of the congregation" (I Peter 2:5, 9, I Thess. 5:11, Smalcald Art., Pt. III, Att. IV).

The remaining theses were specifically directed toward a solution of the problem posed by the Haugean tradition of unregulated lay preaching in America. How to recognize the value and validity of lay activity and yet to safeguard the office of the ministry was the question. Thesis five recognized that God had given "special gifts" to certain individuals and that these gifts, in the possession of the congregation, ought to be employed by the congregation. The reference, of course, was to the gift of preaching. However, this gift was not to be exercised without the call or consent of the congregation and such activity must be supervised by the congregation or its pastor (Rom. 12:6-8, I Peter 5:1-2, Acts 20:28). This thesis was a pointed reference to the unregulated lay preaching encouraged by such Haugean extremists as Eielsen or the "free church" movement both in Norway and America. To offset any unwarranted conclusions from the fifth thesis, which might be made by Norwegian Synod churchmen, the sixth thesis was bold to say that the church was harmed when the "gifts of grace," as above defined, were not used (I Cor. 12:7, 17, 20, 21). Thesis seven returned to thesis five and gave permission to congregations to use pastors and laymen of "good report" from other congregations "to assist in [their] work." This recognized the common practice among Norwegian Lutherans in America of holding evangelistic services conducted by visiting pastors or lay evangelists.[72]

The significant feature of this document is that it was able to state the attitude of the churches on this subject in such a

---

[72] A concluding thesis, No. 8, was not included in the original document of 1906, but was added at the request of Hauge's Synod in 1915, and was drafted by its president, C. J. Eastvold. It sought to avoid any misunderstanding of lay activity by stating that the conferring synods meant what they had said in the preceding seven theses and were agreed that prayer meetings and revivals should not be considered unchurchly or as evidences of religious fanaticism. *The Union Documents . . . E. L. C.*, p. 30. Cf. *Rev. C. J. Eastvold, D.D., 1863-1929, His Life and Work* (Minneapolis: Augsburg Publishing House, 1930), p. 170.

way that, on the one hand, it satisfied the Norwegian Synod which feared lay ministries in the church, and on the other hand, guaranteed to Hauge's Synod the essential preservation of this aspect of the Haugean tradition in America. It should be noted (1) that lay activity was definitely regulated and (2) that regulation was by placing the emphasis not on ordination but on the call and supervision by the church. The mediating position of the United Church, which embraced within its constituency the orderly ecclesiastical tradition as well as the low church emphasis, made it possible for it to hold out hands in two directions and draw the divergent tendencies together.

The report of the union committees which presented the agreement on laymen's activity in the church also included a summary of the joint meeting held March 19-22, 1907, in Minneapolis.[73] It was stated that at the previous meeting it had been decided to consider the doctrines of "the call" and "conversion." The United Church committee was to prepare an introduction to the discussion of the former on the basis of Question 478 in Pontoppidan's *Sandhed til Gudfrygtighed,* and the Synod representatives were to do the same respecting the latter with Question 677 as a basis.[74]

The whole of the March meeting was spent on the first topic. The committees had not anticipated such a time-consuming discussion and therefore, according to the report, found it necessary to hold a second conference in October, 1907. This was followed by a third in April, 1908, at Our Savior's Church, Minneapolis. It was at the last meeting that agreement was reached on the doctrine of the call and conversion, and the committees reported a unanimous acceptance of all the theses pertaining thereto.[75]

---

[73]*Beretning . . . Den f. Kirke . . . 1907,* pp. 64-65.
[74]Question 478: "What is God's Call? That through His Word He moves men's hearts, reveals to them His grace especially through the Gospel, earnestly invites and at the same time bestows power to accept the same." II Tim. 1:9. Question 677: "What is Conversion of the Fallen? When man, fallen from God's grace and dead in sin, is awakened again to the spiritual life by God's power, is reconciled to God through faith, he is thus completely converted and changed." II Tim. 2:25-26; Jer. 3:1, 6, 7; Eph. 2:4, 5; Acts 27:18. Pontoppidan, *op. cit.,* pp. 76 and 108.
[75]*Beretning . . . Den f. Kirke . . . 1908,* pp. 53-63.

The doctrinal agreement on the call contained six theses with the customary "proof" passages. The statement on conversion was more lengthy and detailed, containing eleven paragraphs.[76]

In view of the history of the doctrinal strife between the Norwegian Synod and the other groups and in light of the future difficulties over election, several of the theses in the above documents were noteworthy. Both agreements began with a study in theological anthropology. The first two theses of the former and the first three of the latter described man's natural state as being that of spiritual sleep and death, alienation from and enmity toward God. In this condition man was utterly helpless to effect any alteration in his spiritual status. Therefore, it was God who must "call" and "convert" if man was to be awakened and saved.

Thesis three on the call made it clear that man was not an insensible being coerced by the power of God's call. Rather, it said, "the persons who are called cannot avoid perceiving *in their hearts* [italics added] the operation of the call upon them through the Law and Gospel. . . ." In the same vein, God's conversion of the individual was described as being "brought about by the acknowledgment and repentance of one's sin and faith in Jesus. Two parts therefore belong to conversion: a) sorrow and contrition for sin, and b) faith in the Lord Jesus."[77]

Thesis five urged the sincerity of the call. All the called were met with equal earnestness by God. There was no assigning of "two kinds of calling" to God as done by John Calvin.[78] Furthermore, there was an acknowledgment that not all were called despite the fact that it was God's will that all men be saved

---

[76]English translation in *The Union Documents* . . . E. L. C., pp. 31-38.
[77]The committees' official report to the synods had declared that in addition to Pontoppidan's Question 677, it had been found necessary to use Question 680 as basis for the statement on conversion. *Beretning . . . Den f. Kirke . . . 1908*, p. 53. The above thesis is almost an exact translation of Question 680, except that the original has the additional phrase: "hvis Frugt er en ny Lydighed" ("the fruit of which is a new obedience"). Pontoppidan, *op. cit.*, p. 108.
[78]John Calvin, *Institutes of the Christian Religion*, trans. John Allen (Philadelphia: Presbyterian Board of Christian Education, 1936) II, 227. One call is intended as "a savor of death"; the other is intended for the elect. This involves Calvinism in assigning two contradictory wills to God, or else God's call of the masses, who are predestined to reprobation, is insincere.

and come "unto the knowledge of the truth."[79] The obvious implication of this statement was the fact that God's call was confined to His Word, the proclamation of which was limited by the believers' response to its missionary challenge.

The sixth thesis was perhaps the most significant in view of the future discussions. It stated: "Where God calls by His Word He at the same time bestows power to accept grace."[80] Explanatory statements reiterated the natural man's inability "to accept the offered grace or to contribute anything to his conversion." In addition, emphasis was made that "before regeneration" man did not "receive any indwelling power which he possesses as his own" and which enabled him to decide to accept grace. Nevertheless, God's call was efficacious so that "by virtue of the offered grace, through the drawing of God's Spirit and because of the power which now through the call operates on him" man had "full opportunity and real possibility to be converted or [to] convert himself *(omvende sig)*, to repent of his sin and believe in Christ." In this way, thesis six dealt with the delicate question of the relation between the divine and human factors in the call, assigning to God the initiation of the call and the bestowal of power to accept. Thus the statement sought to avoid vitiating the implications of the Lutheran doctrine of original sin, and at the same time declared that it was *man*, under grace, who repented or "converted himself."

The possibility of man's rejection of grace was indicated throughout both documents,[81] but the most careful attempt at definition of this point was found in the tenth thesis on conversion:

When a person does not become converted, he alone bears the responsibility and the blame, because he would not heed the call; that is, in spite of the fact that God through the call makes it possible for man to be converted or convert himself *[omvende sig]*, he resists and renders ineffective the work of the Holy Spirit through both Law and Gospel, something it is possible for man to do at any stage.[82]

---
[79] I Tim. 2:4.
[80] Cf. Pontoppidan, Question 478, *supra*, p. 147.
[81] See especially thesis six on the call and thesis seven on conversion.
[82] *The Union Documents . . . E. L. C.*, p. 38.

The eleventh thesis made it clear that, though man was responsible for the rejection of grace, God alone was responsible for his acceptance of the same: ". . . the glory belongs to God alone, because it is He who throughout, from beginning to end, without any cooperation on the part of man, works conversion. . . ."[83]

An addendum to the report of the committees had this meaningful statement:

> Dr. Schmidt requested it be added to the minutes that he did not take part in the voting on paragraph eleven [". . . the glory belongs to God alone . . ."]; neither was Dr. Schmidt present at the last meeting when paragraphs 6b and c on the call were adopted.[84]

The fact that Schmidt, the old leader of the Anti-Missourians in the Election Controversy of the eighties, abstained from voting on paragraph eleven can be interpreted as an indication that there might be trouble later on. The hard-hitting phrases of the paragraph apparently were too much for Schmidt who had fought to establish the place of man in conversion.

The next two years saw the essential disagreement flare up in the debate over the old problem of election. This was to be the subject of discussion at the next meeting of the union committee scheduled for November 10-13, 1908, in Minneapolis.[85]

Before turning to the fateful meeting on election, it is well to observe the synodical reactions to the announced doctrinal agreements. President Koren of the Norwegian Synod strangely made no reference to the union movement in his annual report.[86] However, a formal and conventionally phrased resolution expressing gratitude and joy over progress in intersynodical relations was adopted by the Synod.[87]

---

[83]*Loc. cit.* H. G. Stub commented on the results of this meeting that not since the Election Controversy had the Synod and the United Church stood so close. *E. L. K.* XXXVIII (1911), 256-257.

[84]*Beretning . . . Den f. Kirke . . . 1908*, p. 62. Paragraph 6b: "Before regeneration man does not receive any indwelling power which he possesses as his own, and whereby he then is able himself to decide to accept grace."

[85]*Beretning . . . Den f. Kirke . . . 1908*, p. 63.

[86]*Beretning . . . Synoden . . . 1908*, pp. 38-45.

[87]*Ibid.*, pp. 82-83. Votes: 225 ayes, 5 nays, 21 abstentions. Pastor Harstad, who later became a leader in the opposition to union, requested that his name be entered in the minutes as abstaining from voting.

The reaction in Hauge's Synod was mixed. Although President C. J. Eastvold praised the committee on union for its remarkable and unexpected achievements, he admitted that the union interest in Hauge's Synod was not universally enthusiastic. Some comments on the doctrinal agreements had referred to them as newly concocted confessions of faith. In answer to this Eastvold said that such deprecatory remarks were unjustified because the doctrinal statements were based on the Word and the Lutheran confessions. In no way did they supersede the latter or pretend to constitute a new confession. Eastvold continued by referring to reports which he had received from various circuits of the church. In some areas there was little or no interest in union. In other places, there was impatience that the movement was not progressing faster.[88] Viewed as a whole, the attitude within Hauge's Synod was favorable and gave promise of becoming better under the enthusiastic leadership of its union-minded president.

The most hearty response to the union efforts occurred in the United Church. This was to be expected for, as President T. H. Dahl said, the cause of union had been on the program of the United Church "since its birth."[89]

The attitude of the three bodies in 1908 reflected the outlook traditionally associated with them. The Norwegian Synod's cautious but genuine interest, as indicated by its synodical resolution, was quite in character. The hot and cold response in Hauge's Synod was typical of this group, which had a tendency to wear its heart on its sleeve. The all-pervading concern for union in the United Church was congenital and, therefore, not at all unexpected.

At this point it is well to note the presence of a new factor among Norwegian-Americans which exerted a subtle but none the less significant influence on the union movement. The reference is to the appearance of cultural and nationalistic societies which cut across church boundaries and theological differences. As early as 1870 such groups began to form among the

---
[88] *Beretning . . . Hauges Synode . . . 1908*, pp. 9-10.
[89] *Beretning . . . Den f. Kirke . . . 1908*, p. 46.

Scandinavians of the Middle West.[90] They included singing societies, literary clubs, temperance societies, sports associations *(turnforeninger),* welfare groups, and lodges. Perhaps the most significant as far as the church situation was concerned were the Norwegian Society in America *(Det norske selskab i Amerika)* and what was known as the "Bygdelag Movement." The former, founded in 1903, sought to preserve in America the Norwegian language and culture. Although admittedly a non-religious society, its history includes a conflict over the question of confining membership to Norwegians who were Lutherans. This proposal, oddly enough urged by a somewhat anticlerical layman, Professor R. B. Anderson of the University of Wisconsin, was defeated. Nevertheless the membership was largely Lutheran. This fact, combined with the development of friendships and understandings between intellectual and cultural leaders representing divergent synodical and theological allegiances, was to make *Det norske selskab* a positive leaven in the union movement.[91]

Even more important was the "Bygdelag Movement."[92] Natives of a certain *bygd* or district in Norway formed a *lag* or society in America and met annually to cultivate and perpetuate the memories and culture of the motherland. These societies, which were originally organized largely for sentimental reasons, soon developed a more serious purpose, namely, the collecting and publishing of historical and biographical data regarding immigrants who came from the *bygd* whose name was borne by the individual *lag.*

---

[90]Perhaps the most comprehensive survey of the non-religious societies among the Norwegians in America is that by Carl Hansen, "Det norske foreningsliv i Amerika" in J. B. Wist (ed.) *Norsk Amerikanernes Festskrift 1914,* pp. 266-291. Cf. also G. M. Bruce, *The Bygdelag Movement* (Minneapolis: Bygdelagenes Fellesraad, 1937) and Jacob Hodnefield, "Norwegian-American *Bygdelags* and their Publications," *Norwegian-American Studies and Records,* XVIII, 163-222.

[91]Hansen, *op. cit.,* p. 284. It is interesting to observe that the membership of the society embraced such names as Professor Gisle Bothne (Norwegian Synod), Professor J. L. Nydahl (Lutheran Free Church), and Professor P. J. Eikeland (The United Church).

[92]B. E. Bergesen, "Bygdelagenes Betydning" in *Skandinavens Almanak og Kalender, 1928* (Chicago: John Anderson Publishing Company, n. d.), pp. 66-68. L. M. Gimmestad, "Bygdelagenes Kulturbetydning," *ibid.,* 1931, pp. 80-90. Cf. A. A. Veblen, "The Bygdelag Movement" in his *The Valdris Book* (Minneapolis: Folkebladet Publishing Co., 1920), pp. 44-90.

As with the other societies these "lags" were non-religious in character but were destined to exert an even larger influence on the religious scene among the Norwegian-Americans.[93]

Germane to our discussion is the fact that many of the "lags" were led by influential churchmen, and oftentimes within one "lag" pastors of differing theological positions were thrown together. For example, Gjermund Hoyme of the United Church and the Brandts, father and son, of the Norwegian Synod were members of the *Valdreslag*. This group brought together those Norwegian-Americans whose family roots were in the valley of Valdres in central Norway.[94]

It was not strange that the annual meetings of the "lags" occasionally heard addresses on religious and ecclesiastical problems. In 1908, when the churches appeared to be moving toward unity in doctrine, Pastor I. T. Aastad of the Norwegian Synod addressed the *Valdreslag* and dwelt at length and favorably on the cause of church union among Norwegians. Here was a clear indication of the fact that a non-religious society became a medium for promoting ecclesiastical union. In fact, opponents of the cause charged the *Valdreslag* with guilt in opening its meetings to such discussions and in providing the leadership for a movement which would serve only to further "church politics."[95]

We see, therefore, that by 1908, a number of forces among Norwegian-Americans were combining to press upon the people at large the necessity and value of a union of the churches. However, that which gave evidence of success during the years from 1905-1908, was soon to receive a serious setback when the churches could not agree on the doctrine of election. The troublesome question of the eighties was reasserting itself and was not to be settled until 1912.

An ominous silence characterized the year 1909. The various

---

[93]Most of the other societies drew their membership from urban Norwegians, whereas the "lags" found their strength in the rural areas where the church was the chief social as well as religious bond in the community and where the secularizing influences of urbanization were not yet present. *Ibid.*, pp. 78-79.
[94]*Ibid.*, pp. 288-290, 292.
[95]"Foreningsarbeide og kirkepolitik," *Lutheraneren*, XIV (1908), 1236.

synods took little notice of and less action on the problem of union. One example suffices: the president of the United Church, who ordinarily devoted a large portion of his annual report to a consideration of the union of the churches, in a sentence or two reported that the joint committee had reached no agreement on the doctrine of election but was united in the desire to continue its meetings.[96] The reason for the lack of synodical action was obvious. The committees had not yet submitted a report for action.[97] Furthermore, they had agreed that no published account of their proceedings would be made until the discussion of election was "completed . . . sufficiently to give a report."[98]

Despite the absence of official information on the progress of the union meetings, it was clear from articles appearing in the official organs of the Synod and the United Church that all was not going well.[99] In the late autumn of 1909 an official communication to the church press from the union committees indicated that negotiations were at a standstill but that discussions would continue at a meeting on March 29, 1910.[100] Finally, each of the church conventions of that year received a report from the joint committee summarizing the conferences from 1908-1910. For the first time the full story of the impasse was made public, and the hopes for an early union quickly vanished.[101]

The reasons for the abandonment of hope were quite clear from the report, which reviewed the various meetings of the union committees in 1908 and 1909. The first, April 7, 1908, determined the subject for discussion (election) and named a sub-committee to prepare theses for the next colloquy. The second, November 10-13, 1908, fruitlessly debated Stub's theses. The third, March 30-April 2, 1909, served only to reveal

---

[96]*Beretning . . . Den f. Kirke . . . 1909*, p. 47.
[97]"Meddelelse fra komiteen til forhandling angaaende foreningssagen," *E. L. K.*, XXXV (1908), 1326.
[98]"Church News," *Lutheran Herald*, IV (1909), 404.
[99]"Lidt mere om kirkelig enighed," *Lutheraneren*, XIV (1908), 1172; "En forenet røst om foreningsssagen," *ibid.*, p. 1204.
[100]Meddelelse fra foreningskomitteen," *Lutheraneren*, XV 1909), 1321.
[101]*Beretning . . . Hauges Synode . . . 1910*, pp. 151-165; *Beretning . . . Den f. Kirke . . . 1910*, pp. 73-86; *Synodalberetning, 1910, Anden Del*, pp. 82-94.

more clearly the bipolarity of the Missourian and anti-Missourian positions on election. The fourth, November 2-5, 1909, ground to a halt and then referred the subject to a subcommittee whose task was to prepare a new statement for discussion. The subcommittee was unable to reach an agreement. Nevertheless, Dr. Stub found it advisable to call the whole committee together on the previously established date, March 29, 1910. In the interim Dr. Stub had revised his theses which had been the subject of discussion at the earlier meetings. In addition, Dr. Bøckman presented a revised edition of those which he had earlier submitted. Finally, a new set of theses, prepared by President C. J. Eastvold, was placed before the conference. After approving the action of Dr. Stub in calling the meeting,[102] the committee, on Dr. Kildahl's motion, made Eastvold's theses the basis for discussion.[103] However, the representatives of the Norwegian Synod, outvoted by the coalition of the United Church and Hauge's Synod, submitted the following declaration:

> The committee elected by the Norwegian Synod for doctrinal negotiations with committees from the United Church and Hauge's Synod abides by the resolution adopted at the November meeting of the committee: If the so-called subcommittee is unable to present a joint doctrinal declaration, the joint committee will not meet for further doctrinal negotiations.
> In the meantime, the committee will report back to the Synod and await its decision as to whether it will still urge continuation of these meetings in view of the prolonged discussions concerning election and the assurance of salvation.[104]

At this point the representatives of the Norwegian Synod left the meeting; those remaining began a discussion of Eastvold's theses. Since this was obviously a waste of time, the committee voted to adjourn. Before doing so, however, it was decided to publish the proceedings of the past two years. This

---

[102] Agreement in the subcommittee had been the condition upon which Dr. Stub was to call the whole committee together.
[103] *Beretning . . . Den f. Kirke . . . 1910*, pp. 81-84.
[104] *Ibid.*, pp. 85-86. The statement was signed by H. G. Stub, Joh. Ylvisaker, O. E. Brandt, A. Mikkelsen, O. P. Vangsness.

was to be the report of the joint committee to the annual conventions of the three synods.[105]

The official synodical reaction to this record of failure was one of sorrow and misgiving. The auspicious beginning of union negotiations in 1905 had reached a deadlock in the opposing views of election. Thus, in 1910, it appeared the end had come. President Eastvold, however, reported to Hauge's Synod that he felt his church ought not to withdraw as long as there might be some hope of continuing negotiations.[106] President T. H. Dahl told the United Church that essential agreement existed between it and Hauge's Synod on the doctrine of election and that he believed further approaches to the Norwegian Synod might ultimately result in agreement. In keeping with this expression, the United Church passed a resolution stating its approval of continued meetings with Hauge's Synod and the Norwegian Synod.[107]

The Norwegian Synod held district meetings in 1910. Neither the synodical president nor the five district presidents made any reference in their annual reports to the question of union. Nevertheless, resolutions containing oblique hints of interest in the cause of unity were presented to each of the districts. One of the resolutions declared that the doctrine of election in two forms should not be regarded as schismatic.[108] The ray of hope which this statement contained provided the union committees with reason to believe that further discussions would be fruitful. Therefore, another joint meeting was held at the United Church seminary in St. Paul, Minnesota, December 13-14, 1910.[109]

Dr. Stub read a statement to the group that expressed the position of the Norwegian Synod as that of adherence to Article

---

[105]The official reports omitted an important resolution which showed that the union efforts would not be dropped: "Resolved, that we rescind the resolution in regard to discontinuing negotiations on doctrine." Bergh, *Den n. luth. Kirkes Hist. i Am.*, p. 458.
[106]*Beretning . . . Hauges Synode . . . 1910*, p. 81.
[107]*Beretning . . . Den f. Kirke . . . 1910*, pp. 47, 225-226.
[108]*Beretning . . . Østlige Distrikt . . . 1910*, pp. 92-93.
[109]The report of the meeting will be found in *Beretning . . . Den f. Kirke . . . 1911*, pp. 91-96. Present from the Norwegian Synod: Professors Stub, Ylvisaker, Brandt, and Pastor Mikkelsen; from the U. C.: President Dahl, Professors Kildahl, Bøckman, Schmidt, Johnsen, and Weswig; from Hauge's Synod: President Eastvold, Professor Wee, and Pastor Sandven.

XI of the Formula of Concord (the so-called First Form) as the correct form of the doctrine of election. However, the Synod did not consider the use of the Second Form (*intuitu fidei* or Question 548 of Pontoppidan) as a cause for division. Having said this, Stub went on to say that, since the decision of the Synod districts to continue discussions, it had been learned that President Dahl in his message to the 1910 convention of the United Church had charged the Synod theses (Stub's) with being unbiblical and un-Lutheran. Had the Synod known of this earlier it would hardly have agreed to continue the negotiations. In view of this the Synod representatives would make their continued participation in this meeting contingent upon the presentation, by the United Church, of proofs that the Synod position was in error and that these points be made the basis for further deliberation.[110]

The tenor of the meeting was evident from a motion made by Professor E. K. Johnsen in which, with complete disregard for Stub's statement, he urged Pastor Eastvold's theses be made the basis of deliberation. When this motion was adopted, Stub announced that the Norwegian Synod representatives would not participate in the discussion. The United Church committee reminded them that at a previous meeting when the joint committee decided in favor of Stub's theses as over against Kildahl's, the United Church committee did not leave in a huff. Now, however, when a discussion was proposed over statements prepared by one (Eastvold) who had not been a party to the earlier election strife, it was only fair that the Synod acquiesce to the majority.[111] To this Stub replied that at the earlier meeting it was a question of form; now it was a matter of conscience.[112] An attempt to reach a compromise by suggesting that the United Church men present one or more of their points of difference for discussion the next day proved ineffective. The session ended with the Synod delegation withdrawing from further negotiations.

---

[110] *Ibid.*, pp. 91-92.
[111] J. N. Kildahl, "Hvorfor forhandlingerne med Den norske synode stanset," *Lutheraneren*, XVII (1911), 68.
[112] H. G. Stub, "Hvad staar iveien . . . ?" *E. L. K.*, XXXVIII (1911), 369-373.

The next day, December 14, the two remaining union committees discussed the points of difference between the Synod and United Church positions for a time, and then went on to adopt unanimously Eastvold's theses on election with minor changes.[113] The entire orientation of this statement was different from the Synod's presentation of the problem. Unlike Stub's theses which began with a description of God's predestination, these began with a statement of God's will to save all men. Returning to the place of faith in the plan of salvation, the statement asserted that in election faith held a position which was an absolutely necessary correlate. It was not the cause of election, as unbelief was the cause of perdition, but without faith man was outside of Christ and therefore excluded from election. In this sense, election was always *intuiti fidei* or as Johan Gerhard said: "Since the merits of Christ do not profit anyone without faith, we believe that the consideration of faith is a part of the decree of election."[114]

With the adoption of Eastvold's theses, the United Church and Hauge's Synod committees declared themselves to be of the conviction that no differences existed between these two churches and, therefore, that they were now doctrinally prepared for merger. Before adjourning, however, the committees went on record as deploring the withdrawal of the Synod representatives.[115]

The closing of the year 1910 seemed to sound the deathknell of the desired tripartite union, and the future seemed to hold few, if any, signs of hope. During the early winter of 1911, the ecclesiastical and theological overcast was gray and cheerless. Optimism had all but disappeared as the religious and secular presses began to discharge the literary evidences that men were returning to the theological wars. In a short time the atmosphere was charged with recriminations, and the controversy was on.

The chief protagonists of the opposing views were H. G.

---

[113]The original theses will be found in *Beretning* . . . *Den f. Kirke* . . . *1910*, pp. 81-84; the revised theses in *Beretning* . . . *Den f. Kirke* . . . *1911*, pp. 93-96.
[114]*Ibid.*, p. 95.
[115]*Ibid.*, p. 96.

Stub of the Synod and J. N. Kildahl of the United Church. Stub had succeeded U. V. Koren as president of the Synod upon the latter's death in 1910.[116] As the fourth president of the Norwegian Synod, Stub was destined to lead this conservative group into the merger of 1917, to become the president of the new body, the Norwegian Lutheran Church of America, and to be elected the first president of the National Lutheran Council in 1918.[117] But in the early months of 1911, he hardly contemplated any speedy church amalgamation and wrote strong words defending the non-cooperative attitude of the Norwegian Synod. It will be recalled that the United Church president had publicly declared Stub's theses on election to be unbiblical and un-Lutheran and that this charge had been the cause for the later walkout of the Synod delegates. Even before Stub began his polemics, others had taken up the literary cudgels. A layman from the Norwegian Synod wrote a "letter to the editor" of the Chicago-published and widely read Norwegian language newspaper, *Skandinaven*, that he was happy that the Synod had withdrawn from further union negotiations. He took pains to place the blame on the United Church, for had not the Synod always taught that either "form" of election could be held without being a cause for church division? But, he said, the United Church would have nothing of this. Rather it insisted that Schmidt's views were the only correct statement of election and, furthermore, it continued to drag out the old bogeyman *(Busenmand)* of Calvinism and "Missouri doctrine."[118]

A week later the organ of the United Church carried an article by J. N. Kildahl in which he sought to explain how the discussions with the Synod had reached an impasse. After an exhaustive survey of the meetings and a careful presentation

---

[116]In 1905 Koren had been elected for a term of six years and Stub occupied the vice-presidency. When Stub became the fourth president of the Norwegian Synod in 1910, he had been preceded in office by the following: A. C. Preus 1853-1862, H. A. Preus 1862-1894, U. V. Koren 1894-1910. "Fra Kirkens Arbeidsmark," *Skandinaven*, January 11, 1911, p. 4. Cf. "Den norske synodes formand," *E. L. K.*, XXXVIII (January, 1911), 16.

[117]For biographical data see Norlie (ed.), *Who's Who*, p. 563. Cf. Hauge, *Lutherans Working Together*, pp. 37-38.

[118]N. J. Hagen, "Foreningssagen," *Skandinaven*, January 11, 1911, p. 8.

of the issues, Kildahl concluded by saying that the essential reason for the present deadlock was the adamant attitude of the Norwegian Synod.[119]

The Synod committee, of course, defended its position with pointed comments on the outcome of the meeting held in December, 1910. In view of the prevailing attitude in the United Church committee, it said that it saw no prospect of fruitful deliberations. Therefore, nothing remained but to break off negotiations. The apology of the committee concluded:

> We must express our profound regrets, that a task which has so long commanded our best efforts, and for the successful consummation of which we entertained such splendid hopes, should terminate here. We had in all sincerity believed that the United Church men *had approached more closely to us* [italics not in original].[120]

A number of weeks passed with minor skirmishes between lesser belligerents in the fray. Then in March there appeared in the official organs of the two church bodies major statements, one written by President H. G. Stub in defense of his theses and a second by the union committee of the United Church.[121]

Stub reviewed the union negotiations by going back to the first meeting between the United Church and the Synod in 1901. He referred to the actions and words of Dr. Schmidt as being chiefly responsible for the present cul-de-sac. Moreover, the fact that the United Church committee refused to disavow him only served to petrify the situation. He then sought to support his own position and to isolate the United Church by citing, quite unconvincingly, certain contemporary theologians

---

[119]J. N. Kildahl, "Hvorfor forhandlingerne med Den norske synode stanset," *Lutheraneren*, XVII (January 18, 1911), 66-70. This same article had appeared earlier in *Skandinaven*, January 13, 1911, pp. 6, 8.

[120]"Comment by our Committee," *Lutheran Herald*, VI (January, 1911), 7-8. The characteristic Synod attitude is unconsciously revealed in the words: "had approached more closely to us." Since the days of H. A. Preus, the Synod had claimed that it possessed the truth, and therefore it was necessary for others to come to see its point of view.

[121]H. G. Stub, "Hvad staar iveien for det kirkelige enighedsarbeide blandt os?" *E. L. K.*, XXXVIII (1911), 253-258, 281-287, 310-315, 339-344, 366-380. Cf. *Skandinaven*, March 10, 1911, p. 7; and *ibid.*, March 15, 1911, pp. 8-9. This appeared in a pamphlet of forty-seven pages under the same title, including Stub's original theses discussed 1908-1910, and his revised but undiscussed version of 1910 (Decorah, Iowa: Lutheran Publishing House, 1911), pp. 42-47. The "accounting" by the United Church committee appeared as "Fra Foreningskomiteen" in *Lutheraneren*, XVII (1911), 354-359. It was also included in a pamphlet prepared by the United Church committee: *Naadevalget og Foreningssagen* (Minneapolis: Augsburg Publishing House Trykkeri, n. d.), 32 pp.

(Thomasius, Dorner, Kattenbusch, Weidner, and H. E. Jacobs) as advocates of the first form of election.[122]

The document prepared by the union committee of the United Church was essentially a defense of President Dahl's statement at the United Church convention in 1910,[123] that Stub's theses could not be considered biblical and Lutheran. An addendum to the United Church "accounting" expressed its willingness, however, to discuss doctrine further.

The appearance of these two writings served only to entrench each side in its already firmly established position. Despite the gesture of the United Church to continue negotiations, it was patent during the spring of 1911 that union prospects were not encouraging. There seemed to be no possible way out of the deadlock, for each side remained intransigent.

A Theological Log-jam

When one begins to assess and criticize the points of view upheld so tenaciously by both parties and thereby to seek an explanation for the failure of the union negotiations, one is thrust into an area where there is a mingling of historical circumstances, theological presuppositions, and personality conflicts which make it almost impossible to untangle the involved skein of affairs. Nevertheless, a few observations can and ought to be made before surveying the final attempts to reach doctrinal agreement in 1911-1912.

---

[122] Stub, "Hvad staar iveien . . . ?" (pamphlet edition), pp. 3-12, 35-36. Stub also claimed that the official organ of the Swedish Augustana Synod had supported him with these words: "Nobody has the right to accuse the Norwegian Synod of errors in the doctrine of election." "[It] stands on historic evangelical Lutheran ground." *Ibid.*, p. 36. Jacobs is generally considered as one of the chief supporters of the anti-Missourian position. His best-known theological publication gives a thorough discussion of this subject in which he states explicitly that election is "in view of . . . Faith accepting the merits of Christ." H. E. Jacobs, *A Summary of Christian Faith* (Philadelphia: General Council Publication House, 1913), p. 562. Cf. Leander S. Keyser, *Election and Conversion* (Burlington, Iowa: The German Literary Board, 1914), pp. 15-16 *et passim*. Cf. also "Prof. Jacobs Bedømmelse af The Error of Modern Missouri," E. L. K., XXV (1898), 332-334. Despite Jacobs' criticism of *The Error of Modern Missouri*, he finds Schmidt's statement of election sufficiently to his liking to incorporate it into his domatics. Cf. Jacobs, *op. cit.*, p. 562 and F. A. Schmidt, "Intuitu Fidei," in Schodde (ed.), *The Error of Modern Missouri: Its Inception, Development, and Refutation* (Columbus, Ohio: Lutheran Book Concern, 1897), p. 198. Schmidt's formula, used by Jacobs, comes directly from Johann Gerhard. *Ibid.*, pp. 434-435.

[123] "Foreningssagen," *Beretning . . . Den f. Kirke . . . 1910*, p. 47.

In order to do this we have elected to attempt three things: (1) to relate the current controversy to its earlier manifestations in the eighties of the previous century, (2) to review and evaluate the issues involved, and (3) to propose certain explanations for the impasse of 1910-1911.

In the first place, it should be noted that the current debate was in reality a continuation of the old Election Controversy which stemmed out of the Synodical Conference and pitted the leaders of the Ohio and Iowa Synods plus F. A. Schmidt and his followers in the Norwegian Synod against the Missouri Synod under Professor Walther and portions of the Norwegian Synod under the disciples of Walther.[124] Both the Ohio and Norwegian Synods withdrew from the Synodical Conference in the hope that this action would remove them from the controversy. The Norwegian Synod, already threatened by split, discovered that the effort was fruitless. Its treasured "doctrinal unity" was at an end and the Synod divided into "Missourians" and "Anti-Missourians."

The literature produced during the years of the dispute was vast and inconclusive. It is regrettable that the extensive writings were not exhaustive but rather prolific of further literary missiles and drearily repetitious. Unfortunately the great learning displayed on both sides was not directed toward the presentation of two definitive treatises on which each side could have rested its case.

By and large, the first Election Controversy came to center around two opposing charges, one that the Missourians were Calvinists and the other that the Anti-Missourians were synergists. Vehement denials of the charges were forthcoming from both camps. Walther answered the charge of his opponents by saying that the Missourian position set forth both the universal will of God to save men and the particular election of some to salvation, including everything thereto appertaining, viz. faith. Here, said Walther, were two distinct decrees, which though inexplicable, were not contradictory. Therefore, it was

---

[124] J. L. Neve and W. D. Allbeck, *History of the Lutheran Church in America* (Burlington, Iowa: The Lutheran Literary Board, 1934), pp. 207-209.

impossible to harmonize the doctrine of election by grace alone with the universal promises of the gospel.[125] Any attempt to explain or harmonize them would lead inevitably to rationalism and synergism. Why God had chosen to elect some rather than others *(cur alii prae aliis?)* was a question that the Scriptures did not answer. It was a mystery and so it must remain until the end of time.[126] In saying this Walther and the Missourians were actually transcending their theological method without knowing it. The method of "orthodoxy" was often guilty of subordinating biblical interpretation to the "system," thus forcing exegesis to conform to dogmatics.[127]

The Anti-Missourians answered Walther by saying that he had not escaped the rigors of at least semi-Calvinism. If God, through election, could cause faith in the hearts of some men who were stubborn sinners was not this the same as saying that his grace was irresistible? Moreover, the Calvinistic error of the Missourians, despite their loud denials, was most apparent in their theological method. In place of giving the material principle of the Reformation (justification by faith) the pivotal position over against which all other doctrines were to be judged, they had made the fatal mistake of introducing the doctrine of divine sovereignty as the major premise in their theological system. This was apparent when they made faith subject to election.[128] But to seek to avoid the pitfalls of Calvinism by crying, "Mystery," when one was pressed for an explanation why God could cause faith in some and not in others, was to beg the question. One did not escape difficulties by retreating into mystery. To be sure, the formula *intuitu fidei*

---

[125]C. F. W. Walther, *The Controversy Concerning Predestination*, trans. August Crull (St. Louis: Concordia Publishing House, 1881), pp. 13-14. Walther, *The Doctrine Concerning Election Presented in Questions and Answers*, trans. J. Humberger (St. Louis: Concordia Publishing House, 1881), pp. 40-50. Cf. Calvin, *op. cit.*, II, 179-181, 188-199.

[126]F. Pieper, *Zur Einigung der amerikanisch-lutherischen Kirche in der Lehre von der Bekehrung und Gnadenwahl* (St. Louis: Concordia Publishing House, 1913), pp. 14-19. The English translation by W. H. T. Dau, entitled, *Conversion and Election: A Plea for a United Lutheranism in America* (St. Louis: Concordia Publishing House, 1913), pp. 20-26. Subsequent references will be to the English version.

[127]See L. D. Jordahl, "The Theological Tradition of the Wisconsin Synod with Particular Attention to the Work of John Philip Koehler" (Unpublished B.D. thesis, Luther Theological Seminary, 1959), pp. 23 n. 1, 39-43.

[128]Keyser, *op. cit.*, pp. 22-30. Cf. E. Cronenwett, *The Calvinistic Conception in Lutheran Theology* (Columbus, Ohio: n. n., 1883), pp. 5-40 *et passim*.

did not remove the element of mystery, but the *locus* of mystery had been shifted from God to man. In the doctrine of election men were confronted not by a theological mystery, but by an anthropological psychological mystery. Why some men accepted grace and others did not was admittedly a mystery, but to remove this from the temporal theater of man to the eternal decree of God was to weaken man's responsibility in the decision for or against the proffered grace of God.[129]

In this manner, the fundamental question as to the relation of *the general will of God* to save all men to *the specific will of God* in electing a few to salvation began to revolve around the admissibility of the expression *intuitu fidei*. The Missourians charged that it made faith the cause of election. Faith became meritorious and was therefore destructive of *sola gratia*. This was unadulterated synergism.[130] The Anti-Missourians replied that this was a mistaken view of faith. Just as faith was not the cause of our justification, so faith was never the meritorious cause of election. The proper expression was *justificatio propter Christum per fidem* (justification because of Christ through faith), not *propter fidem per Christum* (because of faith through Christ). Likewise the cause of our election rested on the merit of Christ, not in any alleged merit of faith. The nature of faith precluded the idea of merit.[131] Nevertheless, though faith was never the cause of election, election was never apart from faith. Election was in view of faith, not as merit, but as an instrument without which it was impossible to please God. Therefore, one must insist on election *intuitu fidei*.

In this way, it will readily be seen that the ancient problem of God's grace and man's responsibility in salvation had reappeared in American Lutheranism. The one group, exalting the sovereign grace of God at the same time as it denied the Calvinistic implications of this position, claimed that its tenets were set forth in Article XI of the Formula of Concord. This article came to be known as the First Form.[132]

---
[129]Neve-Allbeck, *op. cit.*, p. 213. Cf. Keyser, *op. cit.*, pp. 10-12, 31-40.
[130]Pieper, *op cit.*, pp. 25-26.
[131]Keyser, *op. cit.*, pp. 25-28.
[132]Pieper, *op. cit.*, pp. 11-19.

On the other hand, those who repudiated the teachings of Walther's Missouri Synod claimed that a Second Form of the doctrine, election in view of foreseen faith, was the only proper interpretation of the Formula of Concord and the Scriptural presentation of predestination. Without *intuitu fidei* the teaching on election made of man an automaton moved by the irresistible grace of God to believe in Christ. And what was this but Calvinism!

As to the expression, *intuitu fidei*, the Anti-Missourians admitted that it was not to be found in the Formula of Concord. However, not many years after the signing of the Formula (1577) a controversy appeared in which the Calvinists began to claim that the Lutherans also were teaching, in the Formula of Concord, a special decree of election. It was then that the late sixteenth and the seventeenth century dogmaticians found it necessary to use *intuitu fidei* to explain that there was a difference between the Formula of Concord and Calvinism: the former proclaiming an election conditioned by faith, the latter unconditioned election to eternal life or eternal death.[133]

The Missourians insisted that the First Form, or the Formula of Concord without explanatory phrases, should be the only teaching of the church. On the other hand, the Anti-Missourians in various synods insisted that the denial of the Second Form was a danger not only to personal faith but to "the faith" of the church. A non-American commentator observed, with considerable theological insight, that the Norwegian-Missourians had cured the sickness (synergism) but, in doing so, had slain the patient![134]

It was on this point that agreement could not be reached, and after each side had spent itself in castigating the other, the controversy finally subsided in the nineties. It lay dormant

---

[133] The history of the origin of the Second Form is given in Schmidt, "Intuitu Fidei," in Schodde (ed.), *op. cit.*, pp. 195-198, 449-451, 470-471. Perhaps the most thorough and scholarly presentation of this subject is the work by Geo. J. Fritschel, *Die Schriftlehre von der Gnadenwahl* (Chicago: published by the author at Wartburg Publishing House, 1906). Although a major portion of the book is devoted to an exegetical study of New Testament words which bear on predestination, a detailed account of the origin of the first and second forms is given. See pp. 127-131.

[134] Johan Cordt Harmens Storjohann, *Retfærdiggjørelse og Forsoning til Belysning af vor Tids Lærdomsveir* (Kristiania: Th. Steens Forlagsexpedition, 1892), p. 44.

for over a decade and was all but forgotten by Norwegian church people whose emotions had been stirred by the altercation in the United Church over Augsburg Seminary.

After fifteen years of doctrinal quiescence, the debate on election was resumed. We have taken pains to trace these latter events in detail. It has been apparent that the unresolved tensions of the eighties were projected into the discussions of 1908-1911. This fact together with other circumstances led the churches to the deadlock of 1911. There were at least three possible explanations for this impasse. One centered around the illusive and hardly assessable factor of personalities. The second was the apparent failure to recognize changes in the present situation as over against the old Election Controversy. The third factor was the persisting residuum of antithetical theological method.

One of the chief links which connected the debate of 1908-1911 with the conflict of the previous century was the fact that several of the theologians involved in the earlier phase continued to play dominant roles in the new outbreak. The personal attacks and nasty insinuations of the earlier years were not easily forgotten, and when some of the same men faced each other in the first decade of the twentieth century, they were not inclined to view each other with cordiality. On the Synod side the chief spokesman was H. G. Stub on whom had fallen the mantle of U. V. Koren. Stub had participated effectively in the eighties and now, in the new phase of the debate, his propositions had been made the center of discussion.[135]

On the other side, F. A. Schmidt, who had led the Anti-Missourian secession of 1886-1887, had not changed his views regarding the Synod's essential Missourianism. His untoward

---

[135]In the earlier conflict some of the major pamphlets supporting the Synod position had come from his pen: H. G. Stub, *Om Naadevalget, Guds Ord og den lutherske Bekjendelses Lære derom* (Decorah, Iowa: Den Norske Synodes Bogtrykkeri, 1881), 41 pp. See also H. G. Stub, *Eksegetiske og Dogmehistoriske Bidrag til den Første eller Konkordieformelens Lære typus om Udvælgelsen* (Kristiania: P. T. Mallings Boghandels Forlag, 1882), 104 pp. Stub had been one of the signers of the famed document, "An Accounting," prepared by Koren and sent to the congregations of the Synod in 1884. See *"Til Menighederne i den norske Synode, En Redegjørelse," E. L. K.,* IX (1884), 701-716, (an English translation will be found in Ylvisaker, *Grace for Grace*, pp. 173 ff.). Stub was not an original theologian and so based his theses of 1908 largely on Koren's work of 1884.

actions in 1901,[136] exacerbated the Synod and henceforth he was doubly *persona non grata* in the union meetings. Other men who had participated in the eighties and were now on the union committee of the United Church were M. O. Bøckman and J. N. Kildahl. Especially the latter found himself at theological sword's point with Stub.[137]

It is not strange, therefore, that the tensions which had been caused by the first controversy over election were carried over into the new century in the persons named above. This in itself proved to be a major roadblock on the way to agreement.

The second factor in the deadlock of 1911 was the failure to recognize that there had been some changes in the intervening years. The evidence points to the United Church as the chief offender in failing to note this.

In the eighties the fighting words had been "synergism" and "Calvinism." The Missourians shouted "synergism" on the slightest provocation, and their opponents replied in the same spirit with the charges of "Calvinism." However, in the first decade of the twentieth century there was a noticeable change among the Synod men, especially H. G. Stub. The bogeyman of synergism was less frequently envisioned by them, and, although they retained the Missourian viewpoint by and large, they acknowledged that the Second Form of election ought not to be considered divisive for church unity.[138]

Unfortunately, F. A. Schmidt of the United Church continued to accuse the Synod of Calvinism at every turn. Schmidt could not forget that he was no longer back in the nineteenth century. On occasion, he acted as though he were still fighting Walther. It must be admitted that the presence of Schmidt on the union committee and the hesitation of his colleagues to silence him or to apologize for his occasional inexcusable outbursts played no little part in the cooling union interest among the leaders of the Synod.

---

[136]*Supra*, p. 139.
[137]Kildahl, "Hvorfor forhandlingerne . . . stanset," *Lutheraneren*, XVII (1911), 66-70. Cf. Stub, *Hvad staar iveien* . . . , pp. 26-27.
[138]*Beretning . . . Den f. Kirke . . . 1911*, pp. 91-92. *En Redegjørelse* of 1884 had reluctantly conceded the Second Form as being non-heretical though incomplete and thus dangerous. Cf. Ylvisaker, *op. cit.*, p. 183.

The third factor which contributed to the cessation of negotiations in 1910-1911 was the plain fact that the two theological emphases had not yet been reconciled. This may be seen in at least two instances. In the first place, the debaters approached the doctrine of election from two opposite viewpoints. The Synod had a tendency to begin with God's decree in eternity, and the United Church centered on the actualization of the decree in time. It was this divine-human polarity which was so difficult to resolve.

In the second place, the antithetical theological method of the two sides was seen in the area of Biblical exegesis. Bergh's charge that the failure was due to forsaking the earlier established principle that unity should be based simply on unreserved acceptance of the Word of God and the confessions of the church, neither of which had been denied by any official ecclesiastical action, may seem naive at first glance.[139] However, at the root of this observation was the knowledge that the Missourian tendency in Biblical exegesis was also practiced in the Norwegian Synod. The Synod theologians were led to conclude that a historical and theological interpretation of the Scriptures tended to become rationalism. If two verses of verbally inspired (i.e. inerrant) Scripture appeared contradictory, we must let them stand, each with its own testimony. Since there was no contradiction in God, there could be no contradiction in His Word. It had only the appearance of contradiction. Any attempt to reconcile the apparently contradictory in terms of the doctrine of justification, for example, must be shunned as a rationalistic approach to the Word of God.[140]

These two instances, therefore, were indicative of the funda-

---

[139] Bergh, *Den n. luth. Kirkes Hist. i Am.*, p. 451.
[140] The Missourian view of Scripture is well put in Pieper, *op. cit.*, pp. 89-103. Here Walther is described as "the theologian of the *bare* Scriptures (*nuda Scriptura*)." *Ibid.*, p. 93. Von Hoffman and Delitzsch cannot be called "*Schrifttheologen*" in the same sense as Walther. *Ibid.*, p. 97. The historical-exegetical method of the Erlangen School (*Heilsgeschichte*) as represented by J. C. K. von Hofmann was repudiated by Walther. Von Hofmann stressed the Bible as a history of salvation rather than as doctrine. Doctrine grew out of exegesis which considered the wholeness of Scripture (*die ganze Schrift*). This was a rebuke to the atomistic methodology of the orthodoxists. For a brief study of von Hofmann see Paul Leo, "Revelation and History in J. C. K. von Hofmann," *The Lutheran Quarterly*, X (August, 1958), 195-216. See also J. C. K. von Hofmann, *Interpreting the Bible*, tr. Christian Preus (Minneapolis: Augsburg Publishing House, 1959).

mental theological cleavage between the two groups which in 1911 stood apart from each other after several years of union negotiations. The outlook was dark and the prophecy of Sverdrup's disciple in the Lutheran Free Church, Dr. J. O. Evjen, seemed about to be fulfilled. Said he:

> At present [the United Church] is negotiating with the "Hauge's Synod" and with the Norwegian Missourians. . . . The negotiations will likely be useless, and any attempt to make the Book of Concord or even the Formula of Concord a part of the confessional basis will fall "upon rocky places."[141]

1911-1912: The Opgjør

Not many churchmen in 1911 expected to see the amalgamation of the churches in their time. The prospect had never seemed so hopeless. Surely a major change would be required to alter the situation.

However, a few feeble indications that hope had not died remained on the ecclesiastical horizon. Within the Norwegian Synod there were at least three men of influence who were unwilling to admit the failure of the union movement. H. G. Stub, despite his strong expressions against Schmidt and Kildahl, was a relative "liberal" judged against the standards of certain elements in the Synod.[142] His "liberal" spirit, however, was merely an earnest desire to see the church united. For this he worked unceasingly but invariably within the framework of the Synod's doctrinal position.

Two other men should be noted as embodying this same spirit. One was Dr. Laur. Larsen, president emeritus of Luther College in Decorah, who had been pressured out of the presidency by the ultra-orthodox leader of "the Decorah ring," U. V. Koren, in 1902.[143] Since the days of the earlier Election Controversy, Larsen had aligned himself with Stub, who held

---
[141] J. O. Evjen, "The Scandinavians and the Book of Concord," *The Lutheran Quarterly*, April, 1906, p. 13.
[142] Ylvisaker (ed.), *op. cit.*, p. 95. The slogan of the more liberal element was: "Let us break the Decorah ring!"
[143] Koren's candidate was C. K. Preus, son of the former president of the Synod, H. A. Preus. K. Larsen, *Laur. Larsen*, pp. 306-309.

the view that the church must make room for differences of interpretation in so difficult a matter as election. Koren and the others objected to this display of "liberalism."[144] In later years, Larsen was to uphold and encourage Stub in his efforts to press home the need of a merger with other Norwegian Lutherans.[145]

The third Synod man to give support to the belief that not all hopes for union had been dashed in 1911 was Pastor Rasmus Malmin. One of the sanest articles to appear in the whole controversy came from his pen. Writing in the organ of the Synod, Malmin urged the practice of patience and the withholding of hasty judgments. He suggested that the main difficulty lay in the fact that the two opposing sides began from different premises. Said he: "When the points of departure are different, the doctrinal developments therefrom are necessarily different." This became exceedingly involved when both doctrinal forms (the points of departure) were orthodox, as in the present instance. This was clearly apparent in the immediate controversy in which the Synod judged the conclusions of the United Church as false, because it (the Synod) judged from its own premise; and vice versa. The only way to rectify this, said Malmin, was for each side to judge the doctrinal statements of its opponent from the opponent's premise.[146]

A second factor which kept the union cause alive within the Norwegian Synod was the work which had been done together with the United Church and Hauge's Synod to publish a common hymnal and service book. In 1908 the Synod committee for preparing an English hymnbook approached the United Church committee about cooperation in this endeavor. The United Church accepted the invitation, and continued to cooperate throughout the whole period of doctrinal dissonance.[147]

---

[144] Bergh, *Den n. luth. Kirkes Hist. i Am.*, p. 269.

[145] *Beretning . . . Minnesota Distrikt . . . 1912*, pp. 43-44. Cf. Ylvisaker, *op. cit.*, p. 102.

[146] R. Malmin, "Læreforhandlingerne og deres stans," *E. L. K.*, XXXVIII (1911), 206-208. Malmin became one of the members of the new union committee of the Synod in 1911. Cf. T. A. Hoff, "The St. Paul Convention," *Lutheran Herald*, VI (1911), 747-748.

[147] See "Preface," *The Lutheran Hymnary* (Minneapolis: Augsburg Publishing House, 1913), p. 3.

This indicated that there was an underlying conviction that sooner or later there would be a united church.

A third and not insignificant circumstance which refused to let the union movement die in 1911 was the attitude of the laity in all branches of the church. The feeling prevailed quite generally among laymen that the church ought to be united. Unfortunately for the historian, this pervasive lay sentiment was infrequently expressed in tangible ways and never crystallized into an organized movement.[148] Although the laymen were reluctant to articulate their views through the media of the church and secular press—perhaps due to the fear of becoming lost in abstruse theological terminology—sufficient evidences are at hand to indicate a rather widespread concern among the people for the unity of the church. *Skandinaven*, which carried no brief for either side in the controversy, printed a number of "letters to the editor" written by laymen during the dispute. One unsigned letter remarked that the lay people considered continued disunity foolish *("det er dumt at staa adskilt")*. They could see no major differences between the churches and loved their neighbors whether they were Synod, Hauge's, or United Church members. Up to now the laymen had been obedient to the professors and pastors. If the latter had said, "Go!" the lay people would have gone. But now since the professors and pastors had demonstrated their inability to agree, it was time for the laity to take the situation in hand.[149] Another layman wrote that the churches must quit fighting and surrender to the Spirit of God. Learning and higher education were needful, to be sure, but perhaps sometimes God's mysteries were hidden from the wise. Furthermore, the Roman Catholic menace demanded a united Lutheran church.[150]

Other articles and letters in the same vein appeared in *Skan-*

---

[148]The attitude and influence of the laity is difficult to assess from the sources, as few laymen made literary contributions to the discussions in the period 1908-1911. However, shortly after the *Opgjør* in 1912, there appeared a statement on union signed by ten laymen of the three synods urging the merger of the church. "En venlig Henvendelse," *Lutheraneren*, XVIII (1912), 386-397. Favorable editorial comment appeared in the same issue. "En henvendelse til lægfolket," *ibid.*, p. 400.
[149]"Foreningssagen," *Skandinaven*, January 25, 1911, p. 8.
[150]Peder Haugen, "Slut med Striden!" *Skandinaven*, March 1, 1911, p. 8.

dinaven during the spring of 1911,[151] and, finally, as if in response to this grass-roots sentiment, the Southern Wisconsin Pastoral Conference of the United Church, meeting April 18, 1911, adopted a series of strong resolutions favoring union at once. Specifically, the resolutions declared that ecclesiastical divisions were a sin against God and a serious hindrance to the work of the church. Union on the basis of compromise or error was to be denied emphatically, but to expect more than unreserved acceptance of the Scriptures and the confessions of the Norwegian Lutheran church by the insistence on subscription to explanatory theses was to go beyond the requirements for church unity and to risk the peace of the church. Although it was to be admitted that complete agreement on the matter of election had not been achieved, in the light of the difficulties involved in understanding this doctrine and the limited treatment of it in the Scriptures, the pastors went on record as believing that the conferring bodies had a common teaching on the great basic principle of election. What differences yet remained, it concluded, were of such a nature that they should not divide the church.[152]

By the time the month of June arrived, the delegates to the annual conventions of the three synods were quite aware that the union question was still a live issue. Both the United Church and the Synod met in St. Paul, the former concluding its sessions the day before the latter began its meeting.[153]

The United Church, sensing the demand for union rising from pastors and people, grappled resolutely and effectively with the question and thus paved the way for a resumption of negotiations with the Norwegian Synod. This occurred in a three-fold manner: first, a series of resolutions dealing compre-

[151] It is interesting and informative to note that President Dahl's annual report to the United Church included an explanation of the previous year's judgment on Stub's theses as "unbiblical and un-Lutheran." This explanation, intimated Dahl, was owed to the United Church because *the lay people* were becoming restive about the cause of union. *Beretning . . . Den f. Kirke . . . 1911*, p. 54.
[152] "En henvendelse til vort norske kirkefolk," *Lutheraneren*, XVII (1911), 611. The signers of the document were: O. J. Wilhelmsen, J. A. Bergh, S. Gundersen, G. A. Larson, G. G. Krostu, J. A. Wang, O. G. U. Siljan, C. J. Nølstad, Joseph Green, G. Gunsten, J. A. Aasgaard, Otto Mostrom, J. Brown, P. J. Nestande, P. J. Johnson, Jens Mathiesen, Th. M. Bakke.
[153] United Church: June 15-22, 1911; Synod: June 23-30, 1911.

Union Committee, 1912

Union Committee, 1915

CHURCH PRESIDENTS 1916-1917

H. G. Stub
Norwegian Synod

T. H. Dahl
United Church

C. J. Eastvold
Hauge's Synod

Merger Convention, 1917

OTHER LEADERS IN THE MERGER

J. N. Kildahl
United Church

C. K. Preus
Norwegian Synod

M. G. Hanson
Hauge's Synod

PRESIDENTS OF THE CHURCH 1917-1960

H. G. Stub
1917-1925

J. A. Aasgaard
1925-1954

F. A. Schiotz
1954-1960

PRESIDENTS OF THE SEMINARY 1917-1960

M. O. Bøckman
1917-1930

T. F. Gullixson
1930-1954

A. N. Rogness
1954-

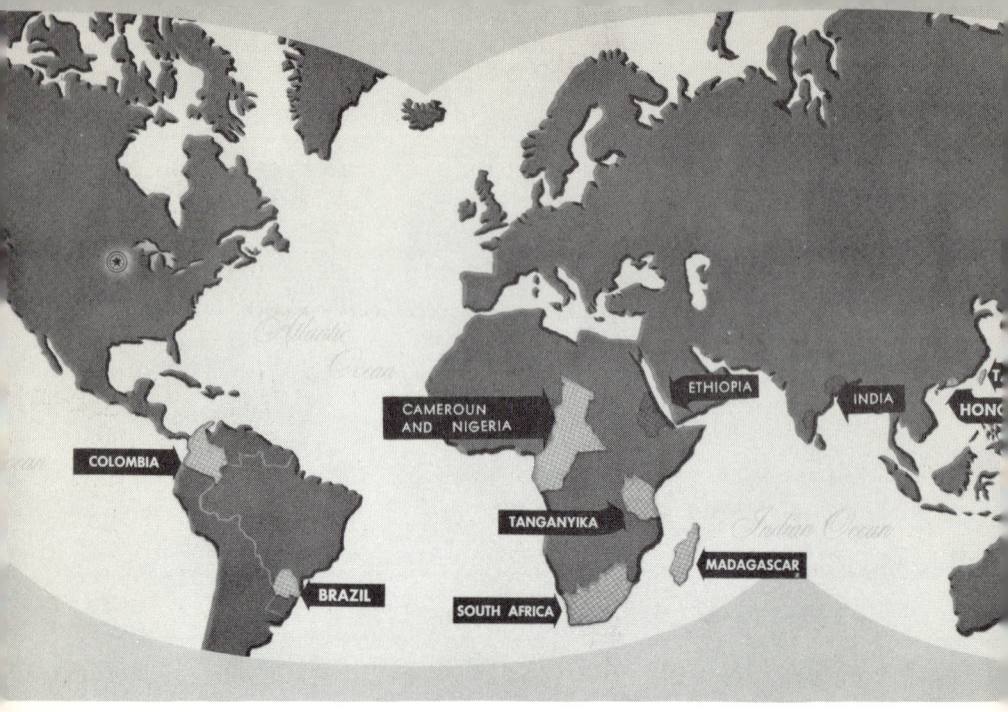

Mission Countries of the ELC

ELC Home Missions (1944-1957)

hensively with the union problems and pointing to a possible solution of the election conflict were adopted; second, an entirely new union committee was elected; and third, a special fraternal delegate to the convention of the Synod, instead of the customary written communication, was appointed.

The resolutions acknowledged the fact that Hauge's Synod and the United Church were, for all practical purposes, in agreement. In regard to the Norwegian Synod, the United Church reiterated its "unalterable principle" that it always stood ready to confer on the matter of union. As far as election was concerned, it was convinced that the *common* Lutheran confessions and the *common* catechism[154] could be interpreted in such a manner as to assure no diminution of God's glory or man's responsibility in salvation.[155]

The election of a new union committee came as a recognition of the fact that the former committee was composed of professional theologians, some of whom had participated in theological strife for most of their careers. From its beginning the United Church had as one of its objectives the realization of a united Lutheran Church in America. This fond hope was now threatened with disaster unless something was done immediately. To this end a series of resolutions was presented to the convention urging that everything possible be done to promote the cause of union.[156] Unanimously adopted by the church, these resolutions prepared the way for the election of the new committee, which consisted of the following parish pastors: P. Tangjerd, G. Rasmussen, S. Gunderson, H. Engh, and M. H. Hegge.[157]

The third item was the naming of a fraternal delegate to the Norwegian Synod convention, Pastor A. Øfstedal.[158] His pres-

---
[154]The words used is *barnelærdom* (the instruction of children), a term associated with Pontoppidan's explanation of the catechism.
[155]*Beretning . . . Den f. Kirke . . . 1911*, pp. 265-266.
[156]The report of the convention in a Twin City Norwegian language newspaper indicated that the resolution was of lay origin and that it set as a goal the union of the churches by the four hundredth anniversary of the Lutheran Reformation in 1917. *Minneapolis Tidende*, June 29, 1911, p. 2.
[157]"Fra Aarsmødet," *Lutheraneren*, XVII (1911), 816-817. Cf. *Beretning . . . Den f. Kirke . . . 1911*, p. 249.
[158]*Ibid.*, p. 255.

ence was recognized by Dr. Stub and his greeting was heard. Following the greeting, President Stub responded:

> ... we of the Norwegian Synod understand how to value the sentiment which has prompted them [the United Church] in sending this greeting. But I would be disloyal to my position and disloyal to the truths which we have sought to uphold if I did not say that I cannot understand how the United Church can send its "fraternal" greetings to a denomination whose doctrines it declares to be unbiblical and un-Lutheran.

After administering this rebuke to the United Church, Dr. Stub went on to say:

> ... we, of the Norwegian Synod, are also possessed of a desire to come to an understanding with those who belong to other Lutheran denominations in this country ... and we hope that Rev. Øfstedal will acquaint the denomination which he represents with the fact that we ... have always been and even now are willing to carry on negotiations with them. ...[159]

Two days later the Synod returned to the union question and after considerable discussion resolved to elect a new committee.[160] Following the pattern set by the United Church, the Synod chose a completely new committee, one whose personnel consisted of parish pastors and not professors of theology or church officials. The following were named: J. Nordby, R. Malmin, J. E. Jørgensen, G. T. Lee, and I. D. Ylvisaker. Alternates were A. H. Eikjarud and N. Bøe.[161]

Earlier during the month of June Hauge's Synod had also elected a union committee, but without changing its membership.[162] The Norwegian Synod had decided at its convention that, should Hauge's Synod participate in the resumed negotiations, the Synod's former committee would take the place of the newly elected committee.[163] Whether in consequence of this decision or not, Hauge's Synod elected to remain outside the coming deliberations. Inasmuch as it had never been in-

---
[159]"The St. Paul Convention," *Lutheran Herald*, VI (1911), 700-701. The convention unanimously approved Stub's position by a rising vote.
[160]*Beretning ... Synoden ... 1911*, p. 87.
[161]"The St. Paul Convention," *Lutheran Herald*, VI (1911), 747-748.
[162]*Beretning ... Hauges Synode ... 1911*, p. 216. Committee members were: C. J. Eastvold, M. G. Hanson, K. C. Holter, A. O. Mortvedt, and J. N. Sandven.
[163]"The St. Paul Convention," *Lutheran Herald*, VI (1911), 748.

volved in the conflict and was now in agreement with the United Church on the matter, it felt that the issue was primarily between the Synod and the United Church. Therefore, when the union meetings were resumed, the committees which met were those recently elected by the United Church and the Synod.

The first meeting of the new joint committee was scheduled to begin November 21, 1911, and was to be held at the Y. M. C. A. in St. Paul, Minnesota. The two synodical committees met separately just before the main meeting and coincidentally agreed on making a concerted effort to demonstrate a spirit of friendliness from the outset.[164] The United Church committee decided that each committee-man should select a member of the Synod committee and befriend him in a special way. The Synod committee agreed that the United Church men should be their guests at lunch.[165] In this way it was hoped to avoid some of the personal antipathies which had developed between members of the former committees.

The St. Paul meeting, November 21-24, was fruitless of theological agreement but served the purpose of acquainting the members with each other. Pastor Nordby of the Synod and Pastor Hegge of the United Church were elected permanent, rotating chairmen. Pastors Lee and Tangjerd were chosen as secretaries.[166] When it was learned that a common understand-

---

[164]How much coincidence there was in these separate decisions is difficult to determine. Rasmus Malmin of the Synod committee informed the writer that a thirty-six-year-old pastor and college president at Forest City, Iowa, by the name of L. W. Boe busied himself at this juncture to press upon leading members of the two committees the necessity of getting acquainted with each other. Interview, April, 1947. Boe later became president of St. Olaf College and a leader in American and world Lutheranism. Cf. Erik Hetle, *Lars Wilhelm Boe* (Minneapolis: Augsburg Publishing House, 1949), pp. 55-89, 131-157.

[165]Writer's interviews with R. Malmin (Synod) and S. Gunderson (U. C.) April 8-10, 1947, and May 22, 1947, respectively. During the summer of 1949 the writer also conferred with G. T. Lee (Synod), one of the secretaries of the joint committee. To illustrate the spirit of *Gemütlickheit* present from the outset, one of the committee members told the writer that "we ate and we drank together." Expressing surprise at the latter, the writer was told that some of the committee met at a German restaurant called "Max's Cafe." When the *formal* sessions adjourned, one member might say to his friend, "Quo vadis?" To this the answer was given, "Ad Max." With that the *informal* sessions began.

[166]"Dagsprotokol. Fællesmøde for Synodens og Den For. Kirkes foreningskomiteer, holdt i St. Paul, Minn., 21-24 nov. 1911. . . . Det 2det Fællesmøde for Synodens og Den For. Kirkes foreningskomiteer afholdtes i Madison, Wis., fra onsdag den 14de til og med torsdag den 22de febr. 1912." (Unpublished handwritten minutes in archives of The Evangelical Lutheran Church, Luther Theological Seminary, St. Paul, Minnesota, p. 1.)

ing of election could not be achieved in the committee as a whole, a subcommittee consisting of Malmin, Lee, Gunderson, and Tangjerd was appointed to draft proposals.[167] The subcommittee, having reported that time did not permit adequate preparation of a statement, was elected as a standing committee to continue its work. A second meeting of the joint committee was planned to be held in Madison, Wisconsin, February 14, 1912. The subcommittee was to place in the hands of the individual members of the joint committee the result of its deliberations in "good season" before the Madison meeting.[168]

The remainder of the St. Paul colloquy was spent in a discussion of the unreconciled viewpoints of the United Church and the Synod. The meeting adjourned after drafting a report which was to be sent to the official organs of the church bodies. Said report closed with the words:

> The deliberations were conducted with earnestness, considerateness, and mutual confidence, and were marked by that love which believes all things, hopes all things . . . So the committees have the best hopes for a good result . . . For this they request our church people to pray.[169]

The subcommittee met at the West Hotel in Minneapolis, Minnesota, during the month of December, 1911.[170] Members of the joint committee had been asked to present proposals to the subcommittee in writing.[171] These were then considered and after thorough deliberation agreement was reached in the subcommittee, and a document embracing the consensus of the four men was prepared.[172]

---

[167] *Ibid.*, p. 2.
[168] *Ibid.*, pp. 2-3.
[169] *Ibid.*, pp. 5-6.
[170] The exact dates are not known. The information about the meeting was given to the writer by R. Malmin in interviews April 8-10, 1947. Malmin was chairman of the four-man committee consisting of Lee, Tangjerd, Gunderson, and himself.
[171] The only proposal discovered by the writer is a hand-written document by the secretary of the U. C. committee: "Past. Tangjerds forslag til subkomiteen." See Item Five in union files, Ev. Luth. Church, Luther Theological Seminary.
[172] The original copy of this report was written on the back side of extra programs of a concert given in Nordsidens Kirke (Zion Lutheran Church, 26th and Lyndale Avenue North, Minneapolis, Minnesota), November 17, 1911. It will be found as Item Six in the union files of the E. L. C., archives and bears the title "Subkomiteen." A printed version of the report was found by the writer in "The G. T. Lee Papers," obtained through the courtesy of his daughter, Mrs. N. K. Neprud, Minneapolis, Minnesota. The printed report contained two parts: (1) the Basis for Discussion, (2) a. The Settlement (*Opgjør*) re

Forward to Opgjør

The second joint committee meeting convened February 14, 1912, at the Park Hotel in Madison, Wisconsin.[173] Naturally the subcommittee's report was the chief item of business. However, upon the suggestion of Pastor Malmin the joint committee turned first of all to a discussion of the doctrine of election as presented in the Formula of Concord, Article XI.[174] This study occupied the committee until Monday, February 19, 1912, at which time it turned to the so-called Second Form of the doctrine, Question 548 in Pontoppidan, *Sandhed til Gudfrygtighed*.[175] When this was completed the negotiators finally turned to the report of the subcommittee. The first point in the proposal read as follows:

> The union committees of the Synod and the United Church, unanimously and without reservation, accept that doctrine of election which is set forth in the Formula of Concord, Part II, Article XI, and in Pontoppidan's "Sandhed til Gudfrygtighed," question 548.

It was resolved to add the following two parenthetical phrases: after Art. XI, "the so-called First Form," and after question 548, "the so-called Second Form."[176]

The next item in the report of the subcommittee was a statement of the relation between the two forms of doctrine. At this point there was disagreement, and it seemed as if another deadlock had been reached. Thereupon, the problem was placed in the hands of a committee of two, Pastors Ylvisaker and Gunderson, "to thrash this thing out." Said the joint committee: "We are going to lock you in a room, and will not open

---

Election, b. Church Union. Equipped with wide margins for insertions, comments, and corrections, the report was placed in the hands of each committee member. *Subkomiteen* [Eau Claire, Wisconsin: "Reform" Printing Company, 1911], 12 pp. This document is essential in interpreting the minutes of the Madison meeting, February 14-22, 1912. The minutes of the latter do not incorporate the report of the subcommittee, but copious references are made to it. The minutes, therefore, are of little value without this document at hand.

[173]"Dagsprotokol," p. 7. Decision was made at the first session to hold the remainder of the meetings in the city library. Arrangements had been made by a local banker, Consul Halle Steensland, an active layman of the United Church, *Ibid.*, p. 25.

[174]*Ibid.*, p. 8-9. Malmin's motive in this suggestion was to forestall the criticism that the committee made a hurried and superficial union agreement. Interview with writer, April 8-10, 1947.

[175]"Dagsprotokol," p. 11.

[176]*Loc. cit.* This item was to become the first paragraph of the Madison *Opgjør*. Cf. *The Union Documents . . . E. L. C.*, pp. 38-39.

the door until you have found the right way of stating this matter."[177]

The eagerly anticipated report of the two-man committee was finally presented with the understanding that a suitable conclusion be appended as a transition to what would follow. Pastor Ylvisaker read the following statement to the joint committee:

> Since both the conferring bodies acknowledge that Article XI of the Formula of Concord presents the pure and correct doctrine of the election of the children of God unto salvation as taught in the Word of God and the Confessions of the Lutheran Church, it is deemed unnecessary for church unity to set up new and more elaborate theses on this article of faith.
>
> However, since it is well known that in presenting the doctrine of election two forms of doctrine have been used, both of which have won acceptance and recognition within the orthodox Lutheran Church, some, in accordance with the Formula of Concord, include under the doctrine of election the whole order of salvation of the elect from the call to the glorification, and teach an election "unto salvation through the sanctification of the Spirit and belief of the truth," while others, with Johan Gerhard, Scriver, Pontoppidan and other recognized teachers of the Church, define election more specifically as the decree concerning the final glorification, with faith and perseverance wrought by the Holy Spirit as its necessary presupposition, and teach that "God has appointed all those to eternal life who He from eternity has foreseen would accept the offered grace, believe in Christ and remain constant in this faith unto the end"; and since neither of these two forms of doctrine, thus presented, contradicts any doctrine revealed in the Word of God, but does full justice to the order of salvation as presented in the Word of God and the confessions of the Church, therefore . . .[178]

Upon motion this was unanimously adopted by a rising vote. Thus was concluded one of the most troublesome problems which had faced the union negotiators since 1908: how to state the relation between the two forms of the doctrine of election,

---

[177]Interview of writer with R. Malmin, April 8-10, 1947. Malmin described the tenseness of the moment by picturing the unemotional Telemarking (descended from natives of Telemarken in Norway), G. T. Lee, softly weeping.

[178]"Dagsprotokol," pp. 12-13. This statement together with the appended phrase, "we find that this should not be a cause for schism within the Church or disturb that unity of the spirit in the bond of peace which God wills should prevail among us," became paragraphs two and three of the Madison Opgjør. The Union Documents . . . E. L. C., p. 39.

both recognized as orthodox, and yet each expressing the viewpoint of one of the opposing parties to the controversy. That this was not to prove completely satisfactory to all members of the Norwegian Synod was to be seen later. But for the majority it became the center of the doctrinal settlement on which the merger of 1917 was based.

Further discussion and the need for editorial changes occupied the committee during the next two days. Finally, on February 22, 1912, "The Joint Report from the Union Committees of the Synod and the United Church" was completed and unanimously recommended to the churches.[179]

The report consisted of two parts: (1) the actual doctrinal agreement *(Opgjør)*, and (2) a committee resolution based upon the agreement. The doctrinal portion of the document consisted of six paragraphs. The first three paragraphs called attention to the two "forms" in which the doctrine was stated. The fourth paragraph dealt with the old battle cries of synergism and Calvinism by rejecting "all errors which seek to explain away the mystery of election." This meant a repudiation of those teachings which would deprive God of His glory (synergism) or "weaken man's sense of responsibility in relation to the *acceptance* [italics not in original] or rejection of grace" (Calvinism). This paragraph was attacked later by a minority in the Synod, which said it was synergistic.[180]

Paragraphs five and six were elaborations of the previous one. The former sought to block all possible avenues for the entrance of synergism by (a) rejecting any human cause of election, (b) denying that God is influenced by "man's good attitude or anything which man is, does or omits to do . . . ," or by denying that (c) faith in Christ is "a product of, or depends upon, man's own choice, power of ability . . . ," or that (d) faith is "the result of an ability and power imparted by

---

[179]*Ibid.*, pp. 17-25. This report is commonly known in The Evangelical Lutheran Church as "The Madison Agreement" *(Opgjør)*. It will be found in *The Union Documents . . . E. L. C.*, pp. 38-41. By resolution of the joint committee the entire Article XI of the Formula of Concord was to be printed together with the report given to the respective church bodies. *Ibid.*, p. 25.

[180]Ylvisaker, *op. cit.*, p. 196.

the call of grace, which therefore now dwell within and belong to the unregenerate heart, enabling it to make a decision for grace."

The final paragraphs sought to avoid the theological pitfalls of Calvinism by listing five teachings which were emphatically rejected. That God acted arbitrarily in electing some and excluding others from salvation was to be denied. Nor could it be said that there were two kinds of saving will in God, one revealed and the other unknown, the latter concerning only the elect to whom were brought "a more cordial love, a more powerful call . . . and greater grace than to those who remain in their unbelief. . . ." Furthermore, when God in conversion removed the resistance of the saved, this was not to be interpreted as though the continuing resistance of the unbelievers was caused by God. The Calvinistic absolute assurance of election and salvation could find no place in a Lutheran whose assurance must always be one of faith, keeping in mind the possibility of falling, but believing that grace would preserve him. Finally, as a sum of all,

. . . doctrines concerning election which directly or indirectly would conflict with the order of salvation, and would not give to all a full and equally great opportunity to be saved, or which in any way would do violence to the Word of God which says that God "would have all men to be saved, and come to the knowledge of the truth"—in which gracious and merciful will of God all election to eternal life has its source.

The second part of the report, the resolution, pointed out that for the unity of the church agreement in the doctrine of the gospel and the administration of the sacraments was necessary. The previous union committees had reached agreement on those portions of the doctrine of the gospel which dealt with the call, conversion, and the order of salvation as a whole. Now agreement had been achieved on election. This led the joint committee to declare "that the essential agreement concerning these doctrines which has been attained is sufficient for church union."

Thereupon, the ten men signed the document, dispatched

the remaining incidental business, approved a report for the church press, and concluded the historic meeting with a devotional service conducted by Pastor Tangjerd.

News of the Madison concord spread rapidly throughout the upper Midwest and was received with much jubilation in the congregations.[181] For over forty years large segments of Norwegian-American Lutheranism had been divided by doctrinal issues, chief of which had been election. The people, of whom it is safe to say few knew much about the theological intricacies of the problem, were weary with the years of strife and were naturally overjoyed at the successful consummation of the union discussions. Once again the hope loomed large that the Norwegian Lutherans in America would merge into one organic whole. This devoutly to be longed for goal was still five years from achievement, but at least the *Opgjør* now gave promise that it would actually come.

The *Opgjør* itself can best be described as the instrument of an ecclesiastical rapprochement rather than as an astute and flawless display of theological finality with regard to the doctrine of election. Both sides, eager for union and weary of conflict, sought desperately to find a way in which they could be delivered from the clutch of bitterness and each could join the other without giving up his own views. It was a case of the victory of heart over head.

After all, what did the *Opgjør* say? It declared that Norwegian Lutherans believed sincerely in the doctrine of election as set forth in two "orthodox" forms. Some accepted election as stated in Form I; others accepted it as stated in Form II. Since both forms were "orthodox," the two views represented by them should not be divisive of church unity. One could

---

[181]Pastor Malmin informed the writer that he immediately dispatched three telegrams with the good news. One went to Dr. H. G. Stub, the president of the Synod and member of the earlier union committee. A second message went to L. W. Boe, president of the United Church's Waldorf College at Forest City, Iowa, and a man who, moving behind the scenes, had a positive though indirect influence on the union movement. A third was sent to Mrs. Malmin who was to inform the sexton to ring the church bell as an announcement to the community. All the churches of the Norwegian Synod and the United Church in Winnebago County, Iowa, had been instructed to ring their bells as soon as word arrived of the agreement. Malmin remarked that one man, a "Yankee" banker in Forest City, was quite carried away when he heard the bells ring. "The Norwegians are united," he exclaimed excitedly. "Now they must build a $10,000 church!"

select the form which pleased him. The Norwegian Missourians had insisted on Form I, but grudgingly gave a subordinate place to Form II. Form I was adequate, they said, by itself; and, in fact, it was the only statement which guaranteed a position beyond the reach of error. Form II was usually suspect. For the true Missourian there was no room, therefore, for a mere condescending toleration of Form II, and certainly not a choice between them as equally good. The "liberal" Norwegian Missourian, generally and charitably speaking, took the former attitude (toleration of Form II); the *Opgjør* took the latter (equal recognition of both). The "orthodox" Missourians and their theological opposites would have difficulty finding their positions expressed in the *Opgjør*. Despite this, most of the Norwegian Missourians and all of the anti-Missourians of the United Church, cognizant of and sympathetic to the feeling expressed in the ground swell of union sentiment found the *Opgjør* to their satisfaction. Madison was not a meeting of minds but of hearts.

Those who were not inclined to be ruled by their hearts soon found much to dismay them in the *Opgjør*. As a consequence, the Synod, whose membership harbored the theological "sharp-shooters" among the Norwegian Lutherans, found itself distraught with dissension over the *Opgjør*. A militant minority, armed with ammunition from St. Louis, soon was directing its fire against the Madison Agreement.

On the other hand, the *Opgjør* was to be welcomed by the great majority of churchmen, and compromise or no compromise, it was seen as the effective device by which men of good will could live together under one church roof. In this way the *Opgjør* marked the successful conclusion of the alternatingly rapid and slogging progress of the negotiators through the jungle of doctrinal problems. There was indeed a lively hope in 1912 that the four hundredth anniversary of the Lutheran Reformation in 1917 would see the Norwegian Lutherans in America united in one major church body.

CHAPTER SIX

The Union of 1917

When the church bells rang to herald the signing of the Madison Agreement on February 22, 1912, no doubt many enthusiastic Norwegian Lutherans in the upper Mississippi Valley considered the union of the churches a virtual *fait accompli*. Surely since the chief obstacle to union had been removed by a common confession regarding the doctrine of election, it would be but a short time until the actual merger was achieved. However, there were practical problems to be dealt with, differences resulting from characteristic emphases to be smoothed out, strong group loyalties to be brought into accord, and even doctrinal viewpoints to be adjusted. The United Church had demonstrated that it was aware of the fact that time would be required to deal with the multitude of merger details, and therefore at its 1911 convention had set the Reformation festival year of 1917 as the goal for accomplishing the union.[1] The wisdom of this lay-sponsored resolution was soon apparent as the churches found themselves requiring year after year to prepare the structure in which they were to dwell together. To be sure, the union was to be consummated in 1917, but it can hardly be said that the senti-

---
[1] *Beretning . . . Den f. Kirke . . . 1911* p. 284.

mental attachments of Lutherans to an historical commemoration fitted the merger neatly into Reformation festivities. It was rather the hard-driving leadership and persistent purposes of the architects of union that made it possible for the merger to coincide with the four hundredth anniversary of the Reformation.

Synodical Reaction to the *Opgjør* 1912-1913

The response to the announcement of the Madison Agreement was spontaneous and jubilant. The church press carried editorials and articles in the weeks leading up to the annual meetings of 1912, indicating that the official synodical reaction would be favorable.[2] The only exception to this was the editorial policy of the *Lutheran Herald*, the English organ of the Norwegian Synod. A restrained and noncommittal attitude in the early weeks soon gave way to open questioning and unqualified advice to proceed slowly.[3] Despite this, however, the general elation over the *Opgjør* gave indication that the churches would take favorable action when they met to consider the reports of their union committees in June, 1912.

The United Church convention was held at Fargo, North Dakota, June 6-12, 1912. The presidential address had these words about the *Opgjør:* "It brought a storm of jubilation among our people. . . . There is an earnest desire for union among the Norwegian Lutheran church people. . . ."[4] Fraternal greetings from the Minnesota District of the Synod were presented by H. O. Thorpe and enthusiastically received by the

---

[2]T. H. Dahl, "Fra Den forenede kirkes formand," *Lutheraneren*, XVIII (1912), 305; "Vil vi forening?" *ibid.*, pp. 368-369. H. G. Stub, "Et glædens budskap," *E. L. K.*, XXXIX (1912), 255-256. "Union Efforts," *The United Lutheran*, V (1912), 72; "The Good News from Madison," *ibid.*, p. 136; "Brethren in the Faith," *ibid.*, p. 153.

[3]"The Committee Completes Its Task," *Lutheran Herald*, VII (1912), 242-243; "Joint Report," *ibid.*, pp. 272-275 (printed without comment); "The Committee's Position," *ibid.*, pp. 602-604; "Make Haste Slowly," *ibid.*, p. 1055. The explanation of this policy lies in the fact that the editor was Theodore Graebner of the Missouri Synod. Graebner had served the Norwegian Synod as a teacher and pastor at Red Wing, Minnesota (1900-1906) and was presently serving a Missouri Synod congregation in Chicago, editing *Lutheran Herald* on the side. Norlie (ed.), *Who's Who*, p. 183.

[4]*Beretning . . . Den f. Kirke . . . 1912*, p. 57.

convention. After considering each paragraph of the union report separately, the whole was unanimously accepted. The approval created the greatest enthusiasm of the convention and the six thousand people gathered in the auditorium rose to sing "Now Thank We All Our God." To add to the joyousness of the occasion the St. Olaf College Choir sang.[5]

With this major item approved, the convention also unanimously accepted the previously submitted reports on absolution, lay activity, the call, and conversion. This prepared the way for the next step which was a resolution to continue negotiations seeking immediate union of the three bodies. A new union committee was elected and instructed to adjust the practical problems pertaining to the merger. It consisted of President T. H. Dahl, Pastors Peder Tangjerd, Severin Gunderson, N. C. Brun, and layman Tollef Sanderson. Another committee, consisting of Dr. J. N. Kildahl and Pastors M. H. Hegge, Gerhard Rasmussen, R. Anderson, and P. J. Reinertson, was instructed to negotiate with the Lutheran Free Church, The Evangelical Lutheran Church in America (Eielsen Synod), and the Church of the Lutheran Brethren.[6]

Hauge's Synod, holding its annual convention in Red Wing, Minnesota, approved the union documents, and elected a new committee on union: President M. G. Hanson, Pastors I. L. Lasseson, T. J. Oppedahl, C. J. Eastvold, and Professor M. O. Wee.[7]

Whereas Hauge's Synod and the United Church met in annual convention, the Norwegian Synod held no general convention in 1912. Instead the five districts convened independently and took action on the union committee report.[8] The earlier reports on absolution, lay activity, etc., were unanimously approved by all five districts, but the Madison Agreement encoun-

---
[5]Benson, *op. cit.*, p. 182. The already famous choir was planning its first European trip, and ecclesiastical dignitaries from Norway attending the United Church convention assured the singers that a welcome awaited them.
[6]*Beretning . . . Den f. Kirke . . . 1912* pp. 217, 232, 234, 250, 252-253. Cf. "United Church Accepts Report," *Lutheran Herald*, VII (1912), 605-606.
[7]*Beretning . . . Hauges Synode . . . 1912*, pp. 105, 194.
[8]The printed district reports are bound together in *Synodalberetning . . . 1912*, each containing a copy of the synodical president's report.

tered some trouble. The main opposition was directed against the doctrinal settlement of election in two forms.

President Stub, anticipating difficulties, had prepared his annual report with utmost care and sought to allay the fears of those who were dubious of the *Opgjør*. Said he:

> To me and others the result appeared almost as a miracle . . .[The committee] found in it the fulfillment of the many ardent prayers which had been directed to the throne of grace for a successful outcome. . . . This agreement, as well as the previous joint reports, is in general an expression of truths which in this connection should be acknowledged. *To demand more would be tantamount to stretching the bow so taut that it would break* [italics not in original].[9]

Realizing that the opponents of the *Opgjør* would attack the first part of the document, Stub quoted from an explanatory statement prepared by Pastors Nordby and Tangjerd of the union committee:

> "Since it has been intimated by members of both parties that the expression 'unreserved' in paragraph 1 and in the conclusion of the resolutions may cause conscientious tensions, since one would not be able in the same sense to vote for the one form as well as the other, we suggest that under the discussion of this point the committee agree to explain as follows: (1) that the expression does not speak of accepting *the two forms,* but of the acceptance of *that doctrine* which is expressed in the two forms; (2) that the meaning of the paragraph is that, in spite of the differences in presentation, everyone shall be free to use the form which his own conviction dictates within the frame fixed by the *Opgjør* itself, without any strictures on fellowship or recognition as a good Lutheran."[10]

The first of the five districts to meet was the Minnesota District, May 30-June 5, at Willmar, Minnesota. In the course of the discussion on the *Opgjør*, Professor Johannes Ylvisaker addressed two questions to those who had participated in drafting the agreement at Madison.[11] The questions and the answers, prepared by Lee, Nordby, and I. D. Ylvisaker of the union committee, were made a part of the record to be sub-

---

[9]*Beretning . . . Østlige Distrikt . . . 1912,* p. 31.
[10]*Ibid.,* p. 32.
[11]*Beretning . . . Minnesota Distrikt 1912,* pp. 118-123.

mitted to the other district conventions.¹² Professor Ylvisaker had asked whether there was an essential difference between paragraphs one and three of the *Opgjør*, and whether the acceptance of paragraph one would be tantamount to a recognition of the Second Form as the doctrine of Scripture and the Lutheran confessions. The first question was answered by a simple "No." To the second question the following answer was given:

> ... In the first paragraph no form of doctrine is accepted, but the doctrine in the two forms. The Synod committee accepts without reservation the first form of the doctrine as that of the Scriptures and the confessions, but can nevertheless recognize as brethren in the faith those who hold the second form of doctrine as seen in the light of the subsequent paragraphs of the *Opgjør*.

Further explanation of this position was given by Pastor I. D. Ylvisaker. He said that it had been discussed twice at Madison where essentially the same questions had been propounded. At that time the Synod men had received the assurance that the first paragraph did not compel acceptance of the Second Form. As for himself, he would be willing to die for the First Form. However, that should not be necessary, for the *Opgjør* did not require the acceptance of two *forms*. The *Opgjør* implied the impossibility of personal subscription to *two* forms. But the two forms stood side by side, thus permitting men to stand side by side in church work, each subscribing to his own form of the doctrine of election. But those who recognized the First Form also recognized the *doctrine* which underlay the Second Form as the doctrine of God's Word.¹³

The motion to adopt the *Opgjør* with this understanding was approved by a unanimous vote of 209. The non-voting advisory members were polled and this resulted in a nineteen to one approval.¹⁴

Three things should be noted about this action: (1) it in-

---
[12] *Ibid.*, p. 120.
[13] A verbatim account of the Willmar discussion is given in "The Committee's Position," *Lutheran Herald*, VII (1912), 602-604.
[14] *Beretning . . . Minnesota Distrikt . . . 1912*, pp. 119-120.

sisted that the Norwegian Synod had not given up its belief in the First Form as the true exposition of the Scriptures on the matter of election; (2) it stated that it was impossible for one man to embrace both forms of the doctrine; and (3) despite the fact that the two forms were mutually exclusive, the *persons* who subscribed to one or the other were not to be mutually exclusive. The old Anti-Missourian position, therefore, was quite thoroughly repudiated. It had held that the two forms were mutually inclusive: the Formula of Concord (the First Form) interpreted "in view of faith" (the Second Form) was a full-orbed Lutheran doctrine of election. In other words, *one person* must embrace *both forms* of the doctrine. But since the former Anti-Missourians were more eager for church union than for precise doctrinal definition, they did not press their position but accepted "The Settlement."[15] The discussion at the Minnesota District convention and the commentary on the *Opgjør* presented by the members of the union committee centered exactly on those points which were to be challenged at a later date by a vigorous and determined group which followed undeviatingly the Missouri line. The Minnesota District had set the pattern by which the other districts of the Synod would deal with the union matter.

When all the districts had met, it was discovered that 591 voting members and sixty-seven advisory members favored the *Opgjør*. Fifteen negative votes were cast and twenty abstained from voting.[16] The Madison Agreement was further supported by the decision of all the districts to continue committee negotiations with the United Church and Hauge's Synod. The committee of five was to consist of President H. G. Stub (*ex officio*), and Pastors D. C. Jordahl (Minnesota), J. Nordby (Eastern), O. P. Vangsness (Iowa), and I. D. Ylvisaker (Northwestern).

[15]That this observation is essentially correct is borne out by the fact that F. A. Schmidt, the chief exponent of Anti-Missourianism, had little good to say for the *Opgjør*. J. N. Kildahl, president of St. Olaf College at the time, reported that Schmidt had come to Northfield to speak to him about the *Opgjør*. He said he would not vote against it but neither would he vote for it. "Laur. Larsen Papers," letter from J. N. Kildahl to Laur. Larsen, December 24, 1912.

[16]For record of votes see *Beretning . . . Minnesota Distrikt . . . 1912*, pp. 119–120; *Østlige Distrikt*, pp. 94-95; *Iowa Distrikt*, pp. 119-120; *Nordvestlige Distrikt*, pp. 95-96; *Pacific Distrikt*, pp. 109-110.

The next step, therefore, was to bring the synodical committees together for further union negotiations. This was complicated by the fact that the Norwegian Synod's original committee on union with Hauge's Synod had never been dismissed and still retained its commission. The Synod now had two committees to deal with Hauge's Synod.[17]

In the meantime, the United Church committee held two separate meetings, July 3 and September 3, 1912, in order to think through and prepare definite union proposals to lay before the other committees.[18] It is obvious from reading the record of these meetings that the United Church was giving forethought to the practical problems of a merger. Several resolutions indicated the aggressive and forward-looking nature of the men of the United Church. The very first resolution set organic union as the goal of their efforts. Another resolution indicated the awareness in the committee of the educational problem which faced three merging synods who would bring their own educational institutions into the union. The pertinent resolution here stated that the new church body should eventually operate one theological seminary, one proseminary,[19] two colleges, and two normal schools. With these resolutions a part of the minutes, the committee spent the remainder of the meeting discussing a proposed constitution for the new church.[20] Before adjourning, the committee indicated its unwillingness to let intersynodical matters slide. Therefore, instruction was given its chairman, President T. H. Dahl, to approach the other committees and, together with them, set a date for a joint meeting.

As a result, the three newly appointed committees met together September 4-5, 1912, to lay plans for the union which

---

[17] Laila Nilsen, "The Genesis and Organization of the Norwegian Lutheran Church of America," (Unpublished M.A., thesis, University of Minnesota, 1933), p. 93.

[18] Minutes of these meetings are to be found in the same secretarial book which contains the minutes of the St. Paul (1911) and Madison (1912) meetings in the archives of The Evangelical Lutheran Church, Luther Theological Seminary, St. Paul, Minnesota.

[19] A "proseminary" was intended for older men who desired to enter the seminary but did not possess a college education.

[20] The basis for this discussion was a constitutional report made to the 1910 meeting of the United Church. *Beretning . . . Den f. Kirke . . . 1910*, pp. 89-96. It is interesting to note that the July committee meeting resolved that the name of the new church should be "The Norwegian Lutheran Church in America," which name was actually adopted in 1917.

now seemed to possess an assured doctrinal basis.[21] At the outset it was clear that the joint meeting would accomplish little or nothing in hastening organic union of the church. Dr. Stub announced that the Synod committee had not been authorized "to discuss actual union," but rather was to deliberate with the others on a *modus vivendi* until the synods themselves determined the date for actual union negotiations to begin. Both the United Church and Hauge's committees expressed themselves as believing that they had been elected for precisely this task, namely, to discuss organic union. President Dahl hoped that the committee of the Norwegian Synod would get proper authorization so that no further delays would impede the plans to have articles of union and a constitution to present to the synods for approval in 1914.[22]

Before charging the Synod committee with delaying tactics and a lack of whole-heartedness for church union, it is well for us to understand the situation which faced Dr. Stub within the Norwegian Synod at this moment. Less than a month previous to this meeting, Dr. Stub had attended the convention of the Synodical Conference in Saginaw, Michigan, at which he felt called upon to defend the *Opgjør* from attacks being made upon it by his German friends in the Missouri Synod.[23] Since the attitude of the Missouri Synod theologians carried much weight among pastors of the Norwegian Synod and was already causing a division of feeling within the Synod, Stub and his colleagues felt justified in "making haste slowly" when they met with the United Church and Hauge's committees in September, 1912. The rising antagonism inside the Norwegian Synod required careful and adroit handling if the cause of union was not to founder again. It was Dr. Stub's task to steer his church between the Scylla of domination by Missouri and the Charybdis of yielding to United Church impatience.

---

[21] The minutes of this meeting, together with the records of the separate meeting of the United Church on September 3, are to be found in the above-mentioned manuscript form in the archives of The Evangelical Lutheran Church. They may also be found in *Lutheraneren*, XVIII (1912), 1232-1233, and *E. L. K.*, XXXIX (1912), 1066-1068.
[22] *Beretning . . . Den f. Kirke . . . 1913*, p. 64.
[23] *Beretning om det Ekstraordinære Synodemøde . . . Synoden . . . 1913*, pp. 30-42.

"Stretching the Bow So Taut . . ."—
Opposition within the Synod

When Dr. Stub presented his presidential message to the districts of the Norwegian Synod in 1912, he had commented on the Madison Agreement as follows: "To demand more than the *Opgjør* would be tantamount to stretching the bow so taut that it would break."[24] During the remaining months of 1912, Stub began to be aware of acute attacks on the Synod for having given the *Opgjør* overwhelming approval at the previous district meetings. The bow was being stretched taut.

When the spring of 1913 arrived, the Synod met in extraordinary convention at the call of the church council because of the seriousness of the union question.[25] Stub's appreciation of the critical state of affairs was apparent in his lengthy presidential message, a major portion of which was devoted to interchurch relations. Apprising the delegates of the fact that the attacks on the Madison Agreement which came out of the Missouri Synod were influencing a number of persons within the Norwegian Synod, he felt it his bounden duty to defend the action taken by the Synod in 1912.[26] With this in mind he had prevailed upon Professor J. Ylvisaker to accompany him to the Synodical Conference convention held at Saginaw, Michigan, in August, 1912, where he had explained and upheld the *Opgjør*.

After Stub and Ylvisaker left Saginaw, the Synodical Conference adopted a statement entitled "An Appeal to the Synod" in which it requested three things of the Norwegian Synod: (1) to eliminate the coordination of the First and Second Forms in the *Opgjør* (paragraphs one to three), since the First

---

[24]*Supra*, p. 186.
[25]A synodical meeting ordinarily would not have been held until 1914.
[26]*Beretning . . . Synoden . . . 1913*, pp. 30-31. The attacks, which Stub describes as unjust, appeared in such Missouri papers as *The Lutheran Witness, Der Lutheraner,* and *Lehre und Wehre*. Perhaps most important was the appearance of a book by Professor Franz Pieper, *Zur Eingung der amerikanisch-lutherischen Kirche in der Lehre von der Bekehrung und Gnadenwahl* (St. Louis: Concordia Publishing House, 1913). The English translation by W. H. T. Dau is *Conversion and Election: A Plea for a United Lutheranism in America*. A review of this book in manuscript by G. T. Lee will be found among "The G. T. Lee Papers." Lee, as will be recalled, was a member of the *Opgjør* committee. He commends certain portions of the book, but severely criticizes Pieper's attempt "to construct an entirely new doctrine of the second form."

Form only had a proper place in the confession of the church; (2) to reject from paragraph five the following doctrine: that the cessation of wilful resistance, either through natural or imparted powers, afforded an explanation of the mystery of predestination; and (3) to enter upon a discussion of conversion and election with the Synodical Conference in order to strengthen the ties of fellowship which in the past had united the Norwegian Synod to the Synodical Conference.[27]

President Stub continued his report to the Synod by calling attention to the literary attacks by Professor Schaller in *Theologische Quartalschrift* of the Wisconsin Synod and by the editor of *Lehre und Wehre* of the Missouri Synod. Stub had considered this an open declaration of war and submitted the whole matter to the church council which supported him in his attitude and prepared protests to the Synodical Conference and the editor of *Lehre und Wehre*.[28]

Stub drew his consideration of the union movement to a close by referring to his requests to the United Church and Hauge's Synod to remove certain formal objectionable aspects of the *Opgjør* which had become apparent at the district conventions of the Synod in 1912. When the *Opgjør* was written, the authors had inserted two parenthetical explanations in the first paragraph: (1) "the so-called First Form" after Article XI of the Formula of Concord, and (2) "the so-called Second Form" after Question 548. These two parentheses, said Stub, might lead some to identify "doctrine" and "doctrinal form," an interpretation not allowed by the Synod. Therefore, would the United Church and Hauge's Synod please adopt the Synod's explanation and remove the offending parentheses?[29]

Despite Stub's detailed *apologia pro vita sua* and evidence to the effect that the Synod, on the whole, stood behind him, the months leading up to the synodical meeting revealed that a belligerently articulate minority had developed within the

---

[27]*Ibid.*, pp. 38-39. A report of the proceedings of the Synodical Conference will be found in *The Lutheran Witness* of mid-September, 1912. Cf. Manuscript union documents, archives, The Evangelical Lutheran Church, St. Paul. See letter from Gustav Stearns to Peder Tangjerd, September 20, 1912.
[28]*Beretning . . . Synoden . . . 1913*, pp. 39-42.
[29]*Ibid.*, pp. 51-53.

church. This was first witnessed publicly in a series of articles and editorials appearing in *Lutheran Herald*.³⁰ The sentiments expressed here and elsewhere culminated in the appearance of an anonymous document known as "The Petition *(Bønskrift)* to the Synod." Circulated among pastors of the Synod, it sought to thwart union with the United Church until complete unity in the faith had been obtained, and to that end it solicited support. The document, according to its authors, was sent only to those who were sympathetic to its declarations. Naturally President Stub was not on the mailing list, but, as usually happens in such cases, circumstances arranged themselves so that a copy came into his hands. Upon reading it, he and Dr. Larsen published a "Warning" in the Synod's Norwegian organ, testifying against its anonymity and factional character.³¹ Thereupon the authors revealed their identity by publishing it over their signatures, without commentary or explanation, in *Evangelisk Luthersk Kirketidene*. The drafters of the document were none other than Stub's colleagues on the seminary faculty, Professors O. E. Brandt, Johs. Ylvisaker, and E. Hove.³²

The preamble of the *Bønskrift* announced that the petitioners did not want their action to be construed as disloyalty to the union movement. In fact, they too were moved by the hope of union, but a *true* union based on unity in faith. This, they feared, did not yet exist between the Synod and the United Church. Several reasons were given for this fear: (1) the Synod interpretation of the first paragraph of the *Opgjør* had not been accepted by the United Church; (2) the United Church had not yet recanted its judgment of the theses on election approved by the Synod in 1910; (3) the leaders of the Synod and the United Church differed in their interpretation of the *Opgjør*, the former claiming it to be a repristination of *Redegjørelse* (1884) and the theses of 1910, and the latter denying this to be the case; and (4) the United Church prac-

---
³⁰See *Lutheran Herald*, VIII (1913), 341, 432-441, 456, 478.
³¹"Advarsel," *E. L. K.*, XL (1913), 483, and "Til den norske synodes menigheder og prester," *ibid.*, pp. 540-541.
³²"Bønskrift i sand troseniheds interesse," *E. L. K.*, XL (1913), 592-593.

ticed fellowship with certain church bodies which the Synod must number as its opponents. For these reasons the petitioners asked that complete unity be reached before organic union be contemplated.

All of this had been taking place during the months of April and May, 1913. Thus, when the Synod met in June, it was to be expected that a division of opinion would be revealed on the union issue. This was demonstrated when the convention heard a majority and minority report from its union committees. The committee of 1911 which drafted the *Opgjør* and the newly-elected committee of 1912 met together before the synodical meeting of 1913 in response to a summons by Stub and formulated the proposals incorporated in the majority report. Anticipating the removal of the parentheses in the first paragraph of the *Opgjør* by the other synods at their 1913 conventions, and anticipating a retraction by the United Church of the judgment on Stub's theses as "unbiblical" and "un-Lutheran," the majority report approved the suggestion of the joint committee meeting of September, 1912, and empowered the Synod union committee to work toward an organic union of the three church bodies.[33] The minority report, signed only by Professor E. Hove, stressed the unsettled doctrinal questions which must be clarified before the union committee be authorized to negotiate a merger. A joint report, signed by all the members of the committee, expressed happiness at the results attained toward union, urged continuation of the committee on union elected the previous year, and gave official sanction to the removal of the parentheses from the first paragraph of the *Opgjør*.[34]

At this point in the proceedings, Professor Brandt asked for the floor and read the *Bønskrift* following it with an explanation of the motivations and purposes of the petition. He said that it grew out of the burdened consciences of many pastors and professors who were dubious of the *Opgjør*. The docu-

---

[33] *Beretning . . . Synoden . . . 1913*, pp. 55-56.
[34] The three reports, majority, minority, and joint, are given in *ibid.*, pp. 61-62. The committee members were Elling Hove, Halvor Halvorsen, Thomas Nilsson, J. Hegg, and Martin Austin.

ment was sent only to those who shared their views. It was consequently private but not anonymous. Its purpose was not to subvert the decisions of the Synod but to emphasize the old Synod principle that cooperation or organic union must be preceded by clear unity in the faith. Feeling that this was not the situation as between the United Church and the Synod the *Bønskrift* sought in good conscience a calm and open discussion of the matter in the convention.[35]

Dr. Stub, as the chief spokesman for the majority, replied in two separate talks: one was a direct answer to the *Bønskrift*, the other an appeal to the Synod to adopt the majority report. In the former, he charged the authors with perpetrating an irresponsible act. Both the manner and the intent of the *Bønskrift* would serve only to harm mutual confidence and further the party spirit in the church.[36] In the latter address, Stub pleaded with the church to give overwhelming approval to the majority report. Not to do so would be to break faith with Hauge's Synod and the United Church. "Therefore," concluded Stub, "I urge you as strongly as possible . . .: do not vote for the minority report, but vote for the majority report! Nothing less is involved than the honor of the Norwegian Synod and the cause of union."[37]

When the vote was taken, the results revealed that 394 ballots favored the majority report and 106 the minority. Despite the favorable vote, it was resolved to submit the whole matter to the congregations for final approval.[38] Supported by the synodical majority and an overwhelming congregational approval,[39] the union committee of the Synod was now prepared

---
[35]*Ibid.*, pp. 64-65.
[36]*Ibid.*, pp. 91-92. A further treatment of the *Bønskrift* will be found in H. G. Stub, *Foreningssagens Gang* (Decorah, Iowa: The Lutheran Publishing House, 1916), pp. 25-26.
[37]*Beretning . . . Synoden . . . 1913*, pp. 87-90.
[38]*Ibid.*, p. 93.
[39]The results of the referendum were announced by President Stub to the convention of 1914. Three hundred ninety-eight congregations voted as follows: 359 for the majority, twenty-seven against. Some of the latter stated that their vote did not indicate opposition to union as such, but found that for sundry reasons they must vote negatively. The parochial report of 1914 shows that in 1913 there were 629 congregations in the Synod. Hence 231 did not report their decisions to the president. Stub's comment was this: "According to the constitution of the Synod, all congregations which did not vote within the time limits set by the constitution are regarded as having endorsed the resolutions of the body." *Beretning . . . Synoden . . . 1914*, pp. 53, 348, 355, 369, and 381. Consequently, no less than 590

to continue merger negotiations with the Hauge's and United Church committees.

This did not mean that the minority opposition was to subside. If anything, it became even more vocal, soliciting and obtaining encouragement from the Missouri Synod. Meanwhile, Dr. Stub made every effort to pacify the minority group and to win their support for the cause of union. Another man who aided in this attempt was Dr. Laur. Larsen, the former editor of the Synod's official organ. In his last years the fundamental issue of union had become so absorbing that he now devoted all his time to promoting it. Convinced that the danger to true Lutheranism in America had been averted in the nineteenth century under the influence of the conservative Missouri Synod, he now felt that the special confessional emphasis of the Missourians, including the Norwegian Synod, had achieved its purpose and that the day had arrived for broader union.[40]

An examination of Larsen's correspondence during the years 1913-1914 reveals a degree of hopefulness that this might soon be achieved.[41] But already by the autumn of 1913, Larsen's optimism regarding an understanding with Missourianism, both within his own synod and in St. Louis, began to fade. He saw the crystallization of opposition in Iowa where C. K. Preus and I. B. Torrison were opposing the *Opgjør* most vigorously. Furthermore, his efforts to approach old friends in the Missouri Synod were, by and large, unfruitful. His espousal of the union movement had made him *persona non grata* in the eyes of the Missourian leaders. When Larsen died in 1915, only a brief note of the event appeared in the periodical of the church in whose seminary he had once taught and with which he had been so closely associated for most of his life.[42] Meanwhile, the attitude of the minority in the Synod was "stretching the bow so taut" that a split seemed about to occur.

---
congregations out of 629 had voted in favor of the merger. It is obvious from this that the chief opposition had come not from the people but from certain professors and a few pastors whose views dominated their congregations.

[40]Larsen, *Laur. Larsen*, p. 338.

[41]"The Laur. Larsen Papers," Kildahl-Larsen correspondence, October 9, 1912, and October 18, 1912. "The Laur. Larsen Papers," letter to Jacob Larsen, July 18, 1913.

[42]Larsen, *Laur. Larsen*, p. 339. Cf. *The United Lutheran*, VIII (1915), 296.

Seeking to Broaden the Scope of Union

It had been the oft-expressed desire of the United Church since the days of its first president, Gjermund Hoyme, to promote an ecclesiastical merger which would embrace all Norwegian Lutherans in America. The idea of a pan-Norwegian Lutheranism organically united received renewed impetus at the 1912 convention of the United Church at Fargo, North Dakota, where a committee was chosen to confer with the Lutheran Free Church, the Eielsen Synod, and the Church of the Lutheran Brethren.[43]

Despite the action of the Free Church in electing a committee to meet with the United Church representatives, it was apparent at the convention of 1912 that this body was only lukewarm. Said Pastor J. Mattson, chairman of its influential committee on organization:

> The Free Church does not desire to reopen the old feuds and controversies, maintaining its position on the principles which have been adhered to by Augsburg Seminary for the past forty years. If the Free Church enters into union with the other denominations, one of two things will happen: Either the principles of the Free Church must be recognized in the consolidated body, or else the Free Church will be untrue to its purpose.[44]

Subsequent meetings demonstrated that the traditional attitudes of the two groups had not altered.[45] The Free Church insisted that *cooperation* precede union; the United Church would have *union* precede cooperation. As a gesture towards better understanding between the bodies, the United Church suggested that both sides forgive and forget the unfortunate circumstances which attended the Augsburg Controversy. The object now ought to be a union of the two bodies on the basis of their common beliefs, and that in the process of consummating the union, joint meetings for discussion and edification ought to be held. The Free Church committee[46] stipulated the

---
[43]*Beretning . . . Den f. Kirke . . . 1912*, pp. 252-253, 270.
[44]"Free Church Enters into Negotiations," *Lutheran Herald*, VII (1912), 606.
[45]Accounts of these meetings are given in *Beretning . . . Den f. Kirke . . . 1913*, pp. 88-91.
[46]Professors E. P. Harbo, Andreas Helland, and Pastor E. F. Gynild.

following condition as the *sine qua non* of union: that the United Church confess that it had acted in an unjust and unchristian manner in the controversy over Augsburg Seminary, especially (1) in its irreconcilable attitude towards the Friends of Augsburg, (2) in its refusal to recognize Sverdrup and Oftedal as delegates to the convention of 1895, (3) in its expulsion of those congregations and pastors who supported Augsburg, (4) in its obstruction to the exercise of the rights of the congregations by denying ordination to properly examined and rightly called ministerial candidates, and (5) in its unbrotherly response to the approaches of the Free Church in regard to the ordination and reception of ministerial candidates graduated from Augsburg Seminary. The committee of the United Church found these conditions completely unacceptable.

This exchange of views revealed that there was little hope of a union in the near future between these two groups. In fact, the next expressions of union feeling in the Free Church, made in 1914 and 1917, did nothing to promote the cause of organic union.[47]

According to its instructions, the committee on union with the Free Church also approached the Eielsen Synod and the Church of the Lutheran Brethren. This approach was made through the chairman, Pastor M. H. Hegge, who during the early part of 1913 received communications from officials of the two bodies. The Eielsen Synod, through President S. M. Stenby, thanked the United Church for being willing to confer with this synod, but since it had never adopted resolutions pertaining to church union, it would be unable to begin such activities. The Lutheran Brethren replied that because of the difference in congregational principles, there was no possibility of a union with other churches. However, a committee from this church would be willing to discuss "cooperation for revival and the saving of souls."[48]

---

[47]*Beretning . . . Den f. Kirke . . . 1914*, pp. 42-43, 196; *Beretning . . . Frikirken . . . 1914*, p. 143. Cf. "Fra frikirkens aarsmøde," *Lutheraneren*, XX (1914), 839-840. See resolution quoted in *Lutheraneren*, XXIII (1917), 176.

[48]The replies of these two churches will be found in *Beretning . . . Den f. Kirke . . . 1913*, p. 92. The best expression of the attitude of the Lutheran Brethren to the question

Despite these rebuffs the United Church decided in 1913 to retain this special committee on union in case any of the church bodies not party to the ongoing merger movement should decide to join the negotiations.[49] But as one might expect, this ended the attempts to broaden the scope of the union to embrace all Norwegian Lutherans in America.

Trilateral Progress

As will be remembered, the Norwegian Synod had adopted the majority report on union with the understanding that the United Church and Hauge's Synod remove the offending parentheses from paragraph one of the *Opgjør*.[50] This was to be done to assure the wary in the Synod that when they voted for the *Opgjør* they were voting for a doctrine and not a doctrinal form. In addition, the Synod had requested the United Church to retract its judgment of Stub's theses on election.

The United Church, in 1913, obligingly sanctioned the removal of the parentheses, but would not withdraw the judgment passed by its union committee in 1910 upon Stub's theses. But in order to eliminate misunderstandings between it and the Synod, the United Church passed a resolution intended to clarify its position. It said that since Stub's theses had never been considered by the church in convention, had never been published through its official organ, and were unknown to the greater part of its membership; and since the three synods had agreed in the *Opgjør* on the doctrine of election, the United Church considered it unreasonable of the Synod to demand that the theses of 1910 be now taken under consideration by the United Church either to judge them anew or to approve the judgment of the 1910 union committee. Since the United

---

of union is given in E. M. Broen, *Gjensvar Til K. O. Lundeberg* (n. p.: Broderbaandets Forlag, 1911), 56 pp.
[49]*Beretning . . . Den f. Kirke . . . 1913*, p. 221.
[50]*Supra*, pp. 192-195.

Church had never expressed itself on Stub's theses, it had therefore never passed "judgment" on them.[51]

Hauge's Synod, on the other hand, did not respond affirmatively to the Synod's request to remove the parentheses. It was said that since Hauge's Synod had not participated in the drafting of the *Opgjør,* it could hardly authorize changes in the document.[52]

A joint meeting of the three synodical union committees was scheduled for the early part of 1914. Fearing that it might not be successful in light of the 1913 actions of the United Church and Hauge's Synod, President Stub arranged a private meeting between himself and Dr. Kildahl of the United Church to consider the objections which had been raised against the *Opgjør.* Together they arrived at a statement which, it was felt, was in agreement with the explanation originally proposed at the convention of the Minnesota District of the Synod in 1912.[53] The second joint meeting of the three union committees was held in Minneapolis, January 21-23, 1914. The Stub-Kildahl "Declaration" was unanimously accepted.[54] With the doctrinal matters disposed of the joint committee turned to some of the other questions which faced the conferring groups. A practical matter, but involving attitude toward doctrine, was dealt with in a joint resolution warning against "unionism," "fanaticism," and inter-church cooperation with non-Lutheran Protestants and those who held to confessions differing from the three deliberating synods.[55]

[51] *Beretning . . . Den f. Kirke . . . 1913,* p. 241. It is to be observed that both the United Church and the Synod passed resolutions in 1913 absolving the church bodies as such of responsibility for unofficial utterances by their members. Nor would they hold other churches responsible for statements of individuals within their bodies. This is noteworthy in view of the "unofficial" attitude within the United Church toward Stub's theses, and the appearance of the *Bønskrift* in the Synod. See Bergh, *Den n. luth. Kirkes Hist. i Am.,* p. 511, and *Beretning . . . Synoden . . . 1913,* p. 125.

[52] *Beretning . . . Hauges Synode . . . 1913,* p. 145.

[53] *Supra,* pp. 186-188. "Erklæring," *E. L. K.,* XLI (1914), 102-103. *Beretning . . . Synoden . . . 1914,* pp. 53-54.

[54] The original manuscript minutes are in the archives of The Evangelical Lutheran Church, St. Paul, Minnesota. A report of the meeting was published in the church organs: "Rapport fra foreningskomiteen," *E. L. K.,* XLI (1914), 131-133.

[55] The word translated "fanaticism" is *sværmeri,* the word Luther used to describe the left-wing agitation of his day. The joint committee adopted an interesting explanatory note: "Sværmeri is not, of course, to be understood as referring to the assembling of people for prayer meetings and the earnest endeavor for awakening and spiritual life."

The joint committee proceeded to name the committee on conditions of union and the committee on constitution. Stub and Dahl, respectively, were named conveners of these committees which were to report at the next joint meeting, March 31, 1914. Before concluding the discussions the committee took occasion to consider the question of synodical institutions and funds. It was decided to make the provision that synodical debts be liquidated before the union.[56]

The meeting of the joint committee, March 31-April 2, 1914, was significant in that the structural framework of the proposed church body was, in the main, erected.[57] Reports from both committees on conditions of union and the constitution were read, together with a minority report from the constitutional committee. Only the report of the first committee, setting forth nineteen articles of union, was considered at this meeting.

Article one required unconditional acceptance of the canonical Scriptures as God's infallible Word and of the confessions of the Norwegian Lutheran Church. Article two asserted that the acceptance of the doctrinal agreements adopted in 1912 (the *Opgjør* as well as the preceding agreements) was a prerequisite for union. The third article denied "unionism" with the Reformed churches and others who did not share the confessions of the uniting bodies.[58] The lengthy fourth article dealt with church rites and ceremonies.[59] Beginning with a citation from the Augsburg Confession (Article VII), which centered church unity not in ceremonies but in doctrine, the article then

---

[56] The separate meeting of the United Church committee in July, 1912, had made this suggestion as a condition of union, and, it will be recalled, also set organic union as the objective of the negotiations. *Supra*, p. 189.

[57] The manuscript minutes are in the archives, The Evangelical Lutheran Church, St. Paul, Minnesota. A report was published by the committee in the church papers: "Rapport fra foreningskomiteen," *E. L. K.*, XLI (1914), 439-442; "Report of the Committee on Union," *Lutheran Herald*, IX (1914), 444-447; "Official Report of the Committee on Union," *The United Lutheran*, VII (1914), 257-259.

[58] In the manuscript minutes of the meeting it is revealed that Dr. Stub sought unsuccessfully to introduce item one of the "Galesburg Rule" at this point: "Lutheran pulpits are for Lutheran ministers only; Lutheran altars are for Lutheran communicants only." In 1925, Stub, as a participant in the Minneapolis Colloquy, saw this rule incorporated into "The Minneapolis Theses."

[59] The detailed prescriptions in this article were necessitated by the widely divergent liturgical traditions represented in the three bodies. Some *modus operandi* had to be composed to which the low-church Haugeans on the one hand and the more liturgical elements in the Synod and the United Church on the other hand could give assent.

asserted the authority of the church to choose those ceremonies which it deemed "most serviceable," but that such church rites which were not contrary to the Word of God and had been honored by long usage should not be discarded except for good and sufficient reason. With these general principles established, the article turned to the specific rites associated with Norwegian Lutheranism, recommending that the liturgy of the Church of Norway be used, that public confession and absolution be administered, according to the congregation's jurisdiction, either by the laying on of hands or by general declaration without the latter, and that private confession and absolution be retained.[60] Finally, the article reiterated the earlier statement on lay activity, asserting that the churches would cherish it and desist from regarding prayer meetings and awakenings as evidences of religious fanaticism.

The second and longer part of the document stipulated that synodical debts be paid before the merger, that one seminary be maintained,[61] that two normal schools (at Sioux Falls, South Dakota, and Madison, Minnesota) be continued, that two senior colleges (Luther at Decorah, Iowa, and St. Olaf at Northfield, Minnesota) be operated, and that other educational institutions connected with any of the three synods be continued and, if under the supervision of the church, subsidized by the church. Further items in the articles of agreement dealt with the perpetuation of existing institutions of mercy and of foreign mission fields, the consolidation of the respective pension funds, publication houses, and periodicals.[62] Incorporation of the new church and the legal transfer of all properties

[60] According to the minutes, one entire session was devoted to the question of absolution. The Church of Norway ritual, followed by the Synod and the United Church, specified the laying on of hands in absolution. This was abhorrent to the Haugean pietists who looked upon the practice as crypto-Romanist.

[61] The three seminaries were located as follows: Hauge's at Red Wing, Minnesota; United in St. Anthony Park, St. Paul, Minnesota; and Synod, in Hamline, also a part of St. Paul. The three merged seminaries would be housed in the St. Paul buildings, while the Red Wing Seminary was to become a "proseminary" and normal school. The teachers and students at the consolidated seminary would be those so engaged at the time of the union.

[62] The publishing interests were to be centered at Augsburg Publishing House (United Church) in Minneapolis. One Norwegian and one English church organ should be published. A Sunday school paper in both languages was also authorized.

were made part of the agreement, and, finally, the union of the synods was not to curtail the rights of congregations to effect mergers or rearrangement of parishes

There were diverse reactions when the articles of union were presented to the three synodical conventions of 1914. Hauge's Synod voted, after some discussion, "that further consideration of the articles of union be postponed until the union committee has reported the draft of the constitution for the proposed body."[63] The United Church had a brisk discussion on the interpretation of article three on "unionism." Would this article permit fellowship with other Lutherans, for example, the Swedish Augustana Synod, the Danish bodies, the English-speaking synods, as well as the other Norwegian groups, so that in the future there might be, not one *Norwegian* Lutheran Church, but *one* Lutheran Church in America? Moreover, would this clause in the articles of union allow participation in the world mission conferences, the Student Volunteer Movement, the American Bible Society, and, in general, the great social movements? Furthermore, could a pastor participate in a funeral service with, for example, a Methodist minister? By way of answer it was stated that it was impossible to go into details at this point. Rather one must be satisfied with the general principle expressed in the clause and then leave the decision in individual cases to the judgment of those concerned as each problem presented itself. Furthermore, it was said that it was self-evident that Lutherans could not cooperate with those who denied God's Word, or with those who either had no confessions at all or who subscribed to a different confession. Not to practice pulpit and altar fellowship with the Reformed churches was not evidence of an intolerant spirit, a persecution complex, or exclusivism; rather, it indicated that Lutherans were not doctrinally indifferent and that it meant something to be a Lutheran. With this explanation, the articles of union were unanimously adopted.[64]

---
[63]*Beretning . . . Hauges Synode . . . 1914*, p. 119.
[64]"Det 25de Aarsmøde," *Lutheraneren*, XX (1914), 816; *Beretning . . . Den f. Kirke 1914*, pp. 214-215.

As one might expect, the Norwegian Synod did not give unanimous approval to the articles. The reports reveal that the spirit of conflict mounted as the discussion alternated between the majority and minority elements.[65] The latter stated that conscience prohibited accepting the articles, an act which would imply that unity in doctrine existed. The majority reminded the opposition that they too possessed consciences—consciences which demanded union. The second day of the discussion was perhaps unique in the history of the Synod: in order to give the laity an opportunity to express itself no pastors were permitted the floor until those laymen who desired to speak had spoken.[66] Lay voices clearly indicated a pro-union sentiment which feared that "the good cause" might be "talked to death," and delayed by unnecessary doctrinal debate.[67] The vote on the articles of union as such resulted in 360 affirmative and 170 negative ballots.[68]

It was clear to all concerned that a serious situation existed within the Synod and that, unless a reconciliation were effected, the church would be irreparably damaged. In view of this, a "Peace Committee" was appointed to resolve the tension and report to the 1916 synod.[69]

The "Peace Committee" met February 22-23, 1915.[70] Two

---

[65]*Beretning . . . Synoden . . . 1914*, pp. 69-141. Cf. *Minneapolis Tidende*, October 22, 1914, p. 8; and "Synod Meeting in Sioux Falls, South Dakota," *Lutheran Herald*, IX (1914), 1042-1043.

[66]*Ibid.*, p. 109.

[67]*Ibid.*, pp. 113-114.

[68]A study of the balloting on this question reveals some interesting facts. In the first place, the ratio between the clerical and lay vote differed widely. The ratio in the affirmative vote was 138 (clerical) to 222 (lay); in the negative 96 (clerical) to 74 (lay). The noteworthy item is the fact that in the negative vote the laymen numbered *fewer* than the pastors in contrast to the affirmative vote which was dominated by the laity. In the second place, the register of names in the roll call ballot shows that some, though voting against the union, later decided to participate in the merger. Names well known in the present Evangelical Lutheran Church are listed in the minority vote, e. g., T. F. Gullixson, J. C. K. Preus, O. J. H. Preus, and N. M. Ylvisaker. *Ibid.*, pp. 137, 139.

[69]"Synod Meeting in Sioux Falls, South Dakota," *Lutheran Herald*, IX (1914), 1043; and *Beretning . . . Synoden . . . 1914*, p. 157.

[70]A typewritten copy of the minutes of this meeting is to be found in "The G. T. Lee Papers." Cf. *Beretning . . . Synoden . . . 1916*, pp. 137-140. G. T. Lee, a member of the committee, was also one of the two secretaries. Lee, a master of Gabbelsberger shorthand, was often used to make verbatim accounts of important meetings even outside the Synod, as for example, the stenographic account of the constituting convention of the United Church in 1890, and the record of the tumultuous Dawson convention of 1892, when the Augsburg Controversy was at its height.

questions, one centering on the doctrinal soundness of the *Opgjør* and the other concerned with "unionism," were fruitlessly argued. When votes were taken, the committee divided evenly. Peace had not been achieved by the "Peace Committee."[71]

More promising and fruitful were the joint union committee meetings of the same year. At the first, April 13-15, 1915,[72] Stub read a statement calling attention to two obstacles to union: (1) the unremoved parentheses in paragraph one of the *Opgjør* and (2) the unretracted judgment of the United Church committee in 1910 over Stub's theses on election. The Norwegian Synod had already removed the parentheses, and the United Church had voted to do so providing the other bodies did. However, since Hauge's Synod had not done so, the joint committee proposed to Hauge's Synod that it agree to the removal. As for the second obstacle pointed out by Stub, the committee resolved to turn this matter over to the separate consideration of the United Church representatives, who later reported that whereas the judgment named was not spoken by the United Church (as the United Church itself had previously declared), the statement could not be retracted by that body. Moreover, since the *Opgjør* ("Settlement") by its very name and nature was the determining word between the synods on the question of election, it annulled all previous articles, judgments, and declarations which contradicted its constituent articles.

The committee of the Norwegian Synod reported its essential agreement with the interpretation given the name *Opgjør* by the United Church committee, and a resolution embodying this was unanimously adopted by the joint committee.

The remainder of the sessions were devoted to the organizational problems confronting the proposed church. In the proposed constitution the article designating the name of the

---
[71]No further meetings were held and by the time its report was presented to the 1916 convention, the union matter had already been disposed of. *Ibid.*, p. 140.
[72]The manuscript minutes are in the archives, The Evangelical Lutheran Church, Luther Seminary, St. Paul, Minnesota.

new church offered three alternatives: (1) "The United Lutheran Synod in America," (2) "The Norwegian Lutheran Church of America," and (3) "The United Norwegian Lutheran Synod in America." A trial ballot resulted in the choice of "The Norwegian Lutheran Church of America."[73] After further discussion on individual articles in the proposed constitution, the committee adopted an explanatory resolution on lay activity to be appended to the articles of union.[74]

When the three synodical union committees again assembled in May,[75] the trial vote on the name of the new church was made official, and the amended constitutional draft was authorized for presentation to the synodical conventions of 1915.

The proposed constitution contained seven chapters, each of which was subdivided. The first chapter on name, creed, and rites committed the new church to the Scriptures as "the revealed Word of God and therefore the only source and rule of faith, doctrine, and life." The confessions commonly held by Norwegian Lutherans were named as a true statement of the doctrine of the Word of God,[76] and liturgical usages were referred, as in the articles of union, to the decision of the congregations, but with strong recommendation for the ritual of the Church of Norway as used in America.

The second chapter delineated in general terms the object of the organization, following the familiar terminology of most church constitutions. Chapters three, four, and five dealt with ecclesiastical polity. The church body was described as composed of congregations who subscribed to the constitution, and pastors, professors, and missionaries who by ordination or other means had been accepted by the church. A congrega-

---

[73]This name had been proposed at the separate meeting of the United Church committee in July, 1912, *Supra*, p. 189, n. 20. It is worth noting that the name approved by the largest number stressed the "Norwegian" rather than the "united" aspect of the new church. This gives credibility to the charge of "racialism" made by Theo. Graebner on the occasion of his resignation from the editorship of the Synod's English organ. *Lutheran Herald*, VIII (1913), 526-527.

[74]See the comments in *The Union Documents* . . . E. L. C., footnote, p. 30.

[75]The manuscript minutes are to be found in the archives, The Evangelical Lutheran Church, Luther Seminary, St. Paul, Minn.

[76]The confessions are: (1 the catholic symbols, the Apostolic, Nicene, and Athanasian; (2) the unaltered Augsburg Confession and Luther's Small Catechism.

tion obtained membership in the church when it had been admitted to one of the districts, the church having been divided into as many of the same as deemed necessary. The church should determine the boundaries and constitution of the districts which should be subdivided into circuits, meetings of which should consider doctrinal, devotional, and practical subjects. The number and size of the circuits should be set by the districts. The fourth chapter specified a general convention each triennium,[77] with special conventions determined by the church or at the call of the president, requested by the church council or at least forty congregations. A distinction was made between voting and advisory members of the convention, the former being active pastors and lay delegates, the latter being pastors without voting rights, permanently elected professors, foreign missionaries, the chairman of the board of trustees, the treasurer, the superintendents of charitable institutions, the editors of official organs, and such as might be voted by the convention. The convention should have legislative jurisdiction on all matters not reserved to the districts by their constitutions, together with those matters appealed from the district conventions. A resolution, which in one and the same year was adopted by at least two-thirds of the districts should have the same validity as if adopted by the church.[78] Matters of doctrine and conscience were not to be decided by majority vote but by the Word and confessions of the church.

The officers of the new body should be a president (elected for a term of six years), a vice-president, a secretary, a treasurer (three-year terms), and district presidents (elected by the districts for three-year terms).[79] A church council, composed of the general president, the district presidents, and one layman from each district, should function as an official board.

[77] Biennial conventions were voted in 1926. See *Annual Report . . . NLCA . . . 1926*, p. 221.
[78] This portion, known as Section 18, was altered in 1926 and 1928 to read as follows: "No legislation for the general Church Body shall be adopted at district conventions." *Report . . . 1926*, p. 103; *Report . . . 1928*, p. 188.
[79] A second vice-president was added later and the terms of the officers (with exception of president) were changed to two years. The district president's term was extended to six years. *Report . . . 1926*, p. 103.

The duties of this council, of the president, secretary, and treasurer were all enumerated and provision was made for the establishment of a board of trustees in accordance with the articles of incorporation. Boards for the supervision of missions, charities, publications, etc., were provided for and their powers and fields of activity were to be defined by the church.

Chapter six assured that the church should maintain schools for the education of pastors, teachers, and missionaries, and colleges for the Christian instruction of the young. Other institutions such as deaconess institutes, orphans' homes, etc., were also sanctioned. Professors and teachers in the schools of the church were to be elected or removed by the church, a two-thirds vote being required. The last chapter made provision for amendments to the constitution.

This constitutional draft was approved for presentation to the synods, and thereupon the joint committee adjourned at the call of the synodical presidents.

When the three synods convened in the late spring of 1915, it was known that the Norwegian Synod would not take action on the question of union.[80] Nevertheless, President Stub made reference to the union movement by saying that no protests against the action of the previous synod on the questions of union had been received from any of the congregations. Furthermore, he read the resolutions prepared by the joint union committee together with the proposed constitution for the new church body.[81]

The United Church, observing its twenty-fifth anniversary at the 1915 convention, unanimously accepted the constitution.[82] A discussion occurred at only four points: (1) the constitution might be construed as defining the church as a body composed of congregations and pastors—should it not be just congregations? (2) the church body might tyrannize the districts; (3) it might be preferable to limit the election of professors at church schools by two-thirds vote to con-

---
[80]*Supra*, pp. 204-205.
[81]*Beretning* . . . *Synoden* . . . *1915*, p. 31-36.
[82]*Beretning* . . . *Den f. Kirke* . . . *1915*, p. 243.

cern only the *permanent* professors; and (4) it might be preferable to have convention representation from *every* congregation, despite how many there might be in a parish.[83] Despite this discussion the constitution was not altered.

The 1915 convention of Hauge's Synod was held in Grand Forks, North Dakota, June 9-16. Some discussion for and against the union was heard at this convention, revealing that a minority element was developing in this body also. The opposition seemed to center about the fear that the theology and spirit of the Norwegian Synod minority might gain the ascendancy in the new church.[84] However, highly regarded men like C. J. Eastvold and E. O. Ringstad spoke favorably for the cause, urging it on the basis that Hauge's Synod was not the only synod which possessed the best and purest principles of church life.[85] Upon motion by the former, Hauge's Synod sanctioned the removal of the parentheses in the first article of the *Opgjør,* thus appeasing the Norwegian Synod.[86] However, the constitution was not approved at this meeting. Because the publication of the constitutional draft did not permit sufficient time for congregational consideration of the instrument, the synod voted, after some discussion, to refer the constitution as well as the articles of union to the congregations for approval. The congregations were instructed to give their delegates power to act conclusively on both documents at the annual convention of 1916.[87]

The synodical meetings of 1915 had revealed that the union was not a foregone conclusion. It was still an open question within both Hauge's Synod and the Norwegian Synod whether these bodies would participate in the merger of 1917. At best, it seemed probable that a minority in both groups would remain unwon for the union cause.

---

[83]"Det 26de Aarsmøde," *Lutheraneren,* XXI (1915), 833-834.
[84]Bruce, "A Brief History of Union Negotiations," *The Union Documents . . . E. L. C.,* p. 21. The previous year had witnessed a growing hesitation about union in some quarters of Hauge's Synod. Cf. "Meeting of the Hauge Synod at Red Wing, Minnesota," *Lutheran Herald,* IX (1914), 582; "The Hauge Synod," *ibid.,* p. 604.
[85]*Minneapolis Tidende,* June 17, 1915, p. 8.
[86]*Beretning . . . Hauges Synode . . . 1915,* p. 162.
[87]*Ibid.,* pp. 179-180.

The Final Steps to the Merger

By 1916, clearly distinguishable minorities had developed in both Hauge's Synod and the Norwegian Synod. The records reveal that of the two the former was considered the more serious. This seems contrary to what one might be led to expect from the history of opposition within the Norwegian Synod. However, the leaders of the churches in 1916 made no secret of the fact that they were more concerned about the Hauge's minority than that which existed in the Synod. President Dahl called specific attention to it in his annual report of that year;[88] the Norwegian Synod took cognizance of the situation;[89] and Hauge's Synod's acting president, J. J. Ekse, bemoaned the threatened rupture in his church.[90] An element in Hauge's Synod was convinced that the merger of the churches would quench the spirit of "true" Haugeanism and make room for "unconverted" ministers and "unworthy" communicants in the church.[91] In view of this, preparations were made in both the United Church and the Norwegian Synod to consummate the merger without Hauge's Synod.

The task which faced two of the synodical meetings in 1916 was the adoption of the constitution.[92] Hauge's Synod had referred this document together with the articles of union to the congregations, and the Norwegian Synod had declared a year's cessation of union discussion. The United Church, as has been noted, had already given unanimous assent to both documents.

Moreover, before the union could be actualized, it was also necessary to prepare legal statements which required the approval of the contracting parties. These so-called "enabling acts" had been formulated by Attorney Andreas Ueland and

---

[88] *Beretning . . . Den f. Kirke . . . 1916*, p. 41.
[89] *Beretning . . . Synoden . . . 1916*, p. 47
[90] *Beretning . . . Hauges Synode . . . 1916*, p. 61.
[91] "The Hauge Synod," *Lutheran Herald*, IX (1914), 604.
[92] Hauge's Synod in 1914-1915 had taken no action on the union documents, so it was faced with adopting the articles of union as well as the constitution. The Synod had adopted the articles, *Supra*, p. 204.

were to be presented for confirmation by the church conventions.[93] The first enabling act provided for the final adoption of all previously ratified documents. The second provided for the consummation of the actual merger of the three bodies, or in case Hauge's Synod withdrew, the union of the United Church and the Synod.[94] The third provided for the transfer of all synodically owned property to the new church.

The United Church convention was held in Fargo, North Dakota, June 15-20, 1916, ". . . the shortest annual meeting in the history of the United Church."[95] On Friday afternoon, June 16, the 1028 voting members turned to the item which held the chief interest for the delegates, the union question. Oddly enough a motion was made that the *Opgjør,* the articles of union, and the constitution be referred to the congregations for approval. A storm of protest preceded the defeat of the motion. It was the sense of the meeting that a referendum at this stage was entirely pointless and supremely inappropriate.[96] When the enabling acts were presented, therefore, the convention voted its unanimous approval.[97] A new union committee, charged with the responsibility of implementing the actions taken by the convention and disposing of the many practical problems of organization, was then elected. It consisted of President T. H. Dahl, Pastors Peder Tangjerd, and Severin Gunderson, Professors J. N. Kildahl and L. W. Boe.[98]

A mere recital of these events fails to convey the mounting gratitude and joy which characterized the convention as it progressed successfully through the final union item. The reporter for the English organ of the United Church described the drama in these words:

---

[93]*Beretning . . . Den f. Kirke . . . 1916,* pp. 60-64.
[94]Identical sets of the enabling acts were presented to the United Church and the Synod. Hauge's Synod received a set which omitted the above stated provision for union of only the United Church and the Synod. *Beretning . . . Hauges Synode . . . 1916,* pp. 231-234.
[95]"The Twenty-seventh Annual Meeting," *The United Lutheran,* IX (1916), 406.
[96]*Ibid.,* p. 390.
[97]*Beretning . . . Den f. Kirke . . . 1916,* pp. 60-63.
[98]*Ibid.,* p. 231. Mr. S. H. Holstad, chairman of the United Church board of trustees, also served as a representative of the board of trustees. Bruce, "A Brief History . . . " in *The Union Documents . . . E. L. C.,* p. 23.

The vast assembly then arose and sang, "Min sjæl, min sjæl, lov Herren," and Dr. Kildahl led in fervent prayer, thanking God for swaying the hearts of the Norwegian Lutheran people so that they ere long will largely constitute only one church body, and invoked the blessings of God upon the union which is to be finally consummated next year. The moment was intensely dramatic. Tears flowed freely down the bronzed cheeks of many of the sturdy [lay] delegates as they caught glimpses of the blessed future which seems to lie in store for the Lutheran church of our land.[99]

While the United Church was in session, Hauge's Synod was meeting in Red Wing, Minnesota.[100] A report on the congregational referendum was given by the synodical secretary, Pastor N. J. Løhre. It showed that sixty-four congregations, representing a membership of 9,081, were unconditionally in favor of union. Eleven congregations, representing 1,379 persons, favored merger "with reservations." Twice this number of congregations with 3,942 members were unconditionally opposed to a union. Six congregations with 1,551 members were opposed "with reservations." Fourteen congregations, numbering 1,296 persons declared that they were neutral.[101]

Before considering the three enabling acts, a motion was made that Hauge's Synod adopt the articles of union and the constitution. The roll call vote on this showed a substantial minority opposing the motion.[102] It was apparent from the discussion that many had voted conditionally, since in their opinion certain questions required clarification before they could vote unconditionally for or against union.[103]

In order to avoid a schism and to secure the largest possible support for the enabling acts, Professor G. M. Bruce presented an "interpretation," previously prepared by Pastor N. J. Løhre, in which the views of Hauge's Synod on certain portions of the articles of union and the constitution were set forth.[104] Special reference was made to that item in the articles of union which

---

[99]"The Twenty-seventh Annual Meeting," *The United Lutheran*, IX (1916), 390.
[100]June 14-21, 1916.
[101]*Beretning . . . Hauges Synode . . . 1916*, p. 68.
[102]The vote: 142 yes, 103 no. *Ibid.*, p. 229.
[103]The account of the discussion is given in *ibid.*, pp. 201-205.
[104]*Beretning . . . Hauges Synode . . . 1916*, pp. 229-231.

forbade unionism and cooperation with non-Lutheran groups. The "interpretation" defined "cooperation" as "organized and continuous activity of a churchly character or also incidental and occasional reciprocal relations in the preaching of the Gospel and administration of the Sacraments." However, the statement continued, such things as occasional participation in weddings, funerals, graduation exercises at public schools, national holiday programs, and the like, where pastors of other churches participated was not to be regarded as unionism. Furthermore, cooperation in such movements as embrace the whole Christian Church (the ecumenical mission Conferences, the Student Volunteer Movement, the Student Christian Federation, and the Laymen's Missionary Movement) was not to be denied.

The "interpretation" continued with a reference to Hauge's Synod's non-liturgical heritage. It was stated that the Haugean emphasis on simplicity of ritual should be given equal standing with the liturgical rites of the Synod and the United Church. Quite in keeping with this explanation was another which would not insist on making confession and absolution a required condition for participation in the Holy Communion. However, those Haugean congregations which retained the practice of confession and absolution should follow the general, conditional absolution without the imposition of hands. In order to perpetuate this custom, Hauge's Synod expected the instruction at the seminary to include a presentation of the Haugean liturgical practices.[105]

The reading of this explanation and its vigorous approval by the convention[106] prepared the way for the presentation of the three enabling acts. Considered one by one, each was adopted by a substantial majority, the vote being 165 to forty, 155 to thirty-one, and 134 to sixteen.[107]

---

[105] Pastor Løhre, the author of the statement, explained to the convention that he had sought to incorporate all the reasons offered by those congregations which had voted "with reservations." *Ibid.*, footnote, p. 204.

[106] The convention approved the statement by a vote of 187 to 18. *Ibid.*, p. 205.

[107] *Loc. cit.* and *ibid.*, p. 234. Hauge's Synod's union committee asked that this statement be referred to the United Church and Norwegian Synod with the request that these

Noteworthy was the fact that discussions at Red Wing were conducted with surprisingly little display of passions. Orderliness and an absence of bitterness characterized the whole proceedings.[108] In this atmosphere a committee was appointed to meet with the Synod and the United Church to complete arrangements for the union. The members were C. J. Eastvold, J. L. Lasseson, J. J. Ekse, M. O. Wee, and G. M. Bruce.[109]

The church council of the Norwegian Synod had called an extraordinary convention for the year 1916 to deliberate the question of union. The "Peace Committee" appointed in 1914 had met and, as we have observed, was unable to report a reconciliation between the majority and minority. In April President Stub had sent out, as a supplement to the synodical organ, his pamphlet, *Foreningssagens Gang* (The Course of the Union Movement), in which he took occasion to defend his personal interest in the union and to refute the arguments of the minority.[110] In answer to this a tract supporting the position of the latter was published. Widely distributed shortly before the opening of the synodical convention in May, it fanned the flames of opposition.[111]

It was in an atmosphere highly charged with conflicting emotions that the Synod met in Minneapolis, May 18-24, 1916. There was no doubt that an organized minority would exert every influence to forestall the union.[112] An animated discussion, in which professors, pastors, and laymen gave heated expression to their views, revealed that the two sides were in no compromising mood.[113]

The test of strength came in the vote on the three enabling acts. The first, providing for final adoption of all previously

---
synods accept those whose views were therein expressed into the union with full recognition. Professor Wee was to present the matter to the Synod and Professor Bruce to the United Church. Approval was given by both churches in 1917. *Beretning . . . Hauges Synode . . . Synoden . . . Den f. Kirke . . . samt Organisationsmøde for Den Norsk Lutherske Kirke i Amerika . . . 1917*, pp. 100, 148, 166, 457, 467. Cf. *infra*, p. 221.
[108]*Beretning . . . Hauges Synode . . . 1916*, p. 222.
[109]*Ibid.*, p. 303.
[110]Stub, *Foreningssagens Gang*, pp. 27-29, 33-48.
[111]O. Turmo (ed.), *Svar paa Tiltale* (Clifford, North Dakota: n. n., [1916], pp. 18-38, 41-44, 52-54.
[112]*Beretning . . . Synoden . . . 1916*, pp. 48-49.
[113]*Ibid.*, pp. 48-110.

accepted documents, was approved by a vote of 522 to 202. The second, pledging the Synod to union with the other bodies, passed by a vote of 491 to 187. The third, authorizing the transfer of property, carried by a vote of 482 to 181.[114]

The hope for reconciliation all but disappeared in the concluding discussion on the union. Pastor N. N. Boe had presented a motion that the church council and all church officers, pastors and professors loyally support the resolutions of the Synod. He explained that the purpose of the motion was to assure peace and to authorize the church council to see to it that the decisions of the church would be carried out by each and every member.

Pastor I. B. Torrison immediately presented a statement which bore the signatures of 176 men. It requested the Synod to advise the other synods that only acceptance of the minority's views would make possible the entrance of this group into the merger. To deny this resolution, the minority declared, would lead to a break in the Synod.[115]

When Boe's proposal was adopted, and the motions to implement the Torrison resolution were laid on the table, it was clear that the sentiments of the minority would quickly crystallize into action.[116] A committee of three was appointed by a "rump" session of the minority to promote the interests of this group. A statement was forthcoming in which the minority asserted that it had never been so strong as at the present moment. Many who had not previously shared the views of the minority were now sympathetic to it because they were opposed to the "autocratic authority which has been given to the church council to cow 'Minority people . . .'" If conditions could not be improved, enough congregations would dissociate themselves from the union movement to be able to assert once again the great motto of the Synod: "The Word alone and Grace alone."[117]

Meanwhile, the Synod made but one alteration in the per-

---
[114]*Ibid.,* pp. 45-48.
[115]*Ibid.,* pp. 98-99.
[116]*Ibid.,* p. 179.
[117]S. C. Ylvisaker (ed.), *op. cit.,* pp. 113-114.

sonnel of its union committee of 1912. The men who were charged with the responsibility of completing the necessary details of the merger, together with representatives of the other bodies, were H. G. Stub, J. Nordby, I. D. Ylvisaker, K. Bjørgo (to replace O. P. Vangsness), and D. C. Jordahl.[118]

The status of the union cause in June, 1916, was clear to all concerned. In the first place the three synods by decisive votes were pledged to an organic merger which should take place the next year. In the second place, each body recognized that no further doctrinal issues faced the contracting parties. The task of the fifteen-man joint union committee would be to provide satisfactory solution for the numerous practical questions involved in merging the varied activities of the three groups. In the third place, it was recognized that in both Hauge's Synod and the Norwegian Synod minority elements threatened to separate themselves from the union movement. In Hauge's Synod the explanatory statement regarding the union documents was calculated to remove the major portion, if not all, of the opposition to the merger. The situation in the Synod, however, was now more serious, as no instrument of reconciliation had been forthcoming from its 1916 convention.

The duties which faced the joint union committee between the conventions of the church bodies in 1916 and 1917 were broad in scope and detailed in nature. Five formal meetings, totalling twenty-eight days, were held between October, 1916, and May, 1917.[119] A member of the committee, G. M. Bruce, has given a concise commentary on the manner in which the committee approached its task. It divided itself into numerous subcommittees, usually with one representative of each of the three synods. The more important problems were handled by subcommittees with two members from each body. These subcommittees would meet with the boards in charge of the finan-

---
[118]*Supra*, p. 188.
[119]Manuscript and published minutes of the meetings are to be found among the union documents in the archives, The Evangelical Lutheran Church, Luther Seminary, St. Paul, Minnesota. The pertinent documents are as follows: Item 14, the meeting of October 10-12, 1916; Item 1, the meeting of December 5-7, 1916; Item 12, the meeting of January 23-27, 1917. Item 2, the meeting of March 20-29, 1917; and Item 19c, the meeting of May 1, 1917.

cial, educational, charitable, missionary, and other institutions and activities of the three churches. Each subcommittee was assigned a particular ecclesiastical department. Reports of findings, recommendations, drafts of rules and regulations were given to the joint committee for final action, often with representatives of the various departments present to press their special interests. On the whole, the joint committee received excellent cooperation, and the many problems were settled in an unselfish and conciliatory spirit. Only two or three decisions of the joint committee were upset by dissatisfied parties, necessitating the carrying over of the dispute into the new church.[120]

The listed accomplishments of the joint committee are impressive. It negotiated successfully with the minority of the Synod; drafted plans for dividing the church into seven districts in the United States and one in Canada, for incorporating the church, for establishing an English Association (composed of English-speaking congregations), and for creating a Board of Education, which had not been included in the constitution. Since no Minnesota law provided for the incorporation of two or more merging ecclesiastical corporations, it drafted a bill to present to the legislature.[121] Besides drafting constitutions for the districts and Luther Theological Seminary, it prepared rules for the various boards: home missions, foreign missions, church extension, pensions, charities, and the trustees. Provisions for consolidating the publishing concerns, the official organs, and the youth work of the three groups were made. The legal documents covering the merger of educational institutions, the transfer of properties, and amendments to charters, constitutions and bylaws were provided. Finally, an agenda for the constituting convention of the Norwegian Lutheran Church of America together with a plan for the equitable distribution of official positions among representatives of the three synods were adopted.

---
[120] Bruce, "A Brief History . . ." in *The Union Documents* . . . *E. L. C.*, pp. 24-25.
[121] A copy is conveniently printed in *The Union Documents* . . . *E. L. C.*, pp. 71-72. Cf. Minnesota Legislative Enactments, 1917, S. F. No. 179, c. 107.

By this time it was evident that the laity of the Synod as well as of the other churches was in favor of union, and the congregations of the minority pastors were not immune to this feeling. In fact, many of the latter found their pastorates intolerable because of the attitude of the pro-union laity.[122] Knowledge of these circumstances led L. W. Boe and J. N. Kildahl of the United Church to conclude that the leaders of the minority might still be won for the union movement. With this in mind, Boe and Kildahl made a special trip to Decorah, Iowa, to interview C. K. Preus and I. B. Torrison relative to further negotiations.[123] This conversation resulted in the decision to have Preus and Torrison present the case of the minority to the union committee. This was done at its meeting, October 10-12, 1916, where Preus and Torrison requested that a separate doctrinal agreement incorporating the desired changes in the *Opgjør* be negotiated with the Synod minority.[124] After a discussion, which included the reading of Attorney Ueland's opinion concerning the legality of such a procedure, the whole matter was placed in the hands of a subcommittee composed of Ylvisaker, Tangjerd, and Wee.[125] Negotiations with Preus and Torrison led the joint committee to submit the following resolution to the 1917 annual meetings of the three synods:

> While the annual meeting reaffirms its position on the unaltered *Opgjør* as the basis for the merger of the three conferring bodies, it expressly takes cognizance of the three reservations ... in the request of Prof. C. K. Preus and the Rev. I. B. Torrison; nevertheless the annual meeting hereby invites that group of men and congregations whose views are expressed in the above cited request to participate in the formation of the new body with full equality and mutual brotherly recognition.[126]

The above resolution proved unacceptable to Preus and Torrison, and consequently a meeting with a newly-appointed

---

[122] Ylvisaker (ed.), *op. cit.*, p. 109.
[123] *Beretning ... Synoden ... 1917*, p. 149. Cf. letter from C. K. Preus and I. B. Torrison to P. Tangjerd, December 11, 1916, in the union documents, Item 29, archives, The Evangelical Lutheran Church, St. Paul, Minnesota.
[124] "Minoriteten i Den norske synode," *Beretning ... 1917*, pp. 460-462.
[125] "Fællesmøde [10 okt. 1916]," p. 2. This document is Item 14 in the union documents at the archives, The Evangelical Lutheran Church, St. Paul, Minnesota.
[126] *Beretning ... 1917*, p. 464.

The Union of 1917

subcommittee was arranged at Austin, Minnesota, where agreement was reached.[127] This was reported to the joint union committee meeting of December 5-7, 1916, at Minneapolis. Here the previously adopted resolution to be presented to each of the synodical conventions was altered to include:

[The annual meeting] declares that there is nothing in the aforementioned request [of Preus and Torrison] which is contrary to Scripture and the Confessions, and that we regard the position taken in that document as a sufficient expression of unity in faith. . . .

Note. It is obvious that the above cited resolution must not be construed to mean that the *Opgjør* as a basis for the union of the three contracting bodies thereby has been abridged or altered.[128]

On this basis the joint committee extended an invitation to the Synod minority to participate in the 1917 merger.

At this point, Preus and Torrison called a meeting of the minority to be held at the West Hotel, Minneapolis, January 17-18, 1917. Most of those who attended agreed to accept the invitation.[129] A report of this decision was made to the joint committee in Minneapolis, January 23-27, 1917, by Lauritz S. Swenson. As the third member of the committee to represent the minority, he read a communication prepared by Preus and Torrison, which conveyed the information that the minority had accepted the invitation of the joint union committee in the form that it was issued, anticipating its approval by the synodical conventions.[130]

When the synodical meetings of 1917 were held, Hauge's Synod, the United Church, and the Synod approved the resolution of the joint committee.[131] In this way, the churches pre-

---

[127]*Beretning* . . . *1917*, p. 149. This colloquy produced what came to be known as the "Austin Agreement." Cf. "The 'Austin Agreement,'" *The Union Documents* . . . *E. L. C.*, pp. 65-66.
[128]*Beretning* . . . *1917*, p. 466.
[129]*Ibid.*, pp. 149-150. A partial listing of the minority may be found in *Beretning* . . . *Synoden* . . . *1916*, pp. 49, 81. Preus and Torrison, in a special visit to St. Louis, solicited the opinion of the Concordia Seminary faculty. Despite an ambiguous reply and consequent misunderstanding, Preus and Torrison recommended union. See J. C. K. Preus, *The Union Movement and the "Minority,"* 1917 (privately printed, 1959).
[130]"Fællesmøde . . . den 23 jan. 1917 og følgende dage," pp. 1-3. This is Item 12 in the union documents in the archives of The Evangelical Lutheran Church, Luther Seminary, St. Paul, Minnesota. Cf. *Beretning* . . . *1917*, pp. 150-151.
[131]For the decisions of the synods see *Beretning* . . . *1917*, pp. 96 (Hauge's Synod), 149 (Norwegian Synod), and 449 (United Church). Only eighteen votes were cast against the resolution within the Norwegian Synod.

pared the way for the acceptance of the Synod minority into the new church, thus allowing the minority to fulfill its real desire for union without losing face. The essentially correct analysis of the union feeling within the minority, made by L. W. Boe and J. N. Kildahl, had thus been confirmed.[132]

It was not completely unexpected, however, that a minority of the minority would not participate in the union. A number of congregations and pastors sought to continue the legal existence of the Norwegian Synod. To this end a meeting was held at the Aberdeen Hotel, St. Paul, Minnesota, during the union convention of 1917. About forty pastors and laymen, equally divided, elected officers to provide *ad interim* leadership. These men were B. Harstad, president; J. A. Molstad, vice-president; C. M. Kittlesen, secretary; and O. T. Lee, treasurer. Inquiry revealed that the Norwegian Synod could not be legally perpetuated, and, therefore, decision was made to establish a new synod. At this meeting a committee of three members from the Synodical Conference assured the assembly that moral support in their contemplated action would be forthcoming from the Synodical Conference. The publication of a pamphlet describing the plans of the little group was then authorized.[133] The next year, June 14, 1918, the Norwegian Synod of the American Evangelical Lutheran Church was organized with the announced purpose of continuing "true Lutheranism" among Norwegians in America.[134]

Meanwhile, the three merging bodies were making final disposition of their synodical affairs and bringing their independent existence to a conclusion.[135] Hauge's Synod, as we

---

[132]President H. G. Stub made special reference in his annual report of 1917 to the outstanding practical sagacity of L. W. Boe in the matter of negotiating the union between the divergent elements. *Ibid.*, p. 131.

[133]"Imod Forening," *Minneapolis Tidende*, June 14, 1917, p. 2.

[134]For an account of the establishment of the new synod and a defense thereof see Ylvisaker (ed.), *op. cit.*, pp. 115-120. This church is colloquially known among Norwegian Lutherans as "the Little Synod" or "The Minority Synod." Application for membership in the Synodical Conference was made in 1919. The following year the synod was received into its membership. *Ibid.*, p. 122. Its name was recently changed to the Evangelical Lutheran Synod.

[135]By the arrangement of the joint union committee each synod was to meet in St. Paul, Minnesota, June 6-8, 1917. The following days they were to meet together as the Norwegian Lutheran Church of America.

have noted, was also plagued with a "minority" problem, settlement of which was anticipated at the synodical conventions of 1917. However, the Hauge's minority held forth the acceptance of the 1916 explanation by the other synods as a condition of joining the new church. In an attempt to settle this matter, the Hauge's Synod union committee met with representatives of the minority[136] and the joint union committee. No decision was reached but the joint committee advised the United Church and the Synod to allow the explanation as a basis for the entrance of Hauge's minority into the merger. Professor G. M. Bruce was instructed to bring the question before the United Church which approved the matter unanimously.[137] Professor M. O. Wee, as the emissary to the Norwegian Synod, encountered serious misgivings. A brisk discussion was followed by Wee's declaration that acknowledgment of those Haugeans who adhered to the specified explanation as members of the new church did not commit the Synod to an approval of the said explanation. With this understanding of the matter the Synod gave its assent, but on the condition that it retained a complete right to witness against the practices enumerated in the explanation.[138] Hauge's Synod, therefore, prepared to enter as a whole into the new church.[139] One obstacle, however, remained to be removed. Hauge's Synod had been unable to comply with that portion of the articles of union which stipulated the payment of all debts before the merger. A resolution requesting a waiver of this provision was approved by the three synods.[140] Finally, Hauge's Synod was the only group to change any of its officers in 1917. Prominent in the union movement, but not presently an officer of the church, C. J. Eastvold was elected president so that he might represent Hauge's Synod in the union festivities.[141]

The major problem confronting the United Church before

---
[136]*Beretning* . . . *1917*, p. 96. Minority committee: Pastors Borgen, Lund, Oppedahl, and Hovland. Other minority leaders were Pastor G. O. Mona and Mr. O. A. Oace.
[137]*Ibid.*, p. 457.
[138]*Ibid.*, p. 166.
[139]*Ibid.*, p. 100.
[140]*Ibid.*, pp. 100-101, 160, 457.
[141]*Ibid.*, p. 95.

it could enter the union was the delicate question of selecting its theological professors for the new seminary. According to the agreement, the Synod and the United Church were to have four professors each, and Hauge's Synod two. The faculty of the United Church consisted of five members. The entire faculty resigned and a new election was held. The vote resulted in the election of Professors M. O. Bøckman, E. Kr. Johnsen, C. M. Weswig, and J. N. Kildahl.[142]

On Friday afternoon, June 8, the three synods ended their separate existence. The next day the three became the Norwegian Lutheran Church of America.

The festive union ceremonies which occurred June 9-10, 1917, have been described by Abdel Ross Wentz as "the greatest church demonstration ever held by Norwegians anywhere in the world."[143] The plan was to devote Saturday to the formal ceremonies of organization. A service of worship, a Reformation festival, and an ordination service were scheduled for Sunday. The remainder of the week through Thursday would be consumed by the business of setting the new church on its course.

On Saturday morning at eight o'clock lay and clerical delegates of the three churches met at the St. Paul Armory from which they were to march together to the St. Paul Auditorium, the scene of the union festivities.[144] The procession began at eight-thirty and was led by Hauge's Synod, the oldest of the three churches. The Norwegian Synod and the United Church representatives followed. Each group was preceded by a flag-bearer.[145] Church officials, professors, pastors, and lay delegates

---

[142]*Ibid.*, pp. 453-454. The fifth professor was M. J. Stolee, professor of missions. At the organizational meeting of the Norwegian Lutheran Church, Stub was elected president, and therefore suggested that, since the Synod had no other candidate to take his (Stub's) place on the faculty (he had been teaching in the Synod seminary as well as being president of the church), the church elect Stolee to his place. This was done. *Ibid.*, p. 502.

[143]Wentz, *A Basic History of Lutheranism in America* (Philadelphia: Muhlenberg Press, 1955), p. 267.

[144]An official account of the proceedings is recorded in *Beretning . . . Den Norsk Lutherske Kirke i Amerika . . . 1917*, pp. 486-494.

[145]These were Governor Peter Norbeck of South Dakota (Hauge's Synod), Mr. John A. Berg, a Wisconsin banker (the Synod), and Hon. Oley Nelson, an Iowa Civil War veteran (the United Church).

followed, the whole procession being led by mounted police. The procession, eight abreast, separated into columns of twos as the marchers entered the auditorium. Already an estimated eight thousand people, a chorus of between 1,500 and 1,800 voices, and the Luther College Band crowded the hall. President Dahl of the United Church read Psalm 103, President Stub of the Synod offered prayer, and Pastor Eske of Hauge's Synod led in the confession of faith and the Lord's Prayer. This was followed by the address of welcome by President Eastvold.

A temporary chairman and secretary were elected in the persons of Dahl and Professor M. O. Wee. After the union committee's report that no hindrances remained to the merger, permanent officers were elected. H. G. Stub was nominated as president, J. N. Kildahl as vice-president, N. J. Løhre as secretary, and Erik Waldeland as treasurer. All were unanimously elected.[146]

When the board of trustees had been duly elected and organized, it announced that it had the necessary documents for the incorporation of the Norwegian Lutheran Church of America, and submitted them for the signatures of President Stub and Secretary Løhre.[147]

Saturday evening the F. Melius Christiansen cantata, *Wondrous Things the Lord Hath Done*, originally prepared for the twenty-fifth anniversary of the United Church, was given by the massed chorus accompanied by the St. Olaf College Band.[148] Sunday morning the first service within the Norwegian Lutheran Church of America was held with President

---

[146]*Beretning* . . . *1917*, p. 491. Stub of the former Synod was nominated by Oley Nelson of the former United Church; Kildahl of the former United Church was nominated by Professor Bruce of the former Hauge's Synod; Løhre and Waldeland were nominated by the nominating committee consisting of Pastors G. T. Lee, N. N. Boe, and Mr. Henry Donhowe of the Synod; Pastors J. N. Sandven, J. A. Quello, and Mr. J. M. Wick of Hauge's Synod; and Pastors G. Rasmussen, C. E. Tiller, and Mr. E. L. S. Evenson of the United Church.

[147]*Ibid.*, p. 492. The articles of incorporation are found in *ibid.*, pp. 527-530.

[148]*Ibid.*, pp. 511-512. The previous evening a "song service" featuring chorales by the St. Olaf Lutheran Choir and sermonettes by Dr. J. N. Kildahl was given. For an account of the origin and development of this unique type of musical-homiletical service see Leola Nelson Bergmann, *Music Master of the Middle West* (Minneapolis: The University of Minnesota Press, 1944), pp. 111-114.

Stub as the preacher.[149] The commemoration of the 400th anniversary of the Reformation was highlighted by three addresses and the premier performance of Christiansen's *Reformation Cantata,* accompanied by the Minneapolis Symphony Orchestra.[150] Sunday evening twenty-seven theological candidates were ordained into the ministry, and the next morning the first service of Holy Communion within the new church was celebrated.

An interesting sidelight which illustrates the practical problems of uniting churches of different tendencies is given in the rubrics for the conduct of the divine services. The joint union committee had arranged that the Sunday morning service should follow the full liturgy with chanted portions by both pastor and congregation; the participating clergy were to wear the traditional vestments. This arrangement was obviously in keeping with the churchly trend represented in the union. On the other hand, the communion service was conducted without ministerial chanting or vestments, and the absolution was pronounced without the laying on of hands. This was an obvious concession to the Haugean element in the merger. At the ordination service the clergy and candidates followed the customs of their congregations in respect to the use of vestments. This, of course, meant that some appeared in full vestments, others in formal dress, and still others in ordinary suits.[151]

The business affairs of the first convention of the Norwegian Lutheran Church were cared for in the sessions of June 11-14. A committee of twenty-four members, with equal representation from each of the former synods, was named to designate officers for the districts. The thought governing this was to see that each of the former bodies was represented on the church council.[152] Property valued at approximately five million dollars was transferred to the new church. Nine districts,

---
[149]*Beretning . . . 1917,* pp. 471-477. That the atmosphere of World War I hung over the merger festivities was evident from Stub's sermon in which he remarked that the natural joy of union was dimmed by the bloodshed among the nations. The concert of the previous evening, incidentally, was announced as a "Red Cross Benefit Concert."
[150]*Ibid.,* pp. 512-514.
[151]*Ibid.,* footnote, p. 494.
[152]*Ibid.,* pp. 495-496, 537-538.

totalling 3,276 congregations, 1,054 pastors, and almost a half-million members, were organized. Boards were elected for the supervision of education, home and foreign missions, charities, finances, publications, and pensions. Uniform regulations governing the eleemosynary institutions were adopted.[153] The fields of activity for home mission work were defined to include slum, seamen's, hospital, prison, deaf, and immigrant missions, in addition to the ordinary work embraced in the term "home missions."[154] Foreign mission fields were those previously supported by the united bodies. They were located in China, Madagascar, and South Africa. In addition, missions among the American Indians and Alaskan Eskimos were placed under the direction of the foreign board.[155] The church schools, colleges, and seminary were to be ordered according to the recommendations made by the union committee.[156] Finally, a number of auxiliary organizations were begun during the course of the convention. These included a youth organization known as the Young People's League, a women's society named the Women's Missionary Federation, an insurance union (unnamed), and an English Association of congregations whose official language was English.[157]

At 12:50 P.M., June 14, 1917, President Stub declared the convention adjourned. His closing words were:

> This convention has been a high point in our lives. But let us not forget, as we separate, that we are called to work. Let us with gratitude to God for the inspiration which we have drawn from this glorious meeting promise to carry out what we here have been reminded is God's call to us. May the Lord God bless the fruits of this convention for us all![158]

---

[153] *Ibid.*, pp. 545-546.
[154] *Ibid.*, pp. 556-558.
[155] *Ibid.*, pp. 559-567. Control of the Zulu Mission was not transferred till 1927.
[156] *Ibid.*, pp. 582-586.
[157] *Ibid.*, pp. 538-539, 600-601, 602-604, 604-606. The insurance society was first called the Luther Union (1918), a name which was changed later to the Lutheran Brotherhood (1920) as its board of directors was altered to include others than members of the Norwegian Lutheran Church of America, thus seeking to serve all Lutherans in America. *Beretning . . . 1919*, p. 108; *Beretning . . . 1920*, pp. 601-602.
[158] *Ibid.*, p. 504.

PART THREE

A Heritage
Meets
a New
Era
(1917-1959)

CHAPTER SEVEN

An Interpretation of the Heritage

The world into which the Norwegian Lutheran Church of America was born was one of violent dislocations and convulsive changes. While Norwegian-American churchmen were struggling to make theological explication of Christian doctrine preliminary to presiding over the birth of a new church, the great world powers were engaged in the carnage and bloodletting of the first World War. Hitherto Norwegian-American Lutherans had lived a relatively isolated existence on the North American continent. Like other immigrant churches, they preached the gospel and administered the sacraments within the walls of a cultural ghetto. An alien tongue and inherited customs were not easily disclaimed and thus quickly became natural obstacles in the new land. The isolation of Norwegian-American Lutheranism, however, ended in 1917. Officially and formally the church was not to recognize it for several years, but nevertheless, the walls of the compound had been broken by the shattering experiences of World War I. From that time forth the church could not insulate itself from the "acids and assets" of American modernity. It was forced willy-nilly to "discover" America and the other churches—Lutheran and non-Lutheran—which shared the opportunities and responsibilities of the Christian witness.

Before attempting to examine the postwar adjustment to the American culture and the encounter with other churches, it is of value to recapitulate the story of Norwegian-American Lutheranism by interpreting and assessing the inheritance which the church of 1917 had received and which it carried into the postwar era.

The formation of the Norwegian Lutheran Church of America in 1917 was unique in at least one particular. For the first time in American church history three European religious emphases were blended in one American denomination. The first was pietism. But it was pietism with a distinctive Norwegian feature in that it was not sectarian or schismatic; it stressed the traditional pietistic characteristics along with doctrinal rectitude and ecclesiastical loyalty within the framework of organized Lutheranism. The second was centuries-old traditions associated with the European Lutheran state church system, which were now transplanted to, and modified by, the American frontier. The third was seventeenth century Lutheran Orthodoxism, reasserted with unyielding rigidity in the face of pressures which seemed to demand surrender to the American socio-ecclesiastical cultural pattern, and coupled with fears which arose from theological insecurity vis-á-vis nineteenth century historical criticism of the Bible. All of this, found in the merger of 1917, was rare, if not unprecedented, in American history. None of the other American Lutheran groups demonstrated an exact correspondence to this development; the major non-Lutheran Protestant denominations—Methodists, Baptists, Presbyterians, Congregationalists—knew nothing quite like this; and surely Roman Catholicism in America could offer no precise parallel.

Actually, of course, these three features were but another arrangement of the age-old issue between "subjectivism" and "objectivism." Norwegian Haugeanism in America represented the subjective tendencies of pietism. On the other hand, the marriage in America of Norwegian state church traditionalism with aggressive Missouri Lutheran "orthodoxy" represented an essential "objectivism." Considering the intrinsic irreconcilability of some of the differing points of view in these tendencies the achievement of 1917 was a notable success, the working out of which after 1917 will be related in the last two chapters.

The study of this phenomenon in American church history leads one to three observations. In the first place, the student who wishes to understand Norwegian-American Lutheranism must exhibit a willingness to come to grips with the position represented by Norwegian Haugeanism on the one hand and the fundamental presuppositions of Lutheran orthodoxism on the other. In the second place, he must be prepared to admit the unique function of a third factor in bringing about a reconciliation of these extremes. Qualitatively different from either Haugeanism or orthodoxism but not as easily defined, this third element can best be described as an attitude of embryonic ecumenicity seen in the emergence of a group of churchmen who were repelled by the exclusivism of extreme Haugeanism and the rigidity of repristination theology but nevertheless sympathetic to their respective emphases on personal Christianity and refined doctrinal definitions. The growth of this attitude was most clearly seen in the formation of the United Church and the subsequent solution of the knotty practical and doctrinal problems associated with the intransigence of the extremes. In the third place, he must make proper allowance for the element of Norwegian nationalism. A common language and culture together with a desire to perpetuate the same in America served as a unifying factor in the area of the religious.

The history of the Christian church includes accounts of men, movements, and incidents which illustrate the tension between the subjective and objective interpretations of the Christian gospel. Always there have been champions of one or the other; seldom have men or churches been committed in practice to both—at least, for long. The tendency has been to assume extreme positions because of fears aroused by tendencies in the opposite point of view. When the objective content of the gospel has been emphasized, the danger has been for religious life to become static, nerveless, and formalistic. When the subjective application of the gospel has received the emphasis, the danger has been to run off into rootless emotionalism, morbid introspection, and contempt for the material. It has been an almost impossible task to keep a balance between the two.

Church life in Norway yielded ample evidence to the presence of the two tendencies, both of which were transplanted root and branch to America. The establishment of Lutheranism as the religion of the state and the Age of Orthodoxy tended to objectify Christianity in Norway. Reactions to this objectivism were forthcoming in the Age of Pietism of the first part of the eighteenth century and in the spiritual movement set afoot by Hans Nielsen Hauge on the threshold of the nineteenth century. In the great migrations which followed, the first Norwegians to come to America carried with them an extreme Haugean view of church life, thus establishing this tendency on American soil. The representatives of state church Christianity, equipped with the prestige of university training and a tradition of culture, arrived a short time later. Before long, this latter group found itself allied theologically and religiously with the Missouri Synod, the American representatives of German Lutheran orthodoxism. Thus the second tendency, objectivism, was rooted among the Norwegian immigrants of the Midwest.

The influence of these two tendencies among Norwegian-American Lutherans has been determinative in almost every area of church life. The Haugean spirit, for example, can be detected in the realms of polity, life, and doctrine. Although the Haugean movement in Norway never broke away from the state church, there was an inbred suspicion of the organized, established church as being unfriendly to spiritual life. The church was not a body of inarticulate members to be governed by an ecclesiastical officialdom. Rather it was a democratic fellowship of believers who had experienced the grace of God. Those who were "born again" and "converted" were living members of the Body of Christ, to which the Head had given not only the *means* of grace in the Word and the Sacraments but also the *gifts* of grace, not least of which was the privilege of the spiritual prophet and priest to testify and pray in public. If the pastors failed to sound the note of repentance and to exhort to "living Christianity," it became the duty of the "awakened" laymen to stir the church by their oral testimony. This highly developed consciousness of the place of the laity in the church quite naturally led to emphasis on congregationalism and individualism with a corresponding failure to appreciate the corporate character of the church.

Closely allied with this view of the church was the Haugean emphasis on "life" and conduct. The "life" of the church and the individual was best cultivated by prayer meetings, evangelistic conferences, home Bible reading, and simple church services. Anything that smacked of formal worship according to an ordered liturgy with prescribed vestments was irrefutable evidence of the flight of the Holy Spirit. Furthermore, the Christian life was to be guarded by setting up rigid standards of personal conduct. Participation in so-called "worldly" pleasures was viewed as inimical to growth in grace, an attitude which not infrequently led to legalistic censure.

In the realm of doctrine the Haugean spirit was likewise evident. Theologically speaking the Haugeans were made of the fabric of conservative Lutheranism. But hand in hand with their emphasis on "life" was an innate fear of the over-refinement of doctrine as an intellectual substitute for a living faith. It was more important to have a personal faith in Christ than belief in a correctly-stated and precise doctrine, as for example, the doctrine of election. Moreover, when it came to doctrinal disputation, the Haugean spirit gave pre-eminence to the subjective application of a doctrine rather than its objective content, and this often led from pure, abstruse theology to theological anthropology. The Haugean stress on "repentance" and "conversion" played a major role in the differing viewpoints over absolution, "justification of the world," and election. In each instance, the Haugean stress was on man's response to God's objective acts.

Because of these emphases the Haugean spirit gave a definite character to certain elements in Norwegian-American Lutheranism. This spirit was not confined to the Eielsen Synod or Hauge's Synod. Both the New School and Old School of the Norwegian-Danish Conference possessed it, as did the Norwegian Augustanans. Moreover, certain leading individuals in the Norwegian Synod, most of whom found themselves drawn together in the Anti-Missourian Brotherhood, were exponents of "living Christianity" as over and against "dead orthodoxy." A striking example of such a person was J. N. Kildahl who played such an effective role in the union movement. Though not a member of Hauge's Synod, he was sympathetic to and appreciative of the Haugean spirit.

The Norwegian Synod is identified with the objective, dogmatic tendency in Norwegian-American Lutheranism. This is not to say that it was content with "dead orthodoxy." To maintain this is to do violence to the truth. One need but read the long articles and extensive reports of synodical discussions on such matters as personal piety, family prayer, temperance, and the frequent exhortations to avoid the dance and the theater to obtain a view of this side of the character of orthodoxism. Nevertheless, the emphasis in the Synod was always on *rene lære* (pure doctrine). Whereas Hauge's Synod invariably began its synodical conventions with a big prayer meeting, the Synod was not properly launched on its annual tasks without the presentation and discussion of a lengthy doctrinal essay. This concern for doctrinal correctness was a part of the theological baggage brought to America by the first pastors. The aristocratic, intelligent, and cultured Preuses, Brandts, and Ottesens who arrived in mid-century were already trained in the categories of Lutheran Orthodoxy. Their theological position was to be enhanced and buttressed by friendship with the Missouri Synod. The alliance soon led the Norwegians to equate Missourianism and true Lutheranism and to rally their forces around such slogans as "God's Word and Luther's Faith" or "It is Written." Against the rising tide of historical criticism of the Scriptures in the second half of the nineteenth century the Synod theologians waged unrelenting warfare. Loyalty to the printed words of the Bible as the inspired, and therefore errorless, Word of God became the criterion of doctrine and church life. The equating of inspiration and inerrancy was the foundation for the position assumed by the Synod theologians in most of the doctrinal controversies. It was a view of Scripture colored by its theory of verbal inspiration which led the Synod to its stand on slavery during and after the Civil War. This was likewise partially true of the attitude taken in the debate over absolution, "justification of the world," and election. Granting the premises of the Norwegian Synod, one must say that it was the most logical and consistent of the parties engaged in the theological wars. But some of its opponents—less logical, less legalistic over against the Scriptures and the confessions—were disquieted by the logical approach of the Synod theologians. For example, C. L. Clausen admitted by his actions that the Synod was logically right in its position on slavery. But he felt that something was nonetheless wrong with the Synod's point of view, and consequently, though unable to articulate his own position with theological precision, he found himself forced to oppose the doctrinal Missourianism of the Norwegian Synod.

Alongside of, or perhaps antecedent to, the doctrinal emphasis in this wing of Norwegian-American Lutheranism there existed a deep reverence for the ecclesiastical tradition. The liturgy, the vestments, and the customs of the Church of Norway were adhered to with scrupulous attention. This attitude was fostered by a high concept of and esteem for the church. To be sure, the final seat of authority was the congregation, but this did not lead the Synod into extreme congregationalism. The church was more than atomistically associated congregations; it was an organic whole made visible before the world as the "true church" by its right doctrine. This unique combination of high churchism and congregationalism had both foreign and domestic roots as did the doctrinal proclivities of the Synod. The ecclesiastical traditionalism can be traced to the Church of Norway; the congregationalism to the writings of Walther on polity, which were translated from the German into Norwegian by the Synod.

These two tendencies, the subjective and the objective, seldom having been fused in the history of the church, were drawn together in the union movement from 1880 to 1917. The resulting church body, the Norwegian Lutheran Church of America, gave evidence within itself that it had not forgotten the rock from whence it was hewn. This church body showed the Haugean trend most clearly in its internal life and activity and the spirit of orthodoxism in its external relations to other Christians. Internally, the church was characterized by Haugean evangelical pietism; externally, it bore the imprint of the Norwegian Synod's traditional caution rather than the United Church's eagerness to sacrifice itself for a greater church.

The merging of these two streams was no simple task. In fact, a close scrutiny will make it apparent that the two tendencies never met head-on but were brought together by a third factor. Not as easily defined as the Haugean practicality or the Synod orthodoxism, but tolerantly sympathetic to the distinctive character of both, this third element was qualitatively different in that it represented an attitude toward inter-Lutheran relations which was incipiently ecumenical. It was in an atmosphere fostered by this attitude that the union movement bore fruit. One must be prepared, therefore, to see the unique function of this third factor in bringing about a reconciliation. We need cite but two or three examples to document this statement.

Already in mid-nineteenth century the two emphases were clearly distinguishable. For fifty years they remained aloof. During those years the divine hand which guides history was shaping a third factor, the mediating element between the two extremes, namely, the United Church. Slowly and arduously a new body which embraced characteristics of both ex-

An Interpretation of the Heritage

tremes began to take form. Strange elements, offshoots of diverse traditions, began to coalesce. First, there was a handful of refugees from Eielsenism which found its way into a new church, the Scandinavian Augustana Synod, by the circuitous route of the Franckean and Northern Illinois synods. From this came in time the Norwegian Augustana Synod, which in turn produced the Norwegian-Danish Conference, under the leadership of a rebel from the ranks of the Norwegian Synod, C. L. Clausen. Finally, a major explosion within the household of the Synod itself propelled a new group, the Anti-Missourian Brotherhood, upon the scene. Then, as we have observed, the groundwork was laid for the formation of the United Church. It was this church, despite being rocked to its foundation by the Augsburg Controversy, that became the instrument of bringing historically antagonistic trends together into one church body. The United Church was, therefore, exhibit A illustrating the function of a third factor in the union movement.

A second and a third example can be found in the settlement of the practical and doctrinal differences of the churches. The first is that which is associated with the Haugean stress on, and orthodoxy's dismay over, the practice known as lay activity. Again the two emphases did not meet head-on. The pure Haugean concept of unregulated lay preaching and orthodoxy's concern for orderly church life finally were introduced to each other through a third concept: regulated lay activity as expressed in the document on "The Lay Ministries of the Church" (1906) which was essentially a restatement of Gisle Johnson's solution of the problem in Norway.

The last and perhaps most convincing illustration of the unique function of the third factor was the disposition of the election controversy. Again, as we have noted, the subjective emphasis of anti-Missourianism and the objectivity of Missourianism, would not admit of solution. Although occasionally petty and personal elements played into the disagreements, it must be admitted that on the whole the differences were rooted in conscience formed convictions and argued with intellectual honesty. Often the conflict took on the air of unreality because the issues did not meet squarely, but nevertheless it would be unfair in the extreme to charge this off as a sham battle over words. But since the two points of view could not be brought to coincide, a reconciliation was possible only through an *Opgjør*, a settlement. The Madison Agreement was introduced as the third element. The two positions, which could not agree with each other, found themselves united in their attachment to a third.

The last conclusion growing out of a study of the union movement points up the role of nationalism in the religious sphere. Although this can be easily over-evaluated, not to make allowance for it would be to neglect a significant item.

No doubt every national group in America has been charged with "clannishness" in the period of its adjustment to the new world. Those who know the Norwegians in America will say that this must be acknowledged by this group as well. But this has not been altogether on the debit side of the ledger. A linguistic or racial island in the American sea made it possible for an inherited cultural and religion to interweave so that the end result contributed to the unity of the church.

As we have pointed out, one of the leaders of the Missouri Synod flayed the union movement as being more nationalistic than religious. This, of course, is to make a statement which is difficult to prove or disprove. We make but one comment: to deny the factor of nationalism would be to be guilty of thoughtlessness and irresponsible judgment. The bond of a common nationality unquestionably knit the Norwegian church groups together, especially at the grass roots level where theologically untutored laymen had difficulty catching the doctrinal nuances so quickly detected by the theologians.

There are at least three evidences of the role of nationalism in the union movement. The first to be noted was the influence of the cultural and social groups typified by what was known as the "Bygdelag" movement. Within these societies which cut across religious lines, pastors and lay people of different synods but from the same community in Norway were drawn together. Acquaintanceship on the social or cultural level often led to better understanding on the religious level.

In the second place, all elements of Norwegian church life in America were bound together by a common *Norwegian* version of Lutheran hymnody and catechetical instruction. They sang the chorales of Brorson, Kingo, and Lindeman as well as the German hymns of Luther, Gerhardt, Nicolai, and Teschner in translation. They learned Luther's catechism with the aid of the explanation of Erik Pontoppidan, the great naturalist-bishop of Bergen. It was definitely a *Norwegian* version of Lutheranism.

Finally, the leaders of the church often gave a nationalistic appeal to their arguments for a united church. How often sentiments like this were expressed: "We look to the day when there shall be one *Norwegian* Lutheran Church in America." The United Church, which played upon this theme, itself looked beyond to the realization of *one* Lutheran Church in America. But it is safe to say that many Norwegians were content with the union on a nationalistic basis. A hint as to this state of mind was the selection of the name of the church. Instead of one of the proposed alternate names such as "The United Lutheran Synod in America," it chose the one with a nationalistic appeal: "The Norwegian Lutheran Church of America."

It is the growth of this church into an organic whole which has been the subject of our study. When this church came into existence in 1917, it represented a hyphenated religio-cultural blend which was still somewhat of a stranger in the New World. Yet the church was convinced it was not an alien; it belonged to America. It must contribute, therefore, some of the riches of its own heritage to the life and thought of this nation. Failing this, it would fail the Lord of the Church. Dr. L. W. Boe, the late president of St. Olaf College, bespoke this in two inspired paragraphs which he called "The Unfinished Task":

Ours is a mediating generation. By training and tradition we live in the spiritual and cultural land of the fathers. With our children we are steadily marching into the land of tomorrow. Ours is the riches of two cultures and often the poverty of the desert wanderer. We live between memory and reality. Ours is the agony of a divided loyalty and joy in the discovery of a new unity. Like Moses of old we see the new but cannot fully enter in. To us has been given the task of mediating a culture, of preserving and transferring to our children in a new land the cultural and spiritual values bound up in the character, art, music, literature, and Christian faith of a generation no longer found even in the land from which the fathers came.

Insofar as these values have been preserved in a Norwegian atmosphere and in the Norwegian language it has been in the form they had when brought over. When released in the language and genius of America they have again become sources of inspiration and power, and in the hearts and minds of a far greater number than our own flesh and blood. Ours is the privilege of releasing for America values that sustained the spirit and life of our forbears for generations. We must become conscious of our responsibility. If we pass on without opening the treasure chest, it will not be done. Our obligation is to translate in the largest sense and to carry over.[1]

---
[1] See P. M. Glasoe, *The Landstad-Lindeman Hymnbook* (Minneapolis: Augsburg Publishing House, 1938), p. 3.

CHAPTER EIGHT

The Church Discovers America

Introduction

Janus-like, the church which emerged in 1917 faced in two directions: towards the past from which it had received its heritage, and towards the future which might easily erode its heritage. The forty years—add or subtract a few—which followed the merger were years of conscious and unconscious tension between the two "faces" of Janus. Almost all of the problems and crises which characterized the era of the two world wars were in some way shaped by this tension. One needs mention but a few to illustrate the point. The language transition was most clearly an example of conflict between the past and the future. Another was the problem of doing "church work" in America, a task which was complicated by the tensions created when churchmen operated with an inherited ecclesiastical point of view in an environment into which the heritage did not fit without some pulling and tugging. Theologically there was the problem of Modernism and the Social Gospel; roughly for two decades Lutheranism was on guard against liberal Protestantism. By the mid-thirties it was clear

241

to some that the battlelines were no longer at the point of liberalism but between Lutheran apologists for a theology of repristination and Lutheran proponents of historically-understood confessionalism. Religiously there was the problem of integrating or blending the various emphases in the heritage without experiencing corrosive influences from the pluralism of America. The massive social and economic changes which accompanied World War I, the Great Depression, and World War II were additional challenges to the inherited reason for and manner of doing things.

When World War I ended, the insular existence of nineteenth century Norwegian-Americans was ended forever. Church work had to be geared to meet the new situation. In the crises which often developed, the church recognized that "something had to be done." Therefore, it went ahead and did it. Necessity drove to action, and action produced programs and institutions which grew "like Topsy." There was little time and perhaps less inclination for theological reflection.

Aside from the Modernist-Fundamentalist flurry in the twenties—in which Norwegian-American churchmen generally sympathized with the Fundamentalists—the church faced its task in the American environment with minimal theological thought. The fear of liberalism drove it into a fundamentalist interpretation of its evangelical tradition where it remained in uneasy security for two decades. Thus the church faced its major postwar tasks pragmatically rather than theologically. The problems which loomed large were (1) How can this Norwegian church become American? and (2) How can this church deal with other churches, Lutheran and non-Lutheran? The first of these is the subject of this chapter; the second, the final chapter.

Americanization: The Language Problem

From its earliest days in America the Lutheran church, perhaps more than any other immigrant church, experienced the bitterness and travail of making the transition from European tongues to English. Why this sociological phenomenon presented such an acute problem to Lutherans it is not our intention to explore. We mention it only as a rather widely accepted fact and as a significant ingredient in the history of the social process.[1]

In Pennsylvania, for example, the transition from German to English was, in some extreme circumstances, accompanied by lawsuits, disorderly congregational meetings, and even fisticuffs. Moreover, the arguments which were to be repeated in other foreign language groups were articulated there: (1) the use of English must be promoted in order to save the second and succeeding generations for the Lutheran church; and (2) the use of German must be continued in order (a) to preserve the true faith which was diluted when Anglicized; and (b) to conserve the cultural heritage.[2]

The Norwegians faced the problem almost immediately upon arrival in America. At mid-century Pastor Paul Andersen, at the time affiliated with the English speaking Franckean Synod, established (1848) a congregation in Chicago where he preached regularly in English to an immigrant congregation. He also began a Sunday school in which the instruction was done in English. Elling Eielsen's "Old Constitution" (Article 13) stipulated that children "must be instructed in both languages, the mother tongue first, provided the district school" be not neglected. In 1851 the pastors of the later Norwegian Synod gave careful attention to an English translation of Luther's *Small Catechism*.[3]

It was the latter who soon found themselves involved in the polar tensions of the problem. A. C. Preus, the first president of the Norwegian Synod, found it necessary in 1858 to defend

---

[1] Adolph Spaeth, "Language Question," *The Lutheran Cyclopedia*, ed. by H. E. Jacobs and J. A. W. Haas (New York: Chas. Scribner's Sons, 1899), p. 270. Cf. H. E. Jacobs, *A History of the Evangelical Lutheran Church in the United States* (New York: Chas. Scribner's Sons, 1893), pp. 327-331; "The Language Situation in the United Church," *The United Lutheran*, VIII (1915), 131-134, 146-150, 186-187. The latter was written anonymously for no apparent reason. The editor, C. O. Solberg, disclosed in 1917 that the author was O. M. Norlie, C. S. Thorpe (ed.), *The First Meeting of the English Association . . . November 13-15, 1917 . . .* (Minneapolis: Augsburg Publishing House, 1918), p. 18.
[2] Jacobs, *op. cit.*, pp. 327-330.
[3] Bergh, *Den n. luth. Kirke i Am.*, pp. 77-78.

the parochial school (which, unlike the public school, used Norwegian) and to warn against the over-hasty transition to English. He maintained that "the language which is the language of the home and the family must be the language of the church and of the religious school. When the English language supplements the Norwegian in the home, our Norwegian speech will have lost its right to be used in the church and in the religious school—but not before."[4]

A. C. Preus and his colleagues were charged in 1859 with opposing Americanization. This they vigorously denied, but added that the Lutheran faith must be kept "uncontaminated by American sects."[5] Moreover, they looked with some concern at other Lutheran groups which, in their opinion, were too rapidly adopting American ways. H. A. Preus and J. A. Ottesen, for example, commented disparagingly of the Scandinavian Augustana Synod in 1866, saying that it was "a Yankified ecclesiastical company" *(et yankificeret Kirkekompagni).*[6] Laur. Larsen, on the other hand, observed that Americanization could not be accomplished without dangers and spiritual losses, but since it was inevitable, it would be folly to work against it.[7]

It was quite clear by the beginning of the twentieth century that the Norwegians were in the midst of the language transition, and that a whole generation was now experiencing the necessity of using two languages simultaneously. On the one side of this generation were those who insisted that the use of Norwegian must prevail in the churches. On the other side were those who impatiently claimed that Norwegian should be given up immediately. The lack of foresight among both extremists only served to accentuate the problem. Meanwhile, however, it became clear to sober observers that thousands of young people were being lost to the Lutheran church because of the reluctance of the older generation, which controlled ecclesiastical policy, to recognize the need for speeding up the

---

[4] "A School and Language Controversy in 1858," tr. and ed. by A. C. Paulson and Kenneth Bjørk, *Norwegian-American Studies and Records,* X, 96-98.
[5] "Missouri-Synodens Mening om 'vore Skole- og Sprogforhold,'" *K. M.,* V (February, 1860), 50-51.
[6] "Beretning om et Møde . . . ," *K. M.,* XI (November, 1866), 328.
[7] "Vor Synodes Jubelaar," *E. L. K.,* V (January 11, 1878), 23.

language transition.[8] O. M. Norlie has pointed out that seventy per cent of the Norwegian-American immigrants did not affiliate with any Norwegian Lutheran synod in America. He claimed further that the United Church alone lost 106,314 in a twenty-one-year period (1890-1911). The causes of the losses were numerous—worldliness, mixed marriages, prosperity, materialism—but high on the list was the refusal of the pastors and the church to recognize how rapidly Americanization was taking place.[9]

A few voices were crying in the wilderness. Pastor Johannes Halvorson of the Norwegian Synod gave an English address at the dedication of Luther Seminary, Hamline, St. Paul, Minnesota, in 1899. Noting the fact that Norwegian Lutheranism in America was predominantly rural, he asserted that it was significant for the future of the church that the seminary had been built in an urban, not a rural, center where the whole complex of problems associated with Americanization would have to be faced.[10] J. A. Bergh, the Nestor of Norwegian-American Lutheran historians, remarked in 1914 "the majority of our congregations want a pastor who can speak English. . . . For the third generation English becomes both the heart and official language. In this emergency the Church must be true to her purpose. If she is to save sinners, she must speak the language which the sinner understands . . ."[11] President T. H. Dahl of the United Church added his voice to those asking that the problem be faced with greater foresight than was being exhibited,[12] but Norlie mentions that "dire threatenings were

---

[8]It was just at this time that the more Americanized Lutheran churches of the East increased their home mission work by establishing English-speaking congregations in the Upper Mississippi Valley, seeking to stop the disastrous losses of second generation German and Scandinavian Lutherans. See G. H. Trabert, *English Lutheranism in the Northwest* (Philadelphia: General Council of Publication House, 1914). Cf. "An English Conference . . .," *Lutheran Herald*, XII (March 8, 1917), 221.
[9]"The Language Situation . . .," *The United Lutheran*, VIII (March 5, 1915), 147. Norlie quotes Gerberding, *Problems and Possibilities*, p. 172, to warn that Norwegian Lutherans might suffer the loss of highly influential men (Victor Lawson, publisher of the *Chicago Daily News*, was one who left the Norwegian Lutheran church because of the language problem; John Wanamaker, Jacob Riis, William August Muhlenberg, the Weyerhauser family, and scores of others were lost to Lutheranism because of the slowness of other Lutherans to make the transition to English).
[10]Copy of address from his grandson, the Rev. John Halvorson, Luther Seminary, St. Paul.
[11]Bergh, *Den n. luth. Kirke i Am.*, pp. 523-524.
[12]*Beretning . . . Den forenede Kirke . . . 1912*, pp. 55-56.

murmured against him [Dahl] for presuming to make such a statement."[13]

As noted in Chapter IV, by 1900 the three main church bodies were employing various devices to encourage church work in the English language. One of the solutions to the problem obviously lay in the seminaries. Hitherto all theological professors used Norwegian in the lecture halls. In 1890, however, the Synod engaged the Rev. Johannes Halvorson as a part-time instructor in English homiletics. Four years later he was succeeded by a full-time "English professor," the Rev. W. M. H. Petersen. The United Church in 1891 elected the Rev. E. G. Lund, a graduate of the Lutheran Theological Seminary in Philadelphia (Mt. Airy) and a member of the English-speaking General Council, to be a professor of theology, using English exclusively. Hauge's Synod's first English professor was Louis H. Chally, who taught from 1898 to 1902.[14]

The Norwegian Synod, moreover, was the first to issue an official organ in English (*Lutheran Herald*, 1905). Hauge's Synod entered the field of English journalism with the publication of *The Lutheran Intelligencer* (1910). The reluctance of pastors and laymen alike to accept this as a necessary part of church life was quickly apparent. The discouraging lack of support led the editor, G. M. Bruce, to announce the discontinuance of the paper, saying, ". . . we do not feel that it is worthwhile to waste any further time and effort on what seems an almost hopeless field for English religious journalism."[15] The United Church provided numerous ways and means for assisting the congregations in making the transition. In 1894 it initiated action to prepare an English hymnal, which was published in 1898.[16] Two years earlier it had organized an "English Conference" to promote the use of English in the synod's congregations.[17] Meeting annually, it joined forces with the editors of the English organ, *The United Lutheran*

---
[13]*Op. cit.*, p. 149.
[14]*The Forward March of Faith*, eds. P. S. Dybvig and R. E. Haugan (Minneapolis: Augsburg Publishing House, 1943), p. 24.
[15]*The Lutheran Intelligencer*, III (June, 1913), 81.
[16]*Beretning . . . Den forenede Kirke . . . 1898*, p. 237.
[17]*Beretning . . . Den forenede Kirke . . . 1896*, p. 184.

(established in 1907), in calling for Americanization.[18] In 1915 Editor C. M. Weswig noted that the union movement had necessarily restricted the goals of the English Conference, but that, come the merger, surely provision would be made for a "real English district."[19] His hopes were never fully realized, although in 1917 the English Association of the Norwegian Lutheran Church of America was organized.[20]

The major language transition in theological instruction occurred between 1917 and 1930. At the time of the union Red Wing Seminary (Hauge's Synod) had three professors. M. O. Wee used Norwegian exclusively; E. W. Schmidt[21] used English exclusively; and the third, G. M. Bruce, offered bilingual courses. At Luther Seminary (Norwegian Synod) Professors H. G. Stub and J. Ylvisaker used Norwegian; O. E. Brandt and Elling Hove used both languages. At United Church Seminary Professors M. O. Bøckman and E. K. Johnsen used Norwegian; J. N. Kildahl and M. J. Stolee, English and Norwegian; C. M. Weswig, English.

Clearly theological instruction in 1917 was still primarily in Norwegian. All students understood it and were able to use it in preaching.[22] After the union of the three faculties to form Luther Theological Seminary in 1917, the pattern remained unchanged, bilingual studies being the rule. Professors' lectures were as follows:

ALL-NORWEGIAN	ALL-ENGLISH	BILINGUAL
Ylvisaker	Bruce	Brandt
Bøckman	Weswig	Kildahl
Johnsen		Wee
		Hove
		Stolee

---

[18]The editorial staff carried the names of J. A. Aasgaard, C. M. Weswig, C. O. Solberg, and Martin Hegland. These were budding leaders in the church.
[19]"The English Conference," *The United Lutheran*, VIII (March 19, 1915), 185.
[20]Thorpe (ed.), *The First Meeting of the English Association* . . . , pp. 9-11. The editor complains that "English did not get very much consideration" at the constituting convention. In fact, when Governor Norbeck of South Dakota addressed the assembly in English, he did so half apologetically. *Ibid.*, pp. 48, 42.
[21]Son of F. A. Schmidt. Was president and professor of theology, 1908-1918. In 1918 he became professor at St. Olaf College. Norlie, *et al.* (eds.), *Who's Who*, p. 517.
[22]Letter, G. M. Bruce–L. O. Tolo, Sept. 29, 1948.

Two of the all-Norwegian professors died shortly, Ylvisaker in 1917 and Johnsen in 1923. Kildahl died in 1920. With these deaths theological instruction in Norwegian suffered loss. Bøckman continued to use Norwegian exclusively until his retirement in 1936. Wee, Hove, and Stolee maintained the so-called bilingual department. But with the arrival of J. Tanner (1925) and the death of Hove (1927), English gained in usage.[23] Faculty meetings were conducted and minutes recorded in Norwegian until the late twenties. In 1930 T. F. Gullixson replaced M. O. Bøckman as president, and from that time the bilingual studies virtually ceased, the only Norwegian lectures being those in New Testament exegesis (Bøckman) and homiletics (Stolee). During the first half of the thirties, an attempt to cultivate and maintain Norwegian among the students was made in the so-called *Norsk Aften,* a weekly social meeting where only Norwegian was spoken. This noble venture evaporated within a few years.

While the seminary was experiencing a relatively gradual transition to English, the agitation for English among some of the church leaders made it appear, for a time at least, that the change in the church as a whole would come more rapidly. In the year before the union, 1916, the use of English was as follows: Hauge's Synod, 17.2 per cent; United Church, 21.6 per cent; and the Norwegian Synod, 25.7 per cent.[24] The year of the union was also the year of America's entry into World War I. With the war and its aftermath came a surge of patriotism which all but forbade the teaching and use of foreign languages in schools, homes, and churches. The NLCA was not immune to this pro-American feeling and almost at once some leaders began agitation to eliminate the word "Norwegian" from the name of the church.[25]

[23]*Ibid.* It should be pointed out that all the students by this time were taking homiletics in English; the Norwegian homiletics sought to make bilingual preachers of at least a few of the students. A student could take a complete English course as early as 1921. Cf. *Lutheran Almanac for 1921* (Minneapolis: Augsburg Publishing House, 1921), p. 54.
[24]See statistical studies, *Report . . . NLCA, 1931,* p. 29. The Norwegian Synod's leadership was due in large measure to the fact that many of the early congregations belonged to the Synod. They naturally faced the language problem sooner than others.
[25]"The Change of Name," *Lutheran Church Herald,* II (May 17, 1918), 305.

The postwar years demonstrated a significant pattern. The first year (1918) witnessed a sustained and vigorous, though in some ways unsuccessful, campaign to hasten the language transition. The English organ of the church, *Lutheran Church Herald,* printed at least twenty-five articles on the language and name questions in 1918. In this context an urgent appeal by President H. G. Stub at the Fargo, North Dakota, church convention (1918) was made to appoint a committee to make proposals for preventing the loss of young people to English-speaking churches, Lutheran and non-Lutheran. Moreover, he added, the church should give serious consideration to dropping the word "Norwegian" from its title and changing it to some such name as "The United Lutheran Synod."[26] This suggestion was enthusiastically received, and the convention voted overwhelmingly (533 to 61) to appoint a committee which prepared a resolution for constitutional amendment to be voted on at the next convention.[27]

Opposition to this action developed immediately and by the next general convention in 1920 sentiment had been so altered that the assembly voted 377 to 296 to retain the name, The Norwegian Lutheran Church of America.[28] There are two probable explanations of this strange shift of sentiment. The first is that the sober realization of the necessity to employ English in church work was given emotional impetus by the political situation in 1918. When these two factors coincided (the actual need and the spirit of patriotism), the convention was swept into abandoning its year-old name.[29] In other words, given normal circumstances the church would perhaps have moved less hastily. A second explanation lies in the fact that the Fargo action united both secular and religious opponents of change. Einar Haugen has pointed out that even before 1918 the Norwegian secular press, the literary societies, the singers' associations, the Norwegian lodges, the "lags," and

---

[26]*Beretning . . . Den n. Lutherske Kirkes . . . 1918,* pp. 20-21.
[27]*Ibid.,* pp. 313-314. Cf. *Lutheran Church Herald,* II (1918), 392.
[28]*Beretning . . . 1920,* p. 247.
[29]Einar Haugen, *The Norwegian Language in America. A Study in Bilingual Behavior* (Philadelphia: University of Pennsylvania Press, 1953), I, 256-257.

especially the *Norske Selskab i Amerika* (The Norwegian Society of America) had spearheaded the opposition to English, which was called "the enemy within the walls."[30] Now, the Norwegian religious press joined forces with the other advocates of preserving the cultural heritage. Although the editor of the English journal of the church maintained that the "average man" did not share this religious myopia, the joint efforts of the opponents had "succeeded in befogging the real issue" and had created the impression that there was "a tremendous sentiment against this change of name."[31] Consequently, the Church Council, without altering its conviction of the need for change, found it advisable to recommend that the next convention rescind the action of 1918. It took this action because "a controversy has arisen which has embittered the minds of many and prevented a discussion of the real issue."[32] It was this resolution which the 1920 convention adopted.

Although there was some sparring between the proponents and opponents of English during the twenties, there was a tendency to avoid any open rupture in the church. In the twenties the advocates of *fædrearven* (the cultural heritage) found their enthusiasm kindled by two things: (1) the wide acclaim given to the novels of one of their own, O. E. Rølvaag, and (2) the celebration of the Norse-American Centennial in 1925.[33] All of this has been described by Einar Haugen as "The Last Rally."[34]

By 1930 it was clear that the language transition was almost complete.[35] P. S. Dybvig, a senior at Luther Theological Seminary in 1930, prepared a careful statistical analysis on the basis

---

[30]*Ibid.*, p. 249.
[31]"Changing the Name of the Church," *Lutheran Church Herald*, III (October 21, 1918), 664.
[32]*Beretning . . . 1920*, p. 15.
[33]Norlie, *History of the Norwegian People in America*, pp. 5-8.
[34]*Op. cit.*, I, 258. Actually the "last rally" occurred in the forties with the invasion of Norway by Nazi Germany (1940) and the celebration of the Centennial of Norwegian-American Lutheranism in 1943.
[35]The minutes of the general convention were published in Norwegian through 1921. The reports of 1922 and 1923 were done in two volumes, one in Norwegian, the other in English. By 1924 publication was in English alone, although some of the individual reports and parts of the daily journal were in Norwegian. This practice continued until 1934.

of which he predicted that "no public services will be conducted in the Norwegian language after 1942."[36] How accurate the prophecy was came to light in a subsequent study (1941) when Dybvig showed that 88 per cent of all services were conducted in English. Had it not been for the temporary resurgence of filial loyalties during the 1940 invasion of Norway and the Centennial celebration in 1943, Dybvig's prediction might well have been completely accurate. A composite of the charts of 1930 and 1941 is herewith reproduced.

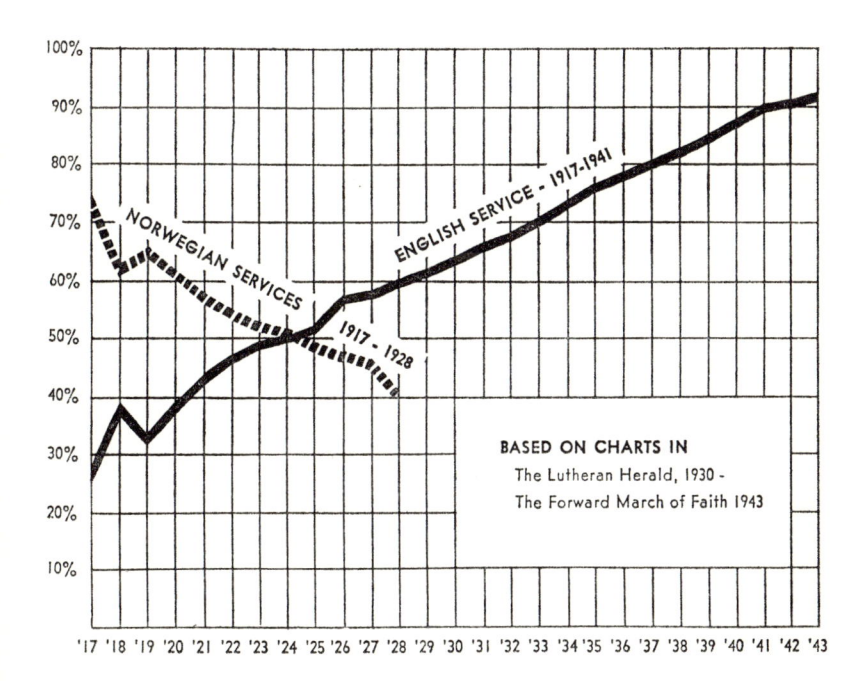

BASED ON CHARTS IN
The Lutheran Herald, 1930 -
The Forward March of Faith 1943

---

[36]P. S. Dybvig, "Facts About the Language Question," *Lutheran Church Herald*, XIV (May 20, 1930), 697-700.

It will be noted that after the unusual upswing in 1918, the percentage of English services was almost predictably steady. Norwegian services dropped about 2.3 per cent annually. "A generation of monolinguals was clearly on the march."[37]

Meanwhile, the question of 1918—should the name be changed?—continued to recur. In 1926, after the Centennial enthusiasms of the previous year had cooled off, advocates of a change were thwarted by approval of a motion to refer the thorny problem to the Church Council.[38] In 1928, less than a two-thirds majority (508-302) approved the change; this was insufficient to make the constitutional change.[39] In 1934 the change was again voted,[40] but two years later when the final constitutional change was presented, a strong opposition defeated the proposal and went on to obtain approval for a resolution to postpone all consideration of name change until after the Centennial of the church in 1943.[41] An effective argument against change of name was an altered version of "Don't-kill-the-goose-that-lays-the-golden-egg." The so-called "Centennial Appeal," an attempt to raise a large sum for the church on the occasion of its one hundredth birthday, might fail should the name be changed. It was believed that the large givers were among the advocates of the status quo.

The proponents of change were restive between 1936 and 1943, but at the first convention after the Centennial they spoke without restraint and voted 766 to 269 for the change.[42] At the next biennial convention, June 13, 1946, the constitution was amended by the necessary two-thirds majority, and henceforth the church was to be known as The Evangelical Lutheran Church.[43] To mollify the opponents of the change and to perpetuate Norwegian interests the church established a "Norwegian Conference" in 1948.[44]

[37] Haugen, *op. cit.*, p. 257.
[38] *Lutheran Church Herald*, X (June 29, 1925), 806.
[39] *Report* . . . *1928*, pp. 186-187.
[40] *Report* . . . *1934*, pp. 16A and 304.
[41] *Report* . . . *1936*, p. 33.
[42] *Report* . . . *1944*, p. 35.
[43] *Report* . . . *1946*, p. 394.
[44] *Report* . . . *1948*, p. 448.

Thus, in thirty years the pendulum had made a full swing. In 1917 a predominantly Norwegian-speaking church had permitted the organization of an "English Association" to promote Anglicization; in 1946-48 an English-speaking church consoled the rapidly disappearing Norwegian minority with the establishment of a "Norwegian Conference" to nurse along the religio-cultural remnants of an immigrant church and to remind the monolingual community that the historical and religious values of another culture were in danger of being relegated to the limbo of forgotten things.

Americanized Church Work

The regime of J. A. Aasgaard as president of the Norwegian Lutheran Church of America (1925-1954) was significant for many reasons. During these years several major domestic and world-wide occurrences had their influence on the church at whose helm he stood. There were the problems of economic "boom and bust" of the twenties and thirties. There was the rise of totalitarianism in Europe with national and international socialism as the common substratum of all. There was in America the emergence of controlled capitalism coming on the heels of the Great Depression. There was the outbreak of the second World War, the ushering in of the atomic age, and the progressive revelation of a postwar East-West conflict. On the church front, there was the defeat of liberalism by a new interpretation of orthodoxy, the quickening of the ecumenical movement, and the great "revival" of interest in religion, especially in the United States. All of these things made the twenty-nine years of Aasgaard's presidency a time of profound seriousness, restless ferment, and exhilarating prospects. When asked to sum up the major accomplishment of his years as president, Dr. Aasgaard modestly replied, "I delivered the Norwegian Lutherans to American shores."[45]

The Americanization of the Norwegian Lutherans took at least two forms. One we have already examined, the language

---
[45]Interview, June 2, 1955.

transition. With this Aasgaard was actively engaged only in his earlier years, when he joined forces with a company of young pastors who made common cause to increase the use of English in the churches. Although his years as president demonstrated a noticeable sympathy towards the bilingual character of his people, he nonetheless recognized the inevitable necessity of a complete language transition.

However, there was no hesitation in his mind on the Americanization of the manner in which the work of the church should be done, whether the language was English, Norwegian, or both. "Doing church work" in America meant preaching the gospel and administering the sacraments in ways that would be most effective in an American setting. This is what Aasgaard meant by delivering "the Norwegian Lutherans to American shores." In order to comprehend this accomplishment, it has been judged best to interpret the activity of the various departments and auxiliaries of the church from the perspective of Americanization rather than to give an exhaustive programmatic chronicle of the church's outreach in missions, education, welfare, and the other services.

Foreign Missions

The foreign mission program during the four decades since 1917 has reflected the fact that the American church has been caught up in the full sweep of international affairs as well as in the task of domesticating the ecclesiastical point of view of a hyphenated constituency. One of the characteristics of the Norwegian Lutheran immigrant church was a genuine enthusiasm for foreign missions. This had grown out of the Haugean revival in Norway and was transplanted, along with the church, to America.[46] In 1917 the Norwegian Lutheran Church of America officially controlled and maintained missions in China and Madagascar.[47]

---
[46]R. A. Syrdal, "Foreign Missions of the . . . Evangelical Lutheran Church," in A. S. Burgess (ed.), *Lutheran World Missions* (Minneapolis: Augsburg Publishing House, 1954), p. 70.
[47]*Supra,* Chapter IV.

In China several Lutheran missions cooperated with the view of forming one Chinese Lutheran Church. The first step was the establishing of The Union Lutheran Theological Seminary at Shekow, near Hankow, supported by the Lutheran United Mission (the three NLCA missions which united in 1917), the Augustana Synod, and two European mission groups: the Norwegian and the Finnish Societies. With the seminary as a focus, the Chinese church was being unified: a common liturgy, a common hymnal, and common publications gave solidarity to the young church.

Meanwhile, one of the products of the 1917 union in America was the intensification of educational and medical programs with the corresponding increase in mission personnel. "An all time high of 125 missionaries" was reached in this period.[48] The birth of The Lutheran Church of China in 1920 marked the beginnings of the indigenous church. Three years later the missions supported by the Norwegian Lutheran Church of America were organized as a synod of The Lutheran Church of China. In 1927 the Nationalist uprising led to a larger measure of independence for the Chinese church. Europeans and other whites found it necessary to step aside from leadership and increasingly gave responsibility to Chinese churchmen.

The brief respite which came to the church before the outbreak of the Sino-Japanese war in 1932 and the ultimate Japanese occupation gave the church a fleeting opportunity to exercise its responsibility in an atmosphere of freedom. Following World War II and the Communist victory of 1949, the American missionaries were withdrawn, leaving the Chinese church without the assistance or the embarrassment of foreigners.

In Madagascar a somewhat similar mission development occurred after 1917. The union intensified the work, especially in education.[49] As in China, a United Lutheran Theological Seminary, serving all the missions, was organized in 1923, and unquestionably was one of the steps which led to the forma-

[48]Syrdal, *op. cit.*, p. 76.
[49]*Ibid.*, p. 83.

tion of an independent church in 1950, The Malagasy Lutheran Church. The church in Madagascar has carried on a strong evangelistic and educational program in which it has received the encouragement of the French Government of the island. Desirous of becoming a part of organized world Lutheranism, it was the first African church to join the Lutheran World Federation and was represented by delegates at the Third Assembly of the Lutheran World Federation in Minneapolis (1957).

In addition to the work in China and Madagascar, the Norwegian Lutheran Church of America recognized in 1917 what was known as the Schreuder mission in Zululand, South Africa, as its official mission. Although control of the mission remained in the hands of a committee in Norway, the NLCA provided missionaries and financial support. Control was transferred to the NLCA in 1927.[50]

The Zulu mission is significant in that it marks the end of what Syrdal has called the "Norwegian influence" on Norwegian-American Lutheran mission interests. Hitherto the missions established by the American church were often directly or indirectly shaped by impulses from Norway. The Zulu field, says Syrdal, marked "a bridge, or overlap, from the period of Norwegian influence to the more independent periods to follow."[51] That is to say, as the church experienced "Americanization" on this continent, its missions on other continents reflected this independence from the church life of the motherland.

From the beginning of mission interest in the nineteenth century the foreign mission enterprise carried on by Norwegian-American Lutherans was an extension of interests originally born in Norway. The three mission fields which received support in 1917 were all closely allied to previous mission work in these general areas by mission societies in Norway. This program continued largely unchanged until the church decided

---
[50]*Ibid.*, pp. 87-88.
[51]Syrdal, "Eras of ELC Foreign Mission History," (unpublished manuscript, 1959).

in 1943 to begin a mission in South America.[52] In that year missionaries were sent to Mexico for training in Spanish. In 1945-1946 the church took over an independent Lutheran mission, known as the Celmosa Mission, in Colombia, South America. This action marked the first alteration in the previous pattern. No influences from Norway characterized this venture; no Norwegian mission work in South America attracted the Norwegian-Americans. Although this was not a consciously planned break with the mission tradition, the "American" aspect of this undertaking was emphasized in that, for the first time, the NLCA shared mission responsibility with another American Lutheran church body, namely, the United (Danish) Evangelical Lutheran Church.

The first two eras of foreign mission history—the period of Norwegian influence and that of independent "American" outreach—were shortly followed by mission contraction and expansion after World War II. The contraction occurred in 1949 with the withdrawal of American missions from Red China. Almost immediately, however, new missions were begun in Hong Kong (1949) and Formosa (1950). Initiated as continuations of the China mission, they rapidly assumed individual characteristics and independent viewpoints. The Formosa venture was unique in that it was a cooperative enterprise by eight American and European missionary groups. Another result of the closing of China was the organizing of the Japan mission in 1949. The Japan mission, like the Colombia mission, was jointly sponsored by the ELC and another American body, this time the Lutheran Free Church. Moreover, the ELC-LFC mission quickly began cooperative efforts with the Japanese Evangelical Lutheran Church (formed earlier by the ULCA and UELC missions); this is already the nucleus for a united Lutheran church in Japan.

Two additional missions have been assumed in the fifties, the Sudan mission in the French Camerouns and Equatorial Africa and a Brazil mission in 1958. The former had an inde-

[52]*NLCA . . . Annual Report . . . 1914*, p. 118.

pendent history back to 1923; the latter, of course, has hardly begun to function.

Two characteristics of the postwar development should be noted: (1) the continuing and intensifying of Lutheran cooperation on the foreign field; and (2) the rising nationalism and self-consciousness of the younger churches.

Cooperation among the home boards has been furthered by the Lutheran Foreign Missions Conference of North America, which includes all American Lutheran bodies. On a global scale the Lutheran World Federation has facilitated united efforts by drawing mission executives into the meetings of its Commission on World Missions.

Perhaps most significant of all has been the drive toward indigenization of the missions. Just as the Norwegian Lutheran Church of America became a self-conscious "American" church, so its mission offspring have shared the vigorous nationalism of Asian and African peoples. More and more the missions are being recognized as autonomous, self-supporting, and self-determining younger churches.

Executive secretaries of the Board of Foreign Missions since 1917 have been: Dr. J. R. Birkelund, 1917-1935; Dr. J. E. Grønli, 1936-1947; and Dr. R. A. Syrdal, 1947 to the present.

Home Missions

The processes of Americanization were most clearly and dramatically evident in the area of home mission activity. It was in this work, for example, that pastors and people felt most acutely the necessity of language transition. Moreover, it was in home missions that the church was closest to the major cultural and sociological problems in America. Consequently, the program of home missions, of necessity if for no other reason, reflected the changing scene. How this occurred during the years between 1917 and the mid-fifties can be seen by abstracting certain key characteristics of three rather distinct periods, 1917-1930; 1930-1944; and 1944 to the present.

1917-1930:Expansion Under a Cultural Pattern.—The work

The Church Discovers America

of home missions before 1917, especially the period from 1890 to the merger, was largely an attempt to win and hold the Norwegian immigrants for the American version of the religion of Norway. The stupendous task of keeping pace with immigration was beyond the church's ability. T. H. Dahl reported that over one million Norwegian-Americans in 1917 were not members of a church.[53] No thought was given to the unchurched "Yankee," or German, or Irishman. The stray German or Irishman who came into a Norwegian-American community was either a lonely individual or a "proselyte of the gate." Forced to conform to the cultural pattern, he soon was indistinguishable from the others. Einar Haugen tells of a Norwegian immigrant who desired to learn English by boarding at the only Irish family in a small Wisconsin town, only to learn to his chagrin that Norwegian was spoken at the family table![54]

The character of the home mission work between 1917 and 1930 was quite unchanged from the pre-1917 years. Norwegian Lutheran pastors sought out Norwegian Lutheran immigrants or sons and daughters of immigrants. Congregations were built on this distinct cultural base.

Before 1917 the home mission division of church activity had been assigned numerous "special missions," some of which could have been more accurately described as inner missions or even parish education. This pattern continued into the twenties. In fact, home missions became a sort of "catchall" for almost a dozen difficult-to-categorize services. There was, for example, a "Book Mission," or tract society, which came to rest in the Department of Home Missions. Likewise the English Association, Indian and Eskimo missions, an immigrant mission, seamen's missions, missions to students at state schools, evangelistic missions, a mission to the deaf, city missionaries (hospital chaplains and slum visitors), even an abortive mission to Russian communities in North Dakota—all were placed under the control of the Board of Home Missions.

---
[53]*Supra*, Chapter IV.
[54]Haugen, *op. cit.*, I, 236.

As early as 1918 some of these activities were transferred to other departments as, for example, the work of the so-called "city missionaries." This was more properly placed under the Board of Charities which supervised the inner mission or social welfare program of the church. Some years later student service was transferred to the Department of Education. However, much of the time and energy and resources of the department continued to be devoted to "special missions."

Three things are to be noted from this period in addition to the over-all "Norwegian" character of the work. The first was the role of the immigrant mission in Brooklyn, New York. "Norway House," as it was called, became a familiar and welcome sight to tourists as well as immigrants.[55] But its historical significance lay in the fact that it was a witness to the rather sharp increase in immigration in the early twenties. When this dropped off, the need for "Norway House" disappeared.[56]

The second item was the role of evangelism, defined not so much as seeking out the unchurched as quickening and "saving" the church members. As noted in Chapter IV, both Hauge's Synod and the United Church maintained the practice of employing evangelists, lay or clerical, who would travel among the congregations conducting series of evangelistic services. In 1918-1920 the church employed one evangelist, the Reverend J. J. Breidablik. He reported in 1919 that he had traveled fourteen thousand miles, conducted three hundred services in twenty-three parishes.[57] In 1921, two evangelists were serving the church; in 1923, a third was added to the staff. This was strong indication that the Haugean emphasis on "living Christianity" and "edifying meetings" was a continuing emphasis in the new church.

The third matter to be noted was the large sums of money appropriated for the cause of home missions. After the first year of existence, the budget request was about $200,000. The

---
[55]*Report . . . NLCA . . . 1925*, p. 277.
[56]*Report . . . NLCA . . . 1936*, p. 104.
[57]*Report . . . NLCA . . . 1919*, p. 62.

next year it was almost $250,000. By 1923 it was over $333,000. Here was striking evidence of the seriousness with which the new church undertook its missionary obligation. However, alongside the large appropriations, there were mounting deficits. Almost annually the executive secretary, the Reverend C. S. B. Hoel, reported expenditures in excess of receipts. In 1924, for example, the fiscal report showed a deficit of $150,100.61. A "Decennial Financial Survey" presented in 1931 indicated that the Department of Home Missions had disbursed over $300,000 more than its income during the so-called "boom years" of the twenties. Other departments were likewise incurring deficits.[58] All of this meant that the church, which had almost unlimited credit at Minneapolis banks, was entering the thirties with fiscal shortages which would sadly cripple it during the difficult years of the Depression.

1930-1944: The Stern Years.—The next period was characterized by a drastically reduced program financially speaking, but an intensification of effort in defining the nature of home mission activity.

With the onslaught of the world-wide Depression and the Midwest drought, the church found it necessary to cut back expenditures and balance the budget. At the pit of the Depression, it was reported that Home Missions had an accumulated deficit of $261,000.[59] One of the first steps taken to remove the imbalance was the curtailment of administrative staff. The church requested Dr. Aasgaard to assume, in addition to his regular duties, the executive direction of two departments, Home Missions and Charities. This he did as of January 1, 1934.[60] The next economy measure was the adoption of a "pay-as-you-go" procedure. This meant the reduction of salaries and mission subsidies and the urging of congregations to repay loans and maintain interest payments. Already in 1934 the department reported an operating balance rather than a defi-

---
[58] See treasurer's summary in *Report* . . . *NLCA* . . . *1925*, p. 96.
[59] *NLCA* . . . *Annual Report* . . . *1940*, p. 93.
[60] *NLCA* . . . *Annual Report* . . . *1934*, p. 68.

cit.[61] By 1940 the Board of Home Missions had removed the entire deficit by using annual surpluses and a large percentage of the Centennial offering. The latter had been initiated in 1936 at the recommendation of Dr. Aasgaard.[62]

The second characteristic of the era of the Depression and the second World War was a new emphasis given to the nature of home missions. Hitherto the "special missions," mentioned above, absorbed much of the attention of the department. Although Aasgaard's direction of Home Missions did not neglect the "special missions," it nonetheless found the focus of the department's activity in an outreach to unchurched Lutherans and the planting of new churches where need existed. During the years before and after the 1917 merger, home missions meant seeking and saving Norwegians. But by 1932 the Norwegian Lutheran Church of America admitted that this was an inadequate policy. In that year it joined with other Lutheran church bodies (ALC, Augustana, LFC, Suomi, United Danish, and ULCA) in the organization of the Lutheran Home Missions Council of America. Its purpose was to coordinate Lutheran home mission activity in the United States and Canada so as to avoid needless competition and duplication of efforts.[63] This Council became the forerunner of Regional Home Mission Committees which supervised comity arrangements between the churches. Implied in this action, of course, was the recognition that Americanization had taken place, and that other bodies were capable of ministering to Norwegians and that the NLCA was capable of ministering to Lutherans of other national origins. In this way, the decade from the early thirties might be characterized as the period of "seeking and saving Lutherans," not merely Norwegian Lutherans. This does not mean that efforts were confined only to reaching unchurched Lutherans—the membership lists of many home mission congregations of these years are evidence to this—but it does mean that when decisions were made to enter a new

[61]*Ibid.*, p. 134.
[62]*Ibid.*, 1936, p. 17.
[63]*Report . . . NLCA . . . 1932*, p. 262.

home mission field, one of the main factors was the percentage of unchurched *Lutherans* living in the area which had been surveyed.

Aasgaard gave vigorous leadership to this phase of the work. As early as 1934 he called attention to the increased population mobility. Vast numbers of Lutherans were moving from their homes to seek employment in the new government sponsored projects such as the Tennessee Valley undertaking and the Fort Peck Dam (Montana).[64]

In 1936 he quoted statistics to show that only four million of an estimated Lutheran population of seventeen million had been drawn into the Lutheran churches of America. Statistics for the Upper Midwest and the Northwest showed that three-fourths of an estimated Lutheran population of four and a half million were not affiliated with the church. From this he concluded: "Most of these millions of unchurched Lutherans are found not out in the vast spaces of Home Mission territory but right within the shadow of large and influential congregations. . . . An active Home Mission program should be a part of the project of every congregation in our Synod."[65]

1944-1954: "Operation New Church": Radical But . . . —The third and contemporary phase of the work of home missions has shown the most marked departures from traditional practices and, in some ways, the most radical innovations in home mission policy by any Protestant church in America.

The change began in 1944. The war had brought on a vast movement of population from one part of the country to another, especially to the West Coast. Every major Christian church in America developed a sharpened interest in reaching the unchurched multitudes. Dr. Aasgaard, as head of the NLCA, shared this concern and declared early in 1944 that the church should have a full-time director of home missions. The Board of Home Missions prepared a series of forward looking resolutions to project plans for the future. Adopted by the church, they called for a full-time executive secretary, regional

---
[64] *NLCA . . . Annual Report . . . 1934*, pp. 64-65.
[65] *NLCA . . . Annual Report . . . 1936*, pp. 97-98.

directors, salaries commensurate with those of pastors in established parishes, and loans from the church's investment funds for the Church Extension Fund.[66]

On September 1, 1944, the Reverend Philip S. Dybvig, professor of religion at St. Olaf College, Northfield, Minnesota, became the Director of Home Missions and almost immediately new energies were released into the program. Before the year was over seventeen new congregations had been established, and plans were being shaped for a dynamic and radically new type of mission activity. The innovation, adopted as policy on October 17, 1945, challenged the methods prevalent in most church bodies at the time.[67] Dybvig shifted the emphasis from long drawn-out salary subsidies to complete financing of a new project by loans to new congregations from funds placed at the disposal of the Home Missions Department. Dybvig called his plan "Operation New Church" and, after successfully introducing it, was asked to explain its workings to the Lutheran mission executives meeting in Chicago, December 6-8, 1948.[68] "Operation New Church" had the following main steps:

1. *Assignment of Field.* This was done on the basis of standard operating procedure of the Lutheran regional committee.
2. *Survey.* This was judged relatively unimportant. If it was an average American community, underchurched, and without evidence of being predominantly Jewish and Roman Catholic, the field was ready for entry.
3. *Calling the Pastor.* He had to be an experienced man with no congregational failures in his background. The salary paid was comparable with that received in the better established parishes. Moving expenses of household goods (but not travel expense) were paid.
4. *The Parsonage.* The practice was to build or buy a good home, not to rent. The idea was, "We are here to stay."
5. *Minimum Equipment.* Each new church was to have a parish record book, thirty hymnals, Sunday school texts and teachers' manuals,

---

[66]H. L. Foss and N. A. Larsen, "A Decade of Home Mission Progress" (Unpublished manuscript), pp. 1-2. The matter of salaries is revealing in that it indicates that, previous to this time, home mission parishes were on a lower financial level than other parishes. This meant they were frequently served by young and inexperienced graduates of seminary or superannuated pastors.
[67]*Ibid.*, pp. 3-5.
[68]P. S. Dybvig, "Operation New Church," in *Policies and Practices in Lutheran Home Mission Development* (Chicago: The National Lutheran Council, 1948), pp. 6-19.

duplex envelopes, Sunday bulletins, communion set, offering plates, mimeograph, and typewriter.
6. *Preparation for the First Service.* The pastor and a parish visitor spent about a month in visitation before the first service. Much depended on a successful (numerically speaking) first service.
7. *Preliminary Committee.* Within a few weeks, the pastor or the worshiping group selected a preliminary committee to work with the pastor arranging for a constitution and formal organization.
8. *Relation to Home Mission Department.* About three months after the arrival of the pastor, there was the first visit by a representative of the Home Mission Department and the District President. Orientation to the general congregational program, financial support (assuming obligations in a specified order from miscellaneous expenses through loan payments to pastor's salary), proposed loan and amortization of same, every-member canvass, and ultimate self-support were discussed.

Under this plan almost phenomenal results occurred. Twenty new churches were organized in 1945; twenty-two (one every seventeen days) in 1946; nineteen in 1947; twelve in 1948; eighteen in 1949; ten in 1950; twenty-three in 1951; nine in 1952; twenty-five in 1953; and at least forty in 1954.

The plan presupposed a large church extension fund. This was arranged by transferring a $300,000 Home Mission Emergency Fund to the Church Extension Fund, to be turned back in the event of dire necessity. Home mission endowment funds were placed into the loan program. With this accomplished, the department implemented the resolution of 1944 to permit borrowing from the church's endowment funds for church extension. Finally, the Home Mission Department received over $800,000 from a church-wide joint appeal for home and foreign missions. Thus, even in periods of economic recession the church had a workable and potentially fruitful plan for home mission expansion.[69]

Three additional activities marked the decade after World War II. One was the inauguration of a "sponsorship plan" whereby a large and well-established congregation would sponsor a new congregation without cost to the Home Mission

---
[69] *Ibid.*, p. 18.

Board. In order to provide capital, the older church would mortgage its property and make a loan to the new congregation.[70]

A second factor in broadening the effectiveness of the home mission program was the establishment in 1945 of a Commission on Rural Life.[71] Recognizing that the NLCA was one of the largest church bodies with a predominantly rural constituency, pastors in the South Dakota District persuaded the church that it had a major responsibility for rural America. Publicizing the plan of the Roman Catholic Church's rural life program as a threat to communities of a Lutheran character, the group soon had enlisted church-wide interest. Recognizing that it had a much greater mission than a mere anti-Roman program, the newly-appointed commission worked for parish realignment, every-Sunday services, promoting interest in and respect for rural life, a heightened attitude of soil stewardship, and cooperation with those interested in rural sociology and economics.

The third phase of activity marked for special comment is that of parish evangelism. In 1945 the Board of Home Missions called a full-time director of evangelism, the Reverend E. C. Reinertson, in order to encourage established congregations in community or parish evangelism.[72] Close on the heels of this appointment came the establishing of a Commission on Evangelism, with Dr. George Aus, professor of systematic theology at Luther Theological Seminary, as chairman.[73] One of the outstanding evangelistic efforts of this commission has been the program nicknamed the "P-T-R" (Preaching-Teaching-Reaching). Begun in 1952 under the direction of the Reverend Conrad Thompson, who had succeeded Reinertson in 1951, the program was a congregation-centered, church-wide attempt at effective parish evangelism.

---

[70]This plan was initiated by First Lutheran Church, Albert Lea, Minnesota, the Reverend M. S. Knutson, pastor, in 1947.

[71]*NLCA . . . Annual Report . . . 1945*, p. 132.

[72]*NLCA . . . Annual Report . . . 1946*, p. 143. The Board of Home Missions continued the inherited practice of calling traveling evangelists. In 1945-1946 there were five. *Ibid.*, p. 135.

[73]Foss and Larsen, *op. cit.*, p. 7.

The plan required that congregations—from three to three hundred—in a given area unite in a simultaneous mission of preaching, teaching, and reaching (visitation evangelism). Each participating congregation invited a guest pastor to conduct a preaching mission from Sunday through Thursday night for the purpose of deepening the spiritual life of believers and of evangelizing the lost.

The "teaching" phase of the mission had three parts. The first was a four-day "mission to pastors," Monday through Thursday during the P-T-R, directed by guest teachers conducting Bible study or presenting theological lectures. The second group to be taught—before the P-T-R began—was the lay visitors who would be conducting the visitation during the mission. The third part was the teaching of adult leadership groups within the congregation by the guest pastor.

The "reaching" phase also consisted of three parts. The first was a "religious canvass" of the community conducted by the congregation in order to establish a "prospect list" for the church. The second—also prior to the mission—was the sending of teams of laymen to visit the members of the congregation to enlist their support for the mission. The third part was the actual "reaching" by the trained laymen who visited the unchurched.

Some of the tangible fruits of the program have been a reexamination of the theology of evangelism, the establishing of year-round programs of parish visitation, the enrollment of thousands in church membership classes, and the growth of Sunday schools and catechetical classes.

In summary, 1917 to 1930 was a period of continuing evangelistic concern for Norwegian immigrants or their descendants; 1930 to 1944 was a time of wider outreach that sought all dislocated and unchurched Lutherans; and 1944 to the present saw an honest attempt at sociologically or ecclesiastically unconditioned evangelism.

Executive secretaries of the Board of Home Missions since 1917 have been: the Reverend C. S. B. Hoel, 1919-1933; Dr. J. A. Aasgaard, 1934-1944; Dr. P. S. Dybvig, 1944 to the present.

Christian Education[74]

The Norwegian Lutheran Church of America began its life in 1917 with a well-established program of education on several levels, elementary, secondary, college, and seminary. We have noted (in Chapter IV) the rise and fall of the academy or church high school movement. The other educational efforts, however, continued in strength throughout the period under survey, weathering the vicissitudes of the Depression and war and demonstrating the church's commitment to a strong program of Christian education.

On all levels, the general pattern of education, as inherited from the pre-1917 years, moved uninterrupted into the new church. Parish education consisted of Sunday schools, pastors' catechetical or confirmation classes, summer "parochial" schools, and, in some instances, weekday schools on the basis of released time from public schools. Adult education on the parish level was inadequate, consisting of a weekly Bible class, infrequent church membership classes, and occasional teachers' training institutes.

On the higher level, the pattern of four-year liberal arts colleges, shaped before 1917, persisted largely unchanged into the twenties and thirties. By the beginning of World War II five senior colleges were associated with the Norwegian Lutheran Church of America: Augustana (Sioux Falls, South Dakota), Concordia (Moorhead, Minnesota), Luther, (Decorah, Iowa), Pacific Lutheran (Parkland, Washington), and St. Olaf (Northfield, Minnesota).

On the professional level only Luther Theological Seminary was operated by the church. By 1939 steps had been taken to establish a second seminary—at Saskatoon, Saskatchewan, Canada.

The influences of the American cultural and religious milieu on the educational program were most clearly evident in parish and collegiate education. Theological education con-

---

[74] For a survey of Christian education in the ELC, see *The ELC . . . Annual Report . . . 1956*, pp. 122-137.

Augustana College, Sioux Falls, South Dakota

Concordia College, Moorhead, Minnesota

Luther College, Decorah, Iowa

Pacific Lutheran College, Parkland, Washington

St. Olaf College, Northfield, Minnesota

*Augustana Academy
Canton, South Dakota*

*Waldorf College
Forest City, Iowa*

Bethesda Home for the Aged, Beresford, S. D.

Aase Haugen Home for the Aged, Decorah, Iowa

Skaalen Sunset Home, Stoughton, Wis.

LUTHERAN COOPERATION

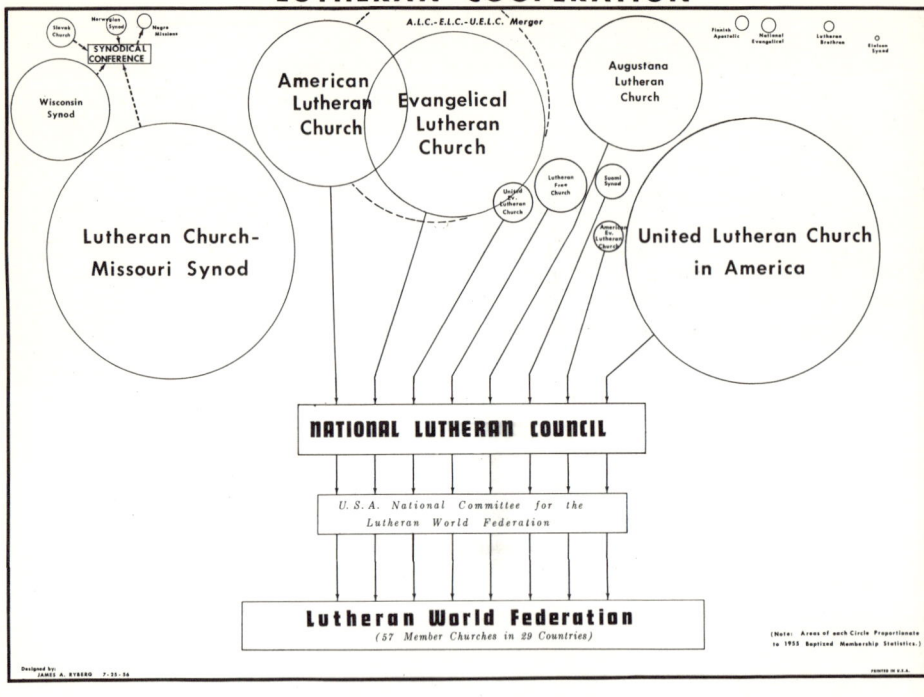

Lutheran Churches in America

Mrs. T. H. Dahl
First President of the
Women's Missionary Federation

L. W. Boe
ELC Pioneer in
Inter-Lutheran Cooperation

tinued in the established manner without noticeable change until the second World War.

In parish education one of the clearest signs of Americanization was the change to monolingual instruction in the pastors' confirmation classes. By the mid-twenties very few children were "reading for the minister" in Norwegian.[75]

A second evidence of change occurred in the summer "parochial" schools. Originally the summer school of religion in the parish served a dual purpose: to indoctrinate the children religiously and to preserve Norwegian culture (instruction was in Norwegian). Sometimes the "parochial" school was called the "Norwegian" school. But the process of Americanization was felt here, too, and by the late twenties and especially the thirties the congregations were beginning to imitate other American Protestant churches by conducting Daily Vacation Bible Schools with, of course, a distinctly Lutheran orientation but without any overt attempt to preserve an inherited culture.

A third example of change was in the textbooks used for Sunday school instruction. Before 1917 and continuing through the twenties instruction was based on graded adaptations of Luther's *Small Catechism*. The "Graded System," as it was called, had been prepared not by professionally trained teachers but by pastors interested in Christian education. In the early thirties a new series of textbooks, this time prepared by teachers, began to make its appearance and has been used to the present. Significant leadership in this area was given by Dr. J. C. K. Preus, executive secretary of the Department of Christian Education. Several projects and programs, some of which became permanent features in parish education, were begun and directed by him during his twenty-five-year period of service.[76]

---

[75]The phrase "reading for the minister" was a literal but not accurate translation of *læse for presten*, which meant the recitation of the catechism in response to the pastor's questions. Although the phrase continued to be used in English, it sounded strange to one who did not understand its background. In 1924 when the writer was "reading for the minister," there was but one out of a class of about thirty who was "confirmed in Norwegian."

[76]*The ELC Annual Report . . . 1956*, pp. 126-129.

In adult education the church was primarily concerned with the training of Sunday school teachers. To this end teachers' institutes using specially prepared textbooks were conducted throughout the circuits of the church and at summer camps. Recently a Christian Service Institute, designed as a school of theology for lay workers in the church, has been sponsored by the Board of Education in connection with the summer program at Luther Theological Seminary.

Church-related liberal arts colleges were also influenced by the American culture. The older schools were distinctly "Norwegian" in character, although the instruction was in English. The students were, in the main, the children of Norwegian-Americans and the campuses on which they lived were colonies of Norwegian-American culture. But, as with other church institutions, the colleges were in the process of "becoming" a part of the American environment. Coeducation, adopted as policy at St. Olaf from the beginning, was distinctly an American way of education. As with other church-related schools the colleges of the NLCA were soon caught up in the tension between the liberal arts and religion. They were forced to ask themselves what their distinctive nature as church colleges was. They asked, Is there a Christian, or specifically Lutheran, philosophy of education? Curricula also showed the influences of Americanization, most noticeably perhaps in the fading of classical emphases. Curricular adjustments to meet the demands of the day were frequently proposed. Increasing interest in vocational courses led some faculties to fear that the liberal arts tradition was being vitiated. In the area of administration the colleges adopted the methods of American business as exhibited in long-range planning, managerial or executive type presidents, offices of public relations, and so forth.

The place of religion on the campus during the past quarter century witnessed a marked change, whether as an influence of Americanization or not is difficult to document. Although the founders, chief supporters, and many of the faculty members were clergymen, there was a conscious trend during the years to avoid identifying religion with the ordained men on campus. Rather there was an effort to bring a theological orientation into the teaching of the non-theological courses. The religious genius of the colleges was not to be sought in the Department of Religion but in the atmosphere of the whole campus. Coupled with this, however, there was a determined effort to make the Department of Religion academically as respectable as the Department of English or the Department of Chemistry.

One of the dominant characteristics of Christian higher education was the vitality exhibited by the colleges. Rapid growth in student enrollments, vigorous expansion of the physical plants, and increased and effective attention to academic standing made the ELC colleges outstanding as sources for lay and ministerial leadership. Presidents of the institutions during this era have been the following: Augustana—H. S. Hilleboe, 1917-1920; C. O. Solberg, 1920-1928; O. J. H. Preus, 1929-1932; C. M. Granskou, 1932-1943; and L. M. Stavig, 1943-. Luther—C. K. Preus, 1902-1921; O. L. Olson, 1921-1932; O. J. H. Preus, 1932-1948; and J. W. Ylvisaker, 1948-. St. Olaf—L. A. Vigness, 1914-1918; L. W. Boe, 1918-1942; C. M. Granskou, 1943-. Concordia—J. A. Aasgaard, 1911-1925; J. N. Brown 1925-1951; and J. L. Knutson, 1951-. Pacific Lutheran—N. J. Hong, 1899-1918; O. J. Ordal, 1921-1928; O. A. Tingelstad, 1928-1943; and S. C. Eastvold, 1943-.

Education on the seminary level showed the least change in the period under survey. In fact, except for the language of instruction, the theological educational process in 1940 was little altered from 1917. This process was characterized by an uncritical acceptance and transmission of the Lutheran tradition for the purpose of training faithful pastors committed to the task of shepherding congregations and preaching the gospel. In keeping with this purpose was the enlargement of the offerings in practical theology by the assignment of students to a year of internship or clinical training in parishes. This departure was authorized by the church in 1934.[77] Only since

---
[77] NLCA Report . . . 1934, p. 307.

World War II has there been a serious consideration of the major theological issues which modern scholarship has thrust upon the seminary horizon, and with this a concommitant curricular concern. Presidents of the seminary since 1917 have been: Dr. M. O. Bøckman, 1917-1930; Dr. T. F. Gullixson, 1930-1954; Dr. A. N. Rogness, 1954-.

Executive secretaries of the Department of Christian Education have been Dr. L. W. Boe, 1917-1918; Dr. L. A. Vigness, 1918-1931; Dr. J. C. K. Preus, 1931-1956; Dr. S. A. Rand, 1956-.

The Work of Charity

The inner mission activities among the Norwegian-Americans were wide and varied by 1917 (Chapter IV), but their common characteristic could be described as institutional social welfare. This took the form of homes for the aged and orphaned children, hospitals and deaconess homes. The task of social missions had not carried the church beyond these enterprises. But, as with the other departmental activities of the NLCA, charities also underwent changes because of the American setting in which the work was done.

There are three periods into which the last forty years quite naturally may be divided: 1917-1933, in which Dr. H. B. Kildahl served as executive secretary; 1933-1944, in which the severities of the Depression forced Dr. Aasgaard to carry the departmental responsibilities; and 1945 to the present, in which Dr. Magnus A. Dahlen has served as executive secretary.

Almost at the outset the newly established church indicated a broadening interest in the nature of its social mission. When H. B. Kildahl was elected secretary of the Board of Charities, he was given the special assignment of home-finding for children.[78] Furthermore, in order to keep abreast of the social developments of the day, the director was authorized to "join the Central Organization for Social Agencies."[79] Concern for

[78] *Beretning* . . . *1917*, p. 568; *ibid.*, *1918*, p. 191.
[79] Minutes of Board of Charities, Dec. 11, 1917.

the mentally ill and inmates of prisons was expressed in a decision to establish chaplaincies in these areas.[80] A day nursery for children of working mothers was in operation already in 1918.[81] By 1920 the Board had expressed itself as being interested in the professional training of social workers.[82] Thus it can be seen that advanced positions in social welfare were being taken in the twenties under the guidance of Dr. H. B. Kildahl.[83]

The economic distresses of the Depression years made the work of direction largely a holding operation.[84] But with the indications of financial recovery at the end of the decade and the pressures of wartime emergencies, expansion of welfare work was deemed imperative. Under these circumstances, M. A. Dahlen was elected full-time executive secretary in 1944, a position he assumed January 1, 1946.

During the decade 1946-1956 the churches of America, including the ELC, made serious attempts to meet the increased emphasis on social welfare. Within the ELC's Department of Charities it was soon evident that the church must make preparations to meet the altered social situation. In 1947 all personnel involved in the social welfare program of the church were called together for what was called the National Charities Conference of The Evangelical Lutheran Church. Although no significant resolution or action originated at the meeting, it nevertheless gave evidence that leaders in this area were conscious of the social ferment occurring in America. In almost every subsequent undertaking of the Board of Charities there was a reflection of what the World Council of Churches has recently called "rapid social change." Acutely sensitive to the American scene, the program of charities—like the program of home missions—became closely involved with the socio-cultural alterations of the age.

One of the first implementations of this awareness of change

---

[80]*Ibid.*, May 14, 1918. Cf. *Ibid.*, Sept. 11, 1920.
[81]*Ibid.*, Nov. 12-13, 1918.
[82]*Ibid.*, April 14, 1920.
[83]For an impressive survey of the social welfare program of the church toward the conclusion of Kildahl's service see *Report . . . NLCA . . . 1931*, pp. 386-410.
[84]*NLCA . . . Annual Report . . . 1934*, p. 98.

was the action of the Board of Charities to initiate a scholarship program for the professional training of social workers. Special attention was given to medical and psychiatric social workers, group workers, workers in children's agencies, hospital administrators, directors of schools of nursing, institutional chaplains and managers.

In 1948 the Department requested Luther Theological Seminary to provide theoretical and clinical training for institutional chaplains. This program, launched in 1952,[85] has been carried through with considerable success.

Perhaps one of the most significant programs of social welfare in the church has been in the area of service to the aged. Public interest in the problems of old persons has mounted as available information has pointed up the increasing longevity of people. Both church and state have concerned themselves with the questions which have grown out of this new situation. Recognizing that it is unwise to remove elderly people from the community where they have had long-time roots, the Board of Charities encouraged the building of new homes for the aged—often with infirmaries attached—in dozens of local communities throughout the church. Furthermore, being persuaded that there was no compromise of the principle of separation of church and state, the Board recommended the use of Federal aid provided through the Hill-Burton legislation.[86] In 1958 there were twenty-nine homes for the aged operating within the ELC.

Other Activities of the Church

During the past forty years the ELC has moved from the position of a church preoccupied with the problems of an immigrant people to a thoroughly American church involved in the great social complex of which it is a part. This has been seen in the work of the church in four of its major fields of activity: foreign missions, home missions, education, and chari-

---
[85] *The ELC Annual Report* . . . 1952, p. 212-213.
[86] *The ELC Annual Report* . . . 1956, p. 249.

ties. Other activities, such as publications, finances, women's, men's, and youth work, all bear witness to basically the same transformation.

Publications.—When the Norwegian Lutheran Church in America was formed in 1917 three publication houses were united: the Hauge Printing and Publishing Society of Red Wing, Minnesota (founded in 1878); the Lutheran Publishing House of Decorah, Iowa (founded by the Norwegian Synod in 1878); and Augsburg Publishing House (established in 1891 by the United Norwegian Lutheran Church). Printing operations were combined in the building at 425 South Fourth Street, which Augsburg had occupied since 1909. The Decorah branch store was operated until 1932.

In 1917 most of the printing was still being done in Norwegian and the major job of the presses was to publish the *Lutheraneren* and the *Lutheran Herald.* In the forty years which have now become history the publishing house has achieved a remarkable success. Evidence of this has been the fact that among thirty-six Protestant publishing concerns in America, Augsburg ranks sixth in dollar volume. The *Lutheran Herald,* the official church paper of the ELC, has a circulation of over one hundred thousand. *Lutheraneren,* which had twice the circulation of the *Lutheran Herald* in 1924 (twenty thousand to ten thousand), had dropped below the *Lutheran Herald* in 1929. When publication of the Norwegian paper was discontinued in 1956 its circulation was two thousand. Editors of *Lutheraneren* since the union have been Thore Eggen, 1917-1920; J. M. Sundheim, 1920-1922; P. Tangjerd, 1923-1924; J. Tanner, 1924-1925; L. A. Vigness, 1925-1939; H. E. Jørgensen, 1939-1956. Editors of *Lutheran Herald* have been G. T. Lee, 1917-1939 and O. G. Malmin, 1939-.

Other parish education materials, such as textbooks and manuals for religious instruction, have made up a large part of Augsburg's output. In these materials the publishing house pioneered in at least two things: the introduction of church history into the Sunday school curriculum and the use of full color in children's texts.

Augsburg has also been a major publisher of music for churches. Choirs of the nation have for years been using the nearly five hundred anthems published by the house. Two Augsburg choral series have been outstanding, the St. Olaf Choir series of 263 anthems, edited by the late Dr. F. Melius Christiansen, director of the St. Olaf choir and a pioneer in a cappella singing, and the Augsburg Choral Library by various authors. The new series now equals the St. Olaf series in volume. Christiansen's arrangement of "Beautiful Savior" has become the nation's best selling choral anthem. Through 1958 sales of this one anthem passed the one million mark. In addition to choral anthems, Augsburg publishes music for organ, vocal solos, music textbooks, as well as junior choir anthems and hymnals. The new *Lutheran Service Book and Hymnal,* a joint project of eight church bodies, was issued in 1958.

A unique product of the Augsburg presses is *Christmas,* an American annual of Christmas literature and art, which has been produced since 1931. Since the first press run of five thousand, the distribution of this book has grown each year until in 1957 it reached one hundred fifty thousand. For several years *Christmas* has made the top of the best seller list (November and December) compiled by the *Retail Bookseller,* the monthly trade magazine of American publishers. The book has been edited by Randolph E. Haugan, the manager of the publishing house since 1929.

The publishing house is the only department of the ELC which is not subsidized from the church budget. In fact, from 1929-57 it had earned a profit of $1,528,908. Eighty per cent of this was given to the ELC for its general budget and pension fund, and the balance was reemployed in the ELC's publishing work. Earnings from the publishing house have largely financed the new $1,250,000 ELC headquarters and publishing house building occupied in 1953.

Finances.—Norwegian immigrants, used to the pattern of a tax-supported state church in Europe, had to make major adjustments in providing systematic financial support for the church which they built in America. The psychological change which the new situation demanded was complicated by the general poverty of the immigrants. Moreover, the money of the church members had to be divided between the local congregation and the benevolent work of the general church body. The local congregation was close at hand and its needs seemed most pressing; but gradually a sense of corporate responsibility was built up for the whole work of the whole church.

By 1917 a pattern began to emerge for the support of the general work. A budget was adopted by the church in convention and allocated to the congregations. However, it was to be the responsibility of the various departments to collect the sums appropriated for their use.[87] The ineffectiveness of this method was soon apparent and revisions in the system were soon forthcoming.[88] By 1920 a more permanent financial organization was worked out. The plan called for the allocation of the church's budget first to the various districts, then to the circuits within the districts, and then to the congregations within the circuits. In this way all were expected to assume a "fair share" of the voted budget.[89] In order to raise the allocation, the congregation most frequently had special offerings for "mission," "education," and the other activities. Weekly or monthly giving was encouraged in the early twenties. Duplex offering envelopes and every-member visitations were increasingly used by the congregations.[90] Promotional secretaries, known as "Field Superintendents," were engaged to visit congregations in the interest of the general work of the church.[91] The success or failure of the congregations to meet their apportionments was made known by publishing an annual report of the assessment and contributions.

The budgetary strains of the Depression years led to the calling of a general field superintendent or stewardship secretary in the person of Dr. A. J. Bergsaker. Assuming office in 1931 and continuing to his death in 1951, Bergsaker together

---
[87]*Beretning* . . . *1917*, p. 569.
[88]*Beretning* . . . *1918*, p. 332.
[89]*Beretning* . . . *1920*, pp. 160-161.
[90]*NLCA* . . . *Annual Report* . . . *1925*, p. 390.
[91]*Ibid.*, p. 373.

with Dr. H. O. Shurson, treasurer of the church (1925-1951) developed a far-reaching consciousness of the stewardship of wealth in ELC congregations. Education in stewardship, workers' conferences, and encouragement of pastors raised the level of giving to new heights. Special appeals such as the Centennial offering in the late thirties, the Luther College Emergency Appeal in 1942, the United Mission Advance in 1946, and several others brought in over five million dollars and, in the process, indicated something of the fiscal potentialities of the church.[92] Meanwhile, World War II led the American Lutheran churches into a cooperative fund-raising effort known as Lutheran World Action. Conducted as a "special appeal" from its beginning in 1943-1944, LWA was made a part of the regular budget of the church in 1955.[93]

Dr. Raymond M. Olson, Bergsaker's successor as stewardship secretary, proposed in 1954 that the church adopt a new fiscal program in view of the approaching merger with the ALC and the UELC. One of the features of the new plan, borrowed from the ALC and originated by the Synod of the Northwest, ULCA (1918-1919), was the discarding of the apportionment plan of raising benevolent funds in favor of voluntarily assumed congregational goals.[94]

Auxiliaries.—Closely related to the general work of the church have been the auxiliary organizations for the laity. The women of the church, the men of the church, and the youth of the church all have had their special organizations. Two women's organizations, The Women's Missionary Federation and the Lutheran Daughters of the Reformation, have provided outstanding leadership and no insignificant support to the general work of the church. The former, established in 1917, and the latter, an outgrowth of the WMF in 1926, have been orientated towards two segments of the church's female constituency. The WMF has directed the religious energies of

---

[92]*NLCA . . . Annual Report . . . 1946*, p. 255.
[93]*ELC Annual Report . . . 1954*, pp. 316, 440.
[94]*Ibid.*, pp. 320, 456.

the housewives and mothers; the LDR, the business and professional women of the congregations.[95]

The WMF under its first president, Mrs. T. H. Dahl, embarked immediately on an intensive program of stimulating "love for the great cause of missions." Confined largely in the beginning to home and foreign missions, it was enlarged shortly to include Christian education and charities.[96] Miss Alice Sanne, elected executive secretary of the WMF in 1945, reported in 1958 that over eight hundred thousand dollars was received by this organization for the work of the church.[97] The LDR, originally known as the DOR (Daughters of the Reformation), has been directed by Miss Arna Njaa since 1936. The organization has urged free-will offerings for the support of its projects, one of which is the support of six missionaries. Recently (1958) the LDR erected a home for unmarried women missionaries on furlough.[98]

The men's auxiliary, The Brotherhood of The Evangelical Lutheran Church, had its roots in the Lutheran Brotherhood, an intersynodical organization organized in World War I to aid military chaplains and to erect service centers for Lutheran soldiers and sailors. The Brotherhood of the ELC did not formally organize, however, until 1930.[99]

Chief among the interests and projects of the Brotherhood have been the promotion of Scouting and boys' work,[100] the pension plan of the church, and parish conservation through a "placement bureau."[101] One of the most farsighted projects has been a program to provide scholarships for postgraduate theological studies. Between 1947, when the project was begun,

---

[95] For details on both organizations see Martha Reishus, *Hearts and Hands Uplifted. A History of the Women's Missionary Federation* . . . (Minneapolis: Augsburg Publishing House, 1958); and *Forward with Christ, The LDR Through 25 Years* (Minneapolis: Augsburg Publishing House, 1954).

[96] Reishus, *op. cit.*, pp. 46, 68.

[97] *ELC Annual Report* . . . *1958*, p. 315.

[98] *Loc. cit.*

[99] *NLCA* . . . *Annual Report* . . . *1930*, p. 21.

[100] *Brotherhood Bulletin*, May, 1950, p. 22, and Report of the Executive Secretary, 1937, p. 3.

[101] Minutes of the Board of the Brotherhood, Feb. 3-4, 1941; Executive Committee, Brotherhood, Sept. 30, 1944.

and the present, a total of forty-one thousand dollars has been invested in this manner. Executive secretaries have been Roy Olson, 1936-1939; A. E. Iverson, 1939-1947; Charles Johnson, 1947-1958; A. E. Doerring, 1959-.

The Young People's Luther League, organized as the "Youth League" *(Ungdomsforbundet)* in 1917, has conducted a vigorous program of education, evangelism, and stewardship during the past forty years. Early in its history, under the leadership of N. M. Ylvisaker, it developed a tradition for huge biennial conventions (nine thousand were registered at the 1957 Missoula, Montana, convention). Enthusiasms of young people have been effectively channeled into the service of the church, and as a consequence, thousands of congregational lay leaders have emerged. A second noteworthy development among the youth has been the so-called Bible Camp Movement. An indication of its extent was the report that more than twenty-five thousand attended the summer camps in 1957.[102] Through the medium of the Bible camps two major emphases of the ELC have been perpetuated: religious indoctrination and religious inspiration. The camps have proved to be an extension of the parish education program of the church whereby Christian principles have been taught. But not only has religion been taught in the Bible camps, it has also been "caught." That is to say, that evangelistic or pietistic emphasis of the church has been freely evident in the movement. It is safe to say that this has been one of the reasons the Bible camps have flourished in the ELC and other pietistically-orientated Scandinavian church bodies. It has been less successful in the German-background Lutheran groups such as the Missouri Synod, the ALC, and the ULCA.

Executive secretaries of the organization have been N. M. Ylvisaker, 1919-1941; Oscar C. Hanson, 1941-1948; Oscar A. Anderson, 1948-1954; Carroll S. Hinderlie, 1954-.

---
[102] *ELC Annual Report* . . . 1958, p. 317.

CHAPTER NINE

The Church Discovers Other Churches

At least two strong factors influenced the Norwegian Lutheran Church of America in its relation to other churches. One was cultural or sociological; the other, theological.

Norwegian-Americans, like most of the other American Lutherans, had lived apart from the main streams of American ecclesiastical life. A foreign tongue and distinctive customs were not easily put aside and thus became natural barriers to communication in the new land. Consequently during the nineteenth century and through World War I the Norwegian-Americans lived in ecclesiastical insularity. Contact even with other Lutherans was infrequent, being limited for the most part to the Midwest and to other Scandinavian Lutherans, especially the Danes and the more numerous Swedes whose languages, culture, and religious spirit were not alien to the Norwegians. Leaders of the Norwegian Synod drew their group into fellowship with the German-speaking Missouri Synod, it is true, but this was primarily a fellowship of leaders and preachers, not of congregations, and limited also by language. But despite the absence of "grass roots" involvement, a large section of Norwegian-American Lutheranism admired the Missouri Synod as the chief representative of "true" and "sound" Lutheranism. As far as the so-called "eastern or English Lutherans" of the General Council, General Synod, and the United Synod, South, were concerned, the Norwegians had almost no contact and very little accurate information. What they had was colored by vague suspicions of their theological position, which, they were told, was Lutheran only in an incomplete or compromising fashion. By the end of World War I, however, the Norwegian-Americans had learned that the Holy Spirit and confessional Lutheranism had not fled from eastern Lutheranism, and they therefore cooperated with the newly-formed United Lutheran Church in America and other non-Synodical Conference Lutherans in organizing the National Lutheran Council. This marked the beginning of the end of sociological-ecclesiastical isolation.

But there was a second factor, theological in character, which played a significant role in the ecumenical relations of Norwegian-Americans. In order to understand it one is driven to make a quick survey of the history of theological thought in nineteenth-century American Lutheranism, and to see Norwegian-American Lutheranism in this context.

Lutheranism in America during the early nineteenth century faced a crisis compounded of rationalism and "Americanization" via revivalism. Religious indifference during the first years of the young republic was seen by the Protestant churches as a serious threat to morals and spiritual life. The Second Awakening and the Great Revival in the West were consequently looked upon as weapons for the defeat of the enemy. In fact, revivalism, which involved unionism, was a vigorous attempt to preserve an evangelical witness in America. But when Lutherans added their strength to this effort to combat religious indifference and rationalism and to preserve evangelical Christianity, they tended to minimize the distinctly Lutheran confessional principle. The movement which resulted was given the descriptive title, "American Lutheranism."[1] The phenome-

---

[1] For a discussion of this phase of American Lutheran history see Vergilius Ferm, *The Crisis in American Lutheran Theology* (New York: The Century Co., 1927), *passim*, and

non was overcome later by an interest in recently imported German neo-confessionalism which arrived in two ways: (1) by the translation of German Lutheran theological literature and its subsequent use in the General Synod just as "American Lutheranism" reached a climax; and (2) by the mass immigration of German and Scandinavian Lutherans beginning about mid-century. The neo-confessionalism which was brought to America in these ways became a movement to combat rationalism, not by the methods of American unionistic revivalism, but by a repristination of the scholastic orthodoxy of the seventeenth-century Lutheran dogmaticians.[2]

The problem which faced American Lutherans was that there was no other option. The historically-conditioned confessionalism of "the Erlangen School" of Lutheran theologians was largely unknown, or if known, was regarded with suspicion.[3] Therefore the choice seemed to be either to repristinate orthodoxism or to abandon Lutheran confessionalism. Confronted with these alternatives, Lutherans chose the former. In this way it came about that Luther's tradition in America was preserved in the rigid forms of scholasticism.

A. R. Wentz, *A Basic History of Lutheranism in America* (Philadelphia: Muhlenberg Press, 1955), pp. 73-156.

[2]The concern of the advocates of "Repristination Theology" was to restore the treasures of Lutheran theology (cast aside by rationalism) by concentrating on the seventeenth century orthodoxist interpretation of the Reformation. It emphasized (1) verbal inspiration of the Scriptures and (2) legalistic use of the confessions. Out of this grew a subsuming of the Material Principle of the Reformation (*sola fide*) under the Formal Principle (*sola scriptura*). One of the leaders of the movement said: "Theology must know that she has nothing new to say, nothing new to discover, but that *her task is to preserve* [italics added] the spiritual treasure that has been given in the Holy Scripture and received by the Church, in such a form that it may be transmitted to future servants of the Church undiminished, certain, and in its most useful form." This, it will be recognized at once, was the application of the ideals of Romanticism to the realm of theology. For discussions of "Repristination Theology" see Hj. Holmquist and Jens Nørregaard, *Kirkehistorie* (København: J. H. Schultz Forlag, 1940), III, 45-47; J. L. Neve and O. W. Heick, *A History of Christian Thought* (Philadelphia: The Muhlenberg Press, 1946), II, 128-131; and especially J. A. Dorner, *History of Protestant Theology* (Edinburgh: T. and T. Clark, 1871), II, 120-140. Hermann Sasse agrees with Dorner at this point. See Robert Preus, *The Inspiration of Scripture* (Edinburgh: Oliver and Boyd, 1955), p. 208.

[3]"The Erlangen School" in mid-century was a dynamic revival of Lutheran theology associated with such names as von Harless, von Hofmann, and F. H. R. Frank. In America its chief exponents were the young Michael Reu and C. M. Jacobs. Reacting both positively and negatively to orthodoxy, pietism, rationalism, Schleiermacher, Hegel and Schelling, its main emphases were: (1) fidelity to the Lutheran confessions historically understood; (2) exposition of the Bible, not as verbally-inspired proof-texts, but as witness to God's redemptive activity in history (*Heilsgeschichte*); and (3) holding to justification by faith as the controlling principle in theology. Cf. *Twentieth Century Encyclopedia of Religious Knowledge*, I, 391.

One of the consequences of this whole development was an estrangement between the Lutherans of the East and the Midwest. Large numbers of post-Civil War immigrants found their way into the "orthodox" Lutheran churches represented by the German and Scandinavian synods in the Mississippi Valley. These tended to judge the eastern brethren by their loyalty or lack of loyalty to the confessionalism of orthodoxy. The Lutherans of the East, some of whom were infected with the virus of "American Lutheranism," suffered as a whole the reputation of being confessionally indifferent and therefore were regarded by Midwestern Lutherans as questionable bearers of the Reformation tradition. But even before the Civil War the eastern Lutherans had generally disavowed "American Lutheranism," and between 1867 and 1895 accepted the neo-confessionalism of the nineteenth century, much as the Midwest Lutherans had done earlier. Thus by 1900 the whole of American Lutheranism was cast into the forms of repristination confessionalism. Consequently no segment of Lutheranism in America was won over to the liberalism of late nineteenth century German theology. Even the confessionally indifferent groups or individuals remaining within the old General Synod were not "liberals" in the sense of European theology. The sole remnants of "Americanization," which continued to irritate the Missouri Synod and others, were differing attitudes toward the questions of unionism, Masonry, and chiliasm, and these were not the concerns of liberal theology.

Thus when the twentieth century dawned, all of American Lutheranism was theoretically committed to a confessionalism of the repristination variety. The first intimation of change, not away from confessionalism but away from repristination theology, came in the newly-formed United Lutheran Church in America (1918), some of whose theologians revealed a preference for the confessionalism of Erlangen and a distaste for extra-confessional requirements for Lutheran unity. Although American Lutheranism rode out the storm of Protestant liberalism in the nineteen twenties, it nevertheless saw itself now divided into two camps—not "liberal" versus "orthodox," but

Erlangen confessionalism versus repristination confessionalism, the former being advocated by a church which more readily than other Lutherans adjusted itself to the American cultural environment.

The Norwegian-American Lutherans, despite the voices of a few significant theologians such as Georg Sverdrup, J. N. Kildahl, and E. K. Johnsen, were clearly in the stream of repristination theology.[4] This attitude with a rich admixture of vitalizing pietism characterized the theological faculty until World War II. It was not at all strange, therefore, that the bulk of the ministers, and therefore the congregations, reflected this point of view. When, for example, the Modernist-Fundamentalist controversy spread across American Protestantism in the twenties, conservative Norwegian-American Lutherans cast their lot with the Fundamentalists. They accepted uncritically the presuppositions of Fundamentalism because their heritage had not equipped them with the knowledge or the tools with which to combat liberalism as Lutherans. The few clergymen who were suspected of heretical leanings—and quickly brought into line—were, in the main, interestingly enough missionaries who, in the context of the new theology, had come in contact with other cultures and religions. The church's reaction to Modernism was to take refuge in its tradition which was spelled out in a set of Fundamentalist-influenced propositions known as "The Minneapolis Theses" (1925).[5]

---

[4]Sverdrup was perhaps the most creative anti-Missourian or anti-repristination theologian among Norwegian-Americans, but lost his influence in the regrettable controversy over Augsburg Seminary. Kildahl and Johnsen at the United Church Seminary were men who feared the scholasticism of orthodoxy, and strove valiantly, but never quite successfully, to break out from the categories of orthodoxist thought. For an interesting example of this struggle, see Kildahl's address on the occasion of his induction to the chair of systematic theology at the United Church Seminary. "Installation Address," *The United Lutheran*, VIII (March 19, 1915), 178-181.

[5]The 1917 constitution contained a general statement on the authority of Holy Scripture which was quite devoid of Fundamentalist overtones: "The Church believes, teaches, and confesses that the Holy Scriptures, the canonical books of the Old and New Testament, are the revealed Word of God and therefore the only source and rule of faith, doctrine and life." Between 1917 and 1925 the Modernist-Fundamentalist controversy, with the Scopes Trial, Clarence Darrow, and William Jennings Bryan as exhibits of the temper of the times, made headlines across the nation. In this milieu Norwegian-American Lutherans, together with other Midwest Lutherans, adopted the so-called Minneapolis Theses as a theological bulwark against liberal Protestantism and some Lutherans who were suspected of "liberalism" because they were trying to deal with the issues as Lutherans rather than as Fundamentalists. The Minneapolis Theses said: "The synods . . . accept without

Since the decade of the thirties a massive cold war between the two theological positions sketched above has characterized relations within American Lutheranism. The Norwegian-American Lutheran leaders, by and large, have given their support to repristination confessionalism, and since World War II have led the church's organizational resistance to the other interpretation of Lutheranism. Their reluctance to accept the ULCA was also due to an honest concern for "spiritual life." The pietism of the ELC was often rebuffed by the ULCA, some of whose pastors and leaders took a seemingly flippant attitude towards the religiously serious and sober mien of the ELC. If there was a relation between "ULCA theology" and a type of piety which appeared to the ELC to be worldly, then the theology, it was concluded, must be responsible.[6] Major consequences of this attitude were the organization in 1930 of the American Lutheran Conference, "a protective league" of Midwest Lutherans within the National Lutheran Council, and the congealing of the two above-mentioned points of view (also within the NLC) thirty years later in two organic mergers.[7]

Lest an erroneous conclusion be drawn, it should be pointed out that Erlangen theology was not adopted by the ULCA *in toto* as providing a final set of theological answers (i.e., repristinated). Rather it offered an orientation which made it possible

---

exception all the canonical books of the Old and New Testaments as a whole, and in all their parts, as the divinely inspired, revealed, and inerrant Word of God, and submit to this as the only infallible authority in all matters of faith and life." Cf. *The Union Documents of the ELC* . . . , pp. 75, 81.

[6] It is sometimes overlooked that to press this is to assume a non-confessional or, at least, extra-confessional position, untenable in a Lutheran approach to unity. The confessions do not posit a certain level of sanctification as a basis for unity. The Augsburg Confession (Article VII) says, "And to the true unity of the Church, *it is enough* [italics added] to agree concerning the doctrine of the Gospel and the administration of the sacraments."

[7] A modified Erlangen confessionalism is roughly represented by the merger embracing the United Lutheran Church in America, the Augustana Lutheran Church, the American Evangelical Lutheran Church, and the Finnish Evangelical Lutheran Church (Suomi Synod). This is scheduled for the early sixties. The other merger, The American Lutheran Church (TALC) (1960-1961) brings together The Evangelical Lutheran Church, the American Lutheran Church, and the United Evangelical Lutheran Church in a union dedicated uneasily and unhappily to repristination confessionalism, which is more closely related ideologically to Missourianism than to Erlangen confessionalism. This explains why the Lutheran Church–Missouri Synod could vote at its triennial convention in June, 1959, at San Francisco, to begin union negotiations with TALC. See *Religious News Service*, June 29, 1959.

to combine adherence to the confessions with such advances in Biblical and theological knowledge as had been made since the Reformation. To a lesser degree the American orthodoxists (e.g., the Missouri Synod) also addressed themselves to new problems and issues, albeit with the seventeenth century presuppositions. Furthermore, it should be noted that the general descriptions given above to the two groups do not fit all persons within them. Both points of view are found in both groups, but the historical orientation of each is as we have described. One of the most hopeful signs for future unity, despite the freezing of organizational forms, is the fact that at no time in American Lutheran history have the various seminary faculties been so theologically congenial, especially in their general uneasiness with and critical evaluation of a theology of repristination.

The remainder of this chapter will be devoted to the tracing out of the confused and oft confusing events which have been leading to 1960. Particular reference, of course, will be made to the role of The Evangelical Lutheran Church, which has continued to bear the tradition of Norwegian Lutheranism modified by the cultural and theological factors described above. This lengthy introduction has been deemed necessary because of the conviction that historians write history best when they assist the reader to see the whole context of events in order to provide a frame in which individual happenings can be properly evaluated.

The periodization of what follows has been somewhat arbitrarily marked out: 1918-1925, The Immediate Postwar Years; 1925-1950, A Quarter Century of Cooperation and Cold War; 1950-1959, The Accomplished Fact; Conclusion: Ecumenical Relations.

1918-1925, The Immediate Postwar Years

Inter-Lutheran relations since World War I have been so complex as to baffle most Lutherans, to say nothing of other Christians and the general American public. The key which unlocks the complicated contemporary situation (1950-1960) lies in the motives and origins of the now defunct American Lutheran Conference (1930-1954). What took place in the years 1925-1930, when the American Lutheran Conference was being shaped, provided the hinge on which considerable history has swung. But to understand what happened in the five years leading to the formation of the American Lutheran Conference one must search the records covering the first years of American Lutheran cooperation through the agency of the National Lutheran Council. Meuser suggests the problem when he observes, "The roots of the American Lutheran Conference are buried somewhere in the 1918 conferences which produced the National Lutheran Council."[8] Meuser leaves the roots buried; actually they must be uncovered if an accurate and full-orbed account of later developments is to be presented.

World War I and its exigencies crystallized the sporadically expressed hopes that American Lutherans might work together in some federal arrangement.[9] Although a federation did not emerge, a functional "agency" known as the National Lutheran Council (NLC) was born in 1918.[10] Participants were the Norwegian Lutheran Church of America, the Augustana Synod, the Joint Synod of Ohio, the Iowa Synod, the Lutheran Free Church, the Danish Lutheran Church, and the three general bodies which shortly became the United Lutheran Church in America. The first president and the first general secretary of the Council were Doctors H. G. Stub and Lauritz Larsen, respectively; both were members of the Norwegian Lutheran Church of America (NLCA). Other significant leaders in the early years of the NLC were Dr. F. H. Knubel, pres-

---
[8]Fred W. Meuser, *The Formation of the American Lutheran Church* (Columbus: The Wartburg Press, 1958), p. 236.
[9]In 1915 J. A. Bergh of the United Norwegian Lutheran Church addressed the Illinois Conference of the Augustana Synod and proposed a federation of all American Lutheran church bodies. C. O. Solberg pointed to the relationship between the General Council and the Augustana Synod as facilitating the federation of all Lutheran groups. *The United Lutheran*, VIII (June 18 and July 30, 1915), 393, 520-521. In addition the Joint Synod of Ohio proposed an all-Lutheran federation. *Beretning . . . Den f. Kirke . . . 1915*, p. 223.
[10]For an account of the steps which led to the formation of the NLC see Osborne Hauge, *Lutherans Working Together* (New York: National Lutheran Council, n. d.), pp. 23-37.

ident of the ULCA; Dr. C. H. L. Schuette, president of the Joint Synod of Ohio; Dr. G. A. Brandelle, president of the Augustana Synod; and such interested individuals as Dr. T. E. Schmauk (ULCA), Dr. C. M. Jacobs (ULCA), Dr. L. W. Boe (NLCA), and Dr. J. A. O. Stub (NLCA), who were not presidents of church bodies.

There were, therefore, in 1918 two main groupings of Lutherans, the Synodical Conference (1872) and the newly-born National Lutheran Council. The largest body in the latter was the United Lutheran Church; in the former, the Missouri Synod. These two were the opposite poles in American Lutheranism. The ULCA was committed to Lutheran unity on the basis of the generally received confessions of Lutheranism. The Missouri Synod went beyond this to require agreement in extra-confessional refinements of doctrine as well as uniformity in practice.

To understand subsequent developments in the Norwegian Lutheran Church of America one must be aware of the fact that this church stood uneasily between these two ecclesiastical colossi; on the one hand cooperating with the ULCA, but suspicious of its doctrinal rectitude; on the other, unhappy with the exclusivism of Missouri but, in large measure, accepting it as "more Lutheran" than the ULCA. Together with other Midwest Lutherans it was *practically* related to the ULCA, but *sociologically* and *ideologically* related to the Missouri Synod.[11] It is clear, therefore, that within the National Lutheran Council there were two distinct, but as yet unarticulated, points of view.

The occasion which brought out the differences was the definition and implementation of the NLC's policy of "cooperation

---

[11] Only a few Norwegians sought to understand and had sympathy for the viewpoint of the ULCA. One was L. W. Boe, the president of St. Olaf College and intimate of J. A. Aasgaard, the second president of the NLCA. Boe wrote Dr. F. H. Knubel, president of the ULCA, assuring him of his complete support and sympathy, trying at the same time to explain that H. G. Stub, the president of the NLCA and the NLC was the leader of the Missourian element among the Norwegians. This accounted for NLCA resistance to the ULCA. See Knubel-Stub correspondence, letter, Boe-Knubel, October 17, 1919, microfilm, Luther Theological Seminary, St. Paul, Minnesota. Cf. Boe's views on Lutheran unity in "The National Lutheran Council," *Lutheran Church Herald*, III (April 29, 1919), 264-266; and *Report . . . NLCA . . . 1928,* p. 471.

in externals." Fearing "unionism" (i.e., fellowship without doctrinal agreement),[11] some of the Midwest Lutherans had insisted that cooperation be limited to *res externae* in contrast to *res internae*. But where was the boundary between the "external" and the "internal"? What could be done cooperatively without doctrinal agreement?[12]

One of the most critical problems after World War I was that of ministering to people who had moved into wartime industrial centers. Clearly this ought to be a cooperative enterprise because the home mission boards of individual church bodies were unable to cope with the situation. The Federal Council of Churches had proposed a joint Protestant undertaking. This, however, was unacceptable to the Lutherans who looked to the National Lutheran Council as the proper agency for this work.[13] It was deemed essential that the Council work with the various Lutheran home mission boards in developing a program. Therefore, a meeting of the NLC executive committee and home mission representatives was called at Columbus, Ohio, December 18, 1918. It produced agreement that the work should be undertaken. However, at the insistence of H. G. Stub a resolution was passed requesting the presidents of NLC member bodies to constitute a "Joint Committee to confer on questions of doctrine and practice, with a view to the coordination of their home mission and other work."[14] Behind this resolution lay the fear of unionism, because home mission cooperation was hardly cooperation "in external things."[15]

---

[11]"Unionism" was originally a term which was applied to pulpit and altar fellowship between Lutherans and non-Lutherans. As such it was often described as "sinful" unionism. It should now be made clear that, under pressures from the Missouri Synod, the term was being carried beyond its original meaning and was being applied currently to inter-Lutheran relations.

[12]Lauritz Larsen, "Unity," *Lutheran Church Herald*, III (April 1, 1919), 194. Cf. Hauge, *op. cit.*, pp. 39-40.

[13]*Annual Report of the NLC . . . 1919*, pp. 13-14.

[14]*Ibid.*, p. 15. Cf. Hauge, *op. cit.*, pp. 41-42.

[15]Stub admits his part in this. See his "Representatives from Eight Lutheran Church Bodies . . . ," *Lutheran Church Herald*, III (March 25, 1919), 180. In a letter to Dr. Knubel, Stub reported that certain elements in the NLCA were attacking the NLC. Moreover, the Church Council of the NLCA, having endorsed the organization of the NLC, refused to approve cooperation with other Lutherans in home mission work. Stub wrote, "I hope, my dear Dr. Knubel, that you will now better understand . . . my specific reasons for having advocated so strongly the meeting in Chicago on doctrine and practice.

The Joint Committee on Doctrine and Practice met March 11-13, 1919, at Chicago.[16] It had been previously agreed that four papers reflecting the viewpoints of their respective churches should be presented by Dr. H. E. Jacobs (ULCA), Dr. C. H. L. Schuette (Ohio Synod), Dr. F. Richter (Iowa Synod), and Dr. H. G. Stub (NLCA). A special NLC resolution had requested Dr. F. H. Knubel "to prepare a statement which shall define the essentials of a catholic spirit as viewed by the Lutheran Church."[17]

After the reading of Knubel's paper on the general principles of catholicity, the particular synodical viewpoints were presented. Jacobs moved that Stub's paper be made the basis of the preliminary discussion before turning to the question of catholicity. Therewith the remaining sessions were devoted to Stub's presentation. After considerable discussion and amendment, the paper was adopted by the group for referral to the churches. The articles contained in it were subsequently known as "The Chicago Theses."[18] The other main paper, Knubel's "The Essentials of a Catholic Spirit," could not be discussed for lack of time. Therefore, a sub-committee consisting of Knubel, Stub, and T. E. Schmauk was appointed to consider the paper and report to a later meeting of the same group. Moreover, the Conference voted to publish both Knubel's and Jacobs' papers, the latter titled, "Constructive Lutheranism."[19]

These papers, Knubel's, Jacobs', and Stub's, have proved to be of profound significance in the shaping of American Lutheranism, setting forth two points of view: catholic confessionalism (Knubel and Jacobs) and repristination confession-

---

If I had not insisted so strongly on this meeting which so many regarded as entirely superfluous, I would have made myself subject to the charge of unionism." Stub-Knubel, 2-20-19, microfilm, Luther Seminary Library, St. Paul. It should be remembered that "unionism" originally referred to relations with other Protestants; now it had been refined to include inter-Lutheran relations.

[16]See microfilm copy of minutes in Knubel-Stub Correspondence, Luther Theological Seminary, St. Paul. NLCA representatives were, besides Stub, J. N. Kildahl and C. J. Eastvold.

[17]*Ibid.*, p. 13.

[18]The original paper is in *ibid.*, pp. 4-8. Cf. H. G. Stub, "Representatives from Eight Lutheran Church Bodies . . . ," *Lutheran Church Herald*, III, 180-182.

[19]"Minutes, Joint Committee . . . March 11-13, 1919," p. 18. The papers by Knubel and H. E. Jacobs were published in *The Lutheran Church Review*, XXXVIII (April, 1919), 187-197, 198-212.

alism (Stub). Later developments among churches of the National Lutheran Council revolved about the positions expressed and implied in these papers. The Knubel-Jacobs thesis insisted that there is an organic union among all parts of God's truth, but a necessary difference of order and importance. The central must ever be distinguished from the peripheral.

> The Gospel is the heart of the whole system, transmitting its vitalizing force into every part. The sacraments are important; but their importance lies in the fact that they are seals of the Gospel. . . . All regenerative and renovating processes are from the center to the circumference, not from the circumference to the center.[20]

In the church, it was argued, it is not always the central doctrines which have been in controversy. Yet, the church must repel attack upon any part of revelation. Sometimes in Lutheranism a "disproportionate emphasis has been laid on certain doctrines, simply because they have been antagonized. But the fact that such doctrines are a part of God's revealed will, and, therefore, to be defended at all hazards . . . does not of itself entitle them to the central place."[21] When it is recognized that the gospel alone is central and constitutive of the church, there is the foundation for a true catholic spirit in the church.

The real problem facing the church, said Knubel, was the question, "What is the Christian Church?"[22] Above all, it does not consist of a group of bodies united on the basis of external principles, if the inner source and bond and power of unity are distinctly minimized. And what are the elements of this inner unity, this "catholic spirit"? An examination of pertinent Scripture passages yielded five:[23] (1) the Father; (2) the Son, Jesus Christ—His Passion, His living Presence, His Parousia; (3) the Holy Spirit, and His work of grace through Word and Sacraments; (4) our faith and its full confession; and (5) works of serving love. Knubel drew three conclusions:

---
[20]*Ibid.*, p. 209.
[21]*Ibid.*, pp. 208-209.
[22]*Ibid.*, pp. 187-189
[23]*Ibid.*, pp. 193-196.

1. In the presence of the constant demands for a statement upon Church unity, we may definitely offer this as a program under which all Christians can consider such an idea.

2. Until such unity is at hand, the Evangelical Lutheran Church must manifestly maintain her identity very clearly as a witness for the truth. As a principle, in agreement with God's Word and our Confession, her pulpits, her baptismal fonts, her altars, her entire use of the Means of Grace, should witness only for the truth she knows. This is our loyalty to and love for our Savior.

3. Upon the question of co-operation with other Christians, we may say that if there be no denial of the first four groups of the above essentials, if nothing be done to diminish their glory, if free utterance concerning them be expected, then some form of co-operation is possible under the fifth—works of serving love (which includes common and necessary testimony upon public matters).[24]

Quoting Dr. T. E. Schmauk, Knubel closed his presentation as follows:

> We are ready to see good wherever it may be found, and we cannot pass by evil wherever it may be found. Hence we cannot join in free and easy laxity on the one hand, nor resort to wholesale condemnation on the other. If our attitude be respected, and our own inner freedom be not compromised, we believe that there are many points in the common problems of the Christian Church in America, and in the world in which a way can be found for common testimony and united action.[25]

Such were the views on "catholic confessionalism" as presented at the first doctrinal conference. As mentioned previously, the papers were only read. Time did not permit a discussion of their contents.

The second point of view enunciated at the Chicago conference can safely be said to have represented Midwest Lutheranism, including the Missouri Synod which was not involved in the discussion.[26] Stub's presentation ("The Chicago Theses") consisted of three parts: (1) a historical introduction; (2) a declaration regarding doctrine; (3) a declaration regarding practice. The first section was not discussed because it was

---
[24]*Ibid.*, p. 197.
[25]*Loc. cit.*
[26]Stub later reported Missouri enthusiasm over "The Chicago Theses." Minutes, Joint Conference on Doctrine and Practice, Chicago, Illinois, January 27-28, 1920 (microfilm copy, Luther Theological Seminary, St. Paul), p. 19.

simply a matter of historical information. The third section on practice set forth Stub's views on pulpit fellowship and the lodge. These views were in essential agreement with those expressed by the ULCA representatives and by Schuette. The second section, however, spelled out specific doctrines, agreement on which Stub felt was essential to "churchly cooperation" or union.[27] The contents may be summarized by using Stub's own words:

> Because even in the Lutheran Church at large disputes and controversies about specific doctrines more or less have disturbed our Church, we regard it both as a duty and as a privilege to declare our position in regard to the following doctrine:
>
> 1. In regard to the Work of Christ, Redemption, and Reconciliation: . . .
> 2. In regard to the Gospel: . . .
> 3. In regard to Absolution: . . .
> 4. In regard to Holy Baptism and the Gospel: . . .
> 5. In regard to Justification: . . .
> 6. In regard to Faith: . . .
> 7. In regard to Conversion: . . .
> 8. In regard to Election: . . .

It was obvious that Stub's presentation did not in any sense attempt to cover all the doctrines and practices of Lutheranism. Rather, he included only those points which had been troublesome in the history of Midwest Lutheranism.[28] There being no general disagreement on the matters which Stub had presented, at least as far as specific content was concerned, the paper was, as noted above, adopted by the conference.

Two things were now clear: (1) Although the National Lutheran Council had called the meeting, the Joint Conference action was not an action of the Council. All enactments would have to be referred to the member churches. (2) The Joint Conference had not completed its task, for the NLC request for a statement "which shall define the essentials of a

---

[27]This was what the Knubel-Jacobs argument described as starting at the periphery rather than the center.
[28]"A Memorable Event in American Lutheranism," *Lutheran Church Herald*, III (March 25, 1919), 184.

catholic spirit as viewed by the Lutheran Church" had not been discussed and adopted.

When Knubel returned home, he set down "A Personal Statement Concerning the Chicago Conference on Faith and Practice,"[29] and sent a letter to Stub seeking to arrange a time for the sub-committee to discuss "the essentials of a catholic spirit."

In "A Personal Statement . . ." Knubel gave a precis of the Chicago meeting, stating his own view that a policy statement on the "essentials of a catholic spirit" was urgently needed because of the pressing problems facing the church in the postwar world. The issues of Bolshevism and other anti-Christian forces in addition to the ecumenical discussion of "Faith and Order" demanded that the Lutherans think through the problem of catholicity.[30]

In November, Knubel, Stub, and Charles M. Jacobs met to carry out their assignment.[31] It was already clear by the fall of 1919 that Stub was not eager to pursue the problem of catholicity. His own theological position (the Chicago paper) was, he felt, the proper point of departure for an approach to other Lutherans.[32] Moreover, certain elements in his own church body, notably pastors of the former Norwegian Synod, were extremely critical of the NLCA's participation in the NLC. L. W. Boe wrote confidentially to Knubel that Stub had become nervous because of the opposition. Therefore, said Boe, "he will insist strongly on the Chicago Theses . . . As I understand it you people feel that the Lutheran Church can-

[29]This statement is in the Knubel-Stub Correspondence, microfilm copy, Luther Theological Seminary, St. Paul.
[30]Knubel was far from satisfied with the Chicago conference. He felt that the Midwest Lutherans were unfair to the ULCA in questioning its Lutheranism. Writing to Stub following the conference he said, "We are not on trial as Lutherans and do not propose that we shall be on trial." Knubel-Stub, 8-26-19. Writing to Schmauk, whose illness kept him from the conference, he remarked that the Joint Synod of Ohio men especially were discourteous. Lenski's outright attack on the ULCA had provoked Knubel's quiet but firm rejoinder. Knubel-Schmauk, 3-18-19.
[31]C. M. Jacobs, professor at Philadelphia (Mt. Airy) Lutheran Seminary, Philadelphia, replaced the ailing T. E. Schmauk. C. M. Jacobs, more than any other individual, was to place the ULCA in the general theological tradition of the Erlangen School of von Hofmann, Frank, *et al.*
[32]See Knubel-Stub Correspondence, letter C. M. Jacobs-Knubel, November 29, 1919. Jacobs says to heed Stub's objections would be to remove the heart from "catholicity."

not get together on a negative declaration, and *I agree with you* [italics added]. Dr. Stub, however, is liable to look at the question from the standpoint of a settlement of . . . old difficulties . . . rather than . . . making a common declaration over against the outside world." Boe went on to assure Knubel that he himself agreed with the ULCA standpoint and hoped "The Chicago Theses" would not be the cause of the NLC's dissolution.[33]

The Joint Conference on Doctrine and Practice met a second time in Chicago, January 27-28, 1920, this time to hear the report of the sub-committee on "the essentials of a catholic spirit." C. M. Jacobs had recast Knubel's earlier paper, which now bore the signature of these two men alone. Stub had requested permission to explain why he had refused to affix his signature.[34] It was this paper which came to be known later as "The Washington Declaration."[35] Consisting of five parts, the paper defined the Lutheran attitude toward cooperative movements, church union, and "organizations, tendencies and movements" within and without the organized church. Part one, "Concerning the Catholic Spirit in the Church," pointed out the ecumenical character of the Lutheran confessions within which frame catholic relations should be fostered. The church, it said, will always be ready:

1. To declare unequivocably what it believes concerning Christ and His Gospel, and to endeavor to show that it has placed the true interpretation upon the Gospel . . . and to testify definitely and frankly against error.
2. To approach others without hostility, jealousy, suspicion, or pride,

---

[33]Knubel-Stub Correspondence, letter Boe-Knubel, 10-17-19.

[34]The minutes of this Joint Conference are in the Knubel-Stub Correspondence, Luther Theological Seminary, St. Paul.

[35]The paper, fully recorded in the minutes, was again reworked by C. M. Jacobs for presentation to the 1920 convention of the ULCA at Washington, D. C., where it was adopted as an official policy of the church. *Minutes . . . ULCA . . . 1920*, pp. 85, 92-101, 449-455. The spirit and purpose of the report, said C. M. Jacobs, grew out of the problems in the history of American Lutheranism. The old General Synod had the habitual attitude of tolerance toward other churches; the General Council, together with most of the rest of American Lutheranism, kept aloof from others. Therefore, in dealing with the problem of catholicity in the church, it was necessary to disregard both of these historical traditions and "endeavor to get down to bed-rock of what is always right and true; to determine, and then to define the principles." C. M. Jacobs, "The Washington Declaration: An Interpretation," *The Lutheran Church Review*, XL (January, 1921), 1-21.

in the sincere and humble desire to give and receive Christian service.
3. To grant cordial recognition to all agreements which are discovered between its own interpretation of the Gospel and that which others hold.
4. To cooperate with other Christians in works of serving love insofar as this can be done without surrender of its interpretation of the gospel, without denial of conviction, and without suppression of its testimony as to what it holds to be the truth.[36]

Part two dealt with relations to other Lutherans and said that there should be no reasons against union where there was subscription to the Lutheran confessions. Part three, "Concerning the Organic Union of Protestant Churches," held that organizational union was less important than agreement in the proclamation of the Gospel and that the church catholic exists "through and under divergent forms of extended organization." Until a more complete unity of confession should be achieved, the Lutheran church was bound in conscience to maintain a separate identity; "and its members, its ministers, its pulpits, its fonts and its altars must testify only to that truth." Part four delineated eight doctrinal essentials as a "positive basis for practical cooperation among Protestant Churches." Part five warned against "Movements and Organizations Injurious to the Christian Faith." Here it was said that lodge members were to be dealt with in an evangelical rather than in a legalistic fashion.

Following Jacobs' presentation of the report, Stub gave several reasons why he could not sign the document. First, it was too voluminous; "The Chicago Theses" (Stub's own product) were short and more easily understood. Second, the Missouri Synod's official organ, *Lehre und Wehre*, had commented that "The Chicago Theses" were excellent. In other words, he implied, one should not risk alienating the Missouri Synod by going beyond a position acceptable to that church. Third, the section on "Cooperative Movements" was inadequate because it did not mention the Bible as "the inerrant Word of God"

---
[36]*Minutes* . . . ULCA . . . *1920,* p. 96.

and the Real Presence in the sacrament. Fourth, the whole position on catholicity was contrary to Article Three of the "Articles of Union" of the Norwegian Lutheran Church of America, which article bound the church to refrain from churchly cooperation with non-Lutherans.[37]

The discussion which followed produced no definite decision regarding "the essentials of a catholic spirit." Knubel and Jacobs pleaded "very earnestly" with the opposition, but to no avail.[38] Before adjournment, however, it was agreed that further meetings would be at the call of Stub, Knubel and Secretary Lauritz Larsen.

It was soon clear that Stub was averse to further conferences.[39] Nevertheless, he agreed to meet in Chicago, March 11-12, 1920. No minutes have been accessible to the writer, but a memorandum by Knubel provides a summary of the discussion.[40] Two things were to the fore: (1) the feeling among Midwest Lutherans that the ULCA was pressing for something contrary to their desires; and (2) the lodge question and unionism. The discussion revealed that Iowa had left the NLC because it feared that the principle of *res externae* was being transgressed. Similar feeling prevailed in Ohio and among the Norwegians. Knubel felt compelled to comment on the phrase, *res externae*. First, he said, the term as now used among American Lutherans had no relation to the use of the term in the Lutheran confessions. Second, the use of the term was not Scriptural and, therefore, not Christian. "There are no *res externae* in the life of the Christian and the Church

---

[37]Minutes, Joint Conference, January 27-28, 1920, pp. 18-27. Stub did not mention that two-thirds of the Norwegian Lutheran Church (United Church and Hauge's Synod) had unanimously accepted an "Interpretation" of Article Three which allowed participation in the ecumenical movement. However, his own former church, the Norwegian Synod, had accepted the "Interpretation" with the stipulation that it reserved the right to "witness against" cooperative practices. Obviously Stub was now speaking, not as president of the NLCA, but as a former member of the Norwegian Synod.

[38]*Minutes . . . ULCA . . . 1920*, p. 454.

[39]Stub wrote Knubel in February that he saw little point in pursuing discussions. The Iowa Synod had dropped out of the NLC, Ohio was objecting to "catholicity," the Norwegians were becoming restive, and even Augustana was uncertain. Stub-Knubel, 2-19-20. Stub was being urged by some members of the NLCA to heed the call to catholicity. His own son, J. A. O. Stub, sought earnestly but unsuccessfully to get him to see the Knubel-Jacobs point of view. Letter, Luther B. Deck-Knubel, 3-31-20.

[40]See "Brief Statement Concerning Meeting in Chicago, March 11 and 12, 1920," in Knubel-Stub Correspondence, Luther Theological Seminary, St. Paul.

(I Cor. 10:31)." Therefore, any attempt to solve the question of inter-Lutheran or other relationships by use of the term would be doomed to failure. Some other solution must be found. For this reason the ULCA insisted on the approach presented by Jacobs and him, and, said Knubel, "The Chicago Theses" would not be put before the ULCA unless some "true foundation be laid for them, as the paper on Catholicity attempts to give."

On the lodge question and unionism Knubel insisted that these matters must not be made the tests or shibboleths of Lutheranism. Said he, "They are not the proofs that a man is a Lutheran, although they are the things to which I believe a Lutheran will come sooner or later."

Once again the Conference broke up without general acceptance of "The Essentials of a Catholic Spirit." It was agreed, however, to refrain from using the phrase *res externae*, although some did not see the utter inadequacy of the term; and by common consent, the "Chicago Theses" were to be discarded for the time being. This action was not to preclude further conferences, nor was it to prevent the ULCA from continuing its study of catholicity at its October (1920) convention in Washington.

Some time between this meeting and April 15, 1920, the NLC presidents agreed to abandon the Joint Conference on Doctrine and Practice.[41] With this decision Lutheranism within the National Lutheran Council came to a parting of the ways. The ULCA moved on to its "Washington Declaration" on catholicity; the Midwest Lutherans picked up Stub's "Chicago Theses" as a banner. Instead of a single-voiced and full-orbed Lutheran testimony within the NLC, there emerged two distinct parties, each waving its own flag. Needless to say, the initial cause—home mission cooperation in industrial areas—was forgotten.

While Stub was exercising his duties as president of the National Lutheran Council, he was also carrying out his responsibilities as president of the Norwegian Lutheran Church

[41] *Minutes . . . ULCA . . . 1920,* p. 85.

of America. In both offices it was his task and desire to see the two organizations, which he headed, prosper. Loath to see such a noble experiment in Lutheran cooperation as the NLC break up, he was quite as reluctant to intrude questions which might keep the heterogeneous NLCA from being welded into a solid body. Added to this two-horned problem was his personal commitment to the "orthodox" or repristination theological point of view. With these attitudes dominating his thought, he faced the district meetings of the NLCA in 1919 (the general convention was not to meet until 1920). He had already given his account of the first Joint Conference of March, 1919,[42] to the church; now he must "sell" the National Lutheran Council as such because there had been no previous opportunity to present the presidents' action of 1918 for the sanction of the church. Full approbation could not come until the summer of 1920, but preliminary acceptance by the 1919 district conventions would enhance the chances of a favorable vote in 1920. In each district Stub received the desired approval.[43] However, the action was not without serious question and some opposition. In the Southern Minnesota District, for example, a substitute motion (that cooperation "in externals" be approved but that closer fellowship should wait upon the ULCA's demonstration of sincerity in its confession) was voted down only after Stub, Kildahl, and Lauritz Larsen spoke against it.[44]

In the year that followed, Stub became increasingly apprehensive about the NLCA's full approval of the NLC.[45] Consequently, in his report to the general convention in 1920, he felt it necessary to assure the church that the NLC was merely an agency for cooperation in external things. Since the con-

---

[42]*Lutheran Church Herald*, III (March 25, 1919), 180 ff.
[43]See *Lutheran Church Herald*, III (June 10 and 24, July 8, 1919), 354, 392, 420; and *ibid.*, IV (April 6, 1920), 216.
[44]*Ibid.*, III (June 24, 1919), 392. Cf. *Beretning . . . Den Norsk Luth. Kirke . . . 1919*, pp. 360-361. That "The Chicago Theses" were looked upon already as a quasi-doctrinal basis for the NLC was evident from the motion to withhold fellowship until it could be determined if the ULCA "lived up to" its acceptance of "The Chicago Theses." What was not realized was that the ULCA, like the other church bodies, had not formally accepted "The Chicago Theses."
[45]*Supra*, p. 298, n. 39.

ference and activity of the past year had been interpreted within the NLCA as "an attempt to work together immediately in the home mission field," he felt it necessary to say:

> Nothing has been farther from my thoughts. I have never thought of cooperation in a churchly sense without unity in doctrine and practice as the essential foundation. This is why I arranged the much discussed *free* conference, held in Chicago in March of last year, where a number of basic paragraphs which relate to doctrine and practice were unanimously adopted, *not by the Council as such,* but by representative men from the synods which through their Presidents were along in the Council. But of course this free conference had no authority to act in behalf of the synod. It is the various synods which must now take up the matter and deal with the named points about doctrine and practice.[46]

For no apparent reason, "The Chicago Theses" were not presented to the convention and thus were not officially adopted by the NLCA.[47] When the question of accepting membership in the NLC came up, a brisk debate took place. But with Stub's explanation and the presentation of three clarifying points—dealing with external cooperation and the autonomy of the individual churches—the church overrode opposition voices from the former Norwegian Synod.[48] Nevertheless, its approval was not without a note of caution. The general convention made certain that participation in NLC activities would be

> under full control of the Church. . . . No action can be taken between the Church meetings except by the advice of the Church Council, which is held responsible to the Church.[49]

And then, as if looking over its collective shoulder at the ULCA, it declared that the

> Church on account of its relation to the National Lutheran Council thereby has [not] acknowledged the doctrinal position and practice of the Church bodies with which it has been connected.[50]

---

[46]*Beretning . . . Den N. Luth. Kirke . . . 1920,* pp. 17-18. It is evident from this that Stub looked upon "The Chicago Theses" as at least a potential doctrinal basis for the NLC.
[47]See Bruce (ed.), *The Union Documents of the ELC,* p. 85, n.
[48]*Beretning . . . Den N. Luth. Kirke . . . 1920,* pp. 248, 277. See also *Lutheran Church Herald,* IV (June 15, 29, July 6, 1920), 377, 409, and 432; *Annual Report . . . NLC . . . 1920,* pp. 7-8.
[49]*Lutheran Church Herald,* IV (July, 1920), 432.
[50]*Ibid.,* p. 410.

In this way, the situation came to an uneasy rest in 1920. The National Lutheran Council had been established, two theological and ecclesiastical points of view had emerged within the Council, and cooperation was theoretically limited to "external affairs."[51] Meanwhile, the churches cooperated in overseas relief for European Lutheran churches. Out of this action there developed an interest for a world organization of Lutherans. This brought the NLCA and others into the Lutheran World Convention (1923). By means of the overseas activity of the NLC and participation in the Lutheran World Convention, the NLCA maintained living contact with the ULCA. Both of these churches provided significant American leadership in world Lutheran cooperation, especially in the persons of John A. Morehead (ULCA) and L. W. Boe (NLCA). Despite this, however, the next few years witnessed the NLCA's pulling away from the ULCA and drawing closer to the Joint Synod of Ohio and the Iowa Synod. One of the contributing factors, in addition to those evident from the previous discussion, was no doubt the Modernist-Fundamentalist controversy of the twenties, in which the Lutherans actually took no part. The Midwest Lutherans, however, felt the ULCA was equivocal on the question of the inerrancy of the Bible. "The Washington Declaration" asserted "the supreme importance of the Word of God" and "the authority of the Scriptures . . . as the only rule and standard by which all doctrines and teachers are to be judged." Stub, Lenski (Joint Synod of Ohio) and others were especially insistent that a statement on the verbal inspiration and consequent inerrancy of Scripture, in the context of Modernism, ought to be promulgated. In this setting, the non-Synodical Conference Lutherans of the Mississippi Valley, especially the Norwegians and the Germans, were moving closer together. Thus, by 1925 a new alignment within the National Lutheran Council was in process.

[51]L. W. Boe, writing to J. A. Aasgaard in 1942, said " . . . the Lord has never permitted it [the NLC] to be only an agency for cooperation in external affairs. Time and again we re-wrote the constitution and regulations . . . to safeguard this line that we arbitrarily set up, only cooperation in externals, but the Lord . . . pushed us across the line every time." Boe-Aasgaard, October 29, 1942.

1925-1950, A Quarter Century of Cooperation and Cold War

To speak of "cooperation" and "cold war" in the same breath seems like a contradiction in terms. Nonetheless, the next quarter century saw both of these occurring simultaneously within the National Lutheran Council. The Council had been organized as an agency to facilitate cooperation. This it did, for the churches continued to use it for those common enterprises which, they felt, their confessional loyalties would permit. At the same time, as we have already noticed, an unmistakable difference in outlook appeared between the ULCA and some of the other member bodies.

The Formation of the American Lutheran Conference

In 1924 the Joint Synod of Ohio elected a new president, C. C. Hein. Whereas the former president, C. H. L. Schuette, was interested in furthering cooperation through the National Lutheran Council, Hein looked toward establishing fellowship with "conservative synods." To Hein's mind Ohio was already at one with the Synodical Conference.[52] As early as 1917, Hein was arguing that one of the first steps towards establishing "orthodox" Lutheranism in America would be to bring Ohio, Iowa, and the Norwegians together.[53]

From the side of the Norwegian Lutherans similar sentiments were expressed by H. G. Stub who wrote to Hein, even before the latter succeeded Schuette, suggesting pulpit and altar fellowship between Ohio and the NLCA.[54] Stub said he looked upon this "as a matter of conscience." He said, "[we] ought to stand together *over against the modernists and all who have another faith* [italics added]."[55]

During the summer of 1925 Stub retired from office and was succeeded by J. A. Aasgaard, whom Hein immediately

---

[52]Meuser, *op. cit.*, pp. 158-159, 171.
[53]*Ibid.*, p. 159.
[54]*Ibid.*, p. 237. It should be remembered that Hein's and Stub's theological roots were in Missourian soil. Both Ohio and the former Norwegian Synod had been partners of the Missouri Synod in the Synodical Conference.
[55]*Loc. cit.* Whether this was an oblique reference to the ULCA cannot be determined. It was certainly clear that he did not consider the ULCA as a possible partner in this task.

invited[56] to a joint conference to discuss a doctrinal basis for fellowship among the following churches: Joint Synod of Ohio, Iowa Synod, Buffalo Synod, and the Norwegian Lutheran Church of America. The meeting was held in Minneapolis, November 18, 1925.[57] The chief results of the colloquy were the formulation of a set of theological propositions known as "The Minneapolis Theses"[58] and the decision to expand by inviting other selected synods to join. Incorporating Stub's "Chicago Theses" of 1919, "The Minneapolis Theses" also addressed themselves to specific points of "opposition to the ULCA."[59] Three areas of concern were spelled out: (1) the inspiration and inerrancy of the Bible, (2) unionism, and (3) the lodge question. On the last point, the following sentence was directed against the ULCA which had inherited the problem of lodgery among two or three per cent of the pastors of the former General Synod: "[We] agree that a Lutheran synod should not tolerate pastors who have affiliated themselves with any anti-Christian society." The statement on unionism was directed against the ULCA's "catholic confessionalism," and denied "cooperation in the strictly essential work of the Church." Here was the old problem of *res externae* versus *res internae*. The chief problem, however, revolved about the first item, the question of inspiration.[60] J. A. Aasgaard reported that the conferees made excellent progress until they reached the question of Biblical inspiration.[61] At this point, the Norwegians learned to their dismay that Dr. Michael Reu of the Iowa Synod was, in their judgment, "a liberal."[62] Reu's "liberalism"

[56]*Report* . . . *NLCA* . . . *1926*, p. 76.
[57]For an account of "The Minneapolis Colloquy" see *ibid.*, pp. 76, 80-83. Cf. Meuser, *op. cit.*, pp. 238-241.
[58]See Bruce (ed.), *The Union Documents* . . . *ELC*, pp. 81-83. Pulpit and altar fellowship was based on those theses.
[59]Meuser, *op. cit.*, p. 238.
[60]Meuser says the chief difficulties were (1) the extent of confessional subscription and (2) the question of predestination. *Op. cit.*, p. 239.
[61]Interview, June 2, 1955. It is significant that the conference completed its work in one day!
[62]There is contradictory testimony at this point. Meuser says that Reu, although strenuously opposing the "Intersynodical Theses" (composed by Ohio, Iowa, Buffalo, Missouri, and Wisconsin synods in 1925) which were couched in the same language as "The Minneapolis Theses," did not protest the Minneapolis statement on Scripture. *Op. cit.*, p. 183.

consisted in this that he held the Scriptures to be inerrant only in that which pertained to salvation, Law and Gospel. When the colloquy was deadlocked on this issue, Aasgaard suggested the technique which had been used to reach agreement on election among the Norwegians in 1912: Reu and Stub would be locked in a room to work out a statement. This was done and Stub's, rather than Reu's, position prevailed: the Scriptures "as a whole, and in all their parts, [are] the divinely inspired, revealed, and inerrant Word of God, and [we] submit to this as the only infallible authority in all matters of faith and life."[63]

The second result of "the Minneapolis Colloquy" was the consensus to invite the Augustana Synod, the United Danish Church, and the Lutheran Free Church to join forces with the original signers of "The Minneapolis Theses."[64]

By 1929 Hein had drafted a constitution for a federation; moreover, by the summer of 1930 all the synods which had assisted in the plans had ratified the proposals. The American Lutheran Conference was organized in Minneapolis, October 29-31, 1930, with the following NLC churches: the American Lutheran Church (Ohio, Buffalo, Iowa Synods), the Augustana Synod, the Lutheran Free Church, the Norwegian Lutheran Church of America, and the United Danish Lutheran Church.[65] Its executive committee (Otto Mees, president, L. W. Boe [later resigned and replaced by T. F. Gullixson], J. P. Nielsen, H. O. Sletten, and P. O. Bersell) was authorized to implement the cooperative functions stipulated in the constitution: home

---

[63]Reu continued to object to this theory of verbal inspiration until sometime after 1930. The formation of the ALC, in fact, was in jeopardy between 1926-1930 because of his opposition to the Missourian or fundamentalist position on Scripture. See *ibid.*, pp. 177-230. Some time after 1932 Reu underwent a theological metamorphosis—for reasons not easily documented—and became progressively pro-Missouri. See his *In the Interest of Lutheran Unity* (Columbus: The Lutheran Book Concern, 1940), and *Luther and the Scriptures* (Columbus: The Wartburg Press, 1944).

[64]Aasgaard reported that Hein had serious misgivings about the "orthodoxy" of Augustana (it had entertained the ecumenically-interested Archbishop Nathan Söderblom of Sweden in 1924 and had also been associated with the General Council until 1918). Moreover, Hein was not sure that the Lutheran Free Church was theologically sound. When Aasgaard assured him about both groups, the decision was made to extend invitations. Interview, June 2, 1955.

[65]"The American Lutheran Conference," *Lutheran Church Herald,* XIV (November 11, 1930), 1587-1593.

missions, inner missions, student service, foreign missions, publications, and exchange of theological professors.[66]

When one seeks to assess the significance of the American Lutheran Conference, he is torn between two evaluations. One is that of the idealist who wanted to see this as a step along the road to ultimate Lutheran union. The other is that of the church politicians who saw this as a means of withstanding the strength of the ULCA, on the one hand, and of persuading the Missouri Synod that true Lutheranism was still alive outside of the Synodical Conference. L. W. Boe expressed both points of view. At the constituting convention he said:

> The United Lutheran Church and the American Lutheran Conference are affiliated in common interests and activities of such a character that they inevitably will approach each other, *unless events are permitted to generate a hostile feeling entirely at variance with the history of the past* [italics added].[67]

Three years later he wrote again. Still expecting the American Lutheran Conference to be a positive influence toward Lutheran unity, his earlier idealism was now noticeably tempered:

> It is, perhaps, the one movement that has started in the Lutheran Church of America pretty much from the top and has worked down. Not many knew about the movement before it was presented all ready for organization. I have the impression that from the standpoint of the administrative officers of the different synods concerned *it was the intention to form a kind of protective league over against other Lutherans* [italics added].[68]

That the American Lutheran Conference possessed the character of a defensive alliance particularly over against the

---

[66]*Ibid.*, p. 1588.
[67]*Ibid.*, p. 1587.
[68]L. W. Boe, "The Church and Its Work," *Lutheran Herald*, XVII (June 27, 1933), 592. Boe wrote to one of the ULCA synodical presidents, "I cannot help but tell you that I wish that [your synod] was with us in our work [in the American Lutheran Conference] and as far as that is concerned, the United Lutheran Church." Boe-R. H. Gerberding, March 9, 1932. Writing to a ULCA layman, interested in Lutheran unity, he said, "Just now we are in a rather difficult situation both because of the depression and . . . the organization of the American Lutheran Conference. It has left us without definite lines when it comes to larger relationships." Boe-J. K. Jensen, April 4, 1932.

ULCA can hardly be denied. When the latter published "The Washington Declaration," the Norwegians and the Ohio and Iowa Germans were convinced that the ULCA lacked doctrinal conviction. Says Meuser, ". . . it was one of the reasons for the determination of the midwestern synods to remain apart from the ULCA."[69] When Stub and Hein prepared theses in anticipation of the 1925 Minneapolis meeting, which in turn prepared the way for the American Lutheran Conference, they did so with "specific points of their opposition to the ULCA" in mind.[70] "The Minneapolis Theses" declared to Lutheranism that the "middle synods" would continue "to protest against the ULCA position."[71] Moreover, President Hein "repeated his hopes for a body bearing testimony against the ULCA" so often that Professor Reu warned that the American Lutheran Conference would hardly prosper if its purpose was simply "to do battle" against other Lutherans.[72]

In relation to the Missouri Synod the new Conference saw no need to be defensive. The reason for this was that according to influential elements in the American Lutheran Conference, the doctrinal position of the Missouri Synod was aggressively and pleasingly Lutheran. Unlike the ULCA it did not pose a theological threat. There was no point in raising defenses against Missouri; rather the task here was to convince Missouri of the doctrinal orthodoxy of the arbitrarily designated "middle group." Exhibit A, as supporting evidence, was the orthodoxist "Minneapolis Theses."

The reaction to the new federation among the leaders of the ULCA was one of profound regret and no little frustration. A member of the ULCA's newly-appointed commission on relations with other Lutherans wrote to President Knubel in 1930 wondering why the ULCA had been excluded. In his reply, Knubel reviewed the history of "The Chicago Theses"

---

[69] *Op. cit.*, p. 232.
[70] *Ibid.*, p. 238.
[71] *Ibid.*, p. 240.
[72] *Ibid.*, p. 245. Meuser suggests that President Fandrey of the Iowa Synod was not "telling the full truth" when he said that the American Lutheran Conference was not conceived in a spirit of antagonism towards any other Lutheran church body.

(and later "The Minneapolis Theses"), showing that at one time (1919) they and the "Essentials of a Catholic Spirit" were intended as two parts of a common effort, around which conferences were held. "Any who were present can tell you that I begged literally with tears that the conferences should not cease." Knubel continued by saying that to follow the line of "The Minneapolis Theses" would turn American Lutheranism into a mere sect and would cast gloom for a long time over the future.

> That is exactly what the Minneapolis Theses standing alone would accomplish. They cannot live ultimately in the life of American Lutheranism for they do not represent pure Lutheranism. Some day before a great while, although not while you and I are alive, American Lutheranism will cast those things aside.[73]

The ULCA withheld comment on the American Lutheran Conference at its Milwaukee (October 7-15, 1930) convention, but its president's opening sermon, "What Does the United Lutheran Church in America Stand For?" included a staunch apology for the ULCA's orthodoxy. Veiled in this was the fact that he and his church had taken umbrage at the UCLA's obvious exclusion from the American Lutheran Conference.[74]

If one can dismiss as insignificant the historical circumstances out of which the American Lutheran Conference emerged and view the activity of the Conference in the abstract, there is no question that it served good purposes. The bringing together of Lutherans of diverse national origins was significant. The vigorous student service program at tax-supported universities and colleges, and the far-sighted all-Lutheran seminars were particularly praiseworthy.[75] But as time went on it became apparent that the American Lutheran Conference, quite as the National Lutheran Council, was of two minds on the problem of Lutheran unity.

---

[73] J. K. Jensen Papers (in possession of the writer); letters, Jensen-Knubel, 9-11-30; Knubel-Jensen, 9-16-30.
[74] *The Lutheran*, October 9, 1930, pp. 5-7.
[75] It has sometimes been overlooked that these purposes have been or could have been accomplished quite as effectively through the National Lutheran Council.

Lutheran Unity Efforts to 1950

During the thirties the Norwegian Lutheran Church of America was preoccupied to a large degree with its own problems. The difficulties which grew out of the Depression and the Great Plains Drought effectively turned its attention to that which seemed more urgent than seeking ways and means to cultivate Lutheran unity. Consequently, during this decade the NLCA played the role of spectator while other Lutherans met to discuss the question of Lutheran unity.

In 1928 the United Lutheran Church in America authorized the appointment of a Commission on Lutheran Unity, later called the Commission on Relationships to American Lutheran Church Bodies. This committee met with a similar group from the Augustana Synod in 1930, but when the latter joined the American Lutheran Conference, conversation ceased. In 1934 the ULCA adopted "The Savannah Declaration," which reaffirmed its adherence to the Scriptures and the Lutheran confessions.[76] "We believe," reads the Declaration, "that these Confessions are to be interpreted in their historical context, not as a law or system of theology, but as 'a witness and declaration of faith as to how the Holy Scriptures were understood and explained on the matters in controversy within the Church of God by those who then lived' (Formula of Concord, Part I, Intro.; ed. Jacobs, p. 492)."

On the basis of this resolution President Knubel was directed to invite other American Lutherans to union discussions.[77] The Wisconsin and Norwegian Synods promptly declined. The Augustana Synod apparently took no action, and the NLCA, though establishing a Committee on Fellowship in 1936,[78] did not enter conversations with the ULCA.[79] Two

---
[76] A convenient collection of official statements by American Lutheran bodies has been assembled and published by the Missouri Synod. See the "Savannah Resolution" in *Doctrinal Declarations* (St. Louis: Concordia Publishing House, 1957), pp. 58-60.
[77] *Minutes . . . ULCA . . . 1934*, p. 416.
[78] *NLCA . . . Report . . . 1936*, p. 32.
[79] It is of some significance that of all the major Lutheran groups in the U.S.A., including the Missouri Synod, the NLCA is the only one which has not had conversations with the ULCA.

groups, however, responded affirmatively, the Missouri Synod and the American Lutheran Church.

Two meetings were held with the Missouri commissioners, 1936 and 1938.[80] Although large areas of agreement were disclosed, the committees reached an impasse on the question of the verbal inspiration of the Bible, particularly as presented in "The Brief Statement" (1932) of the Missouri Synod.[81] As a consequence of this the ULCA felt compelled to set forth its view in a clear and carefully worded statement on the Word of God. This was known as "The Baltimore Declaration" (1938).[82] It ended the discussions with Missouri.[83]

It is necessary at this juncture to pause and note that by 1938 the "Erlangen Theology" had received rather precise formulation in the ULCA. As early as 1918-1920 it was evident that leading ULCA theologians had broken with "Repristination Theology"; but now the documentary witness to the change was complete. Three documents, all shaped in large measure by C. M. Jacobs,[84] explicated for an American audience the Biblical and confessional theology of von Hofmann, Frank, and Ludwig Ihmels. They were "The Washington Declaration" (1920), which claimed the adequacy of the confessions for Lutheran unity; "The Savannah Declaration" (1934), which insisted they must be historically understood;

---

[80]The minutes of the two meetings plus related correspondence are in the J. K. Jensen Papers in the writer's possession.

[81]*Minutes* . . . *ULCA* . . . *1936*, pp. 399-400; *ibid.*, 1938, p. 468. For text of "The Brief Statement" see *Doctrinal Declarations*, pp. 43-57.

[82]*Ibid.*, p. 66. Written largely by C. M. Jacobs (he died before it was published), it points out that the term "Word of God" is used (1) as the Gospel, (2) as God's revelation in history interpreted by inspired men, and (3) the Holy Scriptures.

[83]An editorial in *The Lutheran Witness* (Missouri Synod), LVI (Feb. 23, 1937), 55, charged the ULCA with denying the inspiration of the Bible. "There is a wide gap between bodies that accept the Bible as *being* (not only containing) the Word of God and those who do not believe that the Bible is the Word of God." C. M. Jacobs demanded a correction of this false accusation. "We [at the colloquy] asserted without reservation that the Bible is the Word of God and denied emphatically that the statement, 'The Bible contains the Word of God' describes what we believe." Jacobs-W. Arndt, March 29, 1937, in J. K. Jensen Papers.

[84]See *Minutes* . . . *ULCA* . . . *1934*, p. 416; *ibid.*, 1938, pp. 469-470. Jacobs had studied at Leipzig under Hauck and Brieger who introduced him to the *new* Lutheran confessionalism. Later in his teaching career he showed his admiration for this point of view by translating Werner Elert's *Die Lehre des Luthertums in Abriss* under the title, *An Outline of Christian Doctrine* (Philadelphia: The United Lutheran Publication House, 1927). For biographical information and tributes to Jacobs, see *The Lutheran*, XX[2] (April 13, 1938), 2, 22; *ibid.*, (April 20, 1938), 22, 23, 30.

and "The Baltimore Declaration" (1938) which asserted the divine authority of the Scriptures as *Heilsgeschichte* (history of salvation). Each of these was an "Erlangen" position, hitherto quite foreign to American Lutheranism.[85]

Meanwhile, the ULCA had also been conducting unity negotiations with the American Lutheran Church. Four meetings were held: Pittsburgh, February, 1936; Columbus, April, 1936; Columbus, March, 1938; Pittsburgh, February, 1939.[86] The ALC maintained that the official utterances of the ULCA on Masonry, unionism, and the Scriptures were without fault, but that the ULCA's practice was not in harmony with its official position. Therefore, new statements on these three points were necessary.[87]

Agreement was soon reached on the first two, but the third point revealed a definite clash of opinion. The ALC held a basically fundamentalist view while the ULCA held to Scripture as *Heilsgeschichte*. After extended discussion the two commissions produced what was called "The Pittsburgh Articles of Agreement," which retained a fundamentalist orientation. The significant passage read: ". . . by virtue of a unique operation of the Holy Ghost (2 Tim. 3:16; 2 Peter 1:21), by which He supplied to the holy writers content and fitting word (2 Peter 1:21; 1 Cor. 2:12, 13), the separate books of the Bible are related to one another and, taken together, constitute a complete, errorless, unbreakable whole, of which Christ is the center (John 10:35)."[88] "The Pittsburgh Agreement," quite at variance with "The Baltimore Declaration," was adopted by both the ULCA and ALC in 1940; in the former, under pressure and with opposition, in the latter, as an evidence that the ULCA accepted verbal inspiration.[89] The

---

[85]See translator's (Christian Preus) preface, J. C. K. von Hofmann, *Interpreting the Bible* (Minneapolis: Augsburg Publishing House, 1959), xii.

[86]The minutes of these meetings with related correspondence are among the J. K. Jensen Papers in the writer's possession.

[87]*Minutes . . . ULCA . . . 1936*, p. 401.

[88]*Doctrinal Declaration*, p. 69. The statement breathes the language of Dr. Michael Reu who, since 1932, had forsaken his earlier position on Scripture and now, as a member of the ALC commission, opposed the ULCA. See "Minutes . . . Joint Commission on Fellowship . . . ULCA and ALC, Feb. 6-7, 1936," pp. 6-11, in J. K. Jensen Papers.

[89]"The Pittsburgh Agreement" was presented to the ULCA with a long preamble. Several pastors, three commission members, and Drs. Franklin Clark Fry and Herbert C. Alleman

adoption of the Agreement produced neither organic union (the objective of the ULCA) nor pulpit and altar fellowship (the objective of the ALC).

As stated earlier, the Norwegian Lutheran Church of America stood apart from unity discussion during the thirties. But the forties found the NLCA thrown together with others by the force of the new circumstance, World War II. The National Lutheran Council, which almost experienced extinction during the thirties,[90] suddenly assumed new life in the face of the wartime emergencies. If there were any lingering doubts in the NLCA about the need for the National Lutheran Council, they were dispelled with the Nazi invasion of Norway. The NLCA, through the suggestion of Dr. Aasgaard, made a direct appropriation of $100,000 in order that the NLC might launch immediately a program of wartime services.[91] This began a new effort at Lutheran cooperation which manifested itself in increased attention to the fragmented character of American Lutheranism. The American Lutheran Conference in 1940 called a meeting of all Lutherans to consider the problem of war-orphaned foreign missions and other "matters of common interest." At the same time it ordered a redefinition of the objectives of the Conference to promote "welfare of Lutherans in America as a whole."[92]

The NLCA consequently and subsequently participated in three significant meetings, the All-Lutheran Conference, Columbus, January 20, 1941; The National Lutheran Council and Editors' Meeting, Pittsburgh, January 28-29, 1942; and the second Columbus Conference, May 14-15, 1942.[93] The consensus of all these meetings was the urgency of greater Lu-

---
spoke against adoption. *Minutes . . . ULCA . . . 1940*, pp. 266-267. Alleman wrote an incisive criticism of the Agreement, "The Pittsburgh Agreement and Lutheran Unity," *The Lutheran Quarterly*, in which he called the Articles "The Pittsburgh Disagreement" (p. 14 of reprint in writer's possession). Cf. H. Grady Davis, "Inspiration and the Pittsburgh Agreement," *The Lutheran Church Quarterly*, XV (April, 1942), 154-157.

[90]Hauge, *op. cit.*, pp. 62-64.

[91]*Ibid., op. cit.*, p. 76. It is interesting to note that the Norwegian Lutheran Church did not demand, as in 1919, doctrinal agreement before participating in "churchly cooperation," e.g., Service Commission and Commission on American Missions.

[92]*Journal of Theology of the American Lutheran Conference*, VI (January, 1941), 85-86, 90-91.

[93]*Ibid.*, p. 313; *ibid.*, VII (1942), 390, 542-543, 554.

theran unity and cooperation. The NLC proposed a Lutheran federation; the second Columbus Conference urged the enlargement of the American Lutheran Conference and the calling of a free conference by the NLC. Meanwhile, the ALC declared its willingness to establish fellowship with "either or both" the ULCA and the Missouri Synod.[94]

In this atmosphere of heightened interest in broader Lutheran cooperation the American Lutheran Conference met at Rock Island, Illinois, November 11-13, 1942.[95] Its Commission on Lutheran Unity, created in 1938, said ". . . the American Lutheran Conference must leave the door open, as far as it is concerned, for all Lutheran bodies." It also concurred in the resolution of its Committee on Re-organization: ". . . that the Executive Committee . . . be instructed to negotiate with all other Lutheran bodies, looking toward a more inclusive organization. . . ."[96]

What does not appear in the minutes of this meeting was the resistance of the NLCA to what it considered Augustana Synod pressure to include the ULCA in the American Lutheran Conference. The executive committee (which had been instructed to *negotiate* with other Lutherans) met in Minneapolis, January 26, 1943, and determined that before it could carry out the instructions of the Conference, it would request the Committee on Lutheran Unity to lay out *conditions preliminary to negotiations.*[97]

The result of this action was the drafting of the "Overture on Lutheran Unity" (1944),[98] which together with "The Minneapolis Theses" was sent to all Lutheran bodies in America. The Missouri Synod took no action on it, while the ULCA said it had already covered the same issues in its "Washington

---

[94]*Ibid.*, pp. 859-860.
[95]The January, 1943, issue of the *Journal of Theology* . . . (Volume VIII) is entirely devoted to this important meeting, including reports, minutes, and addresses.
[96]*Ibid.*, p. 84. NLCA representatives on the committee: J. A. Aasgaard, L. W. Boe, T. F. Gullixson, *ibid.*, pp. 28, 33.
[97]*The Lutheran Outlook*, VIII (March, 1943), 12. Cf. *Convention Report . . . Am. Luth. Conf* . . . 1944 pp. 16-17. It is significant that T. F. Gullixson was absent from the Rock Island (1942) meeting and that P. O. Bersell was absent from the Minneapolis (1943) meeting.
[98]*Ibid.*, pp. 19-20. It was written largely by T. F. Gullixson. Interview, 8-25-55.

Declaration."[99] An examination of the contents of the "Overture" reveals why it was not warmly received by the ULCA. The document warned against doctrinal latitudinarianism, insisted on "genuine" acceptance of the confessions, and asserted the necessity of extra-confessional doctrinal theses as testimonies to unity—all of which were clear references to what some considered to be ULCA faults. However, the "Overture" continued, on the basis of "The Minneapolis Theses" (American Lutheran Conference), "The Brief Statement" (Missouri Synod), and "The Pittsburgh Agreement" (ULCA-ALC), pulpit and altar fellowship could be established among Lutherans. The last statement clearly indicated the "repristination" character of the "Overture."[100]

It was evident in the years 1942-1944 that two opposing groups existed within the American Lutheran Conference. One wished to enlarge the Conference to include the ULCA (a view articulated chiefly by Augustana), and the other sought to withhold fellowship until the ULCA demonstrated doctrinal soundness (chiefly upheld by the NLCA).[101] Just as the years 1919-1925 had revealed two attitudes within the National Lutheran Council, so the years 1940-1944 revealed similar variance within the American Lutheran Conference.

The next four years saw no alteration in this pattern. Meanwhile, the ULCA in 1944 had proposed that all Lutherans work together in preparing a joint hymnal and service book.[102] Representatives of five church bodies began work on the project in 1945. The Evangelical Lutheran Church,[103] represented unofficially on the commission by a member of the Board of Publication, evidenced very little interest in the enterprise. In July, 1946, a report was made that the ELC "has indicated that it will not participate in the publication

---
[99]*Minutes* . . . *ULCA* . . . *1944*, p. 241-242.
[100]The "Overture" declared the three statements "to be in essential accord with one another." This was a correct observation.
[101]The editor of *Lutheran Herald* commented in 1944 that the ELC was prepared for fellowship with the Missouri Synod but not with the ULCA. The latter called into question the inspiration of Scripture; unionism was rampant in certain quarters; and some pastors were lodge members. *Lutheran Herald*, XXVIII (1944), 539.
[102]See *Report of the Joint Commission on a Common Hymnal* (n. p.: 1946), p. 1.
[103]The name was changed in 1946.

of the new book."[104] No reasons were given, but when expressions of regret were heard throughout the church, the Church Council appointed two official representatives for the ELC to meet with the commission. The church voted later to give consideration to official use of the common hymnal.[105] Although affirmative action was taken, a residuum of reluctance persisted because it was feared that the spirit and theology of the ULCA would dominate the new book.

The next ten years, 1947-1957, saw the organizational freezing of the two attitudes which had been evident in the National Lutheran Council since 1919. The catholic confessionalism of the ULCA won three additional synodical adherents: the Augustana Lutheran Church, the Suomi Synod, and the American Evangelical Lutheran Church. The repristination confessionalism solidified into a merger of the American Lutheran Church, The Evangelical Lutheran Church, and the United Evangelical Lutheran Church, known as The American Lutheran Church (TALC).

One of the turning points in post-World War II inter-Lutheran and ecumenical relations was the two great assemblies of the Lutheran World Federation (Lund, Sweden, 1947) and the World Council of Churches (Amsterdam, Holland, 1948). Church leaders returned from these meetings impressed with the need for greater unity among Christians. American Lutherans shared this sentiment and soon gave expression to it in definite proposals looking toward closer organizational unity.

Three NLC member bodies met in June, 1948—The Evangelical Lutheran Church, the Augustana Lutheran Church, and the United Evangelical Lutheran Church. Two other major groups, the United Lutheran Church and the American Lutheran Church met in October. Moreover, the American Lutheran Conference convened in November. In all of these meetings, Lutheran unity was a paramount issue.

The first group to meet was the Augustana Church. In response to a memorial from one of its regional conferences, the

---
[104]*The Lutheran Outlook*, XI (July, 1946), 195-196.
[105]*The ELC Annual Report . . . 1948*, pp. 16, 29, 491-492.

synod requested its executive council to invite all NLC churches to discuss organic merger of the NLC or federation as an intermediate step.[106]

The Evangelical Lutheran Church, meeting the same week, anticipated an invitation from the UELC (meeting the following week) to begin merger conversations. Unofficial overtures from UELC officials led ELC officials to draft a "resolution of friendship" for the UELC, and to authorize the naming of a union committee to negotiate with the UELC and "other constituent bodies of the American Lutheran Conference."[107] It should be noted that the resolution excluded the possibility of conversations with the ULCA.

The president of the UELC, Dr. N. C. Carlsen, urged merger with the ELC, but his synod feared its small constituency would be completely swallowed up by the larger ELC. Consequently a new proposal was adopted: that the UELC invite two or more bodies of the American Lutheran Conference to discuss organic union.[108]

When the American Lutheran Conference met in Detroit, November 10-12, 1948, unity resolutions were passed calling for an all-Lutheran free conference under the auspices of the NLC and commending the various efforts for unity being initiated within the Conference and the NLC.[109] Following the convention the five presidents—Aasgaard (ELC), Bersell (Aug.), Burntvedt (LFC), Carlsen (UELC), and Poppen (ALC)—met to consider further steps. Two decisions were reached: (1) that the NLC be petitioned to call a "free conference"; and (2) that dates be determined for meetings which Bersell and Carlsen were contemplating calling to implement the resolutions of their synods. They decided that a meeting of NLC representatives be held at the Augustana headquarters in Minneapolis on January 4, 1949, and that the American Lutheran Conference presidents meet in the ELC headquarters,

---
[106] *Augustana Evangelical Lutheran Church Report* . . . 1948, pp. 28, 36, 406.
[107] *The ELC Annual Report* . . . 1948, p. 482. The resolution was drafted by T. F. Gullixson, Interview, O. G. Malmin, June, 1954.
[108] *UELC Yearbook*, 1948, p. 209.
[109] *American Lutheran Conference Convention Report* . . . 1948, pp. 57-58.

also in Minneapolis, the next day, January 5, 1949.[110] Although the "free conference" was never held,[111] the meetings of January 4 and 5, 1949, proved to be fateful for a large majority of American Lutheranism. In response to Augustana's invitation representatives of the eight NLC bodies (henceforth known as "The Committee of Thirty-Four") convened according to schedule. The ELC representatives, Dr. Aasgaard, Dr. Gullixson, and Mr. S. H. Holstad, were present only as "observers," because they claimed no mandate had been given them by the church.

The proposal before the group was two-pronged: (1) organic merger of the bodies in the National Lutheran Council, or (2) federation of the NLC as an intermediate step.[112] After a full day of discussion, Dr. Emmanuel Poppen, president of the ALC, offered the following resolution: "Resolved, that it is the sense of this group that a closer organizational affiliation of the participating bodies in the National Lutheran Council is desirable and should be sought by all proper means."

In the discussion Dr. F. C. Fry, president of the ULCA, argued forcefully in favor of "a Church with strong federative aspects." Dr. H. F. Schuh, an ALC representative, not only pleaded for such action but insisted that a definite time should be indicated when a federation should become an organic union. "What are we waiting for?" he asked. "We are already

---

[110] Considerable tension developed later around the calling of these meetings. The ELC representatives maintained that the Augustana proposal came as a surprise and seemed intended to undercut the meeting of January 5. Bersell said that Carlsen "graciously" agreed to allow the NLC meeting of January 4. Interview with Bersell, 5-20-59. This is verified by the correspondence of N. C. Carlsen. Writing to the editor of *The Lutheran Standard* (ALC), Carlsen reported that the Detroit meeting of presidents decided on the dates for the discussions. "Dr. Bersell seemed to be quite concerned about getting the meeting which he was calling the day before we had ours. *No objections were made.*" [Italics added.] Carlsen-E. W. Schramm, January 11, 1950.

[111] Dr. Aasgaard was the only one of the five presidents to petition the NLC. He later withdrew his petition. See *Agenda National Lutheran Council. 31st Annual Meeting . . . 1949*, pp. 7, 35. Cf. section on "Minutes," p. 3. For comments on this matter by an Augustana layman see A. J. Bowman, "Lutheran Unity from a Layman's Viewpoint," *The Lutheran Outlook*, XIV (May, 1949), 141-144. The editor of *The Lutheran Outlook* (Feb., 1949, p. 35-36) was grieved that the resolution of the American Lutheran Conference requesting a "free conference" was not carried out. Such a conference would no doubt have included the Missouri Synod. Why only one of the five American Lutheran Conference presidents fulfilled the resolution of the Detroit convention is an unsolved mystery.

[112] See Minutes, "Conference on Lutheran Unity, Augustana Church Headquarters, Minneapolis, Minn., Jan. 4, 1949," J. K. Jensen Papers.

cooperating here at home and in all parts of the world."[113] When a ballot was taken on the resolution, not a dissenting vote was cast. The group then adopted a resolution to appoint a committee of fifteen to prepare a structural plan and report to the full "Committee of 34" the next fall.[114]

Although the records show only unanimous support for the above proposals, at least two churches voiced their objections. President Carlsen of the UELC pointed out that his church would hesitate taking such steps because of the laxity in practice within the ULCA regarding dancing, drinking, and lodge membership of pastors. Dr. T. F. Gullixson, one of the ELC "observers," then objected to Schuh's intimation that the NLC, as it now existed, had outlived its usefulness. Moreover, if there was to be union, it must be on the basis of doctrinal agreement, especially since there were evidences that ULCA seminaries were teaching views on Scripture that were contrary to what had been held in the ELC the last one hundred years.[115]

The next day, January 5, 1949, the representatives of the American Lutheran Conference met in the ELC headquarters under the chairmanship of President N. C. Carlsen. The resolution adopted by this group held that every effort should be made to bring about the plans of the previous day's meeting but that there ought to be no objection to lesser approaches to unity within the Conference.[116]

Three other meetings during 1949 crystallized the points of view evident at the January 4 and 5 conferences. The subcommittee of "The Committee of 34" met in Chicago, April 26-27, 1949. Dr. Aasgaard reminded the group that he and Gullixson

---

[113]"A Move Toward Unity," *The Lutheran Outlook*, XIV (Feb., 1949), 55-56.
[114]*Minutes* . . . *Jan. 4, 1949*, p. 2.
[115]Interview with J. K. Jensen (ULCA member of "Committee of 34"), 1-4-49; and interview with T. F. Gullixson, 6-6-55. It should be noted that a ULCA theological professor, Dr. Joseph Sittler, had just published a book, *The Doctrine of the Word* (Philadelphia: Muhlenberg Press, 1948), which disturbed ELC leaders because it criticized the orthodoxist doctrine of inspiration. Cf. O. G. Malmin's review, *Augsburg Book News Letter*, May, 1949; and *Lutheran Herald*, XXXIII (May 31, 1949), 539-540, 553; and *ibid.* (June 14, 1949), 591-592.
[116]*Minutes of Meeting* . . . *January 5, 1949*, p. 2.

were "observers" without mandate from their church. This meeting prepared recommendations for a structural plan to be submitted to "The Committee of 34." The proposal suggested (1) that the parent committee request the NLC churches to take action on organic union, and (2) that, pending consummation of the same, a National Lutheran Federation be established.[117] "The Committee of 34," meeting in Chicago, September 27, 1949, voted to present the two resolutions to the NLC member bodies."[118]

Meanwhile, eleven days earlier representatives of the ELC, ALC, and UELC met to lay their plans. The informal consensus of the group expressed the judgment that their bodies were not in favor of organic merger of the NLC but preferred a federation of *all* Lutherans in America. Dr. Gullixson then presented a resolution which urged merger of the three bodies and asked that such a resolution be presented to the conventions of the ELC, ALC, and UELC.[119]

During the first week of January, 1950, the final meeting of "The Committee of 34" was held. Of chief importance was the presence of representatives from the Lutheran Church—Missouri Synod, who were invited to cooperate in the common endeavor to form an all-Lutheran federation. President John Behnken said that his group was present only as "observers" to obtain information.[120]

The decisive action in the ELC occurred in 1950. During the winter the Church Council discussed the unity proposals of the previous year and prepared resolutions to be offered to the biennial convention in June. One resolution said "the time is not now at hand for complete organic union" of the NLC churches, and that the implications of a federation produced the conviction "that the National Lutheran Council in its present form is the agency which . . . best can serve the several

---

[117] *Minutes of Sub-Committee . . . April 26-27, 1949,* pp. 4-5.
[118] *Minutes . . . Sept. 27, 1949,* pp. 2-3.
[119] *Minutes . . . Joint Meeting . . . ALC, ELC, and UELC . . . September 16, 1949,* pp. 1-3. What caused Poppen and Schuh to change their minds is not evident in the minutes.
[120] *Minutes . . . Committee of 34 . . . Jan. 5, 1950,* p. 3.

Lutheran bodies in America."[121] The other resolution urged the organic union of the ELC, ALC, and UELC and the appointment of a Joint Union Committee of twenty-seven members, nine from each church. Both of these resolutions were adopted by the ELC.[122] Thus the church was officially launched on the merger program which was to be culminated in the formation of The American Lutheran Church (TALC) in April, 1960.[123]

1950-1959, The Accomplished Fact

After 1950 the ELC was resolutely led by its leaders along the path of the three-way merger. For a short time the Augustana Lutheran Church and the Lutheran Free Church, as members of the American Lutheran Conference, participated in the negotiations.[124] The Augustana Church withdrew in 1952, desiring a more inclusive merger.[125] The Lutheran Free Church, as a result of congregational referendums in 1955 and 1957, found it necessary to remove itself from the projected union. In 1954 the American Lutheran Conference was officially dissolved in *de facto* recognition of the existing circumstances in American Lutheranism. The next year the ULCA and Augustana invited all Lutherans to merger conversations, being ultimately joined by the AELC and the Suomi Synod. Meanwhile, union documents were readied and accepted by the TALC churches. In 1952 the ELC approved a statement on faith and life, "The United Testimony." In 1954 authorization was given the Joint Union Committee to prepare articles of incorporation, a constitution and bylaws, and articles of union. In 1956

---

[121] The idea of a national Lutheran federation was not seriously explored as a live option to organic union. Had it been, ten years (1949-1959) of unhappy inter-Lutheran relations might have been avoided or at least mitigated. The ELC leaders were never enthusiastic about it. They wanted neither merger nor federation if the ULCA was involved. Thus, when Franklin Clark Fry, ULCA president, came out against the idea of federation, this was all that was needed to destroy this alternative to organic union. *The Lutheran*, XXXII (March 8, 1950), 13.

[122] *The ELC Annual Report . . . 1950*, pp. 34-37, 484-485.

[123] It is of more than passing interest that a number of those who voted against the 1917 merger have actively supported the TALC merger, and for essentially the same reason, namely, an honest conviction that such action was the best way to preserve true Lutheranism in America.

[124] The 1950 ELC convention adopted a resolution opening the door to these two bodies. *Ibid.*, p. 521.

[125] *Augustana Ev. Luth. Church . . . Report . . . 1953*, pp. 340-343.

these documents were approved by the ELC for adoption by the constituting convention of TALC.

Thus by the mid-fifties the two points of view which came to light in the National Lutheran Council as early as 1919 had found organizational expression in two merger movements. The forces—overt and covert—which produced them certainly included other than differing theological viewpoints. Personality clashes, sociological differences, and power politics were all in evidence. In spite of the fact that leaders of the ELC occasionally expressed the need of a powerful "middle bloc" with which to face other Lutherans, the efforts to negotiate "from a position of strength" were not confined to the ELC.[126] Furthermore, the continuing feeling in the ELC that the ULCA was casual about "spiritual life," whether a right or a wrong opinion, was a potent factor in molding negative attitudes towards the ULCA. For these and such obvious reasons as proximity to the events, it should be manifest that only succeeding generations will be able to judge the actions of the past forty years with anything approaching comprehensive accuracy. Nevertheless, certain judgments are already almost self-evident. It is clear, for example, that a major change in American Lutheranism has been taking place since World War I. The difficulty all along has been to understand the transformation *while it has been taking place*. The failure to perceive that it has been taking place and inaccurate interpretations of the transformation after it has occurred in certain sections of the church have brought forth suspicions and fears, power politics and personality clashes. The consequent misunderstanding, suffering, and feverish expenditure of energy have been both needless and regrettable.

Moreover, it is now palpable that the objections raised in 1949 to fellowship with the ULCA were unrealistic. The "liberal" ULCA attitude towards the adiaphora (dancing, drinking, etc.) is qualitatively hardly any different from the atti-

---

[126]Richard C. Wolf comments that the ULCA was likewise not guiltless in seeking position and prestige. "Lutheran Unity and Union in Historical Perspective," *The Lutheran Quarterly*, XI (May, 1959), 120-121.

tudes of the Missouri Synod and the American Lutheran Church, both of which the ELC has considered "orthodox." With regard to lodgery, the Augustana Church *alone* has urged upon the ULCA the seriousness of the problem and as a result something positive has already been done. In respect to theological "liberalism" in the ULCA, it should be admitted in all candor that there are pastors and teachers in the ELC who in conscience prefer "The Baltimore Declaration" of the ULCA to the statement on Scripture in "The Minneapolis Theses." It is the latter that has been incorporated verbatim as an unalterable part of the TALC constitution (Article IV). This constitutional provision, however, was no doubt a major factor in influencing the Missouri Synod in 1959 to invite TALC to unity conversations. Meanwhile, the TALC grouping has proposed discussions with the ULCA-Augustana bloc. Considering the history of the past four decades it is difficult to predict what may happen. The diagram on the opposite page, although hardly a crystal ball of prognosticating the future, may serve as a visual summary of the inter-Lutheran family developments since World War I.

Conclusion: Ecumenical Relations

When the Norwegian Lutheran Church of America was formed in 1917, one of the Articles of Union (number three) dealt with the problem of ecumenical relations.[127] The negative content of the article, as already noted, represented largely the concern of the Norwegian Synod. Both of the other uniting bodies, Hauge's Synod and the United Church, had unanimously adopted an "Interpretation" of the article which gave a bit of ecumenical breadth to the statement. However, during the years after 1917, the article *sans* "Interpretation" guided the NLCA and gave it a spirit of extreme caution with regard to other churches, Lutheran and non-Lutheran, which were judged as not sharing "the faith and confession of these bodies."

---

[127]"The three bodies promise one another in all seriousness to observe the rule not to carry on churchly cooperation with the Reformed and others who do not share the faith and confessions of these bodies." Bruce (ed.), *The Union Documents* . . . , p. 58.

The Church Discovers Other Churches

LUTHERAN CONFESSIONALISM IN THE NATIONAL LUTHERAN COUNCIL
1918-1960

The National Lutheran Council
(established 1918)
H. G. Stub, president
Lauritz Larsen, secretary

↓

1919-1920 Conferences on Cooperative Church Work

↓

Two documents, "The Chicago Theses" and "The Essentials of a Catholic Spirit," revealed

TWO CONFESSIONAL VIEWPOINTS:

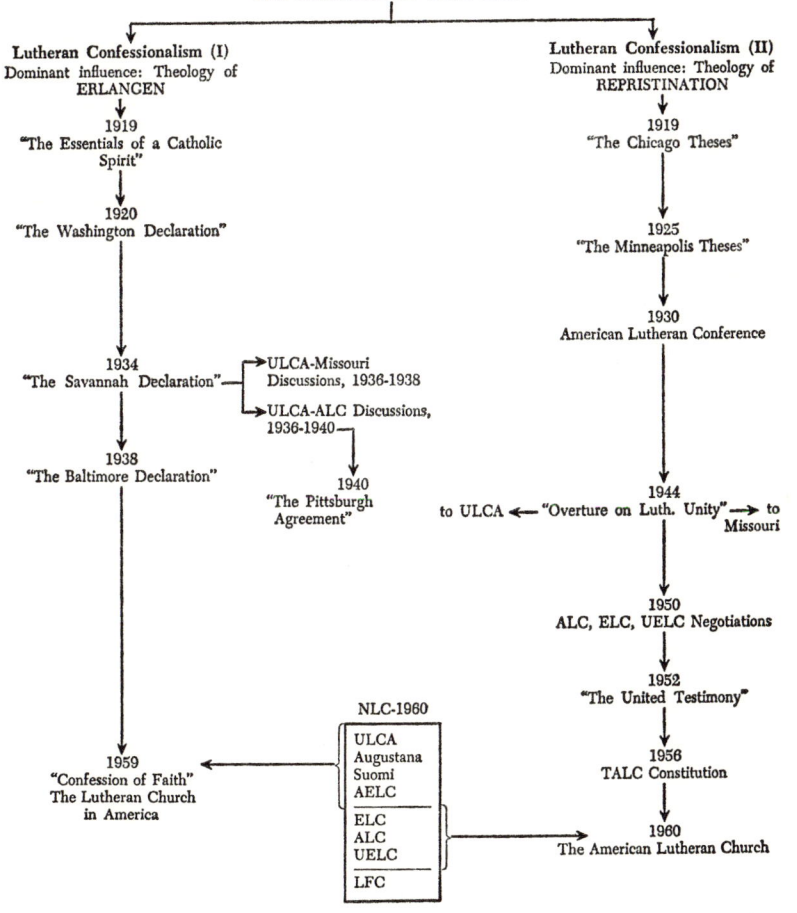

Lutheran Confessionalism (I)
Dominant influence: Theology of ERLANGEN

↓

1919
"The Essentials of a Catholic Spirit"

↓

1920
"The Washington Declaration"

↓

1934
"The Savannah Declaration" → ULCA-Missouri Discussions, 1936-1938
→ ULCA-ALC Discussions, 1936-1940 → 1940 "The Pittsburgh Agreement"

↓

1938
"The Baltimore Declaration"

↓

1959
"Confession of Faith"
The Lutheran Church in America

Lutheran Confessionalism (II)
Dominant influence: Theology of REPRISTINATION

↓

1919
"The Chicago Theses"

↓

1925
"The Minneapolis Theses"

↓

1930
American Lutheran Conference

↓

1944
to ULCA ← "Overture on Luth. Unity" → to Missouri

↓

1950
ALC, ELC, UELC Negotiations

↓

1952
"The United Testimony"

↓

1956
TALC Constitution

↓

1960
The American Lutheran Church

NLC-1960
ULCA
Augustana
Suomi
AELC

ELC
ALC
UELC

LFC

This accounts, in part at least, for the difficulties which H. G. Stub encountered in bringing the NLCA into the National Lutheran Council. When he assured his friends in the former Norwegian Synod, who led the opposition to the NLC, that no "unionism" was involved, and thus no infraction of "Article Three," he was able to lead the church into the Council. Because of this hard-won affiliation with the National Lutheran Council, later support of the Lutheran World Convention and the Lutheran World Federation was not difficult to obtain. However, the content and spirit of "Article Three" effectively served to keep the church out of the Federal Council of Churches and the National Council of Churches of Christ, and most certainly played a large role in the ten-year struggle over membership in the World Council of Churches.

The Lutheran World Convention and The Lutheran World Federation

In Eisenach, Germany, at the first meeting of the Lutheran World Convention (1923), Archbishop Nathan Søderblom of Sweden said: "I have often referred to the fact that the Lutherans of America were the first to appear upon the scene with their ministry of love and help when the war had closed."[128] In a manner far surpassing the expectations of European Lutherans, the American brethren had assumed a role of leadership which the stresses of war had thrust upon them. Working together in the National Lutheran Commission, and later in the National Lutheran Council, Americans had done yeoman work in alleviating postwar distress in Europe. Leaders in this work included several members of the Norwegian Lutheran Church of America. Dr. H. G. Stub, as president of the Council, gave much thought and time to the overseas relief program. Dr. Lauritz Larsen, secretary of the National Lutheran Commission for Soldiers' and Sailors' Welfare, and later executive secretary and president of the National Lu-

---

[128] *The Lutheran World Convention. Minutes, Addresses* . . . *1923* (Philadelphia: The United Lutheran Publication House, 1925), p. 25.

theran Council, was most deeply involved (of the NLCA leaders) in the European outreach of the American Lutherans. Others engaged in the enterprises of 1918-1923 were Dr. M. J. Stolee, professor at Luther Theological Seminary, St. Paul, who was a member of the first American Lutheran team sent abroad to investigate relief needs; and Dr. L. W. Boe, president of St. Olaf College, who had figured in the early negotiations and was destined to become one of the most vigorous leaders of world Lutheranism.[129]

In 1919 Dr. John A. Morehead, chairman of the European Commission of the National Lutheran Council, urgently requested the Council to consider leading the way in forming a world federation of Lutheran Churches.[130] The next year, he and Drs. Stolee and Larsen joined in a formal recommendation "that arrangements be made for holding an international free Lutheran conference."[131] The suggestion commended itself to the Council and in 1921 it appointed an American committee, Dr. C. M. Jacobs, chairman, to make tentative plans for a world congress of Lutherans and to issue a call, together with the *Allgemeine Evangelisch-Lutherische Konferenz* (General Ev. Lutheran Conference) and the *Lutherischer Bund* (Lutheran League) in Germany, for such a meeting.[132] The decision was to meet in Eisenach, Germany, August 19-26, 1923.

When Dr. Stub in his annual presidential address before the NLCA in 1923 referred to the invitation to Eisenach, he commented that the Church Council was recommending that the church be represented at the conference. Later the convention voted to send Stub, who preached the opening sermon at the congress.[133]

The Lutheran World Convention at Eisenach did at least two things which became significant to the NLCA: (1) it adopted a set of resolutions, drafted by a committee of which C. M. Jacobs was chairman, which resolutions included a con-

---
[129]Hauge, *op. cit.*, pp. 25-43.
[130]*Annual Report* . . . *NLC* . . . *1919*, p. 66.
[131]*Ibid.* . . . *1920*, pp. 73-74.
[132]*Ibid.* . . . *1921*, pp. 41-43. The *Bund* did not join in extending the invitation.
[133]*Report* . . . *NLCA* . . . *1923*, pp. 17, 115; *Lutheran World Convention* . . . *Minutes* . . . *1923*, pp. 181-185.

servative (but not fundamentalist) doctrinal statement, and (2) it appointed an executive committee to which Dr. L. W. Boe was named.[134]

The Lutheran World Convention had no constitution and consequently no formal list of members. This meant that there was no way whereby the NLCA and other churches could become *members* of the Convention. It was never to be more than a "free conference." With this in mind Dr. Stub reported the action of the Eisenach meeting to the 1924 convention of the NLCA. He commented on Dr. Boe's appointment as follows: "Dr. Boe represents not only our church but together with Dr. Morehead all the Lutheran churches . . . of the National Lutheran Council. Our Church Council has recommended that Dr. Boe accept the appointment, which surely all the districts will also do."[135] Only one of the districts (Canada) ratified Boe's appointment, while three others (Eastern, Southern Minnesota, Pacific) gave approval to the idea of Lutheran world congresses.[136]

Despite this somewhat less than enthusiastic ratification, Boe continued to serve with uninhibited effectiveness on the executive committee until his death in 1942 (he was succeeded by Dr. J. A. Aasgaard), and kept the NLCA in touch with one of the major developments in modern Christendom. The NLCA was represented at subsequent meetings of the Lutheran World Convention (Copenhagen, 1929, and Paris, 1935) and through Boe's dynamic leadership became involved in the ongoing program of an increasingly self-conscious world Lutheranism.

The fourth meeting of the Lutheran World Convention, planned for Philadelphia in 1940, was prevented by the outbreak of World War II. The war and its aftermath only served to highlight the necessity of a strong world organization. Thus in 1946 the executive committee of the revived Lutheran World Convention drafted a constitution for a new body to be known as the Lutheran World Federation and issued a call

---
[134]*Ibid.*, pp. 10, 14-15.
[135]*Report . . . NLCA . . . 1924*, p. 16.
[136]*Ibid.*, p. 113.

for the First Assembly to be held at Lund, Sweden, in 1947.[137]

Since the call for the Lund Assembly came after the 1946 convention of the ELC (the name was changed that year), President Aasgaard took the responsibility of naming the representatives of the church. They were, besides himself, Drs. A. J. Bergsaker, T. F. Gullixson, J. R. Lavik, Morris Wee, Herman E. Jorgensen, J. W. Ylvisaker, and F. A. Schiotz. The constitution adopted at Lund and signed by Dr. Aasgaard stipulated that "All Lutheran churches previously affiliated with the Lutheran World Convention, which through their representatives participate in the adoption of this Constitution, shall continue to be members of the Lutheran World Federation."[138] Thus, in a rather strange and anomalous fashion the ELC "joined" the Lutheran World Federation. Although the church has never ratified the actions of 1947, neither has it ever repudiated them. In fact, The Evangelical Lutheran Church has been a loyal and enthusiastic member of the Lutheran World Federation. As witness to this has been the large number of ELC members who have served in various capacities as officials and employees of the LWF. Besides Dr. Aasgaard, who served on the executive committee until 1954 (when he was replaced by the new president of the ELC), several others have given generously of their time and abilities to the program of the LWF. Among them Dr. F. A. Schiotz, now ELC president and former director of the NLC's Commission on Younger Churches and Orphaned Missions, was chairman of the LWF's Commission on World Mission. Numerous others participated in the service to refugees, the rehabilitation of war-orphaned missions, and the plans and preparation for the Second and Third Assemblies of the LWF at Hanover (1952) and Minneapolis (1957).[139] In fact, perhaps no other

---

[137] Wentz, *A Basic History* . . . , p. 342; cf. E. T. Bachmann, *Epic of Faith* (New York: National Lutheran Council, 1952), pp. 9-15.

[138] *LWF . . . Proceedings . . . Lund, 1947*, pp. 100-104. See also *The ELC Annual Report . . . 1948*, pp. 18-19.

[139] A quick check of the *Directory of the Lutheran World Federation, 1959* and an unofficial listing of the "LWF family" sent out by the Geneva office, indicates no less than thirty names of ELC personnel as having given service to the LWF or as presently functioning officials in departments or commissions.

American Lutheran group has had proportionately such a large number of its members actively engaged in the program of the Lutheran World Federation. Unquestionably much of this interest has been a fruit of the forthright advocacy of Lutheran cooperation and unity at home and abroad by L. W. Boe.[140]

The ELC and the World Council of Churches

The ELC's relations to non-Lutheran churches have been characterized by extreme caution. Once again it must be said that the conviction embalmed in "Article Three" of the 1917 Articles of Union lay at the root of this attitude. As early as 1915 the United Church had raised serious question about the article; likewise Hauge's Synod in 1916 said it would not enter the 1917 merger unless the article were qualified. Although the above-mentioned ecumenically-oriented "Interpretation" was accepted, no alteration was made in the wording of the original article. For reasons difficult to document, the church in subsequent years was guided by the substance of the article rather than by the "Interpretation" of the article.

A constitution for a World Council of Churches was drafted at Utrecht, Holland, in 1938, and plans were made for its First Assembly to be held in 1941. With the outbreak of World War II, the Provisional Committee with Dr. W. A. Visser 't Hooft as general secretary set up an international office in Geneva, Switzerland. When the war was over in 1945, the WCC, yet unestablished, faced the mammoth task of relief and reconstruction. The following year invitations were extended by the Provisional Committee at Geneva to the churches to unite in the formal organization of the WCC at the First Assembly in Amsterdam in 1948.[141]

Most of world Lutheranism accepted membership in the World Council. The chief exceptions were in America where

---
[140]Erik Hetle, *Lars Wilhelm Boe: A Biography* (Minneapolis: Augsburg Publishing House, 1949), pp. 131-157.
[141]G. K. A. Bell, *The Story of the World Council of Churches* (Harmondswork, Middlesex: Penguin Books, 1954), pp. 32-49.

the Synodical Conference churches, the ELC, and LFC declined the invitations. President Aasgaard explained to the 1946 convention of the ELC that membership did not imply altar or pulpit fellowship "but offers the opportunity to cooperate with other Christian churches where it can be done according to our principles and our confessions." For this reason, he said, the leadership of the ELC was in favor of joining the WCC and the Church Council was presenting a resolution incorporating this sentiment.[142] The resolution was not adopted by the convention, but the whole matter of WCC membership was referred back to the Church Council for study and report to the 1948 convention.[143]

Between 1946 and 1948 a vigorous and, at times, intemperate debate occurred on the question of membership in the WCC. The Church Council and leaders of the church, in general, gave support to the ecumenical movement. A majority of the pastors and lay people, as was soon evident, took the opposite position. The opponents engaged in a widespread pamphlet war charging the WCC with "modernism," "unionism," and ecclesiastical giantism ("a super church"). The Board of Publication of the ELC, in an attempt to have both sides carefully presented, authorized the preparation and publication of a pamphlet entitled, *Should We Join the World Council of Churches?* An affirmative answer was written by Dr. N. Astrup Larsen,[144] a member of the Church Council; the negative position was defended by Pastor R. A. Ofstedal. Larsen sought to answer the strictures of "modernism" and "unionism"; Ofstedal warned that membership in the Council would lead to apostasy.[145]

The battle was joined in 1948 at the general convention of the church and, after lengthy debate, the Church Council's resolution to accept membership in the WCC was decisively

---

[142]*NLCA Annual Report . . . 1946*, pp. 17, 41.
[143]*Ibid.*, p. 438.
[144]Larsen is a son of the first president of Luther College and a brother of Lauritz Larsen who had played such a large role in the NLC and the Lutheran world service program after World War I.
[145]*Should We Join the World Council of Churches?* (Minneapolis: Augsburg Publishing House, 1948), *passim.*

defeated.[146] The defeat of the WCC resolution represented a strange coalition of historically uncongenial elements among the Norwegian Lutherans in America, namely, the pietistic fundamentalists and the Missourian fundamentalists. The coming together of the left- and right-wing segments of the church was brought about by a common fear that the "Word of God" was being denied. In fact, the decisive convention vote was largely influenced by the theological arguments of the opponents rather than by the practical and non-theological appeal of the proponents. Beside the point, at the moment, is the question whether or not the theology of the theological arguments was sound. It was theology, and theology which had a familiar ring. This was enough to defeat membership in the World Council of Churches.

A decade elapsed between the original invitation to join the WCC and the ELC's second—and this time, affirmative—vote on the question. In 1956 the tables were turned and the convention voted decisively to apply for membership in the WCC.

An incomplete but perhaps helpful explanation of the altered attitude in the church is to be found in the following factors: (1) Some of the misinformation and misrepresentation of the WCC had, in the meantime, been corrected. The new president, F. A. Schiotz, for example, was able to present from personal experience a complete and accurate picture of the WCC; this had the effect of allaying many fears. (2) The churches with which the ELC was planning to merge, the ALC and the UELC, were charter members of the WCC. This fact led many to question the reasons given for continued ELC opposition to the WCC. (3) Between 1946 and 1956 the seminary had graduated 723 students. Many of these men were convinced of the wisdom of affiliating with the WCC and now added their voting strength to the supporters of the ecumenical movement.

Thus, in the concluding years of The Evangelical Lutheran

---

[146]*The ELC Annual Report* . . . *1948*, p. 472. The vote was 546 for the resolution, 872 against.

Church, a historically conservative church body has committed itself to the chief non-Roman organization which seeks to manifest before the world the unity of the members of the Body of Christ. It has taken its place in the ecumenical movement, as other Lutherans have done, without renouncing its confessional convictions, but at the same time it has sought consciously a way in which it may witness to its belief that Jesus Christ has created a New Israel, the one, holy, and catholic church. Increasingly, it realizes that such a witness is an inescapable evangelistic necessity in the divine economy, "so that the world may believe . . . so that the world may know."

APPENDIX A

Constitution and Articles of Union[1]

For The United Norwegian Lutheran Church in America (1890)

PROPOSED CONSTITUTION

Chapter I

Name and Confession

1. The name of this church body is "The Norwegian Lutheran Free Church in America."[2]

2. The church believes, teaches, and confesses that the Holy Scriptures, the Canonical Books of the Old and New Testament, are God's revealed Word and therefore the only source and rule of faith, doctrine, and life.

3. As a brief, true, and pure presentation of the teachings of God's Word this church accepts and confesses the Symbols or Confessional Writings of the Norwegian Evangelical Lutheran Church:

a) The ancient Symbols: the Apostolic, the Nicene, and Athanasian;

b) The unaltered Augsburg Confession and Luther's Small Catechism.

---

[1] J. A. Bergh, *Den norsk lutherske Kirkes Historie i Amerika* (Minneapolis: Augsburg Publishing House, 1914), pp. 369-376. Trans. by J. R. Lavik.

[2] Changed November 15, 1888 at Scandinavia, Wisconsin, to "The United Norwegian Lutheran Church in America."

4. The church consists of Lutheran congregations that subscribe to this constitution.

5. When a congregation desires to join the church, it shall send its application to the president of the church. This shall be accompanied by:

 a) A copy of the constitution and bylaws of the congregation as evidence that its doctrine, confession, and church order are genuinely Lutheran;

 b) A properly attested declaration that the constitution of the church has been approved at a public meeting of the congregation. The matter shall be submitted to the church together with the accompanying documents for its decision.

CHAPTER II

The Object of the Church

1. The object of the church shall be:

 a) The mutual brotherly admonition and instruction, guidance and encouragement of its members in accordance with the Word of God;

 b) To consider such doctrinal and practical church questions as from time to time may be considered of importance to the maintenance of the truth and for the good of the congregations;

 c) To provide for the education of future pastors and parochial school teachers for the service of the congregations and instruction of the young;

 d) To seek to compose church conflicts and to give counsel and advice in church problems in cases where the help of the church is requested;

 e) To promote the use and distribution of the Holy Scriptures, orthodox textbooks, hymnbooks, and devotional literature;

 f) On the whole to work for the extension and establishment of the Kingdom of God among our countrymen in America by gathering and organizing Lutheran congregations, provide them with pastors and teachers, and labor for the abundant distribution of the Word of God, also among Jews and heathen, by an energetic participation in the mission work commanded by God. For the attainment of these objectives the members of the church obligate themselves to help one another in word and deed to the best of their ability.

CHAPTER III

Church Conventions and Their Membership

1. The church shall meet in convention at such time and place as the president in accordance with authorization by the church shall determine. The president may also convene other meetings when the church authorizes him to do so, or when at least twenty of the congregations belonging to the church request him to do so.

2. Voting members at such conventions shall be:

a) One representative from each of the congregations belonging to the church.[3]

b) Pastors who are called to serve congregations belonging to the church and who have been ordained in accordance with decision of the church or, in case they have not been ordained by the church, have been admitted into the ministry of the church after necessary examination.

c) The theological professors at the seminary of the church.

Advisory members shall be:

a) The officials of the church who are not voting members.

b) Permanent teachers at the institutions that belong to the church.

c) Pastors who serve Lutheran congregations that do not belong to the church, who have subscribed to the constitution of the church, and who, after necessary examination, have been acknowledged by the annual convention of the church to be in fact Lutheran pastors.

d) Permanent parochial school teachers of congregations which belong to the church.

3. With the exception of amendments to the constitution of the church all matters shall be determined by simple majority. In case of a tie, the vote of the president shall determine; otherwise, the president shall not vote. In regard to admission and expulsion from the church at least two-thirds majority of the votes cast shall be required.

---

[3] Professor Sverdrup requested that it be noted in the minutes that he would move as a minority report that there be two representatives instead of one.

4. If a congregation, for reasons of conscience or because of special conditions, should not be able to carry out some decision of the church, it shall within six months after the decision has been made public send its statement in regard to the matter to the president of the church.

Chapter IV

Ordination

1. The ordination of a candidate shall be determined by the annual meeting of the church or by an ordination committee elected for this purpose.

2. Before anyone can be ordained to the holy ministry the church shall assure itself that he is properly called and examined and has good testimonials for true and living Christianity.

Chapter V

Circuit[4] Meetings

1. The church shall be divided into circuits as may seem necessary.

2. These shall each have one or more meetings each year.

3. The annual convention shall elect a "Visitor" for each circuit.

Chapter VI

Theological Seminary

1. The church shall control and support a theological seminary for the training of pastors and missionaries.

2. The professors and teachers of the seminary shall be elected by the church at its annual meeting by a two-thirds majority of the votes cast.

3. As professors and teachers shall be called and installed such as have satisfactory testimonials for true and living Christianity, who without reservation accept and subscribe to the doctrines and

---

[4]The Norwegian word is *kreds,* customarily translated "circuit." However, the *Haandbog* of the United Church translated it "district."

Confessions of the church and submit themselves to the constitution of the church.

4. The church shall elect a board of directors to supervise the seminary and its affairs.

5. If a professor or teacher at the seminary should be found to teach anything that is in manifest conflict with the Word of God and the Confessions adopted by the church, or to live an offensive and unchristian life, the chairman of the board of directors shall, as soon as he becomes aware of this, at once call a meeting of the board for the purpose of investigating the matter. If the one concerned is found to be guilty, but does not yield to admonition, the accused shall be suspended until the annual convention decides the matter.

Chapter VII

Officers of the Church

1. Officers of the church shall be: a President, a Vice-president, a Secretary, a Treasurer, and Visitors.

2. The president and the visitors shall be elected by the annual convention for three years, the other officers for one year. They shall all be elected from among the members of the church. Election shall be by ballot.

The president, the vice-president, and visitors shall be chosen from among the pastors of the church.

3. The president shall convene and preside over the conventions of the church, provide for the ordination of candidates and their installation, watch over the preservation of peace and order in the church, hold visitations in the parishes of the visitors, submit to each annual convention a report concerning his activities during the past year and concerning the state of the church.

4. The vice-president shall perform the duties of the president in his absence or incapacity.

5. The secretary shall keep a record of the proceedings of the conventions and publish a public report of same; he shall in due time send to each of the pastors of the church a report blank for parochial reports; compile the statistics of the church; carry on the necessary correspondence for the church which it or its president may designate; announce time and place for its conventions at

least six weeks in advance; and keep the seal and the archives of the church.

6. The treasurer shall administer the funds entrusted to him by the church in accordance with its decisions, and submit a report to each annual convention.

7. The visitors shall, if possible, at least once in every three years hold visitation meetings in each of the congregations within their respective circuits.

Chapter VIII

Amendments

1. With the exception of Chapter 1, No. 2 and No. 3, whose contents are unchangeable, and with the exception of this paragraph, amendments to this constitution can be made only in the following manner: Motion to amend shall be submitted to the annual convention of the church. If it approves such motion by simple majority, the motion shall be made public that it may be more fully considered until the next annual convention. At this convention the motion shall be put to a vote, but can be adopted only by two-thirds majority.

ARTICLES OF UNION

The present contracting parties, namely, the Anti-Missourians, the Augustana Synod, the Hauge Synod, and the Conference, for the purpose of forming a church body, each and severally agree to the following conditions:

1. That a theological seminary shall be established and maintained;

2. That this theological seminary shall be Augsburg Seminary in Minneapolis.[5]

3. That the teachers at this school shall be paid from interest on a fund which shall be procured in the following manner:

    a) The Augustana Synod shall contribute its fund of $15,000;[6]

---

[5]Pastor Andreas Wright, ordained at the 1870 meeting of the Norwegian Augustana Synod, which denied that that Conference was the rightful successor to the former Augustana Synod, demonstrated his feeling against Augsburg Seminary of the Conference by requesting that it be noted in the minutes that he did not vote for this article.
[6]Pastor Wright was also unprepared to vote for this.

Appendix A

b) The Hauge Synod shall contribute its fund earlier decided upon of $50,000;

c) The Conference shall contribute its fund of $50,000;

d) The Anti-Missourians shall gather a similar fund, sufficiently large so that the interest on it will pay at least two professors.

Note: The fund shall consist in part of cash, in part of interest-bearing notes, or other acceptable securities.

4. At said seminary six theological professors shall be elected in the following manner:

a) The Anti-Missourians shall elect two theological professors;

b) The Augustana Synod shall elect one theological professor;

c) The Hauge Synod shall elect one theological professor;

d) The Conference shall elect two theological professors.

5. The constitution for said theological seminary shall be worked out as soon as the union is effected.

6. The theological students who already have been admitted to the theological seminaries of the above named church bodies shall by virtue of this admission be admitted to the new theological seminary.

7. The new church body shall be incorporated as soon as possible.

8. To this incorporated church body shall be transferred all school property—both real property and funds—which said church bodies may be in possession of at the time of union.

9. The real property referred to in Paragraph 8 shall, when transferred to the new church body, be free from debt.

10. The preparatory departments at Augsburg Seminary and at Red Wing Seminary and the Academy at Canton shall be conducted in the same way as formerly for at least one year after the union is effected. Also the school at Beloit, Iowa, shall be conducted for at least one year after the union is brought about.

11. At the convention at which the merger of the church bodies is effected a board of directors of twelve members, three from each church body, shall be elected. It shall perform the same functions as the boards of directors formerly performed in each of the church bodies.

12. The theological professors at the seminary of the new church

body shall receive as salary the first year after union is effected $1,250.00 each and free residence.

13. The Anti-Missourians agreed to build two professors' residences for said educational institution in Minneapolis.

14. The church papers that are owned and published by said church bodies shall be combined, so that there will be published one paper for children and an official organ for the church.

15. The book stores and printing establishments of the Hauge Synod and of the Conference shall be transferred to the new church body and be united into one institution.

16. All other debt, which any of the said church bodies may have assumed, shall be paid before union is effected.

17. The merging into one church body shall not involve any limitation of the rights and freedom of the local congregations; neither shall the now existing parishes thereby be interfered with or disturbed.

18. The proposal of the Joint Committee for constitution, for articles of union, and for settlement of doctrinal controversies, shall be submitted to the joint meeting; the decisions of the joint meeting in these matters shall be submitted to the annual conventions of the contracting parties for their consideration. In case the annual conventions in 1889 approve these proposals, the proposed constitution shall be a pending motion for change of constitution in the formerly organized church bodies, and can consequently be adopted by them at their annual conventions in 1890. As far as the Anti-Missourians are concerned, it will be a pending motion for constitution, which can be adopted at their annual meeting in 1890.

19. The proposed constitution and the articles of union shall be sent as motions from the annual conventions in 1889 to the congregations of the respective parties for consideration, the decisions of the congregations in the matter shall be reported as accurately as possible to the annual conventions in 1890.

20. All congregations that do not belong to any organized church body, and which subscribe to said constitution and articles of union, shall be entitled through their pastors and delegates to participate in the organization meeting in which the new church body constitutes itself and elects officers, and shall thereafter be considered members of the new church body.

21. In 1890 all parties shall hold annual conventions at the same

time and place. At these annual conventions the said motion for constitution shall be considered and acted upon. In case two or more of said parties adopt the motion, they shall then and there together with the pastor and delegates mentioned in the preceding paragraph, meet together and elect officers for the new church body.

22. The board of trustees of the respective church bodies, as they were formerly elected by the church bodies, shall continue to function after union is effected until the new church body has been incorporated, after which they at once shall transfer all property which they hold as boards of trustees to the new corporation.[7]

23. At the annual conventions in 1890 a joint committee shall be elected consisting of two members from each party to investigate whether all conditions in this contract have been fulfilled. This committee shall report before the final voting takes place on the proposed constitution. If this committee shall find that any part of the contract has not been fulfilled, it shall submit to the respective annual conventions motion for adjustment thereof.

24. At the annual conventions in 1889 a committee of one member from each party shall be elected to make the necessary legal investigations in regard to the transferring of property and the incorporation.

25. If any of the parties withdraw from this work for union, it shall not hinder the other parties from continuing the work.

---

[7]This article became known as "Article 23" in 1889. *Beretning . . . Konferentsen 1889*, p. 65. This became the article of contention in the Augsburg Controversy, and was referred to as "Article 23."

APPENDIX B

Danish-Norwegian Lutheran Liturgies

16th TO 20th CENTURY

The Ordinance of 1542	Ritualet of 1685-1688	The Rescript of 1802 (Still known as *Ritualet*)	The Liturgy of 1887-1889	American Haugeanism ca. 1900
1. Silent Confession by Minister (kneeling at altar)	1. Opening Prayer (congregation kneeling)	1. Opening Prayer	1. Opening Prayer	1. Opening Hymn
2. Prayer for Word, king, and kingdom (minister) Silent confession (read by kneeling congregation)	2. Kyrie	2. Hymn	2. Hymn	2. Free Prayer (by a layman)
3. Introit	3. Gloria (later a hymn)	3. Collect	3. Confession of Sin	3. Hymn (pastor at altar)
4. Kyrie (sung three times by congregation)	4. Salutation	4. Epistle	4. Kyrie	4. Salutation (congregational response omitted)
5. Gloria in Excelsis	5. Collect	5. Hymn	5. Gloria	5. Collect
6. Salutation	6. Epistle	6. Sermon	6. Salutation	6. Epistle
7. Collect	7. Hymn (in place of Hallelujah)	7. General Prayer	7. Collect	7. Gospel
8. Epistle	8. Gospel	8. Blessing (Benediction)	8. Epistle	8. Hymn
9. Gradual (Hallelujah)	"Praise be to Thee, O Christ" (congregation)	9. Hymn	9. Hymn	9. Sermon
10. Gospel "God be praised for His glad tidings" (congregation)	9. Creed (or hymn)	10. Collect	10. Gospel	10. Free Prayer or General Prayer
	10. Sermon Exordium Union Lord's Prayer Text Sermon	11. Hymn	11. Creed	11. Hymn
	11. General Prayer	12. Closing Prayer (The service of Holy Communion was unchanged)	12. Hymn	12. Collect
	12. Lord's Prayer		13. Sermon Pulpit Prayer Text Sermon Gloria Patri } In Pulpit	13. Benediction
			14. General Prayer Lord's Prayer Apostolic Benediction	14. Hymn
				15. Free Closing Prayer (The service of Holy Communion was sim-

Appendix B

11. Creed (later a creedal hymn)
12. Sermon
    Pulpit Prayer
    Text
    Sermon
13. Confession and Absolution (soon dropped)
14. General Prayer
15. Lord's Prayer
16. Hymn (baptism followed here)
17. Exhortation before Communion
18. Lord's Prayer
19. Words of Institution
20. Distribution
21. Hymn of Thanksgiving
22. Benediction (sign of cross)
23. Hymn
24. Closing Prayer

13. Benediction
14. Hymn (baptism followed)
15. Exhortation
16. Lord's Prayer
17. Words of Institution
18. Distribution
    Agnus Dei sung three times during Distribution
19. Hymn of Thanksgiving
20. Benediction (sign of cross)
21. Hymn
22. Closing Prayer

15. Hymn (baptism may follow)
16. Preface
    Salutation
    Sursum Corda
    Gratias Agamus
    Vere Dignum
17. Sanctus
18. The Exhortation
19. Lord's Prayer
20. Words of Institution
21. Distribution
22. Hymn of Thanksgiving
23. Collect
24. Salutation and Benediction
25. Hymn
26. Closing Prayer and Lord's Prayer

plified, and, as with the rest of the service was not chanted)

Sources:
G. M. Bruce, *Ten Studies on the Lutheran Church* (Minneapolis: Augsburg Publishing House, 1932), pp. 37-38.
Forordnet Alterbog udi Danmark og Norge (Kiøbenhavn: Joachim Schmedtgen, 1688.)
E. K. Johnsen, *I Kirke* (Minneapolis: Augsburg Publishing House, 1913).
———, "The Liturgy of the Norwegian Lutheran Church," *Memoirs of the Lutheran Liturgical Association*, ed. Luther D. Reed (Pittsburgh: The Association, 1906), VII, 35-47.

APPENDIX C

Union Documents
(1906-1912)

I. ABSOLUTION

Absolution, which in accordance with the command of God and in His name is declared to those who request the comfort of the Gospel, is God's own absolving act through the ministry of the Word.

2. In absolution God declares to the sinner the gracious forgiveness of all his sins as a blessing of grace and reconciliation, which has been instituted and acquired through the merits of the blood of Jesus and embodied in the merciful promise of the Gospel for appropriation by the sinner.

3. The instrument by which the sinner receives, appropriates and thus becomes a partaker of the gift and treasure of forgiveness of sins which is offered, declared and bestowed by God in absolution, is faith.

4. Absolution itself is always a real and valid absolution of God, even though it does not profit without faith, and even though the impenitent and unbelieving hypocrite consequently does not become a partaker of the gift of the forgiveness of sin declared to him therein.

5. When it is stated in ecclesiastical language, and rightly so, that only the penitent should be absolved, it is not thereby meant that the one who administers the power of the keys is able to discern the hearts and to pass judgment on the spiritual condition of

the person seeking to be absolved, but only that it is the duty of the ministry to give conscientious attention to the profession in word and deed on the part of the confessors lest the holy be given to the dogs and the pearls be cast before swine. (Matt. 7:6).

II. LAY MINISTRIES IN THE CHURCH

1. God has given the Church, also the individual congregation, the means of grace, the power of the keys, the office of the ministry and the gifts of grace. The congregation and the individual Christian in it therefore possesses all things.

I Cor. 3:21b-23: For all things are yours; Whether Paul, or Apollos, or Cephas, or the world, or life, or death, or things present, or things to come; all are yours;
And ye are Christ's; and Christ is God's.

2. For the purpose of administering the means of grace in the congregation God has instituted the public office of the ministry, which the congregation by its call commits to one or more persons, who are qualified for it according to the Word of God.

Eph. 4:11: And he gave some, apostles; and some, prophets; and some, evangelists; and some, pastors and teachers.
Titus 1:5: For this cause left I thee in Crete, that thou shouldest set in order the things that are wanting, and ordain elders in every city, as I had appointed thee.
See also Acts 14:23; I Cor. 4:1; I Thess. 5:12.

3. When the congregation has committed the office of the ministry to one or more persons, no one, except in a case of emergency, should publicly teach, or administer the Sacraments, without the call of the congregation.

Rom. 10:15a: And how shall they preach, except they be sent?
Heb. 5:4: And no man taketh this honour unto himself, but he that is called of God, as was Aaron.
Aug. Conf. Art. XIV: no man should publicly in the church teach, or administer the sacraments, except he be rightly called.

Note: The above theses on Absolution were reported by the Union Committee under date of March 30, 1906, and approved by the conventions of all three conferring bodies in 1912.

4. This office of the ministry does not, however, do away with the universal priesthood of believers; but it is the right and duty of every Christian as a spiritual priest to work for mutual edification, each in his own station and in accordance with the opportunity and gifts which God has bestowed upon him, either individually, person to person, or in assemblies of the congregation.

I Pet. 2:5, 9: Ye also, as lively stones, are built up a spiritual house, an holy priesthood, to offer up spiritual sacrifices, acceptable to God by Jesus Christ.—But ye are a chosen generation, a royal priesthood, an holy nation, a peculiar people; that ye should shew forth the praises of him who hath called you out of darkness into his marvellous light.

I Thess. 5:11: Wherefore comfort yourselves together, and edify one another, even as also ye do.

Smalcald Art., Part III, Art. IV: the Gospel, which not merely in one way gives us counsel and aid against sin . . . and also through the mutual conversation and consolation of brethren.

5. God also wills that the special gifts which He has bestowed upon certain individuals in the congregation, and which therefore are the possession of the congregation, shall be employed by the congregation, thus also in particular the gift to proclaim the Word of God to an assembly.

In accordance with the Word of God the one who has received this gift shall be called to this service in the congregation at its request or with its consent, and shall use the gift under the supervision of the congregation or of those whom the congregation has called to exercise supervision over the work of the congregation, as taught by the Word of God and the Confessions of our Church.

Rom. 12:6-8a: Having then gifts differing according to the grace that is given to us, whether prophecy, let us prophesy according to the proportion of faith: Or ministry, let us wait on our ministering: or he that teacheth, on teaching: Or he that exhorteth, on exhortation.

See also I Cor. 12.

I Pet. 5:1-2a: The elders which are among you I exhort, who am also an elder, and a witness of the sufferings of Christ, and also a partaker of the glory that shall be revealed: Feed the flock of God which is among you, taking the oversight thereof.

Acts 20:28: Take heed therefore unto yourselves, and to all the flock, over the which the Holy Ghost hath made you overseers, to feed the church of God, which he hath purchased with his own blood.

See also Heb. 13:17; Augs. Conf., Art. XIV.

6. The congregation suffers harm when, either it refuses to make use of such gifts of grace, or those upon whom gifts of grace have been bestowed refuse to serve the congregation with them.

I Cor. 12:7, 17, 20, 21: But the manifestation of the Spirit is given to every man to profit withal. . . . If the whole body were an eye, where were the hearing? If the whole were hearing, where were the smelling? . . . But now are they many members, yet but one body. And the eye cannot say unto the hand, I have no need of thee: nor again the head to the feet, I have no need of you.

7. The congregation may also use pastors or laymen from other congregations, who have good report for doctrine and life, to assist in its work. This work also comes under the rule stated in Sec. 5.

Phil. 2:29: Receive him therefore in the Lord with all gladness; and hold such in reputation.

8. In order to avoid any and all misunderstanding in this matter, the conferring bodies declare that they recognize the Christian lay activity as set forth in the theses on lay activity and that they will cherish it. Consequently, it shall not be considered unchurchly practice or religious fanaticism for people to come together for prayer and the earnest promotion of spiritual awakening and spiritual life.

III. THE CALL

1. The natural man is in a state of spiritual sleep and spiritual death.

Eph. 5:14: Wherefore he saith, Awake thou that sleepest, and arise from the dead, and Christ shall give thee light.

Eph. 2:1: And you hath he quickened, who were dead in trespasses and sins.

2. In order that such a spiritually sleeping and spiritually dead person may be converted and saved, God calls him by His Gospel.

Note: The above theses on Lay Ministries were reported by the Union Committee under date of October 20, 1906, except Section 8, which was reported as an addition on May 5, 1915. The report was approved by the conventions of all three bodies in 1912. Section 8 was approved by the United Church in 1915 and by the other two bodies in 1916. It was formally added to the Articles of Union as Section D of Article IV, but is added here to the above theses as Section 8 to complete the theses on lay activity.

II Thess. 2:14: Whereunto he called you by our gospel, to the obtaining of the glory of our Lord Jesus Christ.

John 6:44: No man can come to me, except the Father which hath sent me draw him: and I will raise him up at the last day.

3. When God thus calls men He moves their hearts by His Word; that is, the persons who are called cannot avoid perceiving in their hearts the operation of the call upon them through the Law and Gospel, that is, certain inevitable thoughts and movements.

Heb. 4:12: For the word of God is quick, and powerful, and sharper than any twoedged sword, piercing even to the dividing asunder of soul and spirit, and of the joints and marrow, and is a discerner of the thoughts and intents of the heart.

Jer. 23:29: Is not my word like as a fire? saith the Lord: and like a hammer that breaketh the rock in pieces?

John 6:60: Many therefore of his disciples, when they had heard this, said, This is an hard saying: who can hear it?

Mark 10:22: And he was sad at that saying, and went away grieved: for he had great possessions.

4. By His call God reveals His grace to the one who is called, that is, He teaches the one called that there is grace available for sinners.

Mark 16:15: And he said unto them, Go ye into all the world, and preach the gospel to every creature.

Acts 9:15: But the Lord said unto him, Go thy way: for he is a chosen vessel unto me, to bear my name before the Gentiles, and kings and the children of Israel.

Rom. 10:18: But I say, Have they not heard? Yes verily, their sound went into all the earth, and their words unto the ends of the world.

Isa. 45:22: Look unto me, and be ye saved, all the ends of the earth: for I am God, and there is none else.

Isa. 1:18: Come now, and let us reason together, saith the Lord: though your sins be as scarlet, they shall be as white as snow; though they be red like crimson, they shall be as wool.

5. By His call, God offers His grace to the one called, and this offer is meant with equal earnestness in relation to all who are called; that is, God offers His grace to all that are called with the earnest purpose that He will bestow it and that the one called shall accept it.

I Tim. 2:4: Who will have all men to be saved, and to come unto the knowledge of the truth.

Isa. 55:6-7: Seek ye the Lord while he may be found, call ye upon him while he is near: Let the wicked forsake his way and the unrighteous man his thoughts: and let him return unto the Lord, and he will have mercy upon him: and to our God, for he will abundantly pardon.

Ezek. 33:11: Say unto them, As I live, saith the Lord God, I have no pleasure in the death of the wicked; but that the wicked turn from his way and live: turn ye, turn ye from your evil ways: for why will ye die, O house of Israel?

6. When God calls by His Word He at the same time bestows power to accept grace.

a) By nature or of himself man has no strength, power or ability to accept the offered grace or to contribute anything to his conversion.

I Cor. 2:14: But the natural man receiveth not the things of the Spirit of God: for they are foolishness unto him: neither can he know them, because they are spiritually discerned.

Eph. 2:1: And you hath he quickened, who were dead in trespasses and sins.

II Cor. 3:5: Not that we are sufficient of ourselves to think any thing as of ourselves; but our sufficiency is of God.

Phil. 2:13: For it is God which worketh in you both to will and to do of his good pleasure.

Eph. 2:8-10: For by grace are ye saved through faith; and that not of yourselves: it is the gift of God: Not of works, lest any man should boast. For we are his workmanship, created in Christ Jesus unto good works, which God hath before ordained that we should walk in them.

See also Rom. 7, where the apostle describes natural man and his powerlessness to do good.

b) Before regeneration man does not receive any indwelling power which he possesses as his own, and whereby he then is able himself to decide to accept grace.

John 8:36: If the Son therefore shall make you free, ye shall be free indeed.

John 1:12: But as many as received him, to them gave he power to become the sons of God, even to them that believe on his name.

c) But God's call is an efficacious call, which mightily works upon the heart of the one called, so that the one called now by virtue of the offered grace, through the drawing of God's Spirit and because of the power which now through the call operates on him, has full opportunity and real possibility to be converted, or can convert himself [omvende sig], can repent of his sin and believe in Christ. And this opportunity and possibility are equally great for all who are called, whether they heed the call or not.

Rev. 3:20: Behold, I stand at the door, and knock: if any man hear my voice, and open the door, I will come in to him, and will sup with him, and he with me.

John 6:44: No man can come to me, except the Father which hath sent me draw him: and I will raise him up at the last day.

Luke 13:6-9: He spake also this parable: A certain man had a fig tree planted in his vineyard: and he came and sought fruit thereon, and found none. Then said he unto the dresser of his vineyard, Behold these three years I come seeking fruit on this fig tree, and find none; cut it down; why cumbereth it the ground? And he answering said unto him, Lord, let it alone this year also, till I shall dig about it, and dung it; And if it bear fruit, well; and if not, then after that thou shalt cut it down.

Matt. 21:32: For John came unto you in the way of righteousness, and ye believed him not: but the publicans and the harlots believed him: and ye, when ye had seen it, repented not afterward, that ye might believe him.

Matt. 12:41-42: The men of Nineveh shall rise in judgment with this generation, and shall condemn it: because they repented at the preaching of Jonas; and, behold, a greater than Jonas is here. The queen of the south shall rise up in the judgment with this generation, and shall condemn it: for she came from the uttermost parts of the earth to hear the wisdom of Solomon; and, behold, a greater than Solomon is here.

Isa. 5:1-4: Now will I sing to my well-beloved a song of my beloved touching his vineyard. My well-beloved hath a vineyard in a very fruitful hill: And he fenced it and gathered out the stones thereof, and planted it with the choicest vine, and built a tower in the midst of it, and also made a winepress therein: and he looked that it should bring forth grapes, and it brought forth wild grapes. And now, O inhabitants of Jerusalem, and men of Judah, judge, I pray you, betwixt me and my vineyard. What could have been done more to my vineyard, that I have not done in it? Wherefore, when I looked that it should bring forth grapes, brought it forth wild grapes?

Jer. 26:2-3: Thus saith the Lord: Stand in the court of the Lord's house, and speak unto all the cities of Judah, which come to worship in the Lord's house, all the words that I command thee to speak unto them; diminish not a word: If so be they will hearken, and turn every man from his evil way, that I may repent me of the evil, which I purpose to do unto them because of the evil of their doings.

Jer. 36:5-7: And Jeremiah commanded Baruch, saying, I am shut up; I cannot go into the house of the Lord: Therefore go thou, and read in the roll, which thou hast written from my mouth, the words of the Lord in the ears of the people in the Lord's house upon the fasting day: and also thou shalt read them in the ears of all Judah that come out of their cities. It may be they will present their supplication before the Lord, and will return every one from his evil way: for great is the anger and the fury that the Lord hath pronounced against this people.

IV. CONVERSION

1. In his natural state man is fallen away from God, alienated from Him and His grace, yes, actually at enmity with Him.

I Cor. 2:14: But the natural man receiveth not the things of the Spirit of God: for they are foolishness unto him: neither can he know them, because they are spiritually discerned.

Eph. 2:12: That at that time ye were without Christ, being aliens from the commonwealth of Israel, and strangers from the covenants of promise, having no hope, and without God in the world.

Rom. 8:7: Because the carnal mind is enmity against God: for it is not subject to the law of God, neither indeed can be.

Col. 1:21a: And you, that were sometime alienated and enemies in your mind by wicked works.

2. In his natural state man is also utterly impotent spiritually, dead in sin.

Eph. 2:1: And you hath he quickened, who were dead in trespasses and sins.

Eph. 5:14: Wherefore he saith, Awake thou that sleepest, and arise from the dead, and Christ shall give thee light.

Col. 2:13: And you, being dead in your sins and the uncircumcision of your flesh, hath he quickened together with him, having forgiven you all trespasses.

3. No ability, or power, is found in man of himself to alter his sad condition, nor to cooperate in the least to effect any change.

John 3:6: That which is born of the flesh is flesh; and that which is born of the Spirit is spirit.

Rom. 8:7-8: Because the carnal mind is enmity against God: for it is not subject to the law of God, neither indeed can be.

Matt. 7:17-18: Even so every good tree bringeth forth good fruit; but a corrupt tree bringeth forth evil fruit. A good tree cannot bring forth evil fruit, neither can a corrupt tree bring forth good fruit.

John 15:5: I am the vine, ye are the branches: He that abideth in me, and I in him, the same bringeth forth much fruit: for without me ye can do nothing.

4. The great change which must take place in man, who has fallen away from God and is dead in sin, Scripture calls conversion.

II Tim. 2:25-26: In meekness instructing those that oppose themselves; if God peradventure will give them repentance to the acknowledging of the truth; And that they may recover themselves out of the snare of the devil, who are taken captive by him at his will.

Acts 2:38: Then Peter said unto them, Repent, and be baptized every one of you in the name of Jesus Christ for the remission of sins, and ye shall receive the gift of the Holy Ghost.

Luke 15:7: I say unto you, that likewise joy shall be in heaven over one sinner that repenteth, more than over ninety and nine just persons, which need no repentance.

5. Conversion is to turn from darkness to light, from the power of Satan to God, and is brought about by the acknowledgment and repentance of one's sin and faith in Jesus. Two parts therefore belong to conversion: a) sorrow and contrition for sin, and b) faith in the Lord Jesus.

Acts 26:18: To open their eyes, and to turn them from darkness to light, and from the power of Satan unto God, that they may receive forgiveness of sins, and inheritance among them which are sanctified by faith that is in me.

Acts 17:30: And the times of this ignorance God winked at; but now commandeth all men every where to repent.

Luke 24:46-47: And said unto them, Thus it is written, and thus it behoved Christ to suffer, and to rise from the dead the third day: And that repentance and remission of sins should be preached in his name among all nations, beginning at Jerusalem.

Mark 1:15: And saying, The time is fulfilled, and the kingdom of God is at hand: repent ye, and believe the gospel.

Jer. 3:12-14: Go and proclaim these words toward the north, and say, Return, thou backsliding Israel, saith the Lord; and I will not cause mine anger to fall upon you: for I am merciful, saith the Lord, and I will not keep anger for ever. Only acknowledge thine iniquity, that thou hast transgressed against the Lord thy God, and hast scattered thy ways to the strangers under every green tree, and ye have not obeyed my voice, saith the Lord. Turn, O backsliding children, saith the Lord; for I am married unto you: and I will take you one of a city, and two of a family, and I will bring you to Zion.

Isa. 55:7: Let the wicked forsake his way, and the unrighteous man his thoughts: and let him return unto the Lord, and he will have mercy upon him; and to our God, for he will abundantly pardon.

Luke 15:21: And the son said unto him, Father, I have sinned against heaven, and in thy sight, and am no more worthy to be called thy son.

Acts 2:37-38: Now when they heard this, they were pricked in their hearts, and said unto Peter and to the rest of the apostles, Men and brethren, what shall we do? Then Peter said unto them, Repent, and be baptized every one of you in the name of Jesus Christ for the remission of sins, and ye shall receive the gift of the Holy Ghost.

See also Luke 7:36-50, about the sinner at the feet of Jesus; and Acts 16:27-34, about the jailor at Philippi.

6. In order that man may come to acknowledgment of his sinful condition and to sorrow and contrition over it, God uses His Law, which by its conviction and judgment works on the intellect, will and conscience; and this Law man must hear and ponder.

Rom. 3:20: Therefore by the deeds of the law there shall no flesh be justified in his sight; for by the law is the knowledge of sin.

Rom. 7:7: What shall we say then? Is the law sin? God forbid. Nay, I had not known sin, but by the law: for I had not known lust, except the law had said, Thou shalt not covet.

II Cor. 7:10: For godly sorrow worketh repentance to salvation not to be repented of: but the sorrow of the world worketh death.

Mark 4:23-24: If any man have ears to hear, let him hear. And he said unto them, Take heed what ye hear: with what measure ye mete, it shall be measured to you: and unto you that hear shall more be given.

Isa. 1:10: Hear the word of the Lord, ye rulers of Sodom; give ear unto the law of our God, ye people of Gomorrah.

Luke 16:29: Abraham saith unto him, They have Moses and the prophets; let them hear them.

7. Even if man by God's work through the Law is brought to the knowledge of sin and judgment, he is thereby not yet converted, for such a person may still, contrary to God's purpose, either despair, or become self-righteous, or fall back into the old sinful life.

Rom. 7:12: Wherefore the law is holy, and the commandment holy, and just, and good.

Rom. 4:15a: Because the law worketh wrath.

Rom. 3:20a: Therefore by the deeds of the law there shall no flesh be justified in his sight.

Acts 24:25: And as he reasoned of righteousness, temperance, and judgment to come, Felix trembled, and answered, Go thy way for this time: when I have a convenient season, I will call for thee.

See also Mark 10:17-24, about the rich young ruler.

8. When the Law gains power over a man's heart, so that he humbles himself before God's judgment, it works broken-heartedness or contrition over sin and thus becomes a tutor to bring him to Christ.

Ps. 51:3, 4: For I acknowledge my transgressions: and my sin is ever before me. Against thee, thee only, have I sinned, and done this evil in thy sight: that thou mightest be justified when thou speakest, and be clear when thou judgest.

Gal. 3:24: Wherefore the law was our schoolmaster to bring us unto Christ, that we might be justified by faith.

9. Only and solely by God's drawing in the Gospel, without coercion, the person who by the operation of the Law has come to the acknowledgment of his sin and repentance, is now brought to faith in Christ, and thus entirely converted and changed; "of a darkened understanding is made an enlightened understanding, and of a rebellious will is made an obedient will, and this Scripture calls to create a new heart." Ps. 51:10: "Create in me a new heart, O God, and renew a right spirit within me."

John 6:44: No man can come to me, except the Father which hath sent me draw him: and I will raise him up at the last day.

Matt. 11:28: Come unto me, all ye that labour and are heavy laden, and I will give you rest.

Eph. 2:8: For by grace are ye saved through faith; and that not of yourselves: it is the gift of God.

Rom. 1:16-17: For I am not ashamed of the gospel of Christ: for it is the power of God unto salvation to every one that believeth; to the Jew first, and also to the Greek. For therein is the righteousness of God revealed from faith to faith: as it is written, The just shall live by faith.

Ezek. 36:26: A new heart also will I give you, and a new spirit will I put within you: and I will take away the stony heart out of your flesh, and I will give you an heart of flesh.

10. When a person does not become converted, he alone bears

Appendix C 355

the responsibility and the blame, because he would not heed the call; that is, in spite of the fact that God through the call makes it possible for man to be converted or convert himself [omvende sig], he resists and renders ineffective the work of the Holy Spirit through both Law and Gospel, something it is possible for man to do at any stage.

Matt. 23:37: O Jerusalem, Jerusalem, thou that killest the prophets, and stonest them which are sent unto thee, how often would I have gathered thy children together, even as a hen gathereth her chickens under her wings, and ye would not!

Jer. 6:16: Thus saith the Lord, Stand ye in the ways, and see, and ask for the old paths, where is the good way, and walk therein, and ye shall find rest for your souls. But they said, We will not walk therein.

Heb. 3:7-9: Wherefore (as the Holy Ghost saith), To day if ye will hear his voice, Harden not your hearts, as in the provocation, in the day of temptation in the wilderness: When your fathers tempted me, proved me, and saw my works forty years.

Isa. 5:4: What could have been done more to my vineyard, that I have not done to it? wherefore, when I looked that it should bring forth grapes, brought it forth wild grapes?

11. When a person is converted, the glory belongs to God alone, because it is He who throughout, from beginning to end, without any cooperation on the part of man, works conversion in the person who becomes converted; that is, acknowledges his sin and believes in Christ.

John 1:12-13: But as many as received him, to them gave he power to become the sons of God, even to them that believe on his name: Which were born, not of blood, nor of the will of the flesh, nor of the will of man, but of God.

Phil. 2:13: For it is God which worketh in you both to will and to do of his good pleasure.

I Cor. 4:7: For who maketh thee to differ from another? and what hast thou that thou didst not receive? now if thou didst receive it, why dost thou glory, as if thou hadst not received it?

See also Eph. 2:14; Rom. 3:20-28, where the apostle describes conversion as an operation of grace by God, for which all glory belongs to God alone.

Note: The theses on the Call and Conversion were reported by the Union Committee under date of the Easter Week, 1908, and were approved by the conventions of all three bodies in 1912.

V. ELECTION
(The Madison Agreement)

1. The Union Committees of the Synod and the United Church, unanimously and without reservation, accept that doctrine of election which is set forth in Article XI of the Formula of Concord, the so-called First Form, and Pontoppidan's Truth unto Godliness (Sandhed til Gudfrygtighed), question 548, the so-called Second Form of Doctrine.

2. Since both the conferring bodies acknowledge that Article XI of the Formula of Concord presents the pure and correct doctrine of the election of the children of God unto salvation as taught in the Word of God and the Confessions of the Lutheran Church, it is deemed unnecessary for church unity to set up new and more elaborate theses on this article of faith.

3. However, since it is well known that in presenting the doctrine of election two forms of doctrine have been used, both of which have won acceptance and recognition within the orthodox Lutheran Church,

some, in accordance with the Formula of Concord, include under the doctrine of election the whole order of salvation of the elect from the call to the glorification (Formula of Concord, Part II, Art. XI: 13-24),[1] and teach an election "unto salvation through the sanctification of the Spirit and belief of the truth,"[2]

while others, with Pontoppidan, in agreement with John Gerhard, Scriver and other recognized teachers of the Church, define election more specifically as the decree concerning the final glorification, with faith and perseverance wrought by the Holy Spirit as its necessary presupposition, and teach that "God has appointed all those to eternal life who He from eternity has foreseen would accept the offered grace, believe in Christ and remain constant in this faith unto the end"; and since neither of these two forms of doctrine, thus presented, contradicts any doctrine revealed in the Word of God, but does full justice to the order of salvation as presented in the Word of God and the confessions of the Church,

we find that this should not be cause for schism within the Church or disturb that unity of the spirit in the bond of peace which God wills should prevail among us.

---

[1] The original has Sections 10-12, according to Norwegian ed. of Book of Concord by Johnson and Caspari.
[2] II Thess. 2:13.

4. Since, however, in the controversy over this question among us, there have appeared words and expressions—justly or unjustly attributed to the respective parties—which seemed to the opposite party to be a denial or to lead to a denial of the Confession,

we have agreed to reject all errors which seek to explain away the mystery of election (Formula of Concord, Part II, Art. XI: 38-64)[3] either in a synergizing or Calvinizing manner, in other words, every doctrine which either on the one hand would deprive God of His glory as only Savior or on the other hand would weaken man's sense of responsibility in relation to the acceptance or rejection of grace.

5. On the one hand we reject:

a) The doctrine that the cause of our election is not solely the mercy of God and the holy merit of Christ, but that there also in us is a cause on account of which God has elected us to eternal life;

b) The doctrine that in election God has been determined by, has taken into account, or has been influenced by man's good attitude or anything which man is, does, or omits to do "as of himself and by his own natural powers";

c) The doctrine that the faith in Christ which is inseparably connected with election is in whole or in part a product of, or depends upon, man's own choice, power or ability (see Formula of Concord, Part II, Art. XI: 45-47 and 64-85);[4]

d) Or that this faith is the result of an ability and power imparted by the call of grace, which therefore now dwell within and belong to the unregenerate heart, enabling it to make a decision for grace.

6. On the other hand we reject:

a) The doctrine that God in election acts arbitrarily and unmotivated, so that He points out and counts a certain arbitrary number of any individuals whomsoever and appoints them to conversion and salvation while all others are excluded;

b) The doctrine that there are two kinds of saving will in God, one revealed in Scripture in the general order of salvation and one that is different from the former and unknown to us, which concerns only the elect and brings to them a more cordial love, a more powerful call from God and greater grace than to those who remain in their unbelief and lost condition;

---

[3] The original has Sections 30-44, Norwegian edition.
[4] Original has reference to Sections 35 and 44, Norw. ed.

c) The doctrine that when the resistance, which God in conversion removes from those who are saved, is not removed from those who are finally lost, the cause for this different result lies in God and a different will to save in His election;

d) The doctrine that the believer can and shall have an absolute assurance of his election and salvation instead of an assurance of faith, drawn from the promises of God, connected with fear and trembling and with the possibility of falling away, which, however, he believes by the grace of God shall not be realized in his case;

e) In brief, all opinions and doctrines concerning election which directly or indirectly would conflict with the order of salvation, and would not give to all a full and equally great opportunity to be saved, or which in any way would do violence to the Word of God which says that God "would have all men to be saved, and come to the knowledge of the truth"—in which gracious and merciful will of God all election to eternal life has its source.

APPENDIX D

Constitution

(1917 Report, pages 480-483)

CHAPTER I

Name, Creed and Church Rites

1. The name of this church body shall be The Evangelical Lutheran Church.

2. The Church believes, teaches and confesses that the Holy Scriptures, the canonical books of the Old and the New Testament, are the revealed Word of God and therefore the only source and rule of faith, doctrine and life.

3. As a brief and true statement of the doctrine of the Word of God, this Church accepts and confesses the symbolical books or confessional writings of the Norwegian Evangelical Lutheran Church:

a) The ecumenical symbols, the Apostolic, the Nicene, and the Athanasian;

b) The unaltered Augsburg Confession and Luther's Small Catechism.

4. In regard to church rites, it is left to each congregation to decide for itself. But in order that there may as a whole be uniform-

---
Changes:
In Section 1, "Norwegian" changed to "Evangelical" and "of America" stricken. Annual Report for 1944, page 410; Report for 1946, page 436.

ity also in church rites, the Church recommends that the congregations use the ritual of the Norwegian Church, modified according to the present common usage among us.

Chapter II

Object

5. The object of the Church shall be to work for the establishment and extension of the Kingdom of God, by:

a) Furthering the knowledge of truth and the development of Christian life in the congregations;

b) Gathering and organizing Lutheran Congregations and helping them to secure pastors and teachers, and assisting them to make use of the spiritual gifts which God has given to His Church;

c) Providing for the education and training of pastors, teachers, missionaries and other workers, for the ministry in the congregations, the instruction of children and young people in the Christian religion, and for the missionary and charity work in the Church;

d) Conducting Home and Foreign Missions and Charity work;

e) Exercising ecclesiastical supervision within the Church, seeking to settle controversies in the Church, and also giving advice in church matters;

f) Furthering the use and distribution of the Holy Scriptures, orthodox textbooks, hymnbooks and other devotional books and papers.

Chapter III

Organization

6. The Church shall consist of congregations which unreservedly subscribe to this constitution and are accepted as members.

7. Pastors, professors and missionaries, who by ordination or admission are accepted by the Church, shall be considered as belonging to the Church, unless they have subsequently withdrawn or have been excluded.

8. A congregation belongs to the Church when it has been admitted to membership in one of the districts.

9. The Church shall be divided into as many districts as may from time to time be deemed necessary.

10. The constitution and the boundaries of the districts shall be determined by the Church.

11. Each district shall be divided into circuits, the object of which shall be to consider doctrinal questions and devotional and practical topics for mutual instruction and establishment of pastors and congregations in the true faith.

12. Each district shall determine the number and the boundaries of the circuit within its territory.

Chapter IV

Church Conventions

13. The Church shall hold a convention every second year, at such time and place as may be determined by the Church itself or by a Convention Committee appointed for that purpose. Special conventions shall be held whenever the Church so determines, or when called by the President on request of the Church Council, or of at least forty congregations.

14. Voting members at these conventions shall be:

a) Pastors who are members of the Church and serve congregations belonging to the Church, and

b) One representative from each parish consisting of one congregation, and two representatives from each parish consisting of two or more congregations belonging to the Church.

15. Advisory members shall be:

a) Pastors who belong to the Church, but do not have the right to vote;

b) Permanently elected teachers at the schools of the Church;

c) Foreign missionaries of the Church;

d) The chairmen of the Boards of Trustees;

e) The treasurer of the Church;

Changes:
Section 13, "Third" changed to "Second," Annual Report for 1926, pages 103 and 220.

f) General secretary of the Church;

g) Stewardship secretary of the Church;

h) The superintendents of the charity institutions of the Church;

i) The editors of the official church papers;

j) Others that may be elected by the convention.

16. The convention shall conduct all elections and shall decide all matters not reserved by the District Constitution for the decision of the districts, also all matters that may be appealed from the District Conventions.

17. All questions, unless otherwise provided for, shall be decided by a majority vote.

18. No legislation for the general Church Body shall be adopted at District Conventions.

19. Matters of doctrine and conscience cannot be decided by majority vote, only in accordance with the Word of God and the symbolical books of our Church.

Chapter V

Officers and Functionaries

20. Officers of the Church shall be:

a) A President, a Vice President, a Second Vice President, a Secretary, a Treasurer and District Presidents;

b) A Church Council consisting of the President of the Church, the Presidents of the districts, and one layman from each district.

21. The Church Council shall be convened at the call of the president, when he deems it necessary, or at the request of at least two of the other members.

Changes:
 Section 15, That Par. h., Sec. 15, of Chap. IV of the Constitution be construed to include all members of Boards, Standing Committees, General and District Officers present at the General Convention, who are not entitled to voting membership. Report, 1930, pages 296:3.
 Section 18, new draft. Annual Report for 1926, pages 103:7 and 109; 1928, 188.
 Section 20, a) Second Vice-president added. Annual Report for 1926, pages 103:5 and 109; 1928, 187.

Appendix D

22. The Church Council shall:

a) Decide questions referred to it by the Church or any of the districts;

b) See that the decisions of the Church are carried out, and work to attain the object of the Church;

c) Supervise the educational institutions of the Church in accordance with their respective constitutions and the decisions of the Church;

d) Ascertain that the candidates for the ministry are rightly called and examined and have satisfactory testimonials as to true and living Christianity;

e) Hold colloquy with pastors applying for admission to the Church and make recommendations concerning them;

f) Mediate in disputes when such service is requested, after the investigation of a President has proven to be of no avail.

23. The President shall be elected for a term of six years and the other officers for a term of two years. They must be members of the Church. The President and Vice Presidents shall be elected from among the pastors of the Church. The officers elected shall enter upon their duties on September 1st following their election.

24. The President shall:

a) Watch over the preservation of peace and order in the Church;

b) As far as possible attend the district conventions;

c) Mediate disputes, when requested;

d) Convene and preside at the conventions of the Church;

e) Make visitation in the parishes of the district presidents in case they serve congregations;

f) Present report to each general convention and district conventions concerning his and the Church Council's official activities and concerning the condition of the Church.

25. The Vice President shall perform all the duties of the President in the latter's absence or incapacity.

Changes:
Section 23, "Three" changed to "Two," and last sentence added. Annual Report for 1926, pages 103:6, and 109.

26. The district presidents shall be elected by the respective districts in accordance with the district constitution.

27. The Secretary shall:

a) Keep a record of the proceedings of the convention of the Church and on the basis of the reports of the district secretaries each year publish an annual report which shall include all the conventions of the Church. This report shall contain the official reports, resolutions, statistics, appendices, parochial reports, and such other matters as the Church may determine;

b) Carry on the necessary correspondence for the Church, as the Church or its President may direct;

c) At least three months in advance publish time and place for the general convention and also matters for consideration;

d) Statistical Work. See footnote.

28. The Treasurer shall administer the funds entrusted to him by the Church, in accordance with the decisions of the Church, and submit a report to each convention of the Church.

29. The Board of Trustees shall be elected, and its powers and duties defined in accordance with the Articles of Incorporation of the Church.

a) The Board of Trustees is authorized and empowered to adjust and regulate the expenditures of the Church so that the budget will be balanced at the end of each fiscal year.

30. The Church shall elect the necessary committees for Home Missions, Foreign Missions, Charities, Publications, etc., as well as the necessary functionaries to carry on the work of the Church, which also defines the field of their activity.

Changes:
Section 27a.
In 1922 the Convention changed the District Constitution by striking from Section 3 of Chapter 12 the following expression: "Compile (utarbeide) and gather parochial reports from the pastors of the District." The Convention adopted the following resolution: "That the General Secretary be the Statistician of the Church and that he collect and compile the statistics of the Church." Annual Report, 1922; English, page 141:37; Norwegian, page 130:37.
Section 29. In 1940 the General Convention resolved that the Constitution of the Norwegian Lutheran Church of America be amended by adding to it the above paragraph, as subdivision a) of Section 29 of Chapter V. 1940. Annual Report, pages 30-31 and 398.

Chapter VI
Institutions of the Church

31. The Church shall manage and maintain schools for the education of pastors, teachers and missionaries, and other higher institutions of learning for the Christian education of the young, also deaconess homes, orphans' homes, homes for the aged, etc.

32. The professors and teachers of the schools of the Church shall be elected and removed by a two-thirds vote of the Church. Their doctrine and life must conform with the Word of God and the confessions of our Church.

Chapter VII
Amendments

33. With the exception of Sections 2 and 3, the contents of which must not be changed, and also this section, amendments to this constitution may be made in the following manner:

A proposed amendment shall be submitted to the Church at its convention; if the convention approves of the amendment by a majority vote, the amendment shall be published that it may be further considered before the next convention. At this convention the amendment shall be voted on, but is adopted only by a two-thirds vote.

This section shall not be construed so as to prevent inserting in Section 3 the remaining Lutheran symbols.

ARTICLES OF UNION
Preamble

Hauge's Synod, the Norwegian Synod and the United Church must first and foremost, both individually and jointly, express a sincere and deepfelt gratitude to God, the Father of all mercy, who has not dealt with us according to our sins, but in grace has brought together that which for years has been separated, uniting us in the same faith and doctrine and evoked a desire to become one also in external matters.

In the next place, we are constrained to confess that during the long and bitter controversy sin has exhibited itself in numerous ways. God requires in His Word that the truth shall be confessed and defended and that error shall be resisted, but frequently unjust accusations have been made by one party or another, and in the heat of conflict things have been done which are now mentioned with grief. Carnal weapons have often been used.

We have all sinned both against God and against one another. This causes our hearts grief, and for all these things we ask the forgiveness of God and of one another, and from the heart we forgive every brother his faults.

In the name of the Triune God we declare jointly and severally our sincere acceptance of the following:

Articles of Union

1. The joint, unanimous and unreserved acceptance of the canonical books of Holy Scriptures as the inerrant Word of God and of the confessional writings of the Norwegian Lutheran Church by the three bodies, we regard as the primary condition of union.

2. Furthermore, the joint reports adopted by the three bodies in 1912 and the "Madison Agreement," as an expression of our common understanding of the points of difference concerning doctrine in the past, must constitute a prerequisite for the union of these bodies and be maintained as such.

3. The three bodies promise one another in all seriousness to observe the rule not to carry on churchly cooperation with the Reformed and others who do not share the faith and confessions of these bodies.

4. CHURCH RITES

A. With respect to church rites, we observe the principles set forth in the confessional writings of the Lutheran Church. These are briefly as follows:

a) To the true unity of the Church it is not necessary that the same church rites are observed everywhere, provided there is unity in doctrine (Augsburg Confession, Art. VII).

b) Therefore the Church of God has the right and authority everywhere and at all times, as far as these matters are concerned, to take such action as it may deem most serviceable (Formula Concord, Art. X).

c) But church rites and ceremonies which are not contrary to the Word of God and which have been in use for some time, promoting peace and good order, should nevertheless be observed everywhere and should neither be altered nor discontinued, except for good and sufficient reason (Augsburg Confession, Art. XV, and the Apology, Art. VIII).

B. In order that there may be general uniformity also in church rites, the Church recommends that the congregations follow the ritual of the Church of Norway in the modified form at present commonly used among us.

C. Public confession and absolution in connection with the Lord's Supper should be administered as determined by the congregations, either by declaring the forgiveness of sins to the individual by the laying on of hands or by a general declaration without the laying on of hands. Private confession and absolution shall be retained.

D. In order to avoid any and all misunderstanding in the matter, the conferring bodies declare that they recognize the Christian lay activity, as set forth in the articles on lay activity, and that they will cherish it. Consequently, it shall not be considered unchurchly practice or religious fanaticism for people to come together for prayer and the earnest promotion of spiritual awakening and spiritual life.

5. Concerning Debt

Each body must, before union can be consummated, pay its own debts.

6. Seminaries

The Church shall establish and maintain one theological seminary. The present property of the United Church at St. Anthony Park and that of the Norwegian Synod in Hamline shall be used for the purposes of this institution. The arrangement of the two departments, theoretical and practical, and the division of the students between the two school buildings, shall be left to the theological faculty in consultation with the Board of Education of the Church. It is recommended that the time of the professors be divided as well as possible between the two places where instruction is given. The Church shall establish and maintain a pro-seminary at the present Seminary of Hauge's Synod at Red Wing. In addition to being used as a pro-seminary, this school shall be used as far as the facilities permit as a normal school or the most prominent preparatory school of the Church for its colleges.

7. TEACHERS

Teachers at the Theological Seminary shall be professors of theology serving as such at the time when the union is effected. Four (4) of these shall be from the United Church, four (4) from the Norwegian Synod, and two (2) from Hauge's Synod.

8. THEOLOGICAL STUDENTS

Theological students who have been admitted to the respective seminaries of the three bodies shall by virtue of such admission be received as regular students by the Seminary of the united body.

9. NORMAL SCHOOLS

The Church shall establish and maintain, until otherwise determined, two normal schools. These shall be, until the Church otherwise decides, Sioux Falls Normal School, Sioux Falls, S. D., and Madison Normal School, Madison, Minn.

10. COLLEGES

The Church shall establish and maintain two standard colleges. These shall be Luther College, Decorah, Iowa, and St. Olaf College, Northfield, Minn. The operating expenses of these schools shall be defrayed from the proceeds of the endowment funds owned by these colleges, general school receipts, and annual appropriations by the Church.

11. OTHER INSTITUTIONS OF LEARNING

The higher institutions of learning which are now connected with either one of the three bodies shall continue their operation. In case the Church exercises supervision over them, they shall receive annual appropriations from the Church. The Board of Education may propose the amounts to be appropriated, but the Church itself shall decide how much each of these schools shall receive each year. Since Jewell College and Augustana College are owned by the Church, they shall be operated as the Church may determine.

12. INSTITUTIONS OF MERCY

All institutions of mercy now owned by the various bodies shall continue their operation as hitherto until the Church may otherwise determine.

13. Missions

All missions now carried on by the respective bodies shall continue in the united body in accordance with plans and methods determined by the Church.

14. The Pension Fund

The pension funds of the respective bodies shall be combined into one and the rules revised to conform with the requirements of such combination.

15. Publication Houses

The bookstores and publishing houses of Hauge's Synod, the Norwegian Synod and the United Church shall be united into one concern, whose chief seat of business shall be Augsburg Publishing House, Minneapolis, Minn.

16. Editorship

The church papers which are owned and published by the respective bodies shall be consolidated, and there shall be published one church organ in Norwegian and one in English and one Sunday school paper in Norwegian and one in English. In the editorship of the organs of the Church all three of the present bodies shall be represented for the present. An editor-in-chief shall be elected for each organ.

17. Incorporation

The united body shall be incorporated as soon as possible.

18. Property

Proper action shall be taken to convey all the property owned by the respective bodies, so that it may become the legal property of the united body.

19. Merging

Merging of the three bodies into one shall in no way curtail the freedom and right of the local congregations to effect mergers or rearranged parishes.

Note: The above articles were reported by the Union Committee under date of April 2, 1914. They were approved by the conventions of the three conferring bodies as follows: 1914 by the United Church unanimously and by the Norwegian Synod by a vote of 360 to 170; 1916 by Hauge's Synod by vote of 165 to 40. See reports of United Church, 1914, pp. 214-215; Norwegian Synod, 1914, p. 139; Hauge's Synod, 1916, pp. 231-232.

"AN INTERPRETATION"

When it is stated in Article 3 of the Union Articles, "and others who do not share the faith and confessions of these bodies," we understand thereby only those who do not accept the confessional writings named in the constitution for the new body proposed by the Union Committee, Article I, Sections 2 and 3. The word "cooperation" we understand to mean organized and continuous activity of a churchly character or also incidental and occasional reciprocal relations in the preaching of the Gospel and administration of the Sacraments. On the other hand, we do not regard as cooperation or unionism, when one occasionally takes part in weddings, funerals, Decoration Day programs, Chatauquas, graduation festivities at public schools, and the like, where ministers of other confessional groups also take part. Furthermore, we do not consider it contrary to this section to participate in such movements, which while they indubitably are of a religious nature, but embrace the whole Christian Church, as for example, ecumenical mission conferences, Student Volunteer Movement, Student Federation and Laymen's Missionary Movement. We consider these Christian religious movements more in the nature of practical enterprises than activities of a pure churchly character.

When it is stated in Article 4 B concerning ceremonies "that the congregations follow the Altar Book of the Norwegian Church or ritual in the modified form at present generally used among us, we understand this to mean that the rule which is observed within Hauge's Synod has official recognition. We enter into the union with the understanding that it shall continue to be fully as much entitled to be observed in the future as the orders used in the other two bodies and that it in the future shall receive full official recognition in the new body and shall be eligible to be employed in the official assemblies of that body.

When in Article 4 C, concerning absolution, it says, "as determined by the congregations," and when it is not said that the Lord's Supper must always be connected with absolution, we accept this section with the understanding that the body will grant full recognition to the form of the administration of the Sacrament which omits absolution, as, for example, the alternative order given on page 23 of the "Altar Book of the Church of Norway," authorized by Oscar II on the 14th of February 1889 (F. Meyer, publisher, 1889), and the order which is approved by Article XIV, Section c, of the constitution of Hauge's Synod, "Confession and absolution shall be diligently employed, but they should not be required as a condition for participation in the Lord's Supper." Also Section d, which reads: "In the congregations which still desire to retain the connection, the hitherto employed usage shall be followed" (a conditional form of absolution without the laying on of hands).

Article I, Section 4, of the proposed constitution is accepted with the same understanding as Article IV of the Union Articles.

Article VII of the Union Articles, The Theological Seminary. This article we accept on the presumption that at the seminary of the Church, instruction shall be given in church rites and the like in the future as at present at Red Wing Seminary. We deem it necessary to have this understanding in order that the congregations that desire to retain our practice, may receive pastors from our Seminary who have received such instruction as will make them acquainted with our practice.

Since there is an earnest desire on our part to have a lasting and brotherly union, Hauge's Synod wishes to remove all possibilities for misunderstandings by accompanying our acceptance of these important union documents with these explanations. We therefore present herewith our understanding of the points cited, although they may not be as detailed as some would like to have them. As we present these statements as our understanding of the union documents involved, we are fully convinced that the brethren in the other two bodies will jointly with us carry on the work of the Church in a manner satisfactory to us and others, to the glory of God and the advancement of His cause. God grant this for His name's sake.[1]

---

[1] Report Hauges's Synod, 1916, pp. 229-231.

Index

Aaker, L. K. 53
Aanstad, O. 53, 57, 63
Aasgaard, J. A. 253, 254, 261, 262, 263, 267, 271, 272, 303, 304, 312, 316, 317, 318, 326, 327, 328
Aastad, I. T. 153
Absolution 7, 39, 128, 144, 185, 234, 235, 344
Adiaphora 321
Alaska Mission 95
Albert Lea Academy 117
Allgemeine Evangelisch-Lutherische Konferenz 325
American Bible Society 203
American Evangelical Lutheran Church 315, 320
American Lutheran Church 280, 305, 313, 317, 330
American Lutheran Conference 286, 288, 305, 306, 307, 308, 309, 310, 311, 312, 313, 314, 315, 316, 318, 319, 320, 322
"American Lutheranism" 282, 283, 284, 286
Andersen, Paul 243
Anderson, Bersvend 91
Anderson, Oscar A. 280
Anderson, R. 185
Anderson, Rasmus B. 152
Anti-Missourians 4, 10, 15, 18, 19, 20, 23, 24, 26, 29, 35, 39, 40, 47, 49, 55, 65, 130, 131, 136, 150, 162, 163, 165, 166, 234, 237
Astrup, Hans 107
Astrup, Johannes 108
Astrup, Nils 107
Atonement and Justification 6
Augsburg College 119

Augsburg Confession 6, 201
Augsburg Controversy 38, 237
Augsburg Corporation 47, 48, 52, 53, 56, 57, 58, 60, 61, 62, 63, 65, 66, 67, 69, 71, 73, 74, 76
Augsburg Publishing House 68, 71, 72, 275, 276
Augsburg Seminary 10, 18, 19, 24, 28, 30, 31, 32, 33, 34, 38, 41, 42, 43, 44, 45, 46, 47, 48, 49, 50, 51, 52, 53, 54, 55, 56, 57, 58, 59, 60, 61, 63, 65, 66, 68, 69, 70, 71, 74, 75, 77, 78, 81, 113, 132, 166, 197, 198
Augustana Academy 10, 28, 41, 119
Augustana College (Canton, S. D.) 113, 119
Augustana College (Sioux Falls, S. D.) 268
Augustana Synod 203, 255, 262, 288, 289, 305, 309, 313, 315, 320, 322
Aus, George 266
Austin Agreement 219

Bacon, Selden 57
"Baltimore Declaration" 310, 311, 322, 323
Bang, A. 126
Behnken, John 319
Beloit Children's Home 109
Bergh, J. A. 8, 15, 32, 168, 245
Bergsaker, A. J. 277, 327
Bergsland, H. H. 5
Bersell, P. O. 305, 316
Bethania High School, Everett, Wash. 121
Bethesda Mission, Brooklyn, N. Y. 97
Bible Camp Movement 280
Bjørn, L. M. 15, 26, 27

373

Index

Birkelund, J. R. 105, 106, 258
Bjørgo, K. 88, 216
Boe, L. W. 211, 218, 220, 239, 272, 289, 295, 302, 305, 325, 326
Boe, N. E. 40
Boe, N. N. 174, 215
Bøckman, M. O. 14, 24, 32, 69, 133, 136, 155, 167, 222, 247, 248, 272
Bønskrift 193, 194, 195
Book of Concord 135, 136
Book Mission 259
Brandelle, G. A. 289
Brandt, Nils 153
Brandt, O. E. 193, 247
Brazil Mission 257
Breidablik, J. J. 260
Brevig, T. L. 95
"Brief Statement" 310, 314
Broen, E. M. 141
Brotherhood of the Evangelical Lutheran Church 279
Brown, J. W. 271
Bruce, G. M. 126, 212, 214, 216, 221, 247
Brun, N. C. 14, 185
Brun, Sven 126
Budbæreren 18
Buffalo Synod 304
Burntvedt, T. O. 316
Bygdelag Movement 152, 238

Call and Conversion 147, 150, 185, 347-355
Canton Academy 10, 28, 41
Canty, Judge 76
Carlsen, N. C. 316, 318
Celmosa Mission, Colombia, S. A. 257
Centennial Offering 278
Charities 108-112, 272
Chicago Conference 291, 293
"Chicago Theses" 291, 293, 297, 299, 301, 304, 307, 323
Children's Homes 109-110
Chiliasm 284
China Missions 104, 255
China Mission Society 93, 104, 105, 107
Christiansen, F. Melius 223, 224, 276
Christian Service Institute 270
Christmas 276
Church Extension 94
City Missions 96, 259
Clausen, C. L. 39, 235, 237
Clausen L. F. 77
Columbia College, Everett, Wash. 121

"Committee of 34" 316, 317, 319
Concordia College 120, 268
Conference 4, 9, 10, 17, 21, 22, 23, 24, 26, 30, 33, 35, 39, 47, 48, 49, 62, 68, 73, 74, 75, 76, 77, 131
"Confession of Faith" 323
"Constructive Lutheranism" 291

Dahl, T. H. 5, 32, 57, 61, 62, 92, 151, 156, 157, 185, 189, 190, 201, 210, 211, 223, 245, 259
Dahl, Mrs. T. H. 279
Dahlen, Magnus A. 272, 273
Deaf, Dumb and Blind Mission 96, 259
Depression 117, 119, 253, 261, 262, 268, 277, 309
Deutsche Messe 123
Doerring, A. E. 280
Donatism 140
Dybvig, P. S. 250, 264, 267

Eastvold, C. J. 151, 155, 156, 157, 158, 185, 209, 221
Eastvold, S. C. 271
Eau Claire Meeting (1888) 4, 8, 10, 17
Educational Institutions 114-115
Egge, A. E. 44, 46
Egge, Thorstein 44
Eggen, Thore 275
Eikjarud, A. H. 174
Eielsen, Elling 3
Eielsen Synod 3, 122, 144, 185, 197, 198, 234, 243
Eisteinsen, J. 5, 18
Eittreim, K. O. 100, 101
Election (Eau Claire Meeting 1888) 7
Election (The Madison Agreement 1912) 356-358
Election Controversy 4, 28, 40, 92, 137, 150, 162, 166, 169
Ellestad, N. J. 5, 32, 90, 93, 97
Engemoen, H. 68, 71
Engh, H. 173
English Association 259
English Conference of United Church 101
Erickson, A. 44
Erlangen Theology 283, 286, 310, 323
Eskimo Missions 259
"Essentials of Catholic Spirit" 291, 308, 323
Evangelical Lutheran Church, The 273, 286, 287, 314, 315, 316, 319, 320, 321, 322, 327, 328
Evangelisk Luthersk Kirketidende 193

Index

Evangelism 98
Evjen, J. O. 169

Federal Council of Churches 290, 324
Finnish Mission Society 255
Fliedner, Theodore 109
Folkebladet 72
Foreign Missions 103-108, 254-258
    Brazil 257
    Colombia 257
    China 255
    Formosa 257
    Hong Kong 257
    Japan 257
    Madagascar 256
    Sudan 257
    Zululand 256
Foreningssagens Gang 214
Formosa Mission 257
Formula Missae 123
Formula of Concord, Article XI (so called First Form) 157, 164, 177
Fort Peck Dam 263
Franckean Synod 237, 243
Frank, F. H. R. 283, 310
Free Conference:
    Lanesboro, Minn. (1897) 137-138
    Austin, Minn. (1899) 138-139
"Friends of Augsburg" 44, 56, 68, 70, 71, 72, 74, 76, 77, 79, 198
Fry, F. C. 317
Fundamentalism 285
Fundamentalists 242

General Council 282
General Evangelical Lutheran Conference 325
General Synod 282, 283, 284, 304
Gerberding, G. H. 112
Glasoe, Oluf 93, 102
Glenwood Academy 117
"Graded System" 269
Granskou, C. M. 271
Grønli, J. E. 258
Guldseth, Olaf 93, 99
Gullixson, T. F. 248, 272, 305, 317, 318, 327
Gunderson, S. 173, 176, 177, 185, 211

Halvorson, Johannes 245, 246
Hanson, M. G. 86, 185
Hanson, Oscar C. 280
Hanson, Østen
Harstad, Bjug 120, 220

Hatlestad, O. J. 5, 27, 57
Haugan, Randolph E. 276
Haugeanism 18, 231, 232, 233, 260
Hauge, Hans Nielsen 232
Haugen, Einar 249, 250, 259
Hauge's Synod 3, 4, 8, 10, 12, 15, 16, 17, 22, 27, 36, 86, 87, 88, 90, 91, 92, 93, 94, 97, 98, 100, 104, 105, 106, 120, 122, 126, 128, 129, 132, 139, 142, 143, 144, 151, 155, 156, 158, 170, 173, 174, 185, 188, 189, 192, 195, 196, 199, 200, 203, 205, 208, 210, 211, 212, 213, 216, 219, 220, 221, 222, 234, 246, 248, 260, 322, 328
Hegge, M. H. 173, 175, 185, 198
Heilsgeschichte 311
Hein, C. C. 303, 307
Helland, Andreas 41
Hendrickson, P. A. 89
Herre, J. C. 98
Hesselberg, W. K. 124
Hilleboe, H. S. 271
Hinderlie, Carroll S. 280
Hoel, C. S. B. 261, 267
Høimesse 124, 125
Hoff, O. 53, 78
Hofmann, J. C. K. von 310
Hogstad, J. P. 104, 107
Holem, H. C. 91, 93
Holstad, S. H. 317
Hong Kong Mission 257
Hong, N. J. 271
Home Missions 28, 85-90, 258-267
Homes for the Aged 110-112
Homme, E. J. 109
Homme Homes, Wittenberg, Wis. 109
Hospital Missions 98
Hove, A. M. 78
Hove, E. 193, 194, 247, 248
Hoyme, G. 5, 13, 19, 21, 22, 26, 27, 32, 34, 38, 50, 51, 52, 57, 61, 62, 65, 134, 135, 139, 141, 153, 197

Ihmels, Ludwig 310
Immigrant Mission 95, 259, 260
Indian Mission 95, 259
Intuitu fidei 157, 158, 163, 164, 165
Iowa Synod 162, 288, 302, 304
Iverson, A. E. 280

Jacobs, C. M. 289, 295, 296, 310, 325
Jacobs, H. E. 161, 291, 298, 299
Jacobson, Axel 95
Jacobsen, N. 53

Index

Japanese Evangelical Lutheran Church 257
Japan Mission 257
Jensen, Gustav 124
Jensen, J. C. 32
Jørgensen, H. E. 275, 327
Jørgensen, J. E. 174
Johnsen, E. K. 123, 157, 222, 247, 248, 285
Johnson, Charles 280
Johnson, Gisle 126, 135, 237
Joint Committee on Doctrine and Practice 291, 294, 296, 299, 300
Joint Meeting. (Scandinavia, Wis. 1888) 11
Joint Union Committee 320
Jordahl, D. C. 188, 216
"Justification of the World" 7, 39, 234, 235
Juul, Ole 95

Kildahl, H. B. 272, 273
Kildahl, J. M. 5, 6, 18, 19, 26, 32, 57, 59, 155, 157, 159, 160, 167, 169, 185, 200, 211, 212, 218, 220, 222, 223, 234, 247, 248, 285, 300
Kittelsen, C. M. 220
Klokker 124
Klove, A. A. 5, 53, 57
Knubel, F. H. 288, 291, 292, 295, 298, 299, 309
Knutson, J. L. 271
Koren, U. V. 130, 131, 134, 135, 150, 159, 166, 169, 170

Landstad's *Salmebog* 127, 239
Language Problem 99-103, 242-251
Larsen, G. A. 93, 97
Larsen, Iver 33, 34, 53, 56, 57, 63
Larsen, Laur. 107, 169, 170, 196, 244
Larsen, Lauritz 298, 300, 324
Larsen, N. Astrup 329
Lasseson, I. L. 185, 214
Lavik, J. R. 327
Lay Activity 8, 18, 20, 146, 147, 185, 237, 345
Laymen's Missionary Movement 213
Lee, G. T. 174, 175, 176, 186, 275
Lee, O. T. 220
Lehre und Wehre 192, 297
Lillegaard, George 106
Liquor Traffic 27
Liturgies 342
"Lodge Question" 297, 298, 299, 304, 322
Løhre, N. J. 86, 212, 223
Lund Assembly 327
Lund, E. G. 69, 245
Lund, Lars 106

Lundeberg, K. O. 140
Lutheran Brethren 140, 141, 144, 185, 197
Lutheran Church of China 255
Lutheran Daughters of the Reformation 278, 279
Lutheraneren 275
Lutheran Free Church 77, 79, 91, 92, 107, 121, 122, 141, 144, 169, 185, 197, 198, 257, 262, 288, 305, 320, 328
Lutheran Free Church "Guiding Rules and Principles" 79-80
Lutheran Herald 102, 184, 193, 246, 249, 275
Lutheran Home Missions Council of America 262
Lutheran Hymnary 102, 124, 170
Lutheran Intelligencer 102, 246
Lutheran Service Book and Hymnal 276
Lutheran World Action 278
Lutheran World Convention 302, 324, 325, 326
Lutheran World Federation 256, 258, 315, 324, 326, 327
Lutheran United Mission 106
Luther College 40, 113, 202, 223, 268, 278
Lutherischer Bund (Lutheran League) 325
Luther League 280
Luthersk Kirkeblad 27, 46, 51, 72
Luther Seminary (Norwegian Synod) 245, 247
Luther's Small Catechism 6, 239, 243, 269
Luther Theological Seminary 217, 268, 274, 325
Lysnes, David 5, 24

Madagascar Mission 106, 255
Madison Agreement 183, 184, 185, 188, 191, 238, (Text) 356-358
Madison Normal, Madison, Minn. 113, 115, 202
Malagasy Lutheran Church 256
Malmin, O. G. 275
Malmin, Rasmus 170, 174, 176, 177
Martin Luther Home, Madison, Wis. 109
Masonry 284, 297, 298, 304, 311, 322
Mattson, J. 197
Mees, Otto 305
Meland, O. C. 137, 138
Meuser, Fred W. 288, 307
Mikkelsen, A. 137
"Minneapolis Theses" 285, 304, 307, 308, 313, 314, 322, 323
Missourianism 6, 136, 162, 163, 164, 165, 167, 196, 234, 235

Index

Missouri Synod 3, 133, 162, 190, 191, 192, 195, 196, 232, 234, 238, 280, 281, 282, 284, 287, 289, 293, 297, 306, 307, 310, 313, 319, 322
Mitchell, Judge 76
Modernist-Fundamentalist Controversy 285
Mohn, Th. N. 30, 43, 46, 57, 64, 65, 131
Molstad, J. O. 220
Morehead, John A. 302, 325, 326
Mormon Mission 95
Muus, B. J. 28, 42, 43, 136, 137

Nielsen, J. P. 305
Njaa, Arna 279
National Council of Churches 324
National Lutheran Commission 324
National Lutheran Council 159, 282, 286, 288, 290, 291, 294, 299, 300, 301, 302, 303, 308, 312, 313, 314, 315, 316, 317, 319, 321, 324
Negro Mission 95
Nelson, Daniel 105
Nelson, Oley 53, 56, 63
Nordby, J. 174, 175, 186, 188, 216
Norlie, O. M. 92, 109, 119, 245
Norske Selskap i Amerika 152, 250
Northern Illinois Synod 237
Norwegian Augustana Synod 4, 10, 15, 21, 23, 24, 29, 35, 49, 78, 91, 131, 237
Norwegian Conference 252
Norwegian Danish Conference 29, 47, 116, 237—Also see Conference
Norwegian Lutheran Church of America 108, 159, 217, 222, 223, 224, 230, 234, 249, 253, 254, 255, 262, 268, 272, 275, 281, 288, 289, 298, 299, 301, 302, 303, 304, 305, 309, 313, 322, 324, 325, 326
Norwegian Lutheran Church of America: Constitution 206-208, 359-365
Organization Meeting 222-225
Articles of Union 365-371
Norwegian Mission Society 104, 106, 107, 255
Norwegian Synod 3, 4, 9, 10, 17, 27, 28, 36, 39, 86, 87, 88, 90, 92, 94, 95, 97, 99, 105, 106, 107, 108, 116, 120, 122, 124, 126, 128, 129, 130, 131, 132, 133, 135, 139, 142, 143, 148, 150, 151, 154, 155, 156, 157, 159, 160, 162, 168, 169, 170, 172, 173, 174, 175, 176, 179, 185, 188, 189, 190, 191, 192, 194, 195, 196, 199, 204, 205, 208, 209, 210, 211, 214, 215, 216, 219, 220, 221, 222, 234, 235, 237, 245, 246, 248, 281, 295, 301, 309, 322, 324
Norwegian Synod of the American Evangelical Lutheran Church 220

Oak Grove Ladies Seminary 119
Øfstedahl, A. 173
Ofstedal, R. A. 329
Oftedal, Sven 13, 22, 24, 30, 33, 44, 45, 53, 56, 59, 60, 62, 63, 64, 67, 68, 69, 70, 71, 72, 73, 74, 77, 198
Ohio Synod 162, 288, 289, 302, 303, 304
"Old Constitution" 128, 243
Olsen, J. 5, 15
Olson, O. L. 271
Olson, Raymond M. 278
Olson, Roy 280
Onstad (Aanstad), O. 56, 57, 63
Opgjør (1912) 129, 179-182, 184, 186, 187, 190, 191, 192, 193, 194, 196, 199, 200, 201, 205, 209, 211, 218, 238
Oppedahl, T. J. 185
Oppegaard, A. O. 93
Ordal, O. J. 271
Østby, P. G. 30
Otte, Heinrich 108
Ottesen, J. N. 244
Outlook College 119
"Overture on Lutheran Unity" 313, 323

Pacific Lutheran Academy 121
Pacific Lutheran College, Parkland, Wash. 120, 268
Pacific Lutheran University Association 120
Parish Evangelism 266
Park Region Luther College, Fergus Falls, Minn. 120
Parochial Schools 269
Passavant, W. A. 108
Pattee, W. S. 57, 60, 61
Paulson, Ole 61
"Peace Committee" (1915) 204, 205, 214
Pedersen, C. O. 98
Petersen, W. M. H. 246
"Petition" *(Bønskrift)* 193, 194
"Pittsburgh Agreement" 311, 314, 323
Pontoppidan's Explanation 6, 135, 177, 239
Poppen, Emmanuel 316, 317
Preaching-Teaching-Reaching Mission 266
Precentor 124
Preus, A. C. 243, 244
Preus, C. K. 196, 218, 219, 271
Preus, H. A. 130, 131, 244
Preus, J. C. K. 269, 272
Preus, O. J. H. 271

Index

Rand, S. A. 272
Rasmussen, G. 173, 185
Rasmussen, P. A. 4, 5, 18, 19, 21, 26, 32, 106
Red Wing Seminary 10, 19, 113, 119, 247
Reformation Cantata 224
Reinertson, E. C. 266
Repristination Theology 284, 310, 323
Reu, Michael 304, 305
Ringstad, E. O. 209
Ritualet 122, 123, 124, 126, 127
Roalkvam, H. 32
Rølvaag, O. E. 250
Rogness, A. N. 272
Ronning, H. N. 104
Ronning, Thea 104
Roseland, Jens 103
Rural Life Commission 266
Russel, R. D. 74, 75

Saeterlie, H. M. 32, 93, 105
Saint Olaf College 28, 29, 30, 31, 32, 39, 40, 41, 42, 44, 45, 46, 47, 52, 54, 55, 60, 64, 65, 66, 81, 113, 119, 132, 185, 202, 216, 223, 239, 268, 270
Saint Olaf Corporation 52, 58, 66
Salveson, C. S. 121
Samfundet 72
Sanderson, Tollef 185
Sandhed til Gudfrygtighed 7, 135, 147
Sanne, Alice 279
"Savannah Declaration" 309, 310, 323
Scandinavia Agreement 133, 142
Scandinavian Augustana Synod 237, 244
Schiotz, F. A. 327, 333
Schmauk, T. E. 289, 291, 293
Schmidt, E. W. 247
Schmidt, F. A. 5, 13, 24, 30, 31, 45, 46, 69, 139, 150, 159, 160, 162, 166, 167, 169
Schreuder, H. P. S. 104, 107, 256
Schuette, C. H. L. 289, 291, 294, 303
Schuh, H. F. 317
Seamen's Mission 95, 112, 259
Should We Join the World Council of Churches? 329
Shurson, H. O. 278
Siloah Scandinavian Mission 112
Sioux Falls Normal School, Sioux Falls, S. D. 202
Skandinaven 18, 44, 159, 171
Skrefsrud, L. O. 73
Sletten, H. O. 305
Søderblom, Nathan 324
Solem, O. A. 21

South African Mission 106
Spokane College, Spokane, Wash. 121
Solberg, C. O. 271
Stavig, L. M. 271
Steensland, Halle 53, 64
Stenby, S. M.
Stolee, M. J. 107, 247, 248, 325
Stub, H. G. 87, 106, 133, 135, 155, 156, 159, 160, 166, 167, 169, 170, 174, 186, 188, 190, 191, 192, 193, 196, 200, 201, 205, 214, 223, 247, 249, 288, 290, 291, 293, 294, 295, 299, 300, 303, 305, 324, 325
Stub, J. A. O. 289
Sudan Mission 257
Sunday Observance 7
Sundheim, J. M. 275
Suomi Synod 262, 315, 320
Sverdrup, Georg 5, 6, 8, 9, 10, 24, 29, 30, 31, 32, 41, 42, 43, 45, 56, 57, 59, 67, 68, 69, 70, 73, 79, 116, 198 285
Swenson, Lars 5, 26
Swenson, Lauritz S. 219
Synodical Conference 95, 162, 190, 191, 192, 220, 289, 303, 328
Syrdal, R. A. 256

Tangjerd, P. 173, 175, 176, 181, 185, 186, 211, 218, 275
Tanner, J. 248, 275
Teachers' Institutes 270
Theologische Quartalschrift 192
The American Lutheran Church 320, 321, 322
"The United Testimony" (1954) 320
Thompson, Conrad 266
Thorpe, H. O. 184
Tingelstad, O. A. 271
Tollefsen, B. 31
Torgerson, T. A. 133
Torrison, I. B. 196, 215, 218, 219
Tou, E. H. 104, 107
Tuve, A. G. 57
Ueland, A. 50, 51, 52, 57, 210, 218
Union Committee Meetings:
  Jan. 17, 1906: 144
  March 27-31, 1906: 144
  Oct. 16-19, 1906: 145
  March 19-22, 1907: 147
  Oct. 1907: 147
  April 1908: 147
  Nov. 10-13, 1908: 150
  March 30-Apr. 2, 1909: 154
  Nov. 2-5, 1909: 155
  March 29, 1910: 155

Index

Dec. 13-14, 1910: 156
Nov. 21-24, 1911: 175
Feb. 14-22, 1912: 176-181
Jan. 21-23, 1914: 200
March 31-Apr. 2, 1914: 201
Apr. 13-15, 1915: 205
May 1915: 206
Oct. 10-12, 1916: 218
Dec. 5-7, 1916: 219
Jan. 17-18, 1917: 219
Jan. 23-27, 1917: 219
Unionism 201, 203, 205, 213, 284, 299, 304, 311, 324, 329
Union Lutheran Theological Seminary, Shekow, China 255
United (Danish) Evangelical Lutheran Church 257, 262, 288, 305, 315, 316, 318, 319, 320, 330
United Lutheran 102, 246
United Lutheran Theological Seminary of Madagascar 255
United Mission Advance 278
United Norwegian Lutheran Church 4, 14, 23, 24, 28, 29, 30, 31, 32, 33, 34, 35, 36, 37, 39, 40, 41, 44, 45, 46, 47, 50, 55, 56, 61, 63, 64, 65, 66, 67, 68, 69, 70, 71, 72, 73, 74, 75, 76, 77, 78, 79, 81, 86, 88, 90, 91, 92, 93, 94, 96, 97, 98, 99, 101, 103, 104, 105, 106, 107, 115, 120, 121, 122, 124, 126, 128, 130, 132, 133, 134, 136, 139, 140, 141, 142, 143, 144, 147, 151, 154, 155, 156, 157, 158, 159, 160, 161, 166, 167, 168, 170, 172, 173, 174, 175, 176, 183, 184, 185, 188, 189, 190, 192, 193, 195, 196, 197, 198, 199, 203, 205, 208, 210, 211, 212, 214, 218, 219, 221, 222, 223, 231, 235, 237, 245, 246, 248, 260, 322, 328
United Norwegian Lutheran Church: Constitution and Articles of Union 9, 333

Seminary 113, 247
United Synod, South 282

Valdreslag 153
Vangsness, O. P. 188, 216
Vigness, L. A. 271, 272, 275
Visser 't Hooft, W. A. 328
Von Hofmann—see Hofmann, von
Vort Blad 24

Waldeland, Erik 223
Waldorf College, Forest City, Ia. 120, 121
Walther, C. F. W. 162, 163, 167, 234
"Washington Declaration" 296, 299, 302, 307, 310, 313, 323
Wee, M. O. 185, 214, 218, 221, 223, 247, 248
Wee, Morris 327
Wenaas, August 19, 39, 78
Wentz, A. R. 222
Weswig, C. M. 222, 247
Whipple School 120
Willmar, Minn. Meeting (1892) 132-136
Wisconsin Synod 192, 309
Wittenberg Normal, Wittenberg Wis. 113
Women's Missionary Federation 278
World Council of Churches 273, 315, 324, 328, 329, 330
Wright, A. 5

Ylvisaker, I. D. 174, 177, 178, 186, 187, 188, 216, 218
Ylvisaker, Johannes 186, 191, 193, 247, 248
Ylvisaker, N. M. 280
Ylvisaker, J. W. 271, 327
Young People's Luther League 280

Zion Society for Israel 104
Zulu Missions 256